Decisions and Dilemmas
Case Studies
in Presidential
Foreign Policy Making

Robert A. Strong

Washington and Lee University

PRENTICE HALL, Englewood Cliffs, New Jersey 07632

Library of Congress Cataloging-in-Publication Data

Strong Robert A.
    Decisions and dilemmas : case studies in presidential foreign
policy making / Robert A. Strong.
      p.   cm.
    Includes bibliographical references.
    ISBN 0-13-200908-0
    1. United States--Foreign relations--1945-1989--Decision making-
    -Case studies. 2. United States--Foreign relations--1989--
    -Decision making--Case studies. I. Title.
E743.S827   1992
327.73--dc20

                          91-33974
                            CIP

Acquisitions editor: Karen Horton
Production editor: Elaine Lynch
Copy editor: Mary Louise Byrd
Editorial assistant: Dolores Mars
Cover design: Ray Lundgren Graphics, Ltd.
Pre-press buyer: Kelly Behr
Manufacturing buyer: Mary Ann Gloriande

 © 1992 by Prentice-Hall, Inc.
A Simon & Schuster Company
Englewood Cliffs, New Jersey 07632

Printed in the United States of America
10 9 8 7 6 5 4 3 2 1

ISBN 0-13-200908-0

Prentice-Hall International (UK) Limited, *London*
Prentice-Hall of Australia Pty. Limited, *Sydney*
Prentice-Hall Canada Inc., *Toronto*
Prentice-Hall Hispanoamericana, S.A., *Mexico*
Prentice-Hall of India Private Limited, *New Delhi*
Prentice-Hall of Japan, Inc., *Tokyo*
Simon & Schuster Asia Pte. Ltd., *Singapore*
Editora Prentice-Hall do Brasil, Ltda., *Rio de Janeiro*

For my parents
who always made the right decisions
in the endless dilemmas
of raising a family

Contents

Chapter 7
Reagan and the Iran-Contra Affair   168

Chapter 8
Bush and the Invasion of Panama   198

Epilogue:
The War with Iraq   226

Selected Bibliography   235

Preface

In the chapters that follow there are eight foreign policy case studies involving nine American presidents who served in the White House from 1945 to 1990. For students of American foreign affairs, the cases are intended to provide informative accounts of events that reflect some of the important international issues affecting the United States in the last five decades. For students of the American presidency, the conclusions at the end of each case have been divided into three sections that roughly correspond to the leading approaches to the study of American executive politics. The conclusions under the subtitle *power* deal with the constitutional language and practices relevant to foreign affairs and with the frequent clashes between presidents and legislators over issues of war and peace and matters of national security. The subtitle *process* introduces observations about the organizations and methods used by various administrations to analyze, discuss, debate, formulate, and implement the policies they have adopted. The final section of concluding remarks, titled *personality*, discusses elements of presidential background and character that may have influenced particular policy outcomes.

The purpose of combining the case studies and the concluding comments about the presidency is to give all readers, including those who may be new to these subjects, the raw material needed for serious discussion and analysis of how individual leaders, complex institutions, and difficult issues have shaped modern American foreign policy.

CASES

The cases have been selected to represent different kinds of foreign policy situations faced by presidents in the years since the Second World War. Some are relatively well known and controversial like Lyndon Johnson's escalation of the war in Vietnam and Ronald Reagan's involvement with the Iran-contra affair. Other cases describe lesser issues. The negotiation of a temporary neutrality in Laos in the early 1960s and the brief invasion of Panama at the end of 1989 are examples of decisions that were quickly overshadowed by subsequent events. Kennedy's response to the situation in Laos, though important during the first year of his administration, was followed by the much more important responses to the Cuban missile crisis and the decisions in Vietnam that returned American attention to Southeast Asia in connection with an increasingly intractable set of political and military problems. President Bush's decision to invade Panama at the end of 1989 was widely seen as the first major military operation of the post-cold war era until it was dwarfed by the larger and far more dangerous operations in the Middle East following the Iraqi invasion of Kuwait. Neither Laos nor Panama tested those administrations in the same way that they were later tested by other challenges. Nevertheless, there are good reasons for studying issues that are less than earth shattering. Most foreign policy decisions do not rock the planet, and there are likely to be important differences between the way our government operates in the midst of a clearly perceived international crisis and the way it performs in more ordinary times.

The cases also vary in the degree to which they involve presidential action. Richard Nixon's development of détente with the Soviet Union and the opening to China were personal initiatives planned in the White House, plotted in private diplomatic messages, and advanced by the secret negotiations of presidential assistants. To an unusual extent in the Nixon years, new policy moves toward China and the Soviet Union were devised and executed by the president, his national security adviser, and a small White House staff. Other decisions bring to the stage a larger cast of characters. The American shift from open support of Panamanian dictator Manuel Noriega to an invasion of his country in order to place him under arrest was a gradual policy change that probably would not have taken place without the efforts of investigative journalists, congressional critics, local law enforcement officials, private attorneys, and a former president. White House concern about Noriega on the part of Ronald Reagan and George Bush came late in the day. President Reagan's most controversial foreign policies, those dealings with Iran and Nicaragua, also involve an odd list of policymakers, both inside and outside the administration, whose actions raise critical questions about how much a president can and should know about what may be done in his name by his subordinates.

A few of the cases that follow produced very little internal debate among presidential advisers. There was almost no deliberation or debate about Jimmy Carter's commitment to renegotiate the 1903 treaty with Panama in 1977 and hardly any dissent to Harry Truman's decision to use nuclear weapons against Japan at the end of World War II. Carter gave simple and straightforward instructions to his negotiators that he wanted new agreements to govern the future of the canal and the Canal Zone in Panama. The story of what followed from that decision draws our attention to what the president needed to do in order to ensure that those new agreements would be ratified by the U.S. Senate. Chapter 6 is a case study in American institutional relations rather than a study of White House foreign policy decision making. Those two subjects are obviously related, and it will be important to consider how debates in the Senate affected relations with Panama and how the anticipated problems with treaty ratification had an impact on the kinds of treaties that emerged from the negotiation process. In the case of Truman's Hiroshima decision, we encounter a group of senior presidential advisers who reached early and nearly unanimous consensus that the new atomic weapons made available in 1945 should be used to bring the war with Japan to a rapid conclusion. The story of the Hiroshima decision describes how the dissenters to that decision, primarily within the scientific community, tried to take their case to the president and failed, and how a few presidential advisers expressed partial reservations to the general consensus that the war must end with an unconditional Japanese surrender brought about by whatever means might be available. The chapter considers whether that consensus was justified and why there was so little serious discussion of the long-range consequences connected with the first use of nuclear weapons.

Though several of the cases, like the examination of Truman's Hiroshima decision, describe events that transpired over a brief period of time, others cover a much broader span. Eisenhower's search for a workable first step in the process of arms control with the Soviet Union went on for his entire eight years in office. The development of détente with China and the Soviet Union during the Nixon and Ford administrations lasted for their combined two terms and beyond. The origins of Reagan's Iran-contra affair began with revolutions that took place during the last two years of the Carter presidency. American involvement in Vietnam extended from the Truman administration to the presidency of Gerald Ford, and the consequences of America's longest war are with us today. It is always difficult to place boundaries on any government decision or action. Policies usually have precedents, and the analysis of any problem is invariably based on assumptions that have their origins in earlier periods. For these reasons, each chapter includes background information and a chronology that will, it is hoped, help to put complicated events in context.

In the selection of cases, some effort has been made to examine important foreign policy problems from the perspective of more than one presidency. The first two cases deal with how Presidents Truman and Eisenhower, the first chief executives to serve in the age of nuclear arms, dealt with the dramatic changes in international politics brought on by the development of these enormously destructive armaments. Chapter 5 returns to this subject briefly in the discussion of arms control in the Nixon and Ford years. The cases from the Kennedy and Johnson administrations both deal with threatened communist guerrilla victories in Southeast Asia and the very different ways that they responded to the impending fall of Laos and South Vietnam. The end of the Vietnam War is discussed briefly in Chapter 5. Two of the cases deal with Panama—one with the new canal treaties negotiated and ratified during the Carter administration and one with the decision to invade that country late in 1989. Several of the chapters, especially the case study of the Iran-contra affair, discuss the laws that were passed in the wake of Vietnam and Watergate that were intended to give the Congress a greater say in the conduct of American foreign policy and what happened to those laws in practice.

Documents have been added at the end of each case in order to provide readers with some firsthand exposure to the papers that presidents and their advisers read, the words they speak, as well as the official treaties, orders, and proclamations they sign.

CONCLUSIONS

Each case ends with concluding remarks organized around three distinct approaches to the study of the American presidency alliteratively subtitled power, process, and personality.

The subtitle *power* is used to suggest the approach to presidential studies taken by Edward Corwin and other students of American constitutional law and practice.[1] Corwin examines both the powers granted to the American chief executive in Article II of the Constitution and the body of precedents and practices that have emerged over 200 years of American history. Some of those foreign policy powers granted to the president by the Constitution are easily understood. The president is the nation's head of state and officially receives foreign ambassadors; thus the power to grant recognition to foreign governments is an exclusive presidential function. Very few presidential functions have that quality. The president is clearly made the commander in chief of the armed forces by the language of Article II, but that duty overlaps with congressional authorities to declare war, provide funds for the raising of armies and navies, and make rules and regulations governing the nation's military forces. The presidential powers to negotiate treaties and appoint cabinet officers and ambassadors are shared with the Senate where consent must be given to all senior appointments and where treaties must be approved by two-thirds of the senators present.

In the American system of separation of powers, foreign policy functions and authorities are divided between the political branches of the national government in accordance with two somewhat contradictory principles. The first involves institutional effectiveness and efficiency. The executive and legislative branches are asked to perform those duties that correspond to the particular strengths inherent in their institutional arrangements. The president as a single individual can speak with one voice to foreign governments and act decisively to defend the country against sudden attack or while in command of the armed forces in time of war. The Congress, as a deliberative and representative body, may, however, be better suited to conduct public debate over matters of budget priorities, trade policy, or decisions to go to war. Saying that each institution should do what it does best does not, of course, resolve those cases where conflict may arise. A commander in chief may perceive a threat to the nation and wish to send troops into combat only to find that the legislature is not at all sure that fighting is necessary. Such conflicts, and the fact that they were anticipated by the Founders, introduces the second justification for separation of powers. Government responsibilities are divided among the branches in order to prevent a dangerous concentration of power and the possibility that such power might be abused. Presidents and Congress are supposed to do what they do best at the same time that they are allowed to meddle in each other's affairs. The resulting checks against abuse of power tend to make our system cumbersome and slow, especially when issues are controversial, partisan differences are sharp, and a climate of distrust exists between the branches.

In the cases that follow, we will explore the power relationships between presidents and Congress on a variety of foreign and military issues—the building of weapons, the making of treaties, the sale of arms to foreign countries, the funding of revolutionary democratic movements, the conduct of covert operations, and the decision to go to war. The question of war powers is central to a number of the cases involving Southeast Asia and Latin America. It remains a question unresolved in the American political system. The boundaries between presidential and congressional powers in foreign affairs have rarely been the subject of Supreme Court decisions and tend to be established by political struggles rather than legal decisions. Moreover, those boundaries shift over time in response to changing circumstances. As the cases will show, there has been considerable shifting over the last fifty years.

The second section of concluding remarks for each case will focus on the *process* by which particular foreign policy decisions have been made. Who gave the president information and advice? How were the various options for action developed and analyzed? What role was played by White House staff and by the bureaucracies that serve the chief executive in the conduct of foreign affairs? Did the president's policies get implemented after they were announced? These are the kinds of questions associated with an approach to presidential studies exemplified by the work of Richard Neustadt.[2] For Neustadt, the question of formal constitutional powers, what he calls authority, provides too narrow a focus for understanding a complex institution like the modern American presidency. It misses too many dimensions of actual presidential behavior, and particularly the way presidents exercise their influence over others and the constraints under which they operate. Occupants of the White House, Neustadt argues, frequently feel restricted by the need to deal with independent subordinates, resistant bureaucracies, fragile political coalitions, and endless demands for their time and attention. Their power, or influence, is primarily a matter of how they use persuasive skills rather than how they exercise constitutionally mandated prerogatives. Decision-making processes within a given administration may be more important than the constitutional powers exercised by a particular president.

Neustadt's insights about the problematic nature of presidential power have tended to draw research attention toward the advisers and organizations that play a role in the formulation and implementation of both domestic and foreign policy. The modern American foreign policy making system includes the bureaucracies and bureaucrats of the State Department, the CIA, the Department of Defense, and a host of large and small agencies, bureaus, and departments, the cabinet officers who lead those organizations, the national security adviser, and the rest of the White House staff. By what procedures do these advisers, officers, and organizations serve or constrain presidential decision making? The study of organizational issues and bureaucratic politics has become a major theme in the examination of the presidency and foreign affairs.[3] The authors who take this approach insist that policy outcomes are affected by the way that options and information make their way to the president's desk, by the standard operating procedures used in all complex organizations, by the unavoidable parochial interests of bureaucracies, and by the bargaining that goes on among presidential appointees and advisers.

In the cases that follow, there are many examples of the kinds of process problems that Neustadt, and others, would lead us to expect. President Truman never fully heard the arguments of the scientists who wanted him to reconsider plans for the bombing of Japanese cities in the summer of 1945. He made the decision to go ahead with the attacks on Hiroshima and Nagasaki without the benefit of their counsel. Bargaining and jealousy among Eisenhower's foreign policy advisers almost killed the 1955 Open Skies proposal. In 1961 and 1962, John Kennedy made clear and frequent statements about his desire to establish a neutral regime in Laos, only to find that the CIA officials on the scene had very different ideas about what American foreign policy in Southeast Asia should be. Richard Nixon dealt with his serious suspicions about the loyalty of the foreign affairs bureaucracies by making decisions in secret and executing policy initiatives with a small White House staff and a national security adviser who became a surrogate secretary of state. Ronald Reagan's political reputation was seriously damaged by the actions of mid-level White House staff members who acted outside normal policymaking routines and withheld information from the public, the Congress, various cabinet officers, and the president himself. The Iran-contra affair was a foreign policy process disaster that very nearly destroyed the standing of an otherwise popular president.

A third approach to the study of the presidency is discussed under the subtitle *personality*. Since the publication of James Barber's *Presidential Character*,[4] observers of American politics have been increasingly concerned with how the personal backgrounds and character traits of presidents and candidates for that office may be used to explain, and perhaps predict, presidential performance. Barber classifies American chief executives in terms of a matrix based on determinations of whether presidents can be said to be active or passive in the level of energy they devote to their political careers and positive or negative in their outlook on the world. Though the cases that follow do not make rigorous use of Barber's classification system, they do include remarks about concepts that Barber helped to promote in the discourse on presidential behavior. Barber urged students of the presidency to consider how individual chief executives may have acquired an identifiable orientation toward life from their early childhood experiences, a unique style that finds expression in the way they speak, deal with others, and handle professional responsibilities, and a worldview that reflects the politically relevant ideas and events in their lives. None of the conclusions in this book attempt to provide an exhaustive personal portrait of the presidents involved; but each chapter does end with a brief consideration of the ways in which elements in presidential personality, background, or character may have contributed to the events that have just been described.

The juxtaposition of separate concluding remarks focused on power, process, and personality naturally invites comparisons among the three approaches to the study of the presidency. Do we learn more about the role of the presidency in American foreign policy by examining the development of constitutional powers and practices, or by studying the complicated interactions of presidential advisers and bureaucratic organizations, or by looking to the personal qualities that make every president a unique individual? Those questions are at the heart of this book and are the subject of an extensive theoretical literature in political science. The cases in this book were written without any predetermined plan to develop, test, or prove specific theoretical propositions about the presidency or American foreign policy. This does not mean that the cases are without connections or relevance to theories in the study of politics. It does mean that readers are left with the difficult task of using the case materials to reach their own conclusions about presidential powers, decision-making processes, and the role of presidential personality in the conduct of American foreign policy.

NOTES

[1]Edward S. Corwin, *The President: Office and Powers. 5th ed.* (New York: New York University Press, 1984).

[2]Richard Neustadt, *Presidential Power* (New York: John Wiley, 1960). The newest edition is titled *Presidential Power and the Modern Presidents* (New York: Free Press, 1990).

[3]See, for example, Graham Allison, *Essence of Decision* (Boston: Little, Brown, 1971); Morton Halperin, *Bureaucratic Politics* (Washington, D.C: Brookings Institution, 1972); I. M. Destler, *Presidents, Bureaucrats and Foreign Policy* (Princeton, N.J.: Princeton University Press, 1974); and Alexander George, *Presidential Decisionmaking in Foreign Policy* (Boulder, Colo.: Westview, 1980).

[4]James David Barber, *Presidential Character* (Englewood Cliffs, N.J: Prentice Hall, 1972).

Acknowledgments

The completion of any book is rarely possible without the help of many people and institutions. Portions of this manuscript have been read and reviewed by a long list of colleagues, teachers, students, and friends. Nancy Baker, James Ceaser, David Clinton, William Connelly, John Gunn, John Handelman, William Kincade, Barry Machado, Henry Mason, Robert Robins, Judy Wey, Lyn Wheeler, and Marshal Zeringue all took time from their busy schedules to review chapter drafts in various stages of development. Elaine Chisek read the entire manuscript and significantly improved both its style and substance. Loch K. Johnson, University of Georgia; William M. Rose, Connecticut College; and Erwin C. Hargrove, Vanderbilt University reviewed the manuscript for the publisher. My editor at Prentice Hall, Karen Horton, provided encouragement throughout the project.

During the summer of 1990 I received a Glenn Grant from Washington and Lee University to complete work on three chapters, and in the fall of that year was awarded a Robert E. Lee Grant, which allowed me to hire a research assistant, Patrick Heffernan, to help with the collection of documents and the final stages of manuscript preparation.

In 1987, an earlier version of Chapter 2 was included in *Reevaluating Eisenhower: American Foreign Policy in the Fifties*, edited by Richard Melanson and David Mayers and published by the University of Illinois Press. In that same year portions of Chapter 6 were presented to the Annual Leadership Conference of the Center for the Study of the Presidency under the title "Jimmy Carter, the Constitution and the Panama Canal Treaties." That paper was later published in the Center's journal, *Presidential Studies Quarterly*, in the spring of 1991. Permission to reprint this material is gratefully acknowledged.

Chapter 1

Truman
and the
Hiroshima Bomb

A NEW PRESIDENT AND A NEW WEAPON

On April 12, 1945, at 7:09 in the evening, Harry Truman took the oath of office as president of the United States. The nation was in shock over the sudden death of Franklin Roosevelt, who had served in the White House for more than twelve years, leading the nation through the dust bowls, the creation of Social Security, the end of Prohibition, Pearl Harbor, and D-day. It was hard for the American people, not to mention their new president, to imagine politics without the man who had dominated the national and international scenes for so long. At a cabinet meeting immediately after the swearing in, Truman asked the leading members of Roosevelt's administration, some of whom he hardly knew, to stay on and help him with the tasks that lay ahead. As the cabinet secretaries filed out of the meeting, Henry Stimson, the aging secretary of war, stayed behind. Taking the president aside, he mentioned briefly that a project was currently underway that could produce a more destructive weapon than any that had ever existed. This was the first that Harry Truman heard about the atomic bomb.

Earlier in the war, Truman had picked up hints about the Manhattan Project, the name used for the vast array of American, British, and Canadian scientific and manufacturing activities needed to produce the new bomb. As a senator from Missouri, he chaired a legislative committee that investigated fraud and abuse in wartime expenditures, but this position had provided him with very little information about the army's largest weapons development program—a project commanding the services of 100,000 people and costing more than $2 billion. When staff members working for this committee began asking questions about major military activities in Hanford, Washington, and Oak Ridge, Tennessee, Stimson appealed to

Senator Truman to have their investigation halted. Truman agreed, as he would later put it, to "call off the dogs," though he had only the vaguest notion of what they were sniffing. During the summer and fall of 1944 when Truman campaigned for the vice presidency, and during the early months of 1945 when he served in that office, neither the president nor any of his advisers ever mentioned atomic research or what it was likely to produce. Truman's friend and former Senate colleague, James Byrnes, who worked for a time in the Roosevelt White House, did say something about a new and powerful explosive that was being developed, but the vice president had no reason to pay much attention to that single comment.[1] Not until after April 12, 1945.

Henry Stimson was seventy-seven years old and in poor health when he mentioned the atomic bomb to President Truman. Stimson had a long and distinguished public career, serving as William Howard Taft's secretary of war and Herbert Hoover's secretary of state. In 1945, he was devoting more and more of his limited energies to the problems surrounding the development and use of the first atomic weapons, and he was beginning to think about what the future might be like for a world entering the nuclear age. In a note to the president on April 24, he reminded Truman of their earlier conversation and asked for an appointment to discuss the subject at greater length.

The next day Stimson gave the new president his first detailed account of S-1, the military code name for atomic research. [Document 1.1] He began a memorandum, which he had carefully prepared for the April 25 meeting, with a blunt statement: "Within four months we shall in all probability have completed the most terrible weapon ever known in human history, one bomb of which could destroy a whole city."[2] The memorandum went on to say that although the development of the atomic bomb was highly secret and enormously expensive, there was every reason to believe that in the future it would become available to many nations, changing the nature of warfare and threatening the very survival of modern civilization. As a result, it was important, Stimson wrote, to begin thinking about how this new technology might be controlled and how the American people, our Russian allies, and the rest of the world would be told of its existence. The only action taken after the president's meeting with his secretary of war was the appointment of a committee to consider the issues they had discussed at greater length. Besides Stimson and his assistant, George L. Harrison, the Interim Committee, as it would become known, consisted of James F. Byrnes, then a private citizen but soon to be Truman's secretary of state; Ralph Bard, undersecretary of the navy; William Clayton, assistant secretary of state; and Drs. Vannevar Bush, Karl Compton, and James Conant, all leading academics who were serving the government in various capacities as science and research administrators. General Leslie Groves, the army officer in charge of the Manhattan Project, was not an official member of the committee but he attended its meetings, as did the army chief of staff, General George Marshall. Additional consultation took place with a panel of leading scientists who were working on S-1, including Robert Oppenheimer, the brilliant physicist and administrator who was in charge of a massive research facility in Los Alamos, New Mexico, where the final steps in the construction of the first atomic bomb were being taken.

The Interim Committee met for extended discussions on May 31 and June 1, along with its panel of science advisers. By this time the war in Europe had ended, and attention was focused on how the new weapon might be used against Japan.

Though much of the meeting was devoted to a general discussion of the future of atomic energy research and the difficulties of sharing atomic secrets with the Russians, the meeting briefly took up the question of what targets should be designated for S-1. For some time military officers had been gathering data about various Japanese cities that might be appropriate, but no specific locations were discussed by the Interim Committee. Instead, the secretary of war expressed what he regarded to be the consensus of the group: "That we could not give the Japanese any warning; that we could not concentrate on a civilian area; but that we should seek to make a profound psychological impression on as many of the inhabitants as possible.... [T]he most desirable target would be a vital war plant employing a large number of workers and closely surrounded by workers' houses."[3] [Document 1.2] The principle of avoiding civilian areas was obviously inconsistent with the suggestion that the military target be surrounded by workers' homes, and the desire to produce a profound psychological impact on a large number of people really meant that the committee was recommending the destruction of a large section of a major Japanese city. In its very first meeting, the Interim Committee agreed to the policy that would eventually be adopted.

Some committee members questioned whether dropping one atomic bomb on a vital war plant surrounded by workers' homes would be enough to lead to a Japanese surrender. The Japanese had already endured enormously destructive air attacks in which American bombers dropped incendiary bombs that started uncontrollable firestorms in densely populated sections of Tokyo and other Japanese cities. These fire bombings had produced some of the largest losses of civilian lives and property in the entire war without apparently bringing the Japanese any closer to surrender. Oppenheimer assured committee members that the visual effects alone of an atomic explosion, which would involve a brilliant luminescence rising to a height of 10,000 to 20,000, feet would have a profound impact on anyone who saw it. Furthermore, "the neutron effect of the explosion would be dangerous to life for a radius of at least two-thirds of a mile."[4] This was one of the rare occasions when senior policymakers were reminded of the radiation that would be produced by an atomic explosion. Stimson had not mentioned it in his April 25 memo to Truman, and the other nonscientists in the room may not have fully grasped what Oppenheimer meant by the "neutron effect."

Because the committee was concerned about maximizing the psychological effect of the atomic bomb, serious consideration was given to dropping two or more bombs simultaneously on different Japanese targets. Though this proposal was abandoned because of the technical and administrative problems it would have created, the fact that it was even considered demonstrates the degree to which the best informed scientists and highest ranking policymakers were still uncertain about what would happen when atomic weapons were actually used and whether their effects would differ very much from the kinds of destruction already carried out against the Japanese. This uncertainty would continue throughout the summer. In July, when the scientists at Los Alamos were ready to test the first atomic bomb, they did what most Americans do in connection with a major forthcoming event. They started a pool. Participants contributed a dollar and their best guess as to the new weapon's destructive capacity. All the scientists and technicians in Los Alamos, save one, guessed too low.[5] In May 1945, no one fully knew what the first nuclear weapons would be like.

A DEMONSTRATION OF THE BOMB?

In the spring and summer of 1945 the individuals with the best claim to nuclear expertise were the scientists who had done the earliest atomic research, before and during the war, and who realized how dangerous their discoveries might be. A group of physicists, chemists, and specialists assigned to government laboratories in Chicago had done the initial studies of the theoretical properties of nuclear fission and developed the technologies for producing enriched uranium and plutonium— the materials being made at Hanford and Oak Ridge. The Chicago scientists, unlike their colleagues in Los Alamos, who were working frantically on last-minute design and engineering problems, had time in 1945 to think about the weapons they had made possible—and they were thinking ominous thoughts.

Leo Szilard, a Hungarian refugee and one of the physicists working on S-1 from the start, was the most active of the Chicago scientists in raising questions about how their creation should be used. Before April 12, he had planned to meet with FDR to express his personal fears about the nuclear future. He was sure that success with the atomic bomb would "precipitate a race in the production of these devices between the United States and Russia."[6] Problems were already developing between the wartime Allies over the administration of occupied Germany and the reluctance of the Soviets to carry out their Yalta Conference promises to hold free elections in Poland. For Szilard, the future of American-Soviet relations and the dangers of a nuclear arms race were far greater problems than any considerations about how the war in the Far East might be ended.

Near the end of May he traveled to Washington with two of his colleagues from Chicago's Metlab, hoping to meet with President Truman. Instead, they were sent to see James Byrnes, still a private citizen, in his Spartanburg, South Carolina, home. There Szilard reported his fears about a Russian-American nuclear rivalry and suggested that the United States might be better off if it did not test the bomb at all and gave the impression that the research efforts had failed. Byrnes responded that it would be impossible to get congressional funding for nuclear research after the war if there was no proof that it was worthwhile. Moreover, he hoped that American possession of enormously destructive weapons would make the Russians more cooperative in the disputes about Poland and Eastern Europe. Szilard was convinced that this was just the opposite of what would happen, but the forceful manner in which he expressed this view did little to persuade Byrnes. The meeting ended with the physicist and future secretary of state mutually unimpressed.

Upon their return to the Chicago laboratories, Szilard and his associates found other scientists equally worried about how the atomic bomb would be used. Many of the scientists working on the project were, like Szilard, refugees from Nazi Europe who had been motivated to develop a bomb for the Allies because of their fears that the Germans would be the first to build atomic weapons and the first to use them. In the summer of 1945 the fear of a German bomb was gone, and the rush to complete the development of atomic weapons for their use against Japan seemed unnecessary and immoral. One of Metlab's highly respected physicists, James Franck, together with Szilard and others, began drafting an unsolicited report to the secretary of war giving their recommendations about what should be done. [Document 1.3]

Their report, completed on June 11, called for an international demonstration of the new weapon in a desert or on a barren island before any atomic attack on

Japan took place. Such a demonstration, the report argued, would make it far easier for the United States to propose a system of international control of nuclear technology once the war was over. And if the Japanese did not surrender following an international demonstration, then the subsequent use of atomic bombs against their cities would be easier for the American public and the world to accept. The Franck report also suggested that there might be some merit in delaying any test or demonstration of the bomb. If efforts to provide for some international controls over nuclear technology after the war were likely to fail and if a postwar nuclear arms race was inevitable, then it might make sense to delay the beginning of that arms race for as long as possible. Answering Byrnes's fears about a congressional uproar over large expenditures that did not produce results, Franck and his colleagues noted that wartime taxpayers had purchased a large stockpile of poison gas that went completely unused. The American people might find the first use of nuclear weapons as offensive as an American initiation of gas warfare. Throughout the report, the authors emphasized the importance of the postwar problems of establishing effective international controls or, in the absence of those controls, dealing with the likely nuclear competition between the United States and the Soviet Union. They were far less interested in how the war with Japan might end. Their advice was never taken seriously in the highest policymaking circles. When the Franck report was carried to Washington by a group of scientists in the middle of June, they were not allowed to see Secretary Stimson or Harrison, his assistant. They left their report with a staff officer.

Though the Franck report attracted little notice in Washington, the demonstration issue was debated by the Interim Committee's scientific panel. Meeting secretly in Los Alamos, Oppenheimer and his fellow panelists considered some of the problems that would accompany a demonstration of nuclear power. There were only three atomic weapons under construction in the summer of 1945 and, therefore, some question about whether or not one of them could be spared for a demonstration blast. The design for two of the three bombs was so revolutionary that a test had already been scheduled for later in the summer. The results of that test were so uncertain that it could hardly have been the occasion for a demonstration. There was even uncertainty about whether the other two weapons, even after the test, would work. What would happen if a demonstration weapon failed to go off or released only a small fraction of its destructive power? If an advertised demonstration at an international location or in a sparsely populated area of Japan were to fail, would the bomb have just the opposite effect of what was intended? Would the Japanese take heart at the American failure and fight longer? If the demonstration were to take place at a desolate site within Japanese territory, how could we be sure that the Japanese would see it? And if we gave them the place and time for the attack, how could we prevent them from defending that location with their remaining fighters or moving American prisoners of war to the demonstration site?

After their debate, the conclusion reached by the scientific panel was cautiously expressed in the negative, "[W]e can propose no technical demonstration likely to bring an end to the war; we see no acceptable alternative to direct military use."[7] Furthermore, the panel in Los Alamos, unlike their colleagues in Chicago, expressed some reticence about offering views on political and military questions. Scientists were among the "few citizens who have had occasion to give thoughtful consideration to these problems during the past few years," but they have "no claim to special competence in solving the political, social, and military problems which are presented by the advent of atomic power."[8] By the end of June, those who did have "competence" in the military and political areas were considering other options to an unannounced atomic attack on Japan.

NEGOTIATING WITH THE JAPANESE OR WARNING THEM?

Outside the scientific community the demonstration idea received relatively little attention, but other alternatives to the proposals made by the Interim Committee were emerging. Some policymakers believed that a negotiated end to the war with Japan might be possible; others were considering giving the Japanese a detailed warning about what would happen if they failed to surrender.

On June 18, the president heard a formal briefing on Operation Olympic, the plan for a conventional invasion of the Japanese home islands. General Marshall told the president that the joint chiefs believed Japan would not surrender solely as a result of the naval blockade and the air attacks that were already taking place. An invasion of the main Japanese islands and a defeat of the large Japanese armies protecting those islands would be necessary, and costly. The invasion of Okinawa in May 1945 had resulted in heavy American casualties in some of the hardest fighting of the Pacific war. Japanese defense of their home islands was likely to involve fanatical resistance. Losses for the invasion of the Japanese home islands were difficult to estimate, but were thought to be as high as half a million American casualties and a much larger number of Japanese soldiers and civilians.[9]

When the briefing was over and a decision to proceed with preparations for Operation Olympic had been made, Truman asked John McCloy, another of Stimson's assistants, for his views. McCloy introduced a possibility that had not been mentioned in the official War Department briefing. He suggested that there might be diplomatic actions that could bring an end to the war without resorting to the extensive military operations then being planned. If the Japanese were offered honorable surrender terms, or given an explicit warning about the atomic bomb, the war might end without either a bloody invasion or a devastating nuclear attack. "I think that our moral position would be better if we gave them specific warning of the bomb."[10] Others in the room then raised some of the same objections marshaled against the demonstration idea. What if the bomb we warned them about failed to go off? McCloy replied that "the moral position that we would have would transcend the temporary disadvantage that might occur from our taking the risk of a dud."[11] Truman expressed interest in the idea of giving the Japanese an ultimatum but had reservations about explicit references to the atomic bomb. He asked McCloy to draft a memorandum for State Department review. As the president already knew, officials in that department were thinking along the same lines.

Three weeks earlier, Acting Secretary of State Joseph Grew had met with the president to argue in favor of a public statement assuring the Japanese people that their imperial dynasty could be retained after the war. Grew, who had served as ambassador to Japan earlier in his foreign service career, was afraid that the Japanese would never surrender, even after they were militarily defeated, if they believed that their emperor would be forced from his throne. Conversely, he was hopeful that some public promise regarding the preservation of the imperial dynasty after the war might lead to an early end to the fighting in the Far East. Truman liked this suggestion and instructed Grew to take it up with Stimson. The following day Grew presented his proposal to Pentagon officials, but because the United States was in the midst of heavy fighting on Okinawa at the end of May, it was feared that a public change in the previously stated policy of unconditional surrender might be interpreted as a sign of weakness. Grew's proposal was temporarily set aside.[12]

By the end of June, the members of the Interim Committee had completed their work without significantly changing the conclusions they had reached at their first meeting. They still called for atomic attacks on populated military targets in Japan, without warning, in an effort to maximize the psychological impact of the new weapon. The list of target cities was not part of the Interim Committee report, but was under consideration throughout the month of June. Stimson personally vetoed proposals to bomb Kyoto, a religious and cultural center in Japan, but approved a number of other potential targets, including Hiroshima. Several days after the final report of the Interim Committee was submitted to Truman, one of the committee's members, Assistant Secretary of the Navy Ralph Bard, began to have second thoughts. He was worried about the moral implications of dropping an atomic bomb on Japan without any prior notification. On June 27, he wrote to the president urging that a warning of two or three days be given before S-1 was used. Such a warning, he said, was in keeping with "the position of the United States as a great humanitarian nation and the fair play attitude of our people."[13] [Document 1.4] Bard was, at that time, preparing to resign from his post in the Department of the Navy, and before he left office, he met briefly with Truman to present his views in person. Bard was confident that the naval blockade would lead to a Japanese surrender without requiring either a massive invasion of the home islands or the use of the atomic bomb. Truman listened to Bard, but was not persuaded to abandon the plans for Operation Olympic or the recommendations of the Interim Committee.[14]

The final resolution of the alternatives put forward by Bard and Grew would take place at the last wartime conference of the Allied leaders, scheduled to begin in the middle of July. At the time Truman talked with Bard, he was preparing to leave for the Potsdam Conference and his first meeting as president with Winston Churchill and Joseph Stalin. As part of that preparation, the separate proposals made by Grew and Bard resurfaced, in diluted form, in a memorandum Stimson sent to the president on July 2. Stimson, who was not scheduled to accompany the president to Potsdam, summarized the prospects for the war in the Far East in the coming months and listed his reasons for believing that Japan would be much harder to defeat by conventional arms than Germany. The Allies would inevitably win, but not before paying a substantial price for their victory. Stimson argued that because that price was potentially so high, it was important for the president to explore every alternative before proceeding with existing plans. He urged Truman to consider giving the Japanese one final formal warning of what was to come and a reasonable opportunity to capitulate. In more tentative language, he proposed that the Allies leave open the possibility of a future form of government for Japan that could involve a constitutional monarchy under the present Japanese dynasty.[15] The warning Stimson proposed did not include any mention of the still untested atomic bomb or any firm guarantees for the Japanese emperor, but it did restate for the president the concerns previously raised by Grew and Bard, and it became the basis for one of the documents that would be drafted in Potsdam.

A FINAL DECISION

The conference of the Big Three leaders officially began on July 17, the day after the world's first atomic bomb was exploded in the New Mexico desert. At 5:30 A.M. on July 16, in a remote section of the Alamogordo air base, a crater 1,200 feet across was produced by an explosion that was equivalent in its power to 20,000 tons of TNT. Before this explosion, the largest bomb used during the Second World War, the "blockbuster" as it was called, exploded with a force equal to ten tons of TNT.[16] The light produced by the New Mexico explosion was brighter than the noonday sun. It was clearly seen by a woman riding in an automobile on a road well outside the perimeter of the air base; her ability to see the light was unusual, not because of her location but because she was blind. The steel tower that had held the bomb in place, some 100 feet above the desert surface, was vaporized by the explosion and no longer existed. Another steel tower a half a mile away was torn from its concrete foundation, twisted, ripped apart, and left in pieces on the ground. Radiation was detected 120 miles from the explosion, but it took several weeks before the strange illness it produced in local animals began to be assessed.[17]

A detailed description of the explosion reached Potsdam on July 21, and clearly excited the president. The successful test meant that Truman no longer needed to solicit Russian assistance in the war against Japan and allowed him to take a harder line in his discussions with Stalin about the future of Germany and Eastern Europe. It also meant that the war in Asia would probably be over before the Russians could make a significant contribution to the fighting there. As a result, the postwar administration of Japan would be an American, rather than an Allied, affair and many of the problems encountered in occupied Germany would be avoided. Truman made sure that Churchill and the British delegation at Potsdam were fully briefed on the results of the New Mexico test. What to tell Stalin about the new weapon was a more difficult problem.

The Interim Committee, in its final report, had recommended that the president provide the Russians with general information about U.S. atomic research before any bombs were used. Stimson, who invited himself to the conference on the grounds that important decisions regarding S-1 would have to be made at Potsdam, advised the president to give the Soviets some minimal information about the New Mexico test. Byrnes objected, but was overruled. Toward the end of a conference session on July 24, Truman approached Stalin and, speaking through the Soviet interpreter, mentioned to the Russian leader that a weapon of a new and powerful type had been perfected and would be used against the Japanese. Stalin asked no questions and seemed unimpressed by Truman's news. The president believed that Stalin had failed to grasp the import of what he was being told, but there is an even more plausible explanation for the Soviet leader's nonchalance. Klaus Fuchs, one of the scientists at Los Alamos, had been passing atomic secrets to Russian agents for some time. Stalin probably received his own reports about what was going on in the Manhattan Project long before Truman mentioned the project's success.

The Potsdam Conference produced very few significant results. The Russians restated their Yalta pledge to enter the war against Japan within three months after the German surrender. The Allies debated issues arising from the administration of occupied Germany, but reached no lasting agreements. The same occurred when they discussed Poland and Eastern Europe. The nations that were then at war with

Japan (the United States, Britain, and China) did agree on a proclamation addressed to the Japanese that closely followed the suggestions Stimson had made before the conference. The Potsdam Proclamation told the Japanese that they would soon face the full force of Allied land, sea, and air power, but it did not mention atomic bombs, directly or indirectly. The shock value of an unanticipated nuclear attack was thought by Truman to be necessary to induce a Japanese surrender.[18] The specific warning that McCloy and Bard had asked for was left out, though their idea was still attracting supporters.

Unknown to the American policymakers in Germany, Leo Szilard and his Chicago colleagues were making yet another attempt to influence atomic decision making. On July 17, they began circulating a petition calling upon the president to issue a precise warning to the Japanese about the impending atomic attack. Their reasons were, like Bard's, primarily moral, but also included the concerns they had expressed earlier about the future of the nuclear age. The petition was signed by sixty-eight of the Metlab scientists, but their views were not unanimous in the scientific community. When an angry General Groves heard about the petition, he ordered a poll to be taken of all the Chicago professionals, and found that many disagreed with Szilard and hoped that the bomb would be used quickly to bring the war in the Pacific to a rapid conclusion. The petition and the results of the poll were forwarded through official channels, which General Groves was careful to make as slow as possible. When the petition arrived in Washington, the Potsdam Conference was already over. The efforts of the scientists to make their case to the president had once again reached a dead end. The Potsdam Proclamation had little in its text that would have satisfied either Bard or Szilard.

The language of the proclamation was harsh. [Document 1.5] It stated the Allied terms with the assurance that "we will not deviate from them. There are no alternatives. We shall brook no delay."[19] As to the future of the emperor, the proclamation was exceedingly vague. It did say that the Japanese people would be allowed to form a new government after the war that would be "in accordance with the freely expressed will of the Japanese people," but it also said that war criminals would be punished and that those who had "deceived and misled the people of Japan into embarking on world conquest" would be removed from positions of authority and influence.[20]

On July 28, Japanese Premier Kantaro Suzuki rejected the Allied ultimatum, or so said the *New York Times*.[21] There is, however, some controversy regarding the meaning of the official response made by the Japanese government. The word used by the premier in his July 28 statement was *mokusatsu*, which, like many Japanese words, is subject to a variety of English translations. It may mean "to kill with silence," or "to take no notice of," or more harshly "to treat with silent contempt," or just simply "to ignore."[22] After the war one of the premier's advisers expressed regret at what may have been a serious diplomatic misunderstanding — none of the translations of the premier's response may have expressed what was intended.

> To interpret *mokusatsu* as "ignore" was a great mistake. Really, we meant "no comment." During the war, the Japanese people were urged not to use the English language—to forget English. Therefore, I could not recall the English term "no comment." I thought the Japanese expression which was most close to "no comment" was *mokusatsu*.[23]

The Japanese may have wanted to respond with "no comment" to the Potsdam Proclamation because they were interested in taking some time to consider the conditions under which they might surrender.   Advocates of surrender among Japanese officials had been heard since 1944. By the summer of 1945, they had gained significant influence in Tokyo and had received some tentative support from the emperor. Messages had been sent to Moscow, earlier in July, asking the Soviet Union if it would serve as a mediator in possible negotiations to end the war. American intelligence officers, who had broken the Japanese codes before Pearl Harbor, intercepted those messages. Their contents confirmed what acting Secretary of State Grew had expected: The Japanese were seeking some modification of the demand for unconditional surrender.

Once the "contemptuous" Japanese response to the Potsdam ultimatum was received, there was no question about proceeding with the plans recommended by the Interim Committee. The official order had been issued from Potsdam earlier in the conference authorizing Pacific military commanders to use the two available atomic weapons against selected Japanese cities after the conference had ended. The order to drop both atomic bombs was given in a single presidential directive, without any apparent consideration that one bomb on one city might be enough to induce surrender. The rejection of the Potsdam Proclamation sealed the fate of the Japanese cities on the approved target list. It only remained for bomb components to be assembled on the Pacific island of Tinian and for the required weather conditions to be present at the designated targets. On August 6, the first atomic bomb to be used in warfare was dropped on the city of Hiroshima. Three days later, on the day after the Soviet Union officially declared war on Japan, a second nuclear weapon devastated the city of Nagasaki. The next day the Japanese communicated their willingness to surrender, but asked the United States to guarantee the survival of the emperor and his dynasty. Though no official change in the policy stated at Potsdam was made, the Allies implied in their response that the emperor could continue on his throne by stating that his powers would be subordinate to those of the Allied supreme commander. On August 14, the Japanese accepted these terms and the Second World War ended.

CONCLUSIONS

POWER

What does the Hiroshima decision tell us about the presidency and foreign policy? Very little need be said about presidential powers in relation to this case—they were never at issue. During the Second World War, there was no question that the president of the United States had broad authority. He could spend billions of dollars on a highly uncertain research project, commission the services of the nation's leading scientists, put vast resources at their disposal, have them develop a powerful new explosive, test it, and order it dropped on enemy territory—all without sharing any of these decisions with the Congress or the public. No substantive consultation occurred between the executive and legislative branches in connection with any of the Hiroshima decisions, and though Russian spies were able to get reasonably good information about what went on in Los Alamos, New

Mexico, the American people could not. By 1945, it was widely recognized that greater accountability to Congress and citizens would return with the end of the war. James Byrnes and others expressed concern about what would happen when members of the legislature finally found out about S-1 and its huge budget. The president's White House military adviser, Admiral William Leahy, even suggested that this was a major factor in the rush to test and use the atomic bomb.[24]

But while it was recognized that the end of the war would bring a change in presidential powers and a return of greater balance among the branches of government, the Hiroshima decision was made entirely in the wartime setting when the extent of presidential power in military and foreign affairs was at its apex. This may, or may not, have been a good thing. Secrecy always has costs.[25] In one respect it was clearly dangerous. The extraordinary power of the presidency during the Second World War did not extend to the vice presidency. Truman and his predecessors were often left out of important wartime decisions and deliberations. Under the U.S. constitutional system the vice president has very few duties beyond casting tie-breaking votes in the Senate and waiting for the president to die. Holders of the office have frequently expressed disdain for the insignificance of their position. John Gardner, one of Franklin Roosevelt's vice presidents during the 1930s, said that the office was "not worth a pitcher full of warm spit."[26] Recent presidents have, in general, treated their vice presidents better than FDR treated his and have tried to ensure that they would be ready to assume the presidency if and when that need arose.[27]

Sharing information and decisions with the vice president is an important precaution for the nation that presidents are well advised to consider. But suppose Roosevelt, or Truman, had shared the Hiroshima decision even more widely. It is interesting to speculate about whether the final outcome would have been different if the use of the atomic bomb had been the subject of a Senate committee hearing, a *New York Times* editorial, or a public opinion survey. None of those rather routine practices in the formulation of American foreign policy took place. In a war that threatened American lives and interests, the secrecy surrounding a new weapon system or the planning of a military operation was clearly deemed to be more important than the maintenance of open decision-making procedures. But what should happen in times of peace, or in international tensions short of war? Some amount of state secrecy is necessary, but how much? And who is to decide which information is to be kept from Congress and the public and which is to be shared? These were not burning questions in the summer of 1945, but in the decades following the war, and in some of the cases described in later chapters of this book, they would become matters of the first importance.

PROCESS

If there are few conclusions to be reached about President Truman's unchallenged power to order the bombing of Hiroshima and Nagasaki, much more may be said about the process by which those decisions were reached. Truman was a new and inexperienced president when he faced a series of important military and foreign policy problems in May, June, and July 1945. He depended heavily on the advisers he inherited from Franklin Roosevelt and he was constrained by the momentum that pushed forward policies set in motion by his predecessor. Scientists and engineers in Los Alamos were busily finishing their work; military planners were preparing an invasion of Japan; diplomats were getting ready for a wartime conference. Decisions needed to be made.

There were at least three important, and interrelated, issues that were considered in the summer of 1945 in connection with plans to use the first atomic bombs. First, there was the question of whether the bomb should be used in a demonstration blast. Second, was the concern over whether the Japanese should be given a specific warning about the kind of weapon soon to be used against them. And finally, there was some discussion about whether the Japanese should be offered an opportunity to surrender on less than unconditional terms with or without a warning specifically mentioning the atomic bomb.

No serious consideration was ever given to suggestions that the atomic bomb be kept secret and not tested or used at all. Szilard offered nonuse as a possibility in his meeting with Byrnes, but Byrnes dismissed it. The Franck report raised it again, but that document was never discussed at the highest policymaking levels. Throughout the war it was simply assumed that any promising weapon that was developed would be used as soon as it was ready. Winston Churchill has recorded his personal response upon hearing at Potsdam of the successful atomic test.

> [T]here never was a moment's discussion as to whether the atomic bomb should be used or not. To avert a vast, indefinite butchery, to bring the war to an end, to give peace to the world, to lay healing hands upon its tortured peoples by a manifestation of overwhelming power at the cost of a few explosions, seemed, after all our toils and perils, a miracle of deliverance....The historic fact remains, and must be judged in the after-time, that the decision whether or not to use the atomic bomb to compel the surrender of Japan was never even an issue.[28]

On each of the three policy questions that were taken seriously—the demonstration, the warning, and the change in surrender terms—Truman turned most often to his new secretary of state, James Byrnes, and to a lesser extent, to Roosevelt's secretary of war, Henry Stimson. Byrnes was confident in the ability of the atomic bomb to end the war in Japan and hoped it would ease the growing tensions with the Soviet Union.[29] Stimson was more reflective about the longer term problems connected with nuclear power, but agreed with Byrnes that the bomb should be used against the Japanese. Both Byrnes and Stimson listened to the advice of other policymakers, but because of the secrecy surrounding S-1, the number of people they consulted was relatively small. Was this enough? Were the right policies adopted? Were effective policymaking procedures followed?

The first of the three policy issues surrounding the use of atomic weapons, the demonstration proposal, died in the Interim Committee's scientific panel. Its death sentence was written by the uncertainty concerning whether the new bombs would work and the difficulty of finding a way to make a demonstration convincing to the Japanese. Invitations to international scientific expositions are difficult to deliver to an enemy during time of war, and even if you could get the Japanese to come, it might have been hard to convince them that what they were witnessing at an international demonstration of atomic power was not some sort of trick. The invitation problem was easily solved by taking the demonstration to Japan and dropping a bomb on a desolate location somewhere on the Japanese home islands. But this possibility also brought forth serious practical objections. If dropped without warning, would a demonstration on Japanese soil be sufficiently noticed to produce the desired result? If detailed warnings were given, in order to ensure that the bomb was noticed, would the target areas be heavily defended or occupied by prisoners of war? Both the demonstration and the negotiated settlement proposed by Grew required some communication and some minimal amount of trust between bitter adversaries. After Pearl Harbor and three and a half years of war, such communication and trust were nearly impossible to achieve. For many policymakers, only an atomic bomb dropped without warning on a Japanese city would provide the kind of communication we could be sure that our enemy would understand.

Behind the demonstration debate, there was a still more important set of foreign policy questions. What would the world be like after the use of the atomic bomb? Would there be a postwar nuclear arms race? Would there be a future war using large numbers of atomic bombs? The scientists who pressed for a demonstration knew that their discoveries could not be kept secret for very long. They hoped that some international mechanism for the control of nuclear technology could be developed, but they realistically predicted a Soviet-American arms race. They understood that the bombs being prepared for use against Japan were small compared to what was likely to follow, and they feared for the survival of humankind. In urging policymakers to think seriously about how the first use of atomic weapons would affect these longer range problems, the scientists were putting forward an entirely different agenda than the one dominating Washington. There the principal goal was to end the war.

Stimson had some of the same concerns about the postwar nuclear world expressed by the scientists and he shared those concerns with Truman in his April 25 briefing and in some of the Interim Committee reports, but he also saw the importance of defeating the Japanese as quickly as possible. So did Byrnes. There were real political pressures to put ending the war with Japan first. The American public was weary of the fighting. Fully mobilized to pursue the war, the public wanted it won and were in agreement that the terms of surrender should be unconditional. Public opinion was also very sensitive to any significant losses of American lives. The Russians would sustain at least 20 million casualties in the Second World War; American casualties would be one fortieth that number. Failing to use a weapon that could bring a rapid end to the war, or even delaying its use, would have had high political costs. On April 16 and again on June 1, when Truman spoke to Congress, he promised to make ending the fighting in the Pacific his primary objective. "There can be no peace in the world," he told the members of the House and Senate, "until the military power of Japan is destroyed."[30] The atom bomb made that objective easier to achieve. The president, in deciding to use it against Japan, and his senior advisers in recommending its use, were giving the American people exactly what they most wanted—an end to the war without undue risk to Allied soldiers.

The conflict between long-term and short-term goals that was evident in the debate over a demonstration, and the tendency of political leaders to be more attracted to immediate rewards, are perennial problems in American foreign policy that will be seen again in later cases. A related question, about the specific decision-making process in connection with Hiroshima, is whether the suggestions of the scientists were intentionally suppressed. Scientists were by no means excluded from S-1 policymaking. The individual who was, perhaps, the most respected of the wartime physicists, Robert Oppenheimer, was an active participant in the Interim Committee deliberations. Nevertheless, both the Franck report and the Szilard petition failed to reach Truman's desk. Similar problems occurred earlier in the war when Neils Bohr, an internationally famous nuclear scientist, tried to present arguments very much like Szilard's to Winston Churchill and Franklin Roosevelt. Bohr's suggestions were dismissed because, as Peter Wyden has observed, the scientists and the politicians were polarized, each speaking their own distinctive language.[31] Part of the problem, as we have already noted, was that the scientists were talking about long-range problems to political leaders who had much more immediate concerns. However, there was more to it than that.

The policymakers, perhaps understandably, were simply slower than the physicists to grasp fully the revolutionary nature of atomic weapons. For them, the atomic bomb may have appeared to be only one more horror in an already long parade of horrors in twentieth-century warfare. Harry Truman had been an artillery officer in the First World War and may have thought about the atomic bomb as a larger and more dangerous explosive than the ones he fired in Europe. In both world wars, large-scale slaughters of soldiers and civilians were routine realities. The massive use of conventional explosives and incendiary devices had made the creation of large wastelands and the destruction of whole cities ordinary events in the conduct of war. Military and political leaders in 1945 may not have fully realized the radical nature of the changes that nuclear weapons would produce in the nature of war and the conduct of international relations. Scientists isolated and removed from the constant life and death decision making of the war, more comfortable with the theoretical and predictive than with the practical and mundane, may have seen the future more clearly without fully recognizing the agonizing choices of the present. The gulf in thinking between physicists and politicians was unavoidably wide. It could probably not have been bridged by making sure that Truman read the Franck report or the Szilard petition.

Furthermore, the president's senior advisers did not suppress all dissent. The president spoke to Bard, who raised many of the moral arguments put forward by the scientists; and Bard was not alone in doing so. When Stimson received a long, unsolicited, and passionate letter from a Manhattan Project engineer raising reservations about the use of the atomic bomb, he immediately sent it to the White House.[32] Later, he encouraged McCloy to bring up the warning issue in the White House meeting on Operation Olympic.[33] Throughout the Hiroshima deliberations, Stimson tried to keep an open mind. He abandoned his original thinking that the Russians should not be told about the bomb before its use, and he incorporated the need for some warning and a sensitivity to the future of the Japanese emperor into his recommendations before Potsdam. Byrnes took a harder line and argued for secrecy and no substantive change in the surrender terms. Because the proclamation written at the Potsdam Conference failed to specifically mention the atomic bomb or clearly guarantee a future for the emperor, it did little to satisfy the critics within the administration who advocated alternatives to Hiroshima. Exactly how viable those alternatives were is subject to serious debate.

The availability of alternate courses of action to the atomic bombing of Japan was dependent on the answer given to a prior question: How close were the Japanese to surrender in the summer of 1945? Some in the navy believed that their blockade would be enough to end the war, but there were good reasons to doubt such a self-serving assessment. General Marshall and the Chiefs of Staff advised the president that more than naval action would be needed to defeat Japan. Intelligence officers intercepting Japanese communications also found evidence of Japanese interest in negotiating an end to the war, but it was never clear if the views found to exist within the Japanese foreign ministry were shared throughout a government still dominated by militarist leaders. Grew could suggest that a modest relaxation of the unconditional surrender terms would lead to a Japanese capitulation, but there was no way to be sure that he was right. At the same time, there were reasons to fear that a change in the long-standing surrender terms would appear to the Japanese war leaders, or to the American people, as a sign of Allied weakness. In the middle of 1945, the evidence on how close the Japanese were to giving up the war was mixed, and American government officials assumed that the bitter fighting on Okinawa was a better indicator of what the rest of the war would be like than any confident naval predictions or intercepted diplomatic messages. In many of the cases described in subsequent chapters, there will be occasions when assessments of a foreign policy situation are difficult to make; in many of these instances the tendency to assume the worst will win out. If that tendency prevails in times of peace, it is even more likely to do so in times of war.

Some revisionist historians have suggested that high-ranking American policymakers were less worried about a long, drawn-out war with Japan than is suggested above, and that their real motive for using atomic weapons against Japan was the impression such action would have on the Soviet Union.[34] There can be no doubt that Truman, Stimson, Byrnes, and others all saw the advantages, in terms of U.S.-Soviet relations, of bringing the war in the Pacific to an early conclusion. Furthermore, there was serious speculation in 1945 about how American possession of new and powerful weapons would improve U.S. ability to get the Russians to do what we wanted in Eastern Europe and occupied Germany.[35] It is, however, a long way from these observations to the conclusion that the real target for the first atomic bomb was the Soviet Union.

The more obvious interpretation of events in the summer of 1945 is that a war-weary nation, focused on bringing its conflict with Japan to an end as rapidly as possible, used all available means to accomplish that end. The process by which the decisions on S-1 were made involved serious policymakers in careful deliberations on what they saw as a rather narrow range of viable options. They believed that the remaining Japanese armies on the home islands would have to be defeated in order to end the war, or that some shock would have to be delivered to the Japanese leadership in order to bring about their decision to surrender. As a result of these assumptions, American foreign policymakers reached an early conclusion that atomic bombs should be used against Japanese cities as soon as they were available, and they never significantly deviated from that conclusion. In the Potsdam Proclamation they elected to give the Japanese a general warning of what lay ahead, but without any specific suggestion that atomic weapons would be used against Japanese cities. They were willing to consider, and eventually accept, a continued role for the Japanese imperial dynasty, but not to compromise publicly the long-standing American demand for unconditional surrender. By such thinking was the Hiroshima decision made.

PERSONALITY

And what are we to say of Harry Truman's role in all of this and the contribution made by his personality to the final policy outcome? Truman was clearly inexperienced in foreign affairs when he became president of the United States, but he was a student of American history and an individual who could act with great determination. One of his most striking characteristics was decisiveness and a willingness to deal promptly with the problems put before him. "He rarely philosophized about the future of the world," observed one State Department official traveling with the president to the Potsdam Conference. "He preferred to address himself to the practicalities of the questions."[36] Unlike his predecessor, Franklin Roosevelt, who was often coy with his cabinet officers and staff assistants, making it impossible for them to know exactly what he was thinking or how he would decide a pending question, Truman was direct and forthright. He told people what he thought, often in blunt language, and he was proud of the sign that would later be placed on his desk announcing that "the buck stops here."

Truman concedes that the Hiroshima decision was a difficult one for him to make, but says in his memoirs that the actions he ordered were the right ones for the circumstances in the summer of 1945.[37] He claims never to have lost any sleep over what he decided to do to the cities of Hiroshima and Nagasaki.[38] That self-confidence was an important asset for a new president faced with a series of difficult decisions, but it may not have been as absolute as Truman sometimes suggested. One of his biographers observed that the former president's personal library contained copies of all of the books written about the Hiroshima decision. In one of them, Truman had underlined a long quote that the author had taken from the final act of Shakespeare's *Hamlet*, where Horatio tells the audience what the tale of Hamlet's life is really about:

> ...let me speak to the yet unknowing world
> How these things came about: So shall you hear
> Of carnal, bloody, and unnatural acts,
> Of accidental judgement, casual slaughters,
> Of deaths put on by cunning and forced cause,
> And, in this upshot, purposes mistook
> Fall'n on the inventor's heads....
> But let this same be presently perform'd
> Even while men's minds are wild; lest more mischance,
> On plots and errors, happen.

The last line was underlined twice.[39]

Chronology of the Hiroshima Decision

1945

Apr 12   FDR dies; Truman becomes president; Stimson first mentions the bomb.

Apr 13   One of several fire bombing raids against Japan destroys the homes of 640,000 residents of Tokyo.

Apr 16   Speaking before the Congress, Truman commits himself to seeking the earliest possible Japanese unconditional surrender.

Apr 25   Stimson gives Truman a detailed briefing on the bomb.

May 8   V-E Day, the war in Europe ends.

May 28   Szilard and two colleagues meet with Byrnes; Grew meets with Truman to suggest leniency for the Japanese emperor.

May 31   Interim Committee meets for the first time, produces memo calling for bombing of Japan without warning.

Jun 11   Franck report completed.

Jun 18   President approves Operation Olympic for the invasion of the Japanese home islands. McCloy suggests a negotiated end to the war and a warning about the atomic bomb.

Jun 21   Final meeting of the Interim Committee calls for bombing of Japan without warning, but advises president to inform the Russians about S-1.

Jun 27   Bard submits his dissent from Interim Committee conclusions; Szilard circulates petition also calling for a warning to Japan.

Jul 2   Stimson memo to Truman, now favoring a warning ultimatum.

Jul 16   Successful Alamogordo test.

Jul 17   First day of the Potsdam Conference.

Jul 21   Detailed account of first atomic test arrives in Potsdam.

Jul 24   Truman has his brief conversation with Stalin informing him of a powerful new explosive; official order to use S-1 is issued.

Jul 26   Potsdam Proclamation issued.

Jul 28   Premier of Japan rejects the Potsdam ultimatum.

Aug 6   The bombing of Hiroshima.

Aug 8   Russians declare war against Japan.

Aug 9   The bombing of Nagasaki.

Aug 10   Japanese communicate willingness to surrender.

Aug 14   Japanese surrender; Second World War ends.

Chapter 1 Documents

Document 1.1
Stimson's Memorandum for President Truman April 25, 1945

1. Within four months we shall in all probability have completed the most terrible weapon ever known in human history, one bomb of which could destroy a whole city.

2. Although we have shared its development with the UK, physically the US is at present in the position of controlling the resources with which to construct and use it and no other nation could reach this position for some years.

3. Nevertheless it is practically certain that we could not remain in this position indefinitely.

> a.   Various segments of its discovery and production are widely known among many scientists in many countries, although few scientists are now acquainted with the whole process which we have developed.
>
> b.   Although its construction under present methods requires great scientific and industrial effort and raw materials, which are temporarily mainly within the possession and knowledge of US and UK, it is extremely probable that much easier and cheaper methods of production will be discovered by scientists in the future, together with the use of materials of much wider distribution. As a result it is extremely probable that the future will make it possible to be constructed by smaller nations or even groups, or at least by a large nation in a much shorter time.

4. As a result, it is indicated that the future may see a time when such a weapon may be constructed in secret and used suddenly and effectively with devastating power by a willful [sic] nation or group against an unsuspecting nation or group of much greater size and material power. With its aid even a very powerful unsuspecting nation might be conquered within a very few days by a very much smaller one, although probably the only nation which could enter into production within the next few years is Russia.

5. The world in its present state of moral advancement compared with its technical development would be eventually at the mercy of such a weapon. In other words, modern civilization might be completely destroyed.

6. To approach any world peace organization of any pattern now likely to be considered, without an appreciation by the leaders of our country of the power of this new weapon, would seem to be unrealistic. No system of control heretofore considered would be adequate to control this menace. Both inside any particular country and between the nations of the world, the control of this weapon will undoubtedly be a matter of the greatest difficulty and would involve such thorough-going rights of inspection and internal controls as we have never heretofore contemplated.

7. Furthermore, in the light of our present position with reference to this weapon, the question of sharing it with other nations and, if so shared, upon what terms, becomes a primary question of our foreign relations. Also our leadership in the war and in the development of this weapon has placed a certain moral responsibility upon us which we cannot shirk without very serious responsibility for any disaster to civilization which it would further.

8. On the other hand, if the problem of the proper use of this weapon can be solved, we would have the opportunity to bring the world into a pattern in which the peace of the world and our civilization can be saved.

9. As stated in General Groves' report, steps are under way looking towards the establishment of a select committee of particular qualifications for recommending action to the Executive and legislative branches of our government when secrecy is no longer in full effect. The committee would also recommend the actions to be taken by the War Department prior to the time in anticipation of the postwar problems. All recommendations would of course be first submitted to the President.

Source: From *A WORLD DESTROYED: THE ATOMIC BOMB AND THE GRAND ALLIANCE* by Martin J. Sherwin. Copyright (c)1973,1975 by Martin J. Sherwin. Reprinted by permission of Alfred A. Knopf, Inc.

Document 1.2
Interim Committee Minutes, selected passages, May 31, 1945

I. Opening Statement of the Chairman:

Secretary Stimson explained that the Interim Committee had been appointed by him, with the approval of the President, to make recommendations on temporary war-time controls, public announcement, legislation and post-war organization. The Secretary gave high praise to the brilliant and effective assistance rendered to the project by the scientists present for their great contributions to the work and their willingness to advise on the many complex problems that the Interim Committee had to face. He expressed the hope that the scientists would feel completely free to express their views on any phase of the subject....

The Secretary expressed the view, a view shared by General Marshall, that this project should not be considered simply in terms of military weapons, but as a new relationship of man to the universe. This discovery might be compared to the discoveries of the Copernican theory and of the laws of gravity, but far more important than these in its effect on the lives of men. While the advances in the field to date had been fostered by the needs of war, it was important to realize that the implications of the project went far beyond the needs of the present war. It must be controlled if possible to make it an assurance of future peace rather than a menace to civilization.

VIII. Effect of the Bombing on the Japanese and Their Will to Fight.

It was pointed out that one atomic bomb in an arsenal would not be much different from the effect caused by any Air Corps strike of present dimension. However, Dr. Oppenheimer stated that the visual effect of an atomic bombing would be tremendous. It would be accompanied by a brilliant luminescence which would rise to a height of 10,000 to 20,000 feet. The neutron effect of the explosion would be dangerous to life for a radius of at least two-thirds of a mile.

After much discussion concerning various types of targets and the effects to be produced, the Secretary expressed the conclusion, on which there was general agreement, that we could not give the Japanese any warning; that we could not concentrate on a civilian area; but that we should seek to make a profound

<u>psychological impression on as many of the inhabitants as possible. At the suggestion of Dr. Conant the Secretary agreed that the most desirable target would be a vital war plant employing a large number of workers and closely surrounded by workers' houses.</u>

There was some discussion of the desirability of attempting several strikes at the same time. <u>Dr. Oppenheimer's</u> judgment was that several strikes would be feasible. <u>General Groves</u>, however, expressed doubt about this proposal and pointed out the following objections: (1) We would lose the advantage of gaining additional knowledge concerning the weapons at each successive bombing; (2) such a program would require a rush job on the part of those assembling the bombs and might, therefore, be ineffective; (3) the effect would not be sufficiently distinct from our regular Air Force bombing program.

Source: From *A WORLD DESTROYED: THE ATOMIC BOMB AND THE GRAND ALLIANCE* by Martin J. Sherwin. Copyright (c) 1973, 1975 by Martin J. Sherwin. Reprinted by permission of Alfred A. Knopf, Inc. The underlining above conforms with the appearance of the original document.

Document 1.3
The Franck Report, selected passages, June 11, 1945

The only reason to treat nuclear power differently from all the other developments in the field of physics is the possibility of its use as a means of political pressure in peace and sudden destruction in war. All present plans for the organization of research, scientific and industrial development, and publication in the field of nucleonics are conditioned by the political and military climate in which one expects those plans to be carried out. Therefore, in making suggestions for the postwar organization of nucleonics, a discussion of political problems cannot be avoided. The scientists on this Project do not presume to speak authoritatively on problems of national and international policy. However, we found ourselves, by the force of events during the last five years, in the position of a small group of citizens cognizant of a grave danger for the safety of this country as well as for the future of all the other nations, of which the rest of mankind is unaware. We therefore feel it our duty to urge that the political problems, arising from the mastering of nuclear power, be recognized in all their gravity, and that appropriate steps be taken for their study and the preparation of necessary decisions....

One possible way to introduce nuclear weapons to the world—which may particularly appeal to those who consider nuclear bombs primarily as a secret weapon developed to help win the present war—is to use them without warning on appropriately selected objects in Japan.

Although important tactical results undoubtedly can be achieved by a sudden introduction of nuclear weapons, we nevertheless think that the question of the use of the very first available atomic bombs in the Japanese war should be weighed very carefully, not only by military authorities, but by the highest political leadership of this country.

Russia, and even Allied countries which bear less mistrust of our ways and intentions, as well as neutral countries may be deeply shocked by this step. It may be very difficult to persuade the world that a nation which was capable of secretly preparing and suddenly releasing a new weapon, as indiscriminate as the rocket bomb and a thousand times more destructive, is to be trusted in its proclaimed desire of having such weapons abolished by international agreement. We have large accumulations of poison gas, but do not use them, and recent polls have shown that public opinion in this country would disapprove of such a use even if it would accelerate the winning of the Far Eastern war. It is true that some irrational element in mass psychology makes gas poisoning more revolting than blasting by explosives, even though gas warfare is in no way more "inhuman" than the war of bombs and bullets. Nevertheless, it is not at all certain that American public opinion, if it could be enlightened as to the effect of atomic explosives, would approve of our own country being the first to introduce such an indiscriminate method of wholesale destruction of civilian life.

Thus, from the "optimistic" point of view—looking forward to an international agreement on the prevention of nuclear warfare—the military advantages and the saving of American lives achieved by the sudden use of atomic bombs against Japan may be outweighed by the ensuing loss of confidence and by a wave of horror and repulsion sweeping over the rest of the world and perhaps even dividing public opinion at home.

From this point of view, a demonstration of the new weapon might best be made, before the eyes of representatives of all the United Nations, on the desert or a barren island. The best possible atmosphere for the achievement of an international agreement could be achieved if America could say to the world, "You see what sort of a weapon we had but did not use. We are ready to renounce its use in the future if other nations join us in this renunciation and agree to the establishment of an efficient international control."

After such a demonstration the weapon might perhaps be used against Japan if the sanction of the United Nations (and of public opinion at home) were obtained, perhaps after a preliminary ultimatum to Japan to surrender or at least to evacuate certain regions as an alternative to their total destruction. This may sound fantastic, but in nuclear weapons we have something entirely new in order of magnitude of destructive power, and if we want to capitalize fully on the advantage their possession gives us, we must use new and imaginative methods....

It must be stressed that if one takes the pessimistic point of view and discounts the possibility of an effective international control over nuclear weapons at the present time, then the advisability of an early use of nuclear bombs against Japan becomes even more doubtful—quite independently of any humanitarian considerations. If an international agreement is not concluded immediately after the first demonstration, this will mean a flying start toward an unlimited armaments race. If this race is inevitable, we have every reason to delay its beginning as long as possible in order to increase our head start still further....

The benefit to the nation, and the saving of American lives in the future, achieved by renouncing an early demonstration of nuclear bombs and letting the other nations come into the race only reluctantly, on the basis of guesswork and without definite knowledge that the "thing does work," may far outweigh the advantages to be gained by the immediate use of the first and comparatively inefficient bombs in the war against Japan. On the other hand, it may be argued that without an early demonstration it may prove difficult to obtain adequate support for further intensive development of nucleonics in this country and that thus the time gained by the postponement of an open armaments race will not be properly used. Furthermore one may suggest that other nations are now, or will soon be, not entirely unaware of our present achievements, and that consequently the postponement of a demonstration may serve no useful purpose as far as the avoidance of an armaments race is concerned, and may only create additional mistrust, thus worsening rather than improving the chances of an ultimate accord on the international control of nuclear explosives.

Thus, if the prospects of an agreement will be considered poor in the immediate future, the pros and cons of an early revelation of our possession of nuclear weapons to the world—not only by their actual use against Japan, but also by a pre-arranged demonstration—must be carefully weighed by the supreme political and military leadership of the country, and the decision should not be left to the considerations of military tactics alone.

One may point out that scientists themselves have initiated the development of this "secret weapon" and it is therefore strange that they should be reluctant to try it out on the enemy as soon as it is available. The answer to this question was given above—the compelling reason for creating this weapon with such speed was our fear that Germany had the technical skill necessary to develop such a weapon, and that the German government had no moral restraints regarding its use.

Another argument which could be quoted in favor of using atomic bombs as soon as they are available is that so much taxpayers' money has been invested in these Projects that the Congress and the American public opinion will demand a return for their money. The attitude of American public opinion, mentioned earlier, in the matter of the use of poison gas against Japan, shows that one can expect the American public to understand that it is sometimes desirable to keep a weapon in readiness for use only in extreme emergency; and as soon as the potentialities of nuclear weapons are revealed to the American people, one can be sure that they will support all attempts to make the use of such weapons impossible....

Source: *Bulletin of Atomic Scientists*, May 1, 1946. Reprinted by permission.

Document 1.4
Bard's Dissent June 27, 1945

Memorandum on the Use of S-1 Bomb

Ever since I have been in touch with this program I have had a feeling that before the bomb is actually used against Japan that Japan should have some preliminary warning for say two or three days in advance of use. The position of the United States as a great humanitarian nation and the fair play attitude of our people generally is responsible in the main for this feeling.

During recent weeks I have also had the feeling very definitely that the Japanese government may be searching for some opportunity which they could use as a medium of surrender. Following the three-power conference emissaries from this country could contact representatives from Japan somewhere on the China

Coast and make representations with regard to Russia's position and at the same time give them some information regarding the proposed use of atomic power, together with whatever assurances the President might care to make with regard to the Emperor of Japan and the treatment of the Japanese nation following unconditional surrender. It seems quite possible to me that this presents the opportunity which the Japanese are looking for.

I don't see that we have anything in particular to lose in following such a program. The stakes are so tremendous that it is my opinion very real consideration should be given to some plan of this kind. I do not believe under present circumstances existing that there is anyone in this country whose evaluation of the chances of the success of such a program is worth a great deal. The only way to find out is to try it out.

Source: From *A WORLD DESTROYED:*THE ATOMIC BOMB AND THE GRAND ALLIANCE by Martin J. Sherwin. Copyright (c) 1973, 1975 by Martin J. Sherwin. Reprinted by permission of Alfred A. Knopf, Inc.

Document 1.5
The Potsdam Proclamation July 26, 1945

(1) We, the President of the United States, the President of the National Government of the Republic of China and the Prime Minister of Great Britain, representing the hundreds of millions of our countrymen, have conferred and agree that Japan shall be given an opportunity to end this war.

(2) The prodigious land, sea and air forces of the United States, the British Empire and of China, many times reinforced by their armies and air fleets from the west are poised to strike the final blows upon Japan. This military power is sustained and inspired by the determination of all the Allied nations to prosecute the war against Japan until she ceases to resist.

(3) The result of the futile and senseless German resistance to the might of the aroused free people of the world stands forth in awful clarity as an example to the people of Japan. The might that now converges on Japan is immeasurably greater than that which, when applied to the resisting Nazis, necessarily laid waste to the lands, the industry and the method of life of the whole German people. The full application of our military power, backed by our resolve, will mean the inevitable and complete destruction of the Japanese armed forces and just as inevitably the utter devastation of the Japanese homeland.

(4) The time has come for Japan to decide whether she will continue to be controlled by those self-willed militaristic advisers whose unintelligent calculations have brought the Empire of Japan to the threshold of annihilation, or whether she will follow the path of reason.

(5) Following are our terms. We will not deviate from them. There are no alternatives. We shall brook no delay.

(6) There must be eliminated for all time the authority and influence of those who have deceived and misled the people of Japan into embarking on world conquest,

for we insist that a new order of peace, security and justice will be impossible until irresponsible militarism is driven from the world.

(7) Until such a new order is established and until there is convincing proof that Japan's war-making power is destroyed, points in Japanese territory to be designated by the Allies shall be occupied to secure the achievement of the basic objectives we are here setting forth.

(8) The terms of the Cairo Declaration shall be carried out and Japanese sovereignty shall be limited to the islands of Honshu, Hokkaido, Kyushu, Shikoku and such minor islands as we determine.

(9) The Japanese military forces, after being completely disarmed, shall be permitted to return to their homes with the opportunity to lead peaceful and productive lives.

(10) We do not intend that the Japanese shall be enslaved as a race or destroyed as a nation, but stern justice shall be meted out to all war criminals, including those who have visited cruelties upon our prisoners. The Japanese government shall remove all obstacles to the revival and strengthening of democratic tendencies among the Japanese people. Freedom of speech, of religion, and of thought, as well as respect for the fundamental human rights shall be established.

(11) Japan shall be permitted to maintain such industries as will sustain her economy and permit the exaction of just reparations in kind, but not those industries which would enable her to re-arm for war. To this end, access to, as distinguished from control of raw materials shall be permitted. Eventual Japanese participation in world trade relations shall be permitted.

(12) The occupying forces of the Allies shall be withdrawn from Japan as soon as these objectives have been accomplished and there has been established in accordance with the freely expressed will of the Japanese people a peacefully inclined and responsible government.

(13) We call upon the Government of Japan to proclaim now the unconditional surrender of all the Japanese armed forces, and to provide proper and adequate assurances of their good faith in such action. The alternative for Japan is prompt and utter destruction.

Source: *Department of State Bulletin* July 29, 1945, pp. 137–138.

Chapter 1 Notes

[1]Merle Miller, *Plain Speaking* (New York: Putnam's, 1973), pp. 199–200.

[2]Henry L. Stimson and McGeorge Bundy, *On Active Service in Peace and War* (New York: Harper & Bros., 1947), p. 635.

[3]Robert C. Williams and Philip L. Cantelon, eds., *American Atom* (Philadelphia: University of Pennsylvania Press, 1984), p. 62.

[4] Ibid., p. 62.

[5] Peter Wyden, *Day One* (New York: Simon & Schuster, 1984), p. 208.

[6] Ibid., p. 141.

[7] Williams and Cantelon, *American Atom*, p. 64.

[8] Ibid.

[9] Harry S. Truman, *Memoirs: Year of Decision* (Garden City, NY: Doubleday, 1955), p. 265.

[10] Wyden, p. 173.

[11] Ibid.

[12] Joseph Grew, *Turbulent Era, Vol. II* (Boston: Houghton Mifflin, 1952), pp. 1423–1425.

[13] Wyden, *Day One*, p. 175.

[14] Martin J. Sherwin, *A World Destroyed* (New York: Vintage Books, 1977), p. 216.

[15] Stimson and Bundy, *On Active Service*, p. 623.

[16] *The Simon and Schuster Encyclopedia of World War II* (New York: Simon & Schuster, 1978), p. 69.

[17] The full text of General Groves report on the first atomic test is reprinted in Williams and Cantelon, pp. 47–55. See also Wyden, pp. 203–218.

[18] Margaret Truman, *Harry S. Truman* (New York: Pocket Books, 1974), p. 301.

[19] Charles L. Mee, Jr., *Meeting at Potsdam* (New York: Evans, 1975), p. 314.

[20] Ibid., p. 315.

[21] On July 30, the *New York Times* headline read "Japan Officially Turns Down Allied Surrender Ultimatum;" see Wyden, *Day One*, p. 229.

[22] Sherwin, *A World Destroyed*, p. 236.

[23] Len Giovannitti and Fred Freed, *The Decision to Drop the Bomb* (New York: Harper & Bros., 1959), p. 231.

[24] William D. Leahy, *I Was There* (New York: McGraw-Hill, 1950), p. 441.

[25] For reflections on the role of secrecy in the Hiroshima decisions, see McGeorge Bundy, *Danger and Survival: Choices About the Bomb in the First Fifty Years* (New York: Random House, 1988), pp. 76–77.

[26] Quoted in Joseph Conlin, *The Morrow Book of Quotations in American History* (New York: Morrow, 1984), p. 118.

[27] Paul Light, *Vice Presidential Power* (Baltimore: Johns Hopkins University Press, 1984).

[28] Winston S. Churchill, *Triumph and Tragedy* (New York: Houghton Mifflin, 1953), p. 63.

[29] James F. Byrnes, *Speaking Frankly* (New York: Harper & Bros., 1947).

[30] Quoted in Robert J. Donovan, *Conflict and Crisis* (New York: Norton, 1977), p. 65.

[31] Wyden, *Day One*, p. 142.

[32] Ibid., p. 154.

[33] Walter Isaacson and Evan Thomas, *The Wise Men* (New York: Simon & Schuster, 1986), pp. 293–296.

[34] Gar Alperovitz, *Atomic Diplomacy: Hiroshima and Potsdam*, 2nd ed. (New York: Penguin, 1985). For a review of historiography on the Hiroshima decision, see Barton J. Bernstein, "The Atomic Bomb and American Foreign Policy, 1941–1945: An Historical Controversy," *Peace and Change* 2, (Spring 1974), 1-16; and J. Samuel Walker, "The

Decision to Use the Bomb: A Historiographical Update," *Diplomatic History*, 14 (Winter 1990), 97–114.

[35] For a discussion of early thinking about the anticipated role of the bomb in postwar diplomacy, see Gregg Herken, *The Winning Weapon* (New York: Knopf, 1980).

[36] Chip Bohlen, quoted in Donovan, *Conflict and Crisis*, p. 72.

[37] Truman, *Memoirs*, pp. 419–422.

[38] Miller, *Plain Speaking*, p. 227.

[39] Ibid., pp. 230–31.

Chapter 2

Eisenhower and Arms Control

THE NUCLEAR AGE

Between the bombing of Hiroshima in 1945 and the election of Dwight D. Eisenhower in 1952, important changes took place in the development of nuclear weapons and in the nature of Soviet-American relations, changes that affected almost every aspect of foreign policy in the Eisenhower administration and in the cold war presidencies that would follow.

The three atomic bombs that were tested or exploded on enemy targets during the Second World War had been difficult to design and expensive to produce. The enriched uranium and plutonium used in their cores could only be purified or manufactured by slow, laborious, and costly processes. The three bombs used in the summer of 1945 represented the entire American wartime stockpile. After the Japanese surrender, the arsenal was rebuilt, slowly at first, but more rapidly as the methods for manufacturing fissionable material became cheaper and more efficient. By 1948, according to some estimates, the United States had fifty atomic bombs in its possession,[1] a sizable nuclear force given the fact that the United States was the only nation in the world with access to these new and powerful weapons. Within a year, the American nuclear monopoly was over.

In 1949, radioactive fallout was detected in upper atmosphere locations that could not be explained by any American nuclear testing. The Soviet Union had tested its own atomic device. This news came at a time when relations between the United States and the Soviet Union had already shifted from wartime alliance to postwar animosity. A Soviet-backed coup in Czechoslovakia, the failure to hold promised free elections in the rest of Eastern Europe, the blockade of West Berlin, the Soviet rejection of the American-proposed Baruch Plan for the international control of nuclear technology, and a series of confrontations over a long list of international issues had led the two most powerful nations in the postwar world into the intense international competition that came to be known as the cold war. After

1949, the cold war was complicated by the kind of dangerous nuclear arms race that some of the Manhattan Project scientists had feared. That arms race involved the vast expansion of existing stockpiles, the development of small nuclear weapons for use on European battlefields, the persistent search for new and improved ways of delivering nuclear weapons of all sizes to enemy territory, and most importantly, the development of hydrogen (or thermonuclear) weapons.

The decision to accelerate the development of the hydrogen bomb was made in the Truman administration shortly after the reports of a Russian atomic explosion reached Washington. Where atomic bombs were capable of producing explosions measured in thousands of tons of TNT, hydrogen bombs could be constructed to release energy equivalent to millions, and tens of millions, of the now old-fashioned tons of dynamite. A whole new unit of measure for each million tons of TNT, the megaton, had to be invented by military planners contemplating the age of thermo-nuclear weapons. Single bombs could now be designed to destroy not only small cities like Hiroshima and Nagasaki but large cities like New York and Moscow. And they could now be constructed in virtually unlimited numbers. By the end of the 1950s the American nuclear arsenal had a total destructive capacity of approx-imately 19,000 megatons, or 19 trillion tons of TNT.[2] As Eisenhower said in his final State of the Union address, with "both sections of this divided world in possession of unbelievably destructive weapons, mankind approaches a state where mutual annihilation becomes a possibility. No other fact of today's world equals this in importance; it colors everything we say, everything we plan, and everything we do."[3]

President Eisenhower presided over the most dramatic changes in military technology to occur in the twentieth century—the arrival of the hydrogen bomb, the rapid growth of the superpower nuclear arsenals, the deployment of interconti-nental bombers, and the birth of the missile age. Reflecting on these changes in his memoirs, he observed:

> I have pondered, on occasion, the evolution of the military art during the mid-fifties. The Army in which I was commissioned a second lieutenant in 1915 underwent phenomenal changes in the thirty years from then until the German surrender in 1945. ... But those changes, startling as they were, faded into insignificance when compared to those of the postwar period.[4]

Throughout his presidency, Eisenhower attempted to deal with these changes by moderating the pace of the arms race, without endangering American security, and by seeking some first step toward the control of the new and enormously destructive technologies that were being developed. His success in pursuing these goals was not great, but analyzing the problems he faced and the attempts he made to address them illustrates some of the enduring dilemmas that all presidents have confronted in the nuclear age.

Atoms For Peace

Eisenhower received a secret briefing from the Atomic Energy Commission on the first American thermonuclear test shortly after his victory in the 1952 presidential election. Nine months later he learned that the Soviets had successfully developed their own hydrogen bomb. Eisenhower came to the White House at the outset of the thermonuclear revolution. That revolution would require some serious adjustments on the part of the American people and their president. The experimental thermonuclear explosion that Eisenhower heard about in November 1952 was a 10-megaton blast that took place on a small Pacific island. After the test, the island no longer existed; all that remained was an underwater crater 1,500 yards in diameter.[5] The typical hydrogen bomb built during the Eisenhower presidency was roughly a thousand times more powerful than the bombs used against Japan in 1945. Late in the decade the Soviets would test a single bomb with the explosive equivalent of 58 to 60 megatons. The United States never built or tested any weapon that large, but only because it could not think of a good military reason for doing so. Beyond a certain point, it made no sense to make the craters deeper or the rubble bounce higher. The scale of destruction made possible by this new technology was difficult to imagine, even for those who had seen the horrors of World War II and the consequences of Hiroshima and Nagasaki. For Winston Churchill, "the entire foundation of human affairs was revolutionized" by the development of the hydrogen bomb.[6]

Eisenhower was fully aware that a military revolution was underway in the early years of his presidency, and he was very cautious about how he informed the American people about the realities connected with these new and awesome weapons. After a joint press conference with Lewis Strauss, Eisenhower's appointee as chairman of the Atomic Energy Commission, where Strauss freely admitted that hydrogen bombs could be made to destroy completely any city, even New York, the president chided his commission chairman and expressed concern about how the American public would learn about the hydrogen bomb.[7] Revolutions are not easily announced. Nor are they easily incorporated into existing policies.

The changes in nuclear technology in 1953 pushed the Eisenhower administration in two different directions. They led to a greater dependence on nuclear weapons as the basis for the nation's defense and diplomacy and to a serious search for some way to begin the process of controlling the new power available to the nations of the world. Eisenhower's "New Look" in defense involved an explicit emphasis on nuclear weapons and the means for delivering them to enemy targets as a way of reducing the costs associated with conventional armed forces. Keeping overall defense spending within manageable limits was important for Eisenhower, because he was convinced that the long-run health of the American economy was just as important in the cold war as the strength of the military. His approach to the stalemated Korean negotiations was an implicit threat to expand the war "without inhibition in our use of weapons,"[8] a thinly veiled reference to nuclear arms, if a satisfactory armistice was not signed promptly. At the same time that Eisenhower was acknowledging the growing importance of nuclear weapons in the nation's defense and foreign policies, he was also warning his fellow citizens and the world about the costs and dangers that accompanied the thermonuclear age.

In his first major foreign policy address as president, Eisenhower told the American Society for Newspaper Editors in April 1953 that "we had come down a dread road with no turning, where the worst threat was atomic war and the best hope was a life of perpetual terror and tension with the cost of arms draining the wealth and energies of all peoples."[9] The costs were high not only in terms of strained domestic economies, but also in terms of deferred world development. In a global equivalent of his domestic budget decisions, he pledged to devote "a substantial percentage of the savings achieved by disarmament to a fund for world aid and reconstruction."[10] The Chance for Peace speech did not contain new or detailed disarmament proposals but instead made a general case for reducing the burdens and dangers of an accelerating arms race. These were familiar American sentiments, but because they came from a new president and were addressed to a new group of Soviet leaders taking over after Stalin's death, they were well received by the press and public. Eisenhower's next major speech on these issues would contain a more specific and wholly new arms control proposal.

The early drafts of what eventually became the Atoms for Peace speech were prepared throughout 1953, and were intended to provide a detailed explanation to the American people of the dangers that accompanied the hydrogen bomb and the accelerating arms race between the United States and the Soviet Union.[11] Such a speech had been proposed by a government advisory group led by Robert Oppenheimer in 1952, but the suggestion, contained in a document called the "Candor Report," had not been acted on in the final months of the Truman administration.[12] Eisenhower saw merit in Oppenheimer's suggestion and ordered the creation of his own "Operation Candor." Even after Oppenheimer became embroiled in a controversial security clearance hearing in which his loyalty and reliability were publicly challenged, Eisenhower remained committed to the Oppenheimer proposal that an honest and complete picture of the dangers in the thermonuclear age should be drawn for the American people. Eisenhower directed C. D. Jackson, his White House adviser on psychological warfare, to write a major presidential address with a full explanation of the destructive power now available to the United States and the Soviet Union. The first dozen drafts of the speech were all rejected. Apparently, they were too candid, and Eisenhower complained that they "left the listener with only a new terror, not a new hope."[13]

The hope that was later inserted into the speech was a proposal for the creation of an international agency to administer a limited amount of enriched uranium for scientific research and energy production. In what must be one of the rare occasions of a modern president developing a major policy initiative by himself, the idea for an "atom bank" originated with Eisenhower shortly after the announcement of the Soviet thermonuclear test.[14] The idea was simple. Both the United States and the Soviet Union, and perhaps Great Britain, would divert nuclear material currently destined for defense projects to an international agency that would use the materials for peaceful endeavors. At the beginning the amounts of fissionable material would be small, but if the agency grew, its activities might eventually slow the growth of nuclear arsenals. More importantly, if the United States and the Soviet Union could cooperate in this project, it would, Eisenhower wrote to his brother Milton, get the atomic armaments problem off "dead center."[15]

Atoms for Peace was not popular in the Eisenhower cabinet. The secretaries of defense and state raised questions about the wisdom of announcing such a program in a public speech and speculated about the negative impact that it might have in Europe, where our allies were still debating the establishment of a European Defense Community and might be suspicious that a major agreement between the two superpowers was being made at their expense. The whole idea of sharing atomic materials and presumably atomic technology with other countries was also controversial with those members of Congress and bureaucrats who had a stake in the administration of atomic energy and the strict secrecy that surrounded it. Legislation to restructure the Atomic Energy Commission and the coordination of commercial and military nuclear research was pending in the Congress during the first two years of the Eisenhower administration and gave critics of the atom bank an excellent opportunity to restrict the president's proposal. This was, however, a case where cabinet resistance to the president's wishes and anticipated congressional difficulties were not particularly important. The objections raised to the idea of an atom bank were either ignored, resolved, or postponed until detailed negotiations with the Soviet Union could begin. After consulting with British Prime Minister Winston Churchill in Bermuda, a final draft of the Atoms for Peace speech was rapidly prepared while the president flew to New York to address the United Nations. [Document 2.1]

In a long diary entry Eisenhower explained the purposes that he tried to achieve in the speech. First and foremost, he regarded Atoms for Peace as a serious arms control endeavor. Because it was a modest program that would divert small amounts of fissionable material and would not require any inspection of the Soviet Union, it would avoid the obstacles that were preventing progress in all other disarmament discussions. And, if we could "get the Soviet Union working with us in some phase of this whole atomic field that would have only peace and the good of mankind as a goal...[it] might expand into something broader." The "world is racing toward catastrophe," Eisenhower wrote in his diary, and "something must be done to put a brake on this movement."[16] This sincere hope for a beginning to Soviet-American cooperation in halting the arms race was tempered by the recognition that the "U.S. could unquestionably afford to reduce its stockpile by two or three times the amounts that the Russians might contribute to the United Nations agency, and still improve our relative position in the cold war and even in the event of the outbreak of war."[17] Atoms for Peace was modest in its objective, but even more modest in the risks it posed for the United States. In fairness, it must be noted that Eisenhower was willing to make a much larger American commitment of fissionable material to the program than would have been expected from the Soviet Union or Great Britain.[18] But such a concession would not have changed the essence of Atoms for Peace, which was always more important for its symbolism than its substance.

The speech to the United Nations succeeded in combining an honest explanation of the power of hydrogen bombs with a hopeful description of the peaceful uses of atomic energy and, like the Chance for Peace speech earlier in the year, won immediate public praise. The president received an unusually long standing ovation from the General Assembly delegates in the United Nations and nearly universal praise from the media. Winston Churchill, speaking to the House of Commons shortly after the speech, called it "one of the most important events in world history since the end of the war. . . . As I mediated on the President's proposals, limited though they are in scope, and shrouded in technicalities as they are for laymen, I could not help feeling that we were in the process of what might prove to be a turning point in our destiny."[19]

If destiny turned in the aftermath of the Eisenhower proposal, it did so very slowly. Initially, the Russians insisted that any agreement about the formation of an atom bank be accompanied by an agreement repudiating the use of all nuclear weapons—the favorite Soviet arms control proposal of the day. The United States was willing to talk about a wide range of subjects along with Atoms for Peace, but found very little that was worthwhile in the completely unenforceable Soviet non-use agreement. For most of 1954 the negotiations were stalemated on the issue of how broad the agenda should be.[20] Frustration with this slow progress led the

United States temporarily to abandon hopes for an international agency and instead negotiate a series of bilateral agreements for the construction of nuclear research and energy-producing reactors in a number of developing countries. Late in the year, the Soviets surprised the administration by dropping their demand for a broad-based disarmament agreement and by agreeing to resume talks on Atoms for Peace. The rejuvenated negotiations did not, however, lead to a quick agreement. The Soviets raised legitimate questions about the dangers of nuclear proliferation that Eisenhower had seriously underestimated in his UN speech, saying only that "the ingenuity of our scientists will provide special safe conditions under which such a bank of fissionable material can be made essentially immune to surprise seizure."[21]

By the time the International Atomic Energy Agency (IAEA) was fully in operation in 1958, nearly four years after the Atoms for Peace speech, it was a rather different institution than the one that Eisenhower had envisioned. In practice, the IAEA became an international inspection agency that provided oversight for bilateral nuclear development projects rather than the principal owner and operator of third world nuclear reactors. Moreover, the stockpiles of weapons and fissionable material on both sides by the late 1950s were so large that no commitment to the worldwide development of atomic energy, whether internationally operated or bilaterally negotiated, could be regarded as an arms control measure. Throughout Eisenhower's eight years in the White House, both the fears of the nuclear age, which Atoms for Peace tried to alleviate, and the search for a first step in arms control, which Atoms for Peace tried to provide, would continue to be presidential preoccupations.

Open Skies

The lack of progress on Atoms for Peace throughout the mid-1950s and the inconclusive negotiations on comprehensive disarmament that were conducted in various committees of the United Nations left the Eisenhower administration without a realistic arms control proposal at a time when the president was conscious of the growing dangers of the arms race and under pressure to explore the diplomatic opportunities created by the change in Soviet leadership. The middle years of Eisenhower's first term as president saw rising hopes that the cold war tensions between East and West might be reduced. The war in French Indochina was brought to an end in 1954 with a Geneva agreement that temporarily divided Vietnam into a communist north and a noncommunist south. In 1955, the uncertain alignment of Austria in Central Europe was resolved when the Soviets signed a peace treaty that accepted Austrian neutrality. In May of that year Soviet negotiators put forward disarmament proposals that included limited inspection procedures within Soviet territory, the first time they had ever suggested international inspection of facilities inside their borders. When Eisenhower accepted an invitation to join Soviet, British, and French leaders in a July four-power summit in Geneva, he did so amid high expectations that a new and more peaceful relationship might be forged between the Western nations and the Soviet leaders who had replaced Joseph Stalin. The Geneva summit would be the first meeting of Soviet and American heads of state since the end of the Second World War. As the date for the summit approached, members of the Eisenhower administration debated various arms control proposals that could be announced or negotiated at the summit meetings.

The Open Skies initiative emerged from a conference between academics and administration officials arranged by Nelson Rockefeller, C. D. Jackson's successor in the peculiarly cold war position of psychological warfare adviser.[22] The conference met at the Marine base in Quantico, Virginia, in June to consider, among other things, proposals for the scheduled Geneva summit. One of the proposals that members of the conference favored was the possibility of exchanging blueprints of military bases with the Soviet Union and permitting each superpower to photograph the other's installations from the air. The idea had a number of attractive features. It was simple and would be easily understood by the American people and the nations of the world. Opening up both sides to regular aerial inspection would reduce the chances that either side could exaggerate the strategic power of the other or prepare in secret for a surprise attack. The proposal would test Soviet sincerity on the issue of inspection that had most often held up previous arms control negotiations. If the overflights were accepted and became routine, any disarmament agreements in the future would be much easier to verify. If the overflights were rejected, Soviet efforts to win over world opinion with various disarmament proposals would be exposed as mere propaganda.

Eisenhower read the Quantico Conference report despite efforts by Secretary of State John Foster Dulles to prevent him from seeing it,[23] and was particularly enthusiastic about the suggestion for mutual aerial inspection. Calling Dulles immediately, Eisenhower urged the secretary to study the idea carefully because "it might open a tiny gate in the disarmament fence."[24] Rockefeller prepared a memorandum for the president outlining the advantages of mutual aerial inspections [Document 2.2], but Dulles continued to oppose any suggestions that Geneva should be more than an exploratory meeting of government leaders. Dulles was afraid that in serious negotiations the Western allies would be unable to remain united. It was not clear at the outset whether the skies being opened by Rockefeller's idea would be the skies over American and Soviet territory alone, or whether there would be inspection flights above European nations. Dulles was also concerned that during the summit the president's good nature would lead him to accept some ill-considered Soviet offer or response.[25] There may also have been some institutional prejudice against an idea that had come from a group of academic outsiders rather than the foreign policy experts in the Department of State.[26] For a variety of reasons Dulles urged caution, and for a time his sentiments prevailed.

Throughout mid-summer of 1955, and even after the president had arrived in Geneva, bureaucratic maneuvering among Eisenhower's advisers kept Open Skies alive. Rockefeller enlisted support from the chairman of the Joint Chiefs of Staff, Admiral Radford, from the president's adviser on disarmament, Harold Stassen, and from Andrew Goodpaster, the president's trusted staff secretary. He also made sure that drafts of the aerial inspection proposal and some of the experts who had worked on it were close at hand during the Geneva meetings. On the eve of the conference session in which disarmament was the scheduled topic, Eisenhower met with his leading foreign policy advisers in Geneva. At that meeting he decided to insert into a formal statement on the problem of inspection, which he would deliver the next day, a personal proposal that the two superpowers exchange information about the location of military establishments and the right to conduct aerial reconnaissance. [Document 2.3] The president's introduction of Open Skies was brief and general, and he expressed a willingness to consider any Soviet suggestions regarding details.

Although some members of the Soviet delegation expressed interest in Eisenhower's remarks, Nikita Khrushchev immediately announced his opposition. During the Geneva Conference, Khrushchev displayed his emerging dominance of the Soviet collective leadership, and the president spent the remaining sessions trying "to persuade Mr. Khrushchev of the merits of the Open Skies plan, but to no avail."[27] The Soviets criticized Open Skies as inspection without disarmament, and they were justified in doing so. Like Atoms for Peace, Open Skies was only a first step in the disarmament process, and a step that would have been more painful for a secretive society like the Soviet Union than for an American government that regularly announces its defense plans in official reports and newspaper leaks. Unfortunately, the Soviet alternative to inspection without disarmament was disarmament without inspection, at the time an even more unacceptable proposition.

Open Skies, like Atoms for Peace, was well received in American and international public opinion, but failed to produce meaningful progress in arms control negotiations. It remained an American priority and was proposed to the Soviet Union both alone and along with other arms control ideas in a number of forums. The plan was consistently rejected. In practice, a kind of covert open skies arrangement was unilaterally carried out by the United States in the form of unauthorized overflights of Soviet territory by the newly developed high-altitude U-2 spy plane. These flights helped American intelligence agencies verify the slow pace of Soviet deployment of intercontinental bombers and missiles. The flights were never legal, and after one of the U-2 pilots was captured when his plane was shot down in 1960, they were no longer secret. But the U-2 flights were extremely important in giving the president a balanced assessment of Soviet military capabilities at a time when exaggerated estimates had considerable political sway.[28] Ironically, it was the Soviet Union rather than the United States that finally established the precedent for acceptable aerial inspection when Sputnik and the other early Soviet satellites flew unimpeded over American territory. Shortly thereafter, satellite-based photography became an integral part of intelligence operations for both sides and one of the major instruments of verification for the arms control agreements of the 1970s and 1980s.

Throughout his administration, Eisenhower clearly regarded arms control as an important subject. He made it the centerpiece for two of the major foreign policy initiatives during his first term—Atoms for Peace and Open Skies. He consistently appointed able assistants to work on arms control policy and generally gave them the support they needed to make headway against the more cautious members of his administration. He was personally convinced that arms control negotiations were necessary. In a letter Eisenhower wrote in 1956, he stated the central dilemma of the nuclear age about as well as anyone could:

> The true security problem . . . is not merely man against man or nation against nation. It is man against war. . . . When we get to the point, as we one day will, that both sides know that in any outbreak of general hostilities, regardless of the element of surprise, destruction will be reciprocal and complete, possibly we will have sense enough to meet at the conference table with the understanding that the era of armaments has ended and the human race must conform its action to this truth or die.[29]

Atoms for Peace and Open Skies were modest attempts to get us to the conference table by beginning with relatively simple and straightforward limitations on the amount of fissionable material available for weapon construction and the level of secrecy surrounding strategic deployments. The hope was that success with these proposals would lead to further and more fruitful negotiations. Throughout the 1950s, Eisenhower sought some agreement with the Soviet Union that would generate a better relationship between the superpowers. Writing to General Alfred Greunther about the importance of Open Skies, he emphasized the need to reduce the fears felt by both sides. "But if we assume that the kind of inspection to which I referred would eliminate the danger of devastating surprise attack, the agreement for such inspection and this result would yield an immense gain in mutual confidence and trust. This means that we would thus have established a truly realistic basis for studying disarmament."[30] Trust was hard to come by in the early years of the cold war, and both Atoms for Peace and Open Skies failed to become the first step that would lead to more wide ranging arms control negotiations. Serious reductions in superpower armaments and in the easing of the tensions that fueled the cold war competition would not come until much later in the postwar period.

CONCLUSIONS

POWER

The constitutional powers of the president as commander in chief did not change during the Eisenhower administration, but the physical properties of the weapons available to modern military commanders did undergo dramatic escalation. Beginning in the Eisenhower era, it became possible for a single presidential order to result in the death of millions, and perhaps billions, of people across the globe. By some estimates, a large-scale nuclear war of the kind that became possible in the mid-1950s could have created climatic changes that would have ended human existence on the planet. During the Eisenhower administration the image of the president of the United States with a finger hovering above a "nuclear button" became a widely accepted symbol of the military power available to a modern American president.

There is, of course, no button. Instead, special communications codes are carried in a briefcase by a military officer who travels with the president at all times. Use of these codes makes it possible to verify that any orders that might be given with regard to nuclear weapons have come from the commander in chief. Under normal circumstances, presidents retain complete authority over decisions involving the use of nuclear weapons. Most of the weapons are locked in an inactive state and cannot be armed by local military personnel unless the locks are released following a clearly communicated presidential order. Maintaining constant and reliable means of communication between the president and the nation's operational nuclear commanders is not always easy and occupies the time and energy of a large staff of White House technicians. The task is further complicated whenever the chief executive leaves Washington and must ensure that comparable communication capabilities are available at each planned destination.

The enormous importance of decisions surrounding nuclear weapons puts tremendous pressure on modern presidents and enhances concern for issues arising from presidential succession or disability. The Constitution provides for the succession of the vice president to the presidency if a sitting president dies or resigns.

In addition, the Twenty-fifth Amendment to the Constitution [Document 2.4] establishes a system for filling vacancies in the vice presidency by presidential appointment and confirmation in both houses of Congress. If a president dies or resigns while the vice presidency is vacant, or if both the president and vice president die or resign simultaneously, legislation currently designates that succession will pass to the Speaker of the House of Representatives and then to the president pro tempore of the Senate. Because all the nation's senior political leaders could conceivably be killed in a surprise attack on Washington, D.C., it must be assumed that provisions have been made for this possibility. The exact nature of planning for such contingencies is naturally classified, but it is often discussed in general terms by experts in military strategy who suggest that in the event of an attack aimed at America's political leadership command of nuclear retaliatory forces would pass to specially trained and protected senior military officers.[31] Though presidential succession is guided by obscure constitutional provisions, legislative acts, and secret military plans, in today's world it is extremely important. In the confusion that followed the assassination attempt against President Reagan in 1981, Secretary of State Alexander Haig mistakenly announced that he was in charge of the federal government when, in fact, Vice President George Bush, who was then flying back to Washington, was the constitutionally designated national leader. In the nuclear age, it is essential that there be minimal confusion about who is in charge in a national emergency.

Presidential disability, even more than presidential succession, involves complicated and largely untested constitutional provisions. The same amendment that provides procedures for filling vacancies in the vice presidency also outlines what is to be done when a president is ill or otherwise unable to carry out official duties, including the command of nuclear and other military forces. Presidents may voluntarily, and temporarily, surrender their responsibilities to a vice president if illness or incapacity briefly makes it impossible for them to carry out their duties. After the Twenty-fifth Amendment became binding in 1967, at least one president, Ronald Reagan, used its procedures when undergoing surgery.[32] Even before the amendment was ratified, President Eisenhower set important precedents by making specific arrangements to transfer his responsibilities temporarily to Vice President Richard Nixon in the event of presidential incapacity. These formal arrangements were made after Eisenhower had suffered from three serious illnesses—a stomach operation, a heart attack, and a stroke—each of which raised legitimate questions about the president's abilities to perform his duties. If a president knows that he or she is unable to carry out White House duties and willingly accepts a temporary transfer of responsibilities to a vice president, there can be no question about who is in charge of the American government. But things become much more complicated and troublesome if a president is incapacitated and refuses to acknowledge that fact. Who, then, would have control over our vast nuclear arsenal?

The Twenty-fifth Amendment outlines procedures by which the vice president and cabinet could theoretically remove a physically or mentally ill chief executive who refuses to acknowledge his or her illness, but these procedures have never been tried in practice and are full of difficulties that would be very hard to resolve in the midst of the political crisis that would almost certainly surround a contested public debate about a president's disability. In its history the United States has had presidents who continued in office during illnesses or periods of questionable mental capacity. Woodrow Wilson had a crippling stroke during the last year of his presidency and, for a time, government decisions were executed by his wife, who held a pen in the president's otherwise motionless hand and signed Wilson's name to official documents. At the height of the Watergate affair, near the end of Richard Nixon's presidency, there were widely circulated rumors that the president was depressed, drinking too much, and prone to take irrational action. As a precaution, Nixon's secretary of defense, James Schlesinger, instructed all military commanders to report unusual orders that did not come through the normal chain of command.[33] In taking this action Schlesinger may well have been acting beyond the constitutional authority of a cabinet officer, but in a world in which the president of the United States controls weapons of an immensely dangerous nature, it is not surprising that those around the president would be extremely sensitive to any behavior that threatened the security and safety of the nation and the world.

Since the presidency of Harry Truman, all American presidents have had the power to control nuclear weapons, to order a nuclear attack against another nation, or to use these destructive weapons in retaliation for an attack on the United States. All of these momentous actions could presumably be taken without any expectation of formal or informal congressional consultation. As we will see in subsequent chapters, the line between the war powers of the Congress and the president's authority as commander in chief of the armed forces is often difficult to draw. During Truman's presidency at the end of the Second World War, there was a widely accepted consensus that the chief executive had extraordinary powers during hostilities with Germany and Japan. The cold war would begin with a similar consensus that special presidential powers were necessary to protect us from the Soviet threat, but that consensus would be shaken by the Vietnam War and other events in the 1960s and 1970s. At no time, even at the height of the controversy surrounding war powers in the aftermath of the Nixon presidency, has it been seriously suggested that the president of the United States would be expected to do anything but act alone in the horrifying national emergencies involving nuclear attack against this nation. The vulnerability of the United States, and every other nation, to massive destruction in the nuclear age and the speed with which weapons can reach their targets when delivered by ballistic missiles dictates this concentration of power in presidential hands. The power to make life and death decisions for hundreds of millions of people, and perhaps for the whole human race, is not specifically granted by the Constitution or written into legislation. It is a function of the realities of modern warfare that emerged during the Eisenhower administration.

Eisenhower responded to these realities by accepting presidential responsibility for national security, building an adequate arsenal of nuclear weapons, developing the most efficient means for delivering them to enemy territory, and making it clear that any attack on this nation or its closest allies would result in devastating retaliation. He was uncomfortable with all of these decisions. They gave the nation unprecedented military strength and some security, but at a very high cost. Weapons and their delivery systems were growing ever more elaborate and expensive, and fears of Soviet superiority were fueling a rapidly accelerating arms race. Nuclear deterrence provided, at best, a tenuous security and forced the American people and their leaders to live with the possibility of almost unimaginable national and global disaster if deterrence ever failed. All of the postwar presidents have been conscious of the fact that the nuclear weapons at the heart of the nation's security are so powerful and dangerous that their use could easily destroy the very values they are intended to defend. For that reason, Eisenhower, and all of his successors, have taken the power of modern weaponry, and the power of the presidency to control that weaponry, as a very mixed blessing. From Eisenhower on, each of the postwar presidents, in one way or another, has attempted to negotiate limitations on the numbers and qualities of nuclear arms.

PROCESS

In the Eisenhower administration, arms control negotiations with the Soviet Union produced very little progress, and both Atoms for Peace and Open Skies had their greatest impact when they were first announced as American negotiating suggestions. Arms control in the 1950s was, for the most part, a matter of spoken words rather than written treaties. This does not mean that nothing of consequence in the control of strategic weapons occurred during the Eisenhower presidency. The importance of presidential speeches and announcements should not be underestimated. Theodore Roosevelt is famous for calling the presidency a "bully pulpit" and drawing attention to the ability that a president has to set the national and international agenda by the words that are spoken in public forums. Understanding the process by which presidents and their advisers decide on the language to be used in formal speeches and international conferences is fundamental to understanding modern American foreign policy. In this regard, Atoms for Peace and Open Skies provide interesting and contrasting lessons about presidential involvement in the decisions surrounding important public statements.

In the case of Atoms for Peace, Eisenhower took personal charge over the drafting of the speech that would eventually be delivered to the United Nations in December 1953. He decided early in his first year in office that he wanted to give a major address on the subject of the hydrogen bomb and how the enormous power of this new weapon would affect the lives of American citizens and people throughout the world. He stuck to that commitment even after the scientist who had suggested a candid explanation of nuclear realities, Robert Oppenheimer, became the subject of a controversial security investigation. Eisenhower commissioned C. D. Jackson, who was by training a journalist and a professional writer, to draft the candid address on nuclear weapons and gave Jackson considerable personal direction regarding the content of the speech. Eisenhower understood from the outset that this would be an important presidential statement and was in no hurry to go before the American people with a poorly conceived message. He waited for nearly a year until he felt that he and his staff had developed the best possible speech and then used an invitation from the United Nations to guarantee a large international audience. The president was involved throughout the development of the Atoms for Peace speech. He read and rejected early drafts because they failed to offer any hope, and he personally came up with the idea that would constitute the hopeful half of the presentation. Presidents often take great care in preparing particular speeches and occasionally write what they wish to say without the aid of speechwriters, but it is somewhat unusual for the chief executive to develop a major policy proposal alone. In this case, it is a mark of how much importance Eisenhower placed on the message to the American people that would be developed as part of Operation Candor.

The systematic involvement of the president in the preparation of what became the Atoms for Peace speech meant that the development of serious cabinet opposition to the idea of an international atom bank was easily overcome. Many administration officials were not told about the pending speech, including all the members of the Atomic Energy Commission, except its chairman.[34] Those who did know about Operation Candor and had reservations about giving away atomic secrets, like Secretary of Defense Charles Wilson, also knew that candor was important to Eisenhower and that the idea for an international atomic energy agency had come directly from the president's desk. That information had the effect of moderating opposition. Presidential advisers criticize each other's positions much more freely than they criticize presidential proposals. Given the high level of presidential involvement and interest, Atoms for Peace was guaranteed the most serious possible consideration. Open Skies had none of these advantages and was almost lost in the bureaucratic shuffle.

The idea for a negotiated agreement to permit mutual aerial reconnaissance came from a group of government officials and academic outsiders who helped Nelson Rockefeller prepare agenda items a few weeks before the Geneva summit. Several factors nearly killed the idea before it even reached presidential attention. In the summer of 1955, Nelson Rockefeller was a relatively new member of Eisenhower's White House staff who lacked the speechwriting credentials that C. D. Jackson had brought to the position of psychological warfare adviser. Rockefeller's Quantico Conference was one of his first efforts to influence a major presidential decision and made him a potential competitor with John Foster Dulles for foreign policy power within the administration. Rockefeller was in a relatively weak position for advocating a major new policy initiative at a time when Dulles favored a low profile for the upcoming summit. The fact that Open Skies had come from an informal meeting with outsiders further weakened its chances. According to one of the participants at Quantico, the general attitude of foreign policy officials at the conference was "one of irritation at the idea that some smart outside one-shot kibitzers will be able to suck out of their thumbs something that the professionals who work 365 days a year won't already have thought of, and probably discarded."[35] Rockefeller had a great deal of bureaucratic resistance to overcome.

He was able to overcome these obstacles for a number of reasons. The existence of a scheduled summit in July meant that the administration faced a rapidly approaching deadline. The president would go to Geneva and would need something to say to the American people upon his departure and something to show for his efforts upon his return. Superpower summits, particularly when they have not occurred for some time, generate enormous public interest, media coverage, and expectations that the meeting will make a difference. Though Dulles did not want to use the summit for the introduction of new foreign policy proposals, his cautious advice ran against the tide of political pressures generated by the first meeting of Soviet and American leaders in a decade. They also ran against the inclinations of the president, who wanted to make progress in the arms control arena.

Throughout the Eisenhower presidency, and for years thereafter, commentators were convinced that John Foster Dulles, rather than President Eisenhower, was the guiding force behind American foreign policy in the 1950s. More recently, scholars examining the materials in the Eisenhower presidential library have concluded that Eisenhower practiced a "hidden-hand" leadership style in which he used his cabinet officers to take controversial public stands but ensured that behind the scenes he was fully in control of the major decisions in his administration.[36] Dulles would ultimately fail to keep Open Skies off the Geneva agenda because Eisenhower was frustrated with the slow progress on Atoms for Peace in 1955 and wanted new arms control ideas for the summit. Initially, he looked for those new ideas to come from his United Nations disarmament negotiator, Harold Stassen, who briefed the National Security Council on a new set of American negotiating positions prior to the Geneva meeting. Unfortunately, those new positions were comprehensive, complicated, and unlikely to lead to any breakthrough in the near future. Moreover, the verification necessary in connection with the arms control agreements that Stassen favored would have required substantial and highly intrusive inspection procedures. The president needed a simple idea, like the atom bank, that could be clearly understood, and rapidly agreed to, if he was going to get anything done at Geneva. Rockefeller provided the president with exactly what he wanted.

Eisenhower's initial favorable response to the Open Skies idea when he read the Quantico Conference report did not automatically place the subject of aerial reconnaissance on the agenda for Geneva. The issue was referred to Dulles, who promised to investigate it, but failed to become an enthusiastic supporter. Rockefeller, who was not invited to accompany the president to the summit, continued to lobby for Open Skies after it had been turned over to Dulles. He had the assistance of his predecessor, C. D. Jackson, who participated at Quantico and wrote to the president praising the surprisingly good results that had come from a group "containing an alarmingly large number of Ph.D.'s."[37] He was also able to win the support of a number of the president's personal and military advisers who understood the value of a regularized and legitimate opportunity to spy on Soviet territory. As the summit approached, the circle of advocates for the Open Skies idea had become wider, and though Rockefeller was not invited to be with the president in Switzerland, he made sure that he and key members of his staff were close by in Paris. No commitment to Open Skies had been made when the president flew to Geneva, but no decision against it had been made either. On the night before the summit disarmament session, after several days of inconclusive talks, Eisenhower asked for a review of Open Skies. By that time, the staff work for the proposal was completed, the number of presidential advisers in favor of the plan was substantial, and those most knowledgeable about the issue could easily be brought to Geneva.

Though Eisenhower's introduction of Open Skies was meant to appear casual and spontaneous, it was, in fact, a carefully prepared and orchestrated presidential statement. Unlike Atoms for Peace, it was not a pet project of the chief executive that went through months of review and revision. Instead, it emerged rather quickly as the summit deadline loomed and only after a fair amount of bureaucratic infighting. When Open Skies caught the imagination of the world watching the summit's progress, the few words spoken by Eisenhower as a departure from his official text easily became one of the lasting legacies of the 1955 four-power meeting. What presidents say, even if it is not followed by concrete international action, can have significant consequences for foreign affairs. In both Atoms for Peace and Open Skies, President Eisenhower, the hero of the Second World War and the only postwar president with extensive military experience, made clear to his nation and to the world that he favored policies that would ease tensions with the Soviet Union and begin to bring nuclear arms under some sort of control. In the long run, those words would make it easier for Eisenhower's successors to advocate détente and arms limitations that, in the 1950s, never quite got past the speechmaking stage.

PERSONALITY

Why did Eisenhower, in the midst of the cold war, when the United States was extremely distrustful of Soviet action try as hard as he did to get started with arms control negotiations? Why did someone who had been a military officer throughout most of his adult life and the commander of the largest army ever assembled by the democratic nations of the world want to limit the arms available to fighting forces in the second half of the twentieth century? Why did someone who earned his fame as a leader in war want, more than anything else, to leave a legacy of peace? The contradictions here are not as great as they may at first appear.

Eisenhower's long years of experience in the military may have made it easier for him to understand the devastating consequences of the nuclear revolution and the dangers that it posed for the world. As a participant in the wartime decisions to bomb German cities with conventional weapons, Eisenhower had firsthand knowledge of the moral dilemmas that arise when civilians become prime targets in military operations. He knew what conventional bombing could do, and when he was asked by Stimson at the Potsdam Conference for his opinion about the forthcoming use of atomic weapons against Japanese cities, he recommended that they not be used.[38] The years of the Second World War may have sensitized Eisenhower to the moral consequences of modern warfare. His last military post as the first commander of NATO forces in Europe would have taught him about the dangers of war with the Soviet Union and the likelihood that such a war would quickly become nuclear. Because of these personal and professional experiences, Eisenhower understood, from the outset of his administration, the serious military and diplomatic dangers with which he would have to grapple.

As president, Eisenhower never took those dangers lightly or tried to avoid them. He was willing to lead an administration that openly based American defenses on the power of nuclear weapons and promised "massive retaliation" to any nation that threatened vital American interests. But he never regarded nuclear deterrence and massive retaliation as the final answers to the problems raised by the existence of nuclear weapons and resisted suggestions that nuclear war would ever be an acceptable alternative in less than desperate situations. Nuclear threats were made against the Chinese in connection with the Korean armistice negotiations and consideration was given, at various times in the Eisenhower presidency, to the use of nuclear weapons in other regional disputes. But no actual use of the weapons was ever authorized, and it is impossible to know whether any of the threats that were made would ever have been carried out.

In private, Eisenhower urged those around him to be aware of the devastation that would accompany any use of nuclear weapons. "Any notion that 'the bomb' is a cheap way to solve things is awfully wrong," he told his cabinet early in 1953. "It is cold comfort for any citizen of Western Europe to be assured that—after his country is overrun and he is pushing up daisies—someone still alive will drop a bomb on the Kremlin."[39] In June 1954 he told a group of military officers that they should never expect easy victories in the nuclear age:

> No matter how well prepared for war we may be, no matter how certain we are that within 24 hours we could destroy Kuibyshev and Moscow and Leningrad and Baku and all the other places that would allow the Soviets to carry on war, I want you to carry this question home with you: Gain such a victory, and what do you do with it? Here

would be a great area from the Elbe to Vladisvostok and down through Southeast Asia torn up and destroyed without government, without its communications, just an area of starvation and disaster. I ask you what would the civilized world do about it? I repeat, there is no victory in any war except through our imaginations, through our dedication, and through our work to avoid it.[40]

Eisenhower's personal experiences in the military ironically may have made him one of the least militaristic of the postwar presidents. He was elected on a promise that he would go to Korea, and an implication that he would bring a rapid end to the fighting there. He was hesitant throughout his presidency to commit American combat forces overseas and avoided using American troops to save the French in Southeast Asia, to liberate the Hungarians after their revolt, or to assist America's European allies in Suez. He did make serious military threats against the Chinese in order to preserve Taiwanese control over two relatively small offshore islands and against the Soviets in order to guarantee the freedom of Berlin. But his eight years in the White House are remarkable, in retrospect, for their peace and prosperity.

Eisenhower ended his presidency with a personal warning to the American people regarding the dangers posed by the emergence of a military-industrial complex. [Document 2.5] His Farewell Address is perhaps his best remembered and most often quoted speech. In it he pointed out that the important decisions being made about modern weaponry were increasingly complex, technical, and beyond the capacity of political leaders, much less ordinary citizens, to understand fully. This new complexity raised the possibility that important decisions would be made by experts in the military-industrial complex rather than through the democratic processes and institutions that traditionally shaped American defense policy. The existence of an independent academic community with its own expertise capable of checking the influence of military and industry specialists was also endangered. Government-funded scientific research on campuses across the country was creating a scientific and technological elite that could no longer afford to criticize the departments, agencies, and corporations that financed their scientific activities. As a result important opportunities for public debate were being closed off.

Eisenhower was not afraid of the sort of waste, fraud, and abuse among military contractors that so often makes headlines today. His warning to the nation was about a far more subtle threat. Well-meaning scientists, engineers, and industrialists, believing that they were acting in the best interest of the nation, might urge the construction of more weapons and more dangerous weaponry than would, in fact, be wise. Researchers dependent on government support would be unlikely to raise serious objections to these endeavors. Citizens and political leaders without expert knowledge of their own might not be able to understand the issues that were before them and might defer to specialists from industry, the Pentagon, and the academic community. Eisenhower, the only genuine military expert to hold America's highest elected office in modern history, ended his presidency by warning us against putting too much faith in the very people he knew best. He wanted us to look beyond the military-industrial complex and the scientific-technological elite to form our own judgments about the dangers of the nuclear age and what we should do to reduce those dangers. Eisenhower's unique personal background gave that sobering message enormous power and persuasive appeal.

Chronology of Eisenhower's Arms Control Decisions

1952

Nov 2   U.S. tests first thermonuclear explosive.

Nov 7   President-elect Eisenhower briefed on H-bomb test.

1953

Mar 6   Stalin's death announced by Kremlin officials.

Apr 16   President gives Chance for Peace speech.

Aug 12   Soviets test their first hydrogen bomb.

Dec 4-7   Eisenhower meets with Churchill in Bermuda.

Dec 8   Atoms for Peace speech to the United Nations.

1954

Apr 12   Hearings begin on removal of Robert Oppenheimer's security clearance.

Jul 27   Atomic Energy Act of 1954 passed by the Congress.

1955

May 10   Soviets offer to allow some stationary inspection sites on their territory as part of a future disarmament agreement.

Jun 5-9   Conference at Quantico, Virginia develops aerial inspection idea.

Jun 30   NSC reviews Stassen's disarmament plan and Open Skies proposal.

Jul 6   Rockefeller memo to the president recommending Open Skies.

Jul 21   Eisenhower makes Open Skies offer at Geneva summit.

Sep 23   Eisenhower suffers heart attack.

1956

Sep 20   UN conference debates establishment of IAEA.

Oct 23   Conference unanimously adopts creation of IAEA.

1957

Oct 1   First meeting of IAEA in Vienna.

Nov 25   Eisenhower suffers a stroke.

1958

Sep 1   Second international conference on the peaceful uses of atomic energy convenes in Geneva.

1961

Jan 17   Eisenhower's Farewell Address.

Chapter 2 Documents

Document 2.1
Atoms for Peace Speech, selected passages, December 8, 1953

. . . I feel impelled to speak today in a language that in a sense is new—one which I, who have spent so much of my life in the military profession, would have preferred never to use.

That new language is the language of atomic warfare.

The atomic age has moved forward at such a pace that every citizen of the world should have some comprehension, at least in comparative terms, of the extent of this development of the utmost significance to every one of us. Clearly, if the peoples of the world are to conduct an intelligent search for peace, they must be armed with the significant facts of today's existence.

My recital of atomic danger and power is necessarily stated in United States terms, for these are the only incontrovertible facts that I know. I need hardly point out to this Assembly, however, that this subject is global, not merely national in character.

On July 16, 1945, the United States set off the world's first atomic explosion. Since that date in 1945, the United States of America has conducted 42 test explosions.

Atomic bombs today are 25 times as powerful as the weapons with which the atomic age dawned, while hydrogen weapons are in the ranges of millions of tons of TNT equivalent.

Today, the United States' stockpile of atomic weapons, which, of course, increases daily, exceeds by many times the explosive equivalent of the total of all bombs and all shells that came from every plane and every gun in every theatre of war in all of the years of World War II.

A single air group, whether afloat or land-based, can now deliver to any reachable target a destructive cargo exceeding in power all the bombs that fell on Britain in all of World War II.

In size and variety, the development of atomic weapons has been no less remarkable. The development has been such that atomic weapons have virtually achieved conventional status within our armed services. In the United States, the Army, the Navy, the Air Force, and the Marine Corps are all capable of putting this weapon to military use.

But the dread secret, and the fearful engines of atomic might, are not ours alone.

In the first place, the secret is possessed by our friends and allies, Great Britain and Canada, whose scientific genius made a tremendous contribution to our original discoveries, and the designs of atomic bombs.

The secret is also known by the Soviet Union.

The Soviet Union has informed us that, over recent years, it has devoted extensive resources to atomic weapons. During this period, the Soviet Union has exploded a series of atomic devices, including at least one involving thermo-nuclear reactions.

If at one time the United States possessed what might have been called a monopoly of atomic power, that monopoly ceased to exist several years ago. Therefore, although our earlier start has permitted us to accumulate what is today a great quantitative advantage, the atomic realities of today comprehend two facts of even greater significance.

First, the knowledge now possessed by several nations will eventually be shared by others—possibly all nations.

Second, even a vast superiority in numbers of weapons, and a consequent capability of devastating retaliation, is no preventive, of itself, against the fearful material damage and toll of human lives that would be inflicted by surprise aggression.

The free world, at least dimly aware of these facts, has naturally embarked on a large program of warning and defense systems. That program will be accelerated and expanded.

But let no one think that the expenditure of vast sums for weapons and systems of defense can guarantee absolute safety for the cities and citizens of any nation. The awful arithmetic of the atomic bomb does not permit of any such easy solution. Even against the most powerful defense, an aggressor in possession of the effective minimum number of atomic bombs for a surprise attack could probably place a sufficient number of his bombs on the chosen targets to cause hideous damage.

Should such an atomic attack be launched against the United States, our reactions would be swift and resolute. But for me to say that the defense capabilities of the United States are such that they could inflict terrible losses upon an aggressor—for me to say that the retaliation capabilities of the United States are so great that such an aggressor's land would be laid waste—all this, while fact, is not the true expression of the purpose and the hope of the United States.

To pause there would be to confirm the hopeless finality of a belief that two atomic colossi are doomed malevolently to eye each other indefinitely across a trembling world. To stop there would be to accept helplessly the probability of civilization destroyed—the annihilation of the irreplaceable heritage of mankind handed down to us generation after generation—and the condemnation of mankind to begin all over again the age-old struggle upward from savagery toward decency, and right, and justice. . . .

So my country's purpose is to help us move out of the dark chamber of horrors into the light, to find a way by which the minds of men, the hopes of men, the souls of men everywhere, can move forward toward peace and happiness and well being. . . .

To hasten the day when fear of the atom will begin to disappear from the minds of people, and the governments of the East and West, there are certain steps that can be taken now.

I therefore make the following proposals:

The Governments principally involved, to the extent permitted by elementary prudence, to begin now and continue to make joint contributions from their stockpiles of normal uranium and fissionable materials to an International Atomic Energy Agency. We would expect that such an agency would be set up under the aegis of the United Nations.

The ratios of contributions, the procedures and other details would properly be within the scope of the "private conversations" I have referred to earlier.

The United States is prepared to undertake these explorations in good faith. Any partner of the United States acting in the same good faith will find the United States a not unreasonable or ungenerous associate.

Undoubtedly initial and early contributions to this plan would be small in quantity. However, the proposal has the great virtue that it can be undertaken without the irritations and mutual suspicions incident to any attempt to set up a completely acceptable system of world-wide inspection and control.

The Atomic Energy Agency could be made responsible for impounding, storage, and protection of the contributed fissionable and other materials. The ingenuity of our scientists will provide special safe conditions under which such a bank of fissionable material can be made essentially immune to surprise seizure.

The more important responsibility of this Atomic Energy Agency would be to devise methods whereby this fissionable material would be allocated to serve the peaceful pursuits of mankind. Experts would be mobilized to apply atomic energy to the needs of agriculture, medicine, and other peaceful activities. A special purpose would be to provide abundant electrical energy in the power-starved areas of the world. Thus the contributing powers would be dedicating some of their strength to serve the needs rather than the fears of mankind. . . .

Against the dark background of the atomic bomb, the United States does not wish merely to present strength, but also the desire and the hope for peace.

The coming months will be fraught with fateful decisions. In this Assembly; in the capitals and military headquarters of the world; in the hearts of men everywhere, be they governors or governed, may they be the decisions which will lead this world out of fear and into peace.

To the making of these fateful decisions, the United States pledges before you—and therefore before the world—its determination to help solve the fearful atomic dilemma—to devote its entire heart and mind to find the way by which the miraculous inventiveness of man shall not be dedicated to his death, but consecrated to his life.

I again thank the delegates for the great honor they have done me, in inviting me to appear before them, and in listening to me so courteously. Thank you.

Source: *Public Papers of the Presidents of the United States: Dwight D. Eisenhower, 1953* , pp. 813–822.

Document 2.2
Rockefeller Memorandum for the President July 6, 1955

SUBJECT: Disarmament Proposal for Four Power Conference

Basic U.S. policies, with exception of disarmament, are considered in NSC 5524, Basic U.S. Policy in Relation to Four Power Conference, which is up for consideration Thursday, July 7. The U.S. position on disarmament, which was studied separately by Governor Stassen, was considered at last Thursday's NSC meeting. As a result of that consideration, you directed Governor Stassen to study further and in detail the problem of inspection to determine if a workable, satisfactory inspection method exists and, if so, how it affects his plan. The results of this study will not be available for the Big Four conference.

The subject of disarmament is of outstanding importance in connection with preparations for the Big Four conference because:

1.   It is so closely related to the establishment of lasting peace, our primary long-term objective.

2.   Our former U.S. position is outmoded and we have not developed a new one.

3.   The Soviets are almost certain to press discussion of this subject at the Geneva Big Four conference.

4.   The Soviets have the initiative in this field by virtue of their May 10, 1955, proposals which represented, for them, great concessions.

5.   More than any other world problem it has universal appeal and decided psychological aspects.

6.   If we come to a wrong position, we will sacrifice our security either through loss of our allies or loss of the strength with which to defend ourselves.

In last week's NSC discussion of disarmament three main points stood out:

1.   Inspection is the key to disarmament.

2.   We must have something we can talk about.

3.   We must educate the people as to what a satisfactory disarmament entails.

I believe that you should give serious consideration to the proposal on the part of the U.S. at the forthcoming conference for an agreement for mutual inspection of military installations, forces and armaments without limitations provisions. This proposal for testing an inspection system before limiting or reducing armaments seems to me to be a step in the direction of meeting all three points I have listed above. I cannot see any aspect of it—even if the Soviets accept it, which is highly doubtful—which in any way seriously jeopardizes our security. Instead, it would offer many advantages beyond the main one of testing to determine the practicability of an inspection system. Among the collateral advantages are the following:

1.   Regains the initiative in disarmament negotiation; provides us a position at Geneva.

2.   Helps break down the Iron Curtain.

3.   Provides us intelligence.

4.   Poses a difficult decision for the Soviets.

5.   Focuses on a practical and immediate aspect of disarmament which people in general can understand.

6.   Exposes the phoniness of the proposed Soviet inspection system— the Korean-like type that provides for international inspectors at ports, major airfields, etc.

7.   Demonstrates first hand to the Soviets our greater war potential.

RECOMMENDATION

That, subject to concurrence of the Secretary of State, the Secretary of Defense, and Governor Stassen, and, further, subject to coordination with the British and the French, you offer at the forthcoming Big Four conference a proposal for mutual inspection of military installations, forces, and armaments, without any arms limitations provisions.

Nelson A. Rockefeller

Source: Dwight D. Eisenhower Library, Abilene, Kansas: White House Office, Office of the Special Assistant for National Security Affairs (Robert Cutler, Dillon Anderson, and Gordon Gray): Records, 1952-61, NSC Series, Briefing Notes Subseries, Box # 8, Folder "Four Power Heads of Government Meetings (4)."

Document 2.3
Eisenhower on Open Skies at the Geneva Summit,
selected passages, July 21, 1955

. . .Gentlemen, since I have been working on this memorandum to present to this conference, I have been searching my heart and mind for something that I could say here that could convince everyone of the great sincerity of the United States in approaching this problem of disarmament. I should address myself for a moment principally to the delegates from the Soviet Union, because our two great countries admittedly possess new and terrible weapons in quantities which do give rise in other parts of the world, or reciprocally, to the fears and dangers of surprise attack.

U.S. PROPOSAL

I propose, therefore, that we take a practical step, that we begin an arrangement, very quickly, as between ourselves—immediately. These steps would include:

To give to each other a complete blueprint of our military establishments, from beginning to end, from one end of our countries to the other; lay out the establishments and provide the blueprints to each.

Next, to provide within our countries facilities for aerial photography to the other country—we to provide you the facilities within our country, ample facilities for aerial reconnaissance, where you can make all the pictures you choose and take them to your own country to study; you to provide exactly the same facilities for us and we to make these examinations, and by this step to convince the world that we are providing as between ourselves against the possibility of great surprise attack, thus lessening danger and relaxing tensions.

Likewise we will make more easily attainable a comprehensive and effective system of inspection and disarmament, because what I propose, I assure you, would be but a beginning. . . .

Source: *Bulletin of the Department of State*, 33 (July-December 1955), 174.

Document 2.4
The Twenty-fifth Amendment to the Constitution
ratified February 1967

Section 1. In case of the removal of the President from office or of his death or resignation, the Vice President shall become President.

Section 2. Whenever there is a vacancy in the office of the Vice President, the President shall nominate a Vice President who shall take office upon confirmation by a majority vote of both Houses of Congress.

Section 3. Whenever the President transmits to the President pro tempore of the Senate and the Speaker of the House of Representatives his written declaration that he is unable to discharge the powers and duties of his office, and until he transmits to them a written declaration to the contrary, such powers and duties shall be discharged by the Vice President as Acting President.

Section 4. Whenever the Vice President and a majority of either the principal officers of the executive departments or of such other body as Congress may by law provide, transmit to the President pro tempore of the Senate and the Speaker of the House of Representatives their written declaration that the President is unable to discharge the powers and duties of his office, the Vice President shall immediately assume the powers and duties of the office of Acting President.

Thereafter, when the President transmits to the President pro tempore of the Senate and the Speaker of the House of Representatives his written declaration that no inability exists, he shall resume the powers and duties of his office unless the Vice President and a majority of either the principal officers of the executive departments or of such other body as Congress may by law provide, transmit within four days to the President pro tempore of the Senate and the Speaker of the House of Representatives their written declaration that the President is unable to discharge the powers and duties of his office. Thereupon the Congress shall decide the issue, assembling within forty-eight hours for that purpose if not in session. If the Congress within twenty-one days after receipt of the latter written declaration, or, if Congress is not in session, within twenty-one days after Congress is required to assemble, determines by two-thirds vote of both Houses that the President is unable to discharge the powers and duties of his office, the Vice President shall continue to discharge the same as Acting President; otherwise, the President shall resume the powers and duties of his office.

Document 2.5
Farewell Address to the Nation,
selected passages, January 17, 1961

... We face a hostile ideology—global in scope, atheistic in character, ruthless in purpose, and insidious in method. Unhappily the danger it poses promises to be of indefinite duration. To meet it successfully there is call for not so much the emotional and transitory sacrifices of crisis but rather those which enable us to carry forward steadily, surely, and without complaint the burdens of a prolonged and complex struggle—with liberty the stake. Only thus shall we remain, despite every provocation, on our charted course toward permanent peace and human betterment.

Crises there will continue to be. In meeting them, whether foreign or domestic, great or small, there is a recurring temptation to feel that some spectacular and costly action could become the miraculous solution to all current difficulties. A huge increase in newer elements of our defense; development of unrealistic programs to cure every ill in agriculture; a dramatic expansion in basic and applied research—these and many other possibilities, each possibly promising in itself, may be suggested as the only way to the road we wish to travel.

But each proposal must be weighed in the light of a broader consideration: the need to maintain balance in and among national programs—balance between the private and the public economy, balance between cost and hoped for advantage—balance between the clearly necessary and the comfortably desirable; balance between our essential requirements as a nation and the duties imposed by the nation upon the individual; balance between actions of the moment and national welfare of the future. Good judgment seeks balance and progress; lack of it eventually finds imbalance and frustration.

The record of many decades stand as proof that our people and their Government have, in the main, understood these truths and have responded to them well in the face of stress and threat. But threats, new in kind or degree, constantly arise. I mention two only.

IV

A vital element in keeping the peace is our military establishment. Our arms must be mighty, ready for instant action, so that no potential aggressor may be tempted to risk his own destruction.

Our military organization today bears little relation to that known by any of my predecessors in peacetime, or indeed by the fighting men of World War II and Korea.

Until the latest of our world conflicts, the United States had no armaments industry. American makers of plowshares could, with time and as required, make swords as well. But now we can no longer risk emergency improvisation of national defense; we have been compelled to create a permanent armaments industry of vast proportions. Added to this, three and a half million men and women are directly engaged in the defense establishment. We annually spend on military security more than the net income of all United States corporations.

This conjunction of an immense military establishment and a large arms industry is new in the American experience. The total influence—economic, political, even spiritual—is felt in every city, every State house, every office of the Federal Government. We recognize the imperative need for this development. Yet we must not fail to comprehend its grave implications. Our toil, resources and livelihood are all involved; so is the very structure of our society.

In the councils of government, we must guard against the acquisition of unwarranted influence, whether sought or unsought, by the military-industrial complex. The potential for the disastrous rise of misplaced power exists and will persist.

We must never let the weight of this combination endanger our liberties or democratic processes. We should take nothing for granted. Only an alert and knowledgeable citizenry can compel the proper meshing of the huge industrial and military machinery of defense with our peaceful methods and goals so that security and liberty may prosper together.

Akin to, and largely responsible for the sweeping changes in our industrial-military posture, has been the technological revolution during recent decades.

In this revolution, research has become central; it also becomes more formalized, complex, and costly. A steadily increasing share is conducted for, by, or at the direction of, the Federal Government.

Today, the solitary inventor, tinkering in his shop, has been overshadowed by task forces of scientists in laboratories and testing fields. In the same fashion, the free university, historically the fountainhead of free ideas and scientific discovery, has experienced a revolution in the conduct of research. Partly because of the huge costs involved, a government contract becomes virtually a substitute for intellectual curiosity. For every old blackboard there are now hundreds of electronic computers.

The prospect of domination of the nation's scholars by Federal employment, project allocations, and the power of money is ever present—and is gravely to be regarded.

Yet, in holding scientific research and discovery in respect, as we should, we must also be alert to the equal and opposite danger that public policy could itself become the captive of a scientific-technological elite.

It is the task of statesmanship to mold, to balance, and to integrate these and other forces, new and old, within the principles of our democratic system—ever aiming toward the supreme goals of our free society. . . .

VI

Down the long lane of history yet to be written America knows that this world of ours, ever growing smaller, must avoid becoming a community of dreadful fear and hate, and be, instead, a proud confederation of mutual trust and respect.

Such a confederation must be one of equals. The weakest must come to the conference table with the same confidence as do we, protected as we are by our moral, economic, and military strength. That table, though scarred by many past frustrations, cannot be abandoned for the certain agony of the battlefield.

Disarmament, with mutual honor and confidence, is a continuing imperative. Together we must learn how to compose differences, not with arms, but with intellect and decent purpose. Because this need is so sharp and apparent I confess that I lay down my official responsibilities in this field with a definite sense of disappointment. As one who has witnessed the horror and the lingering sadness of war—as one who knows that another war could utterly destroy this civilization which has been so slowly and painfully built over thousands of years—I wish I could say tonight that a lasting peace is in sight.

Happily, I can say that war has been avoided. Steady progress toward our ultimate goal has been made. But, so much remains to be done. As a private citizen, I shall never cease to do what little I can to help the world advance along that road.. . .

Source: *Public Papers of the Presidents of the United States: Dwight D. Eisenhower, 1960–61*, pp. 1037–1040.

Chapter 2 Notes

[1] Estimate as of June 30, 1948, in Thomas B. Cochran et al. *Nuclear Weapons Databook, vol II. U.S. Nuclear Warhead Production* (Cambridge, Mass.: Ballinger, 1987), p. 15.

[2] Ibid., p. 18.

[3] State of the Union Address, January 7, 1960. *Peace and Justice: Selected Speeches of Dwight D. Eisenhower* (New York: Columbia University Press, 1961), p. 207.

[4] Dwight D. Eisenhower, *The White House Years: Mandate for Change, 1953–1956* (Garden City, N. Y.: Doubleday, 1963), p. 457.

[5] Richard G. Hewlett and Jack M. Holl, *Atoms for Peace and War 1953–1961* (Berkeley: University of California Press, 1989), p. 3.

[6] Winston S. Churchill, speech in the House of Commons (1 March 1955). Reprinted in David Cannadine, ed., *Blood, Toil, Tears and Sweat* (Boston: Houghton Mifflin, 1989), p. 341.

[7] Stephen Ambrose, *Eisenhower: The President* (New York: Simon & Schuster, 1984), p. 169.

[8]Eisenhower, *White House Years*, p. 181.

[9]This is Eisenhower's summary of the speech given in his memoirs and not an exact quote from the text of the speech. See ibid., p. 145.

[10]*Public Papers of the Presidents of the United States: Dwight D. Eisenhower 1953* (Washington, D. C.: Government Printing Office, 1960), p. 186.

[11]John Lear, "Ike and the Peaceful Atom," in *Eisenhower as President*, ed. Dean Alberton (New York: Hill & Wang, 1963), pp. 87–111.

[12]Gregg Herken, *Counsels of War* (New York: Knopf, 1985), pp. 67–103.

[13]Eisenhower, *White House Years*, p. 252.

[14]Ibid.

[15]Ibid., p. 254.

[16]Robert H. Ferrell, ed., *The Eisenhower Diaries* (New York: Norton, 1981), p. 261.

[17]Ibid., p. 262.

[18]Ambrose, *Eisenhower*, p. 147.

[19]Speech to Parliament, 17 December 1953. Quoted in Martin Gilbert, *Winston S. Churchill: Never Despair 1945–1965* (Boston: Houghton Mifflin, 1988), p. 940.

[20]*Department of State Bulletin* (October 1954), 478–489.

[21]*Public Papers*, p. 256.

[22]There is some dispute over where the idea for Open Skies originated. Both Stassen and Rockefeller claim credit for it. See John E. Eisenhower, *Strictly Personal* (Garden City, N.Y.: Doubleday, 1974), p. 178. The best source on the development of the Open Skies proposal is Walt W. Rostow, *Open Skies* (Austin: University of Texas Press, 1982). Rostow is convinced that the idea originated with the participants at the Quantico Conference which he attended.

[23]Herken, *Councels of War*, p. 110.

[24]Memo of phone conversation between Eisenhower and Dulles, July 6, 1955. Quoted in Rostow, p. 46.

[25]See Appendix H to Rostow, pp. 159–164.

[26]There is some suggestion of this in C. D. Jackson's account of how the Open Skies proposal developed. See Appendix D to Rostow, pp. 120-129.

[27]Ibid.

[28]For a full account of the U-2 flights and the 1960 affair, see Michael R. Beschloss, *Mayday: Eisenhower, Khrushchev and the U-2 Affair* (New York: Harper & Row, 1986).

[29]Quoted in Herbert Scoville, Jr., *MX: Prescription for Disaster* (Cambridge, Mass.: MIT Press, 1982), p. 1.

[30]Quoted in Thomas Soapes, "A Cold Warrior Seeks Peace," *Diplomatic History*, 4 (Winter 1980), 61-62.

[31]See, for instance, Paul Bracken, *Command and Control of Nuclear Forces* (New Haven, Conn.: Yale University Press, 1982).

[32]Ronald Reagan, *An American Life* (New York: Simon & Schuster, 1990), p. 500.

[33]Stanley I. Kutler, *The Wars of Watergate* (New York: Knopf, 1990), pp. 546–547.

[34]Hewlett and Holl, *Atoms for Peace and War*, p. 75.

[35]Rostow, *Open Skies*, p. 120.

[36]Fred I. Greenstein, *The Hidden-Hand Presidency* (New York: Basic Books, 1982).

[37]Ibid., p. 165.

[38]Eisenhower, *White House Years*, pp. 312–313.

[39]Quoted in John Emmet Hughes, *Ordeal of Power* (New York: Atheneum, 1963), p. 101.

[40]Quoted in Robert H. Ferrell, ed., *The Diary of James C. Hagerty* (Bloomington: Indiana University Press, 1983), p. 69.

Chapter 3

Kennedy and the Negotiated Neutrality of Laos

AMERICA AND LAOS IN THE 1950s

On the day before his inauguration, John F. Kennedy met for several hours with Dwight D. Eisenhower to review the international problems that the new administration was about to inherit. [Document 3.1] The foreign policy issue dominating their conversation had not been seriously debated in the 1960 presidential campaign; nor was it a problem now remembered as a major foreign policy controversy of the 1960s. The focus of their attention was not arms control, Berlin, Cuba, or Vietnam. The issue at the top of their agenda was the crisis in Laos.[1]

Laos was one of four new states created in Southeast Asia after France, the former colonial ruler of Indochina, withdrew from the region in the years after World War II. Its 91,000 square miles (a bit smaller than the state of Oregon) contained some of Southeast Asia's most rugged and mountainous terrain and a small, but varied, population including more than forty different tribal clusters speaking five distinct languages. The mixture of different peoples within one nation was further complicated by the fact that Laotian ethnic groups, in general, chose their homes by elevation without regard to any political or administrative boundaries. The fierce Méo tribesmen tended to live in the highest regions of the northern and eastern provinces where opium was the leading cash crop. The politically and economically dominant Lao population lived in the lowlands along the Mekong River in the west and in the narrow valleys that could be found throughout the more mountainous sections of the country. A variety of tribes, many with ethnic and linguistic ties to Laotian neighbors—Thailand, Vietnam, Cambodia, Burma, and China—occupied the foothills and plains between the Lao villages in the valleys and the mountaintop homes of the Méo. According to one careful observer of

Southeast Asia, Laos was "neither a geographical nor an ethnic or social entity"; it was "merely a political convenience."[2] And what was politically convenient for French colonial administrators turned out to be highly inconvenient for the Laotian leaders who tried to mold a new nation in the decades after the Second World War.[3]

Laotian political history in the 1950s was a story of royal intrigue, foreign interventions, guerrilla warfare, military coups, and constantly shifting personal and ideological allegiances. The porous borders of Southeast Asia made it easy for conflicts in neighboring countries to have an impact on Laotian affairs. In the early years of the decade, when the French were still trying to maintain military control over Vietnam, communist Viet Minh guerrillas moved freely in the northern and eastern sections of Laos. There the Vietnamese provided assistance and encouragement to the Pathet Lao, a small Laotian communist movement led by Prince Souphanoubong. After the Geneva Conference of 1954 brought a temporary end to the fighting in Southeast Asia and divided Vietnam into a communist North and a noncommunist South, efforts were made to restore stability throughout the region.

By 1954, Laos had become a constitutional monarchy with a Buddhist king in the traditional capital of Luang Prabang, a legislative assembly in the political capital of Vientiane on the border with Thailand, and a small band of communist guerrillas in control of two northeastern provinces. Long and complicated negotiations took place between Laotian government officials and representatives of the Pathet Lao. Eventually, a government of national unity was established under the leadership of Prince Souvanna Phouma (Souphanoubong's half brother), who adopted a policy of international neutrality and included both communist and pro-Western politicians in his cabinet. Guerrilla warfare between the Pathet Lao and government forces was brought to an end and a general cease-fire was observed by an International Control Commission (ICC) created by the Geneva conferees. In 1958, Souvanna Phouma's government was defeated in national elections and replaced by one more sympathetic to the West under Prime Minister Phoui Sananikone. Shortly after the change in government, the Pathet Lao forces that were scheduled to be integrated into the Royal Laotian Army returned to the hills of the north and resumed guerrilla warfare. Phoui's troops could not defeat the Pathet Lao; the ICC, which had never been very effective, was no longer available to enforce a cease-fire; and late in 1959 the Laotian government was overthrown in a coup led by General Phoumi Nosavan.

These events, which took place in a remote, sparsely populated, poor country thousands of miles from our shores were of little concern to most Americans. Diplomats assigned to Laos referred to it as the "end of nowhere;"[4] and one foreign policy expert in the United States found it difficult to decide whether the change in Laotian leadership from Phoui to Phoumi was "a significant event or a typographical error."[5] The United States was, however, deeply involved in the domestic and international affairs of Laos and the other countries of Southeast Asia. Internationally, the United States was formally pledged to defend Laotian independence. In 1954, just after the Geneva Conference, the United States negotiated the creation of a Southeast Asia Treaty Organization (SEATO) in which several nations in the South Pacific—Australia, New Zealand, the Philippines, Pakistan, and Thailand— the former colonial powers Great Britain and France, and the United States guaranteed the security of the signatories from foreign intervention and communist subversion. A protocol to the treaty extended this protection to South Vietnam,

Laos, and Cambodia. Beginning in 1955, Laos received extensive American military and economic assistance, which sustained a large Royal Laotian Army and simultaneously disrupted the local economy. Whenever significant shipments of American military equipment, large groups of technical advisers, and sizable infusions of dollars are introduced into a developing country, they tend to produce inflation, currency speculation, and inevitable American involvement in local corruption. All of these problems occurred in Laos.[6] Though average American citizens may not have realized it, the United States was heavily committed to the stability and security of Laos in the 1950s and heavily involved in its domestic politics.

The election that brought Phoui to power had been welcomed by American officials uneasy about the role of communists in Souvanna Phouma's government; the coup that replaced Phoui with Phoumi also met with Washington's approval (and probably involved the CIA[7]) because it was hoped that Phoumi would be more aggressive than his predecessor in opposing the growing strength of the Pathet Lao. His efforts in this regard were, however, largely ineffective; the Royal Laotian Army was neither trained nor equipped to deal efficiently with a guerrilla enemy. Furthermore, Phoumi's government could not end widespread corruption or win lasting public support. In August 1960, Phoumi was deposed by yet another coup, this one led by Captain Kong Le, who brought back Souvanna Phouma as prime minister. Kong Le captured the capital city of Vientiane, but could not take control of the entire Laotian army. Phoumi staged a countercoup. For a time in the fall of 1960, there were at least two Laotian governments, one led by General Phoumi and his political ally, Prince Boun Oum, the other under Kong Le and Souvanna Phouma. There were also two Laotian armies, both receiving American supplies and subsidies and both completely unable to fight the Pathet Lao, who were consolidating their position in rural areas throughout the country. American policymakers in the final months of the Eisenhower administration sided with General Phoumi, increased the size of his air force, and cut off all American aid to Kong Le. Phoumi recaptured the capital city, sending Souvanna Phouma into exile and Kong Le to the north, where he and his troops joined forces with the Pathet Lao and began receiving direct Soviet military assistance airlifted from North Vietnam.

George Ball, who later became undersecretary of state in the Kennedy administration, describes Laotian politics in his memoirs as a "preposterous long-running serial that, more than anything else, resembled a Kung Fu movie."[8] But while the frequent changes in government and shifting alliances in Laos did have a comic quality for distant observers, events in Laotian politics were tragic for the people of that country, who were caught in the midst of a growing civil war, and they were dangerous for the United States and the Soviet Union, which found themselves in a confrontation neither really wanted but from which neither could easily back away.

Throughout the Eisenhower administration, American policy in Laos had been aimed at strengthening the Laotian government and army so that they might serve as a bulwark against the spread of communism in Southeast Asia. This was consistent with the general policy of "containment," adopted in the late 1940s, which committed the United States to opposing any Soviet, and later Chinese, expansionism. And it was also consistent with Eisenhower's "domino theory"—the fear that other countries of the South Pacific would fall to communism if one was pushed in that direction. Neither of these fundamental American foreign policy objectives—stopping the spread of communism or the falling of dominoes—changed when Kennedy replaced Eisenhower. What did change was a recognition that no pro-Western government in Laos—not one under Phoui, or Phoumi, or Boun Oum—had much chance of stopping the Pathet Lao. The choice then faced by Kennedy and his advisers was whether the United States should introduce its own military forces into the jungles, mountains, and plains of Laos in order to defend that country from a communist military victory, or whether it should support a negotiated return to Laotian neutrality under the kind of coalition government that had briefly existed in the late 1950s.

In the end, Kennedy used threats of American military intervention to bring about a restoration of Laotian neutrality under Prince Souvanna Phouma. Kennedy took this course against the advice of many members of his administration who wanted a large-scale military deployment in Southeast Asia. Understanding why the United States decided *not* to intervene in Laos, and what diplomatic tools were used to win Soviet acceptance of a neutral Laotian government, provides an interesting case of superpower conflict and cooperation in the third world. It may also provide some important insights for our later analysis of why we *did* intervene in South Vietnam.

THE LAOTIAN CRISIS OF 1961

Kennedy talked about Laos at his very first presidential press conference, calling for the transformation of the nation into a "peaceful country—an independent country not dominated by either side."[9] [Document 3.2] Proposing peace and neutrality for Laos was, of course, much easier than bringing those conditions into existence. There were many obstacles on the road to Laotian neutrality. The Pathet Lao had no real reason to compromise with the forces of General Phoumi, which were engaged in a leisurely pursuit of Kong Le and had never shown much success against guerrilla tactics. Souvanna Phouma, the Laotian most likely to lead a new coalition government, was bound to be suspicious of American promises to support neutrality when the United States had enthusiastically welcomed his earlier fall from power. Moreover, the Kennedy administration was constrained in the flexibility it could show in the Laotian crisis because the problem had become, in part, a cold war confrontation with the Soviet Union. Presidents of the United States, in the decades when the cold war was at its coldest, faced serious domestic and international political criticism if they showed weakness in dealing with the Soviet Union. Laos was a complicated problem for Kennedy. According to one of his advisers, the president spent more time on the Laotian crisis during the early months of his administration than on any other domestic or foreign problem.[10] His first step was to establish a Laos task force made up of White House, CIA, and State, and Defense department officials from whom he demanded daily reports. The reports were not encouraging.

During the first few months of 1961, the civil war in Laos was being won by the Pathet Lao and Kong Le. In February and March, Phoumi's army was beaten in skirmishes with Kong Le's troops, which held the strategically important Plaine des Jarres where Soviet supplies, airlifted from North Vietnam, continued to arrive. Communist and neutralist forces also managed to capture a vital section of the only road connecting the two Laotian capitals. The Royal Laotian Army, despite years of American training and funding, seemed unable, or unwilling, to mount an active defense of their government. According to one Kennedy adviser, the fighting ability of the entire Lao nation was "clearly inferior to a battalion of conscientious objectors from World War I."[11]

On the diplomatic front, though Kennedy had made an early public appeal for peace and neutrality in Laos, very little effective international action was being taken. The British proposed a resumption of ICC inspections in Laos and a return to Geneva negotiations, but the Soviet Union (Great Britain's co-chair of the 1954 Geneva Conference) did not respond to the British proposal. In February, the king of Laos, following an American suggestion, called for the establishment of a different international commission made up of representatives from Burma, Cambodia, and Malaya that would take the responsibility for overseeing a new cease-fire. This idea was quickly rejected by the Burmese, the Cambodians, the Russians, and the Chinese. Without any signs of diplomatic movement and with continuing reports of Phoumi's failure to deal with the military challenges he faced, the Kennedy administration was forced to consider some rather unpleasant alternatives.

On March 20 and 21, the National Security Council met to review American policy in Laos. With the government of General Phoumi under serious military threat, there were only three options available to the United States—doing nothing and allowing Laos to fall under communist control, ordering an American military intervention to save the Phoumi regime, or negotiating a cease-fire and the creation of a new neutral government under Souvanna Phouma. Though Kennedy told the nation's leading correspondent, Walter Lippmann, that doing nothing was really the most popular alternative,[12] he realized that "losing" a country to communism, as Harry Truman had "lost" China in 1949, would be a serious setback in the policy of containment with damaging domestic and international political consequences. His real choice was between military intervention and neutralization.

American military operations in Laos posed serious problems. The country is landlocked, so troops and supplies had to be transported across Thailand or brought in by air to one of two airfields in the Laotian territory still under government control. Defending those airfields would be difficult. According to General Lyman Lemnitzer, the chairman of the Joint Chiefs of Staff, we could easily put American troops into Laos. "It's getting them out again that worries me."[13] There was also some confusion about what American troops in Laos would do. Would they defend the territory under government control, essentially the lowlands and the Mekong River valley, or would they pursue and attempt to defeat the forces of Kong Le and the Pathet Lao? Would air power be used extensively against communist forces and supply lines, or would ground forces bear the brunt of the burden in the operations being proposed? Would military action be limited to Laotian territory, or would the fighting be taken to North Vietnam where Soviet supplies were positioned for airlift to Laos? And what would we do if the North Vietnamese, or the Chinese, or the Russians actively entered the fighting in support of their Pathet Lao allies? So much confusion surrounded proposed military operations in Laos that, in one meeting with the five members of the Joint Chiefs of Staff, Kennedy listened to five different accounts of what needed to be done in the Laotian crisis. According to one of his advisers, the president "literally and figuratively threw up his hands and walked out of the room."[14] When the Joint Chiefs finally reached some consensus in their recommendations, they called for a significant American intervention with an initial force of 60,000 troops and assurances that there would be no limitations regarding where American forces could fight or what weapons they would be allowed to use. The president's military advisers wanted an all-out war in Southeast Asia or no use of military force at all. For the time being, Kennedy rejected the military option and sought a political solution to the deteriorating situation in Laos.

There was some reason to believe that neutrality was a viable option in the early months of 1961. In Souvanna Phouma, there already existed a natural leader for a coalition government; and although some American officials had a low opinion of Souvanna's leadership abilities and feared that he would be manipulated by the communists, Kennedy's roving ambassador, Averell Harriman, met Souvanna in New Delhi, and later in Paris, and urged the president to trust the Laotian prince and to have faith in his commitment to genuine neutrality. Early diplomatic communications between Kennedy and Khrushchev were also hopeful. The Soviet leader told both Harriman and the American ambassador to Moscow that he was not interested in having a superpower confrontation over Laos. There was, however, no benevolence in Khrushchev's moderate position: "Why take risks over Laos," he told American Ambassador Llewellyn Thompson, "It will fall into our laps like a ripe apple."[15]

The problem with the neutrality alternative was the absence of any incentive for the local Laotian communist forces to negotiate with General Phoumi at a time when the communists were enjoying a series of military victories. Only the threat of American armed intervention could force them to consider a cease-fire, but such a threat returned Kennedy to a consideration of the military option he was trying to avoid. Neutralization and military force were not really alternative courses of action in Laos; they were interrelated policies that needed to be carefully coordinated if the United States was going to develop an effective strategy for dealing with the Laotian civil war. And the longer the United States took to develop that strategy, the more ripe Khrushchev's apple became.

After meeting with the NSC and consulting with members of Congress, Kennedy ordered a number of limited military preparations for later actions that might be taken in Laos. Ships of the Seventh Fleet, including the aircraft carrier *Midway*, were ordered to sail for the Gulf of Siam; a military task force in Okinawa and a contingent of marines also stationed in Japan were put on alert; and a base on the Thai-Laotian border was provided with the supplies, equipment, spare parts, and technicians that would be needed should the base become a major center of American military operations. Though these military preparations were not formally announced, no effort was made to hide them from the national or international media. On March 23, Kennedy began his regular press conference with a long discussion of Laos and the threats it faced. [Document 3.3] Pointing to large-scale maps prepared for that evening, he showed how the Laotian territory under communist control had been growing in recent months. Repeating his support for a neutral Laos, he added a cautiously worded warning that continued advances by the communist forces in Laos would force the United States and its allies to make some response. "We will not be provoked, trapped, or drawn into this or any other situation; but I know that every American will want his country to honor its obligations."[16]

The ship movements, troop alerts, and the public press conference were accompanied by a series of diplomatic steps to make clear that the United States was still seriously interested in a neutral Laos as the final solution to the problem.

Messages were sent to India's Prime Minister Jawaharlal Nehru (India was one of the three nations in the original ICC) asking for his support of a cease-fire and his assistance in communicating to the Chinese both our desire to negotiate and our willingness to use force if needed. On the 26th, the president met with British Prime Minister Harold Macmillan, who reluctantly agreed to a limited British participation in a Laotian intervention if all efforts to secure a negotiated settlement failed. The next day, Secretary of State Dean Rusk met the foreign ministers of the SEATO nations in Bangkok, and although he was unable to win unanimous support for the American position, he found at least some of the SEATO countries willing to join in a last resort intervention. Kennedy also met with Soviet Foreign Minister Andrei Gromyko, who visited Washington shortly after the Laos press conference. The president took special care to warn Gromyko not to misunderstand or miscalculate American intentions in Laos. We were willing to support a neutral government, but we would not accept a communist military victory. This message apparently had some effect, because during the first week in April, the Soviets publicly accepted the British proposal for a resumption of the Geneva Conference and urged their Southeast Asian allies to support a "cease-fire in Laos" in order "to create a favorable atmosphere for negotiations."[17] The Soviets had not yet accepted the American condition that an effective cease-fire would have to precede any Geneva negotiations, but their new statement was close to the American position and raised hopes in Washington that the crisis could be resolved.

General agreement between Washington and Moscow was, however, easier to achieve than real progress in bringing peace to the fighting factions in Southeast Asia. Throughout the month of April, communist forces continued to increase the territory under their control and to threaten both Laotian capitals. On April 18, Kennedy ordered the 400 American military personnel who were assisting Phoumi's army and were technically in Laos as civilians (the 1954 Geneva agreements prohibited official American military advisers from serving in Laos) to put on their service uniforms and accompany Royal Laotian Army units into combat zones. Six days later the British and Soviets announced the reactivation of the ICC and the date for a new Geneva Conference. Once again progress among the great powers seemed to have little effect on the fighting in Laos. By late April, the National Security Council was again holding a series of meetings to consider American military intervention.

Members of the administration were bitterly divided at the NSC meeting on April 27.[18] Walt Rostow, a member of the NSC staff and the Laos task force, proposed sending limited numbers of U.S. troops into Thailand as a further signal of America's willingness to intervene should the need arise. Averell Harriman, who was then in Vientiane, supported the task force proposal because it would give the United States something to bargain with at the hoped-for Geneva negotiations. The Joint Chiefs, however, once again opposed any use of American military force that was not all out. Members of the JCS continued to have different ideas regarding policy in Laos but, in general, called for a massive American intervention beginning with 140,000 men.

Kennedy was increasingly suspicious of the military advice he was receiving. Earlier in April, he had suffered the first major disaster of his administration, the failure of the CIA-sponsored invasion of Cuba at the Bay of Pigs. He now doubted that an invasion of Laos would go as planned, and at one NSC meeting asked a series of probing questions: "How many [U.S. troops] will be able to land [at the two Laotian airfields]? How many troops of the Communists are in the surrounding area? Now, what's going to happen if on the third day [of our airlift] you've landed three thousand men and then they bomb the airport? And then they bring up five or six thousand more, what's going to happen?"[19] Eventually he was told that tactical nuclear weapons might be needed in Laos with further nuclear attacks against North Vietnamese and Chinese targets if those countries became more heavily involved.[20] The military option still looked bleak. When Kennedy again consulted with members of Congress, he found no enthusiasm for the kind of intervention favored by the JCS. In the series of NSC meetings devoted to Laos in late April and early May, Kennedy did authorize additional CIA covert operations in Southeast Asia, including increased arms for the Méo tribesmen who fought as guerrillas against the communists,[21] but he ordered no new American military preparations or overt signals. He once again waited to see what diplomacy could achieve.

     This time, waiting did not make matters worse. Another series of diplomatic messages and meetings in India, in Moscow, and at the United Nations finally produced some results. On May 3, the Pathet Lao and the Laotian government reached general terms on a cease-fire, and shortly thereafter representatives of the ICC arrived in Laos to confirm that fighting was actually being brought to a halt. On May 16, after several delays caused by cease-fire violations, the new Geneva Conference convened with Averell Harriman as the chief American negotiator. The following month, when Kennedy and Khrushchev met in Vienna for what was generally an unsuccessful summit, they managed to agree on at least one point— both superpowers reiterated their commitment to a peaceful and neutral Laos. Kennedy had achieved his goal of taking the Laotian question off the battlefield and putting it on the conference table. But even if the United States, the Soviet Union, and the rest of the Geneva conferees now agreed that peace and neutrality were the destinations they hoped to reach, the road to those destinations would be much like the muddy roads in the Laotian countryside—dangerous, slow, and only passable during certain months of the year.

THE LAOTIAN CRISIS OF 1962

The prospects for a quick Geneva Conference that would resolve all the international and domestic problems afflicting Laos were not very good. When the Chinese delegates arrived in Geneva in May 1961, they signed six-month leases on their villas;[22] they ended up living in the Swiss city for more than a year. During the fourteen months of Geneva deliberations two separate sets of problems had to be addressed—the details regarding a new Laotian coalition government and the responsibilities of the international conferees pledged to support Laotian neutrality. For the most part, the political problems within Laos were more difficult and had to be settled before the conference participants could agree on their roles in preserving regional peace and security.

     One of the earliest issues to be addressed in Geneva was the number of Laotian delegations. The government of General Phoumi and Prince Boun Oum sent representatives, as did the Pathet Lao; both delegations were readily accepted. Problems arose regarding the status of Souvanna Phouma, who remained the object of considerable suspicion within the American military and intelligence establishments. Though Souvanna was clearly the logical leader of a new coalition government, he held no official position in Laos and the troops led by Kong Le that were loyal to Souvanna were much smaller in number than the military forces supporting Phoumi or the Pathet Lao. Souvanna handled this delicate delegate situation extremely well and arranged some informal meetings of the three princes, Boun Oum, Souphanoubong, and himself, representing the right, left, and center in Laotian politics. Those meetings established a clear precedent for the equal treatment of all three Laotian factions, and Souvanna won a place at the negotiating table.

He also won Averell Harriman's respect, and therefore had a powerful American ally to support his diplomatic efforts in Geneva and in Laos. Throughout the Geneva meetings the American negotiator, who became undersecretary of state for Far Eastern affairs late in the fall of 1961, played a pivotal role. Harriman was seventy years old by the time the conference ended. His work for the Kennedy administration came near the end of a long and distinguished career as a businessman and public servant, including a tour as ambassador to the Soviet Union during World War II. He understood both international politics and the workings of the American foreign policy bureaucracies. Before matters in Laos could be resolved, he would use that knowledge to good effect.

Though Harriman, Kennedy, and most Laotian leaders had concluded that there was no viable political alternative in Laos to a neutral government under Souvanna Phouma, not all American policymakers fully accepted that conclusion. Throughout 1961 and much of 1962, the United States continued to provide generous financial support for the government of Prince Boun Oum and for the army of General Phoumi. American officials even authorized the expansion of the Royal Laotian Army during the course of the Geneva meetings. Until a new coalition government was formed, Boun Oum remained the prime minister officially recognized by the United States; and until permanent peace was brought to the region, the army of General Phoumi remained the only military force available to counter communist cease-fire violations. Phoumi, himself, was not above violating the cease-fire provisions when it suited his own political purposes. After the Laotian negotiators in Geneva had tentatively agreed that Souvanna Phouma would lead a new coalition government, both left and right wing Laotian politicians held out for the best possible representation in the new cabinet that would be formed. For months controversy centered on which faction would control the important defense and interior ministries that in turn controlled the army and internal security. Phoumi wanted the defense ministry for himself and was encouraged to seek it by at least some American officials.[23]

This was not Harriman's policy. On January 19, 1962, he announced that the United States and the Soviet Union had agreed in Geneva that the controversial military cabinet positions should be held by neutralists. Earlier in the month, Harriman arranged for a temporary suspension of American economic aid to Boun Oum in order to pressure his government to accept a compromise on coalition cabinet assignments. The CIA, following its own policy in Laos, provided intelligence agency funds to Boun Oum and Phoumi as a substitute for the suspended State Department assistance and continued to encourage Laotian officials to stall in the neutrality negotiations. The CIA apparently believed that it was still possible to maintain a pro-Western military force in Laos. When Harriman discovered that his efforts were being counteracted by others within his own government, he ordered a halt to economic and some military aid for the month of February and insisted that key CIA personnel assigned to Vientiane be removed. These were controversial steps, and only after considerable bureaucratic resistance did the energetic septuagenarian succeed. The CIA officials who supported Phoumi were sent home.[24]

At the same time that Harriman was putting political and economic pressure on Boun Oum, Phoumi, and the CIA, the Pathet Lao was doing the same thing in the northwestern jungles. Throughout the early months of 1962, a series of cease-fire violations by communist and Royal Laotian forces took place in the province of Nam Tha and in the provincial capital of the same name. Eventually the Pathet Lao (reportedly supported by the North Vietnamese and, in a few unconfirmed reports, by Chinese troops) surrounded and attacked the city of Nam Tha. Phoumi, against the advice of Harriman and the American ambassador to Laos, sent 5,000 reinforcements to the threatened provincial capital, increasing its military and symbolic importance. Phoumi was confident that he could hold the city and by doing so win leverage in his dealings with both Washington and the Geneva negotiators. He was wrong.

On May 6, Royal Laotian troops abandoned Nam Tha and retreated in the direction of the Thai-Laotian border. The American adviser accompanying the Laotian government troops in their retreat was not altogether discouraged. "The morale of my battalion is substantially better than in our last engagement," he reported. "The last time, they dropped their weapons and ran. This time, they took their weapons with them."[25] But the loss of Nam Tha was more important than the officer on the scene realized. It once again suggested that the communists might be willing, and able, to take all of Laos by force. The fall of Nam Tha produced a repeat performance of the spring 1961 Laotian crisis in which the options faced by the United States were essentially the same ones that had been considered the year before.

On May 10, 1962, the NSC met to review policy in Laos and to consider proposals put forward by Harriman and another State Department official, Roger Hilsman. Harriman and Hilsman recommended ship movements to the Gulf of Siam and limited troop deployments to the Thai-Laotian border, together with new diplomatic assurances that the United States still hoped for progress in the neutrality negotiations. The Joint Chiefs of Staff made their familiar criticisms of military commitments that were less than total, and though they were willing to go along with a naval show of force, they opposed sending limited numbers of American troops to the Laotian border. After some hesitation, Kennedy ordered the ship movements and scheduled another NSC meeting for May 12, when Secretary of Defense Robert McNamara and General Lemnitzer would be returning from an overseas trip that included stops in Southeast Asia. At the May 12 meeting, McNamara agreed that the State Department proposals should be adopted; Kennedy ordered about 3,000 American troops to the Thai-Laotian border and authorized a series of improvements to supply lines and communications in Thailand that would be necessary for a larger American operation in Laos.

Once again military moves were accompanied by diplomatic efforts to ensure all concerned that an American intervention would be a last resort to prevent a communist military victory and that the real goal was neutralization. The Soviet Union criticized the American military moves, but publicly agreed with the United States that a neutral Laos was the best solution to the situation in Southeast Asia.[26]

While the Kennedy administration reassured the world about the goal of its policy in Laos, it also continued to put pressure on Boun Oum and Phoumi. Aid to Laos was restricted throughout April and May, and eventually the military threat to the communists, the diplomatic support for the neutralists, and the financial pressure on the Royal Laotian government brought all three factions together. On June 11, Souvanna announced agreement on the composition of a new Laotian cabinet. There would be four communists in his government and four pro-Western ministers; the controversial military cabinet posts would be held by neutralists. Three days later, American aid to Laos was restored and when the first meeting of the new coalition government was held on June 23, a nationwide cease-fire was proclaimed.

It took another month for the Geneva conferees to finish their negotiations. Their agreement called for the complete withdrawal of all foreign forces from Laos and contained a vague prohibition against North Vietnamese use of the Ho Chi Minh Trail (actually a series of roads, trails, and footpaths through the jungles of eastern Laos that were used by the North Vietnamese to resupply guerrillas in South Vietnam) that had little chance of being respected in practice. The final Geneva document also contained an official statement that the co-chairs, Great Britain and the Soviet Union, would accept responsibility for enforcing the cease-fire and neutrality with their allies and an unofficial agreement between Harriman and the Soviet negotiator, Georgi Pushkin, that each superpower would encourage restraint on the part of the nations and politicians under its respective influence. This meant that the Soviet Union was pledged to play a role in controlling North Vietnamese actions in Laos. American policymakers expected that there would be violations of Laotian neutrality by North Vietnamese forces, but hoped that the Soviets would help to keep those violations at modest levels.[27] On July 23, the fourteen nations in Geneva signed the Declaration on the Neutrality of Laos, and the people of Laos achieved a limited peace and neutrality. [Document 3.4]

The resolution of the Laotian crisis was far from perfect. Fighting in Laos would later resume, eventually resulting in a Pathet Lao victory. But in the summer of 1962, the political arrangements in Laos endorsed by the Geneva Conference were much better than any that had existed for the past four years.

CONCLUSIONS

POWER

On at least two occasions in 1961 and 1962, President Kennedy seriously contemplated sending American military personnel into combat in order to defend Laos from a communist military takeover. Had he followed the recommendations of his senior military advisers, he would have sent tens of thousands of soldiers into Southeast Asia, he would have authorized bombing missions against North Vietnam and China, and he would have considered the use of tactical and strategic nuclear weapons against a variety of Southeast Asian targets. He would, in other words, have taken the United States to war.

The Constitution clearly states in Article I that the power to declare war belongs to the Congress, and not to the president. Along with the war power,

Congress is given complete control over military spending and must pass legislation authorizing and appropriating all defense expenditures. The constitutional language on war and purse powers is unambiguous.[28] Article II of the Constitution, which deals with the executive branch, does give the president the position of commander in chief of all American armed forces. It also gives the chief executive a number of duties, some of which are shared with the Senate, to receive ambassadors, to negotiate treaties, and to appoint diplomatic representatives. Taken together, these duties arguably make the president our principal foreign policy official. The Constitution does not make clear, however, how the presidential military and foreign policy functions are related to the congressional war and purse powers. Can a treaty, like the SEATO agreement, negotiated by the president and ratified by the Senate obligate the United States to go to war without a formal congressional declaration? Is a president who orders troops into combat as commander in chief always in violation of the constitutional requirement that wars be declared by the Congress? In situations less than all-out war, must the commander in chief seek the explicit concurrence of the branch that pays the bills for military operations? In the aftermath of Vietnam, these would become serious questions for Americans, but before that war had left its mark on American public opinion, the exact relationship between the executive and legislative branches in the area of war and peace was not at all clear. In the words of one scholar, the "Constitution, considered only for its affirmative grants of powers capable of affecting the issue [of foreign affairs], is an invitation to struggle for the privilege of directing American foreign policy."[29] In the early 1960s, there was very little struggle, because Congress acquiesced to a dominant executive role in foreign policy.

At the time, there was no real challenge to this arrangement. Members of Congress knowingly accepted compromises to their foreign policy powers. When asked on a television news program to comment on congressional reaction to a possible Kennedy decision to send troops into Laos, Senate Majority Leader Mike Mansfield made a statement that would have been typical for the period: "[W]e must remember that under the Constitution, the President is charged with the conduct of our foreign policy, and he is the Commander in chief of our armed services, and furthermore, we do have this treaty (SEATO) which we are obligated to adhere to."[30]

Postwar congressional leaders had a number of reasons for deferring to the executive in matters of war and peace. As we noted in Chapter 2, in the nuclear age, when the warning that the United States was under attack might be received in a matter of minutes before an attack began, no time would be available for a congressional debate on the wording of a legal declaration of war. If the attack was against the city of Washington, there might not be any members of Congress alive to hold such a debate. In the crisis confrontations, which were a routine part of the cold war between the United States and the Soviet Union, a prompt response to changing situations in Berlin, Cuba, or the Middle East was often required. Use of a long and drawn out constitutional procedure in these situations could have weakened American foreign policy. Furthermore, in the guerrilla warfare that was taking place in many third world countries, there was often no nation against which one could legally declare a state of war. Had we actively entered the fighting in Laos, the United States would have been using force against the Pathet Lao, a guerrilla organization with no officially recognized status as a nation. Protecting a legitimate Laotian government from internal subversion would not normally require a declaration of war under accepted practices of international law. In the early 1960s, when nuclear war was a real threat, cold war confrontations commonplace, and a number of American allies under challenge from guerrilla forces, much of the war power granted to the Congress by the Constitution had, in fact, been transferred to the executive branch.

But even if Kennedy had the power necessary to take the United States into Southeast Asian hostilities without a formal declaration of war, he could hardly do so without giving some consideration to congressional opinion and to the political responses that would follow such an action. Kennedy consulted, informally, with a number of his former colleagues in the Congress and with leading figures in both the Democratic and Republican parties during the Laotian crises of 1961 and 1962. On several occasions he was warned against committing the United States to a guerrilla war in Laos. This is what he heard from Senator William Fulbright, the chairman of the Senate Foreign Relations Committee, and also from retired General Douglas MacArthur.[31] Senator Mansfield, in the same interview in which he endorsed Kennedy's constitutional right to initiate hostilities in Southeast Asia, warned that long and costly fighting in Laos would have real political costs. "[A]s soon as the first significant casualty lists are published...it will not be long before the approval of 'stand firm' gives way to the disapproval of 'Kennedy's War' and 'what are we doing in Laos?'"[32]

Kennedy took the warnings he received, both public and private, into account throughout his decision making. His power to act in Southeast Asia may not have been limited by the Constitution, as it was interpreted in the early 1960s, but it was limited by political realities. Neither Congress nor the American public wanted a presidential foreign policy that imposed high costs in defense of a remote Southeast Asian nation.

PROCESS

A bigger problem for Kennedy than dealing with the Congress was dealing with lower level policymakers within his own administration. At the highest levels of foreign policy making, Kennedy managed to coordinate the process reasonably well. He appointed an interdepartmental task force and paid close personal attention to what they reported and recommended. He listened carefully to his Joint Chiefs of Staff and was fully aware of the variety in their opinions and advice. Even though there was usually no consensus among the president's advisers about what should be done in Laos, Kennedy was well informed about their differences of opinion and knowledgeable about the arguments made in support of the various alternatives. The president could make his difficult decisions in the Laotian crises with reasonable certainty that he had heard a wide range of advice; he could not, however, have confidence that his policies would be carried out.

Throughout America's relations with Laos, differences among departments and agencies played a large role. In the 1950s, before Laos had become a crisis worthy of presidential attention, confusion reigned in American policy toward Southeast Asia. Roger Hilsman believes that that confusion was produced by the different missions and perspectives of the Americans sent to work in the region.

American military officers were in Laos to build a modern army that could fight against communist invasion or subversion and naturally became allied to the local generals, like Phoumi, who were effective military leaders. The Agency for International Development (AID), which had representatives in Laos to advise on the management of the local economy, became convinced that corruption was at the heart of Laotian political problems and that domestic reforms and economic progress would prevent the spread of communism much more effectively than a modern army. State Department officials dealing with the members of the ancient royal families who were now modern Laotian politicians became aware of the complexities of the local culture and politics and were, for the most part, advocates of negotiated resolutions to Laotian problems. Agents of the CIA working in the jungles with the Méo tribesmen and taking part in several Laotian coups were busy supporting any individuals or groups willing to take an active role in the fight against communism. According to Hilsman, before Laos became a major presidential issue, the debates between and among these various departments and agencies produced policy failures in both Vientiane and Washington.

> Each of the American agencies concerned with Laos—the State Department, the Pentagon, the Agency for International Development (AID), and the CIA—sent people there to carry out their agency's programs, people with money to spend and influence and leverage to exert. Each had different interests and views on how to handle Laos as a foreign policy problem for the United States and each had its own private channels of communication to Washington, where the battles were carried on just as vigorously in the larger arena. In time, the differences between the agencies and departments became more marked and the exchanges sharper, with the CIA and the Pentagon generally on one side and the State Department and AID on the other. Each agency came to pursue its own programs and policies with less and less regard for the others, and with little relationship to an over-all American policy....[T]he tragedy was that neither the Lao nor our allies could tell who really spoke for the United States.[33]

Even after Kennedy took an active role in reviewing the Laotian situation and directing the policymaking process, lower level bureaucrats actively worked against his decisions. Kennedy was fortunate that the individual he entrusted with much of the day-to-day responsibility for Laotian policy, Averell Harriman, was a tenacious and effective bureaucratic politician, nicknamed the "crocodile" by those with whom he worked.[34] We have already noted Harriman's decisive action against the CIA officials in Vientiane, but there were other instances of his ability to deal with bureaucratic resistance. When the ambassador arrived in Switzerland to lead the American Geneva delegation, he selected a young foreign service officer, William Sullivan, to serve as his assistant. Harriman was immediately informed by the State Department that this appointment could not possibly be made because many of the foreign service officers sent to Geneva outranked Sullivan. Harriman's response was to order his delegation cut in half, with everyone senior to Sullivan among those sent back to Washington. Harriman got the assistant he wanted.[35]

Throughout the foreign policy making process of this and other administrations, half the problem is deciding what to do and the other, sometimes neglected, half is making sure that it gets done. Implementation of decisions is just as important as the making of them, and Kennedy's implementation problems in Laos were more difficult than most. The president was consciously pursuing a complicated policy. He was making military preparations to intervene in Laos, but holding back on a full-scale invasion of the country. He was supporting the creation of a neutral government under Souvanna, but without fully abandoning General Phoumi, whose support would be needed if negotiations ever broke down. He was publicly appealing for peace and neutrality in Laos, and secretly financing covert operations and the arming of Méo tribesmen as pro-Western guerrillas. Under such circumstances, it is not difficult to imagine that different agencies in the government would be acting in opposition to each other. Kennedy was lucky to have skillful subordinates, like Averell Harriman, who both understood the complexities of the president's thinking and knew how to push, prod, and occasionally bulldoze the departments and agencies in the implementation of presidential policy.

PERSONALITY

Kennedy's personality also played a role in the resolution of the two Laotian crises. Kennedy was a skeptic who frequently refused to accept the advice he received, particularly after the Bay of Pigs. In the days following the Cuban disaster, the president confessed to one of his closest assistants that his failure had been a willingness to trust what the CIA and JCS had told him. "All my life I have known better than to depend on experts. How could I have been so stupid?"[36] The president's reaction to the mistakes made in the planning of the Cuban invasion was to reinforce his tendency to question assumptions, to be suspicious, and to be cautious. "Thank God the Bay of Pigs happened when it did," Kennedy told one of his leading advisers in September 1961. "Otherwise we'd be in Laos by now—and that would be a hundred times worse."[37]

Kennedy consistently asked probing questions of military officials. He wanted to know not only what the United States would do in the early days of a military confrontation in Southeast Asia, but what it would do after the Pathet Lao, or the North Vietnamese, or the Chinese, or the Russians had responded. He wanted those around him to think beyond the first step of an international crisis to the second or the fifth or the tenth, and when they did this he found that elaborately planned and documented military ventures were often careless and dangerous enterprises. This practice of pushing crisis decision making as far into the future as possible was repeated in the Cuban missile crisis later in his presidency,[38] and in both cases to good effect. It made the president shy away from large-scale military operations that could easily provoke our enemies, and introduced a measure of caution into American foreign policy decision making.

Caution was necessary because Kennedy was afraid that mistakes and miscalculations would lead to results that neither the United States nor the Soviet Union wanted. Preventing miscalculation was the theme in Kennedy's first private talks with Gromyko in Washington and later with Khrushchev at the Vienna summit. It was an obvious concern in the conduct of his diplomacy. When the president wanted to send a message to the Soviets or the Chinese, he did so redundantly through various channels so that they would be sure to hear what he had to say. His desire for a neutral Laos was repeated publicly in speeches and press conferences and reinforced by Harriman's actions in Geneva and Vientiane. His decisions to move ships to Southeast Asian waters, to place troops on alert, and later to move troops to the Thai-Laotian border were designed to signal only that the United States would not accept a communist military victory in Laos. Kennedy always combined these military moves with diplomatic messages reassuring the world about the limited nature of the goals being sought. The president carefully "combined bluff and real determination in proportions he made known to *no one*,"[39] but with an awareness that what he was doing was always subject to misinterpretation. He seemed to give equal attention to what his decisions would be and to how they would look to the other side,[40] balancing policy and perception in an effort to avoid both a serious confrontation with the Soviet Union and an embarrassing loss of a country to communist takeover.

The result of all of these efforts was to give Laos a few years of peace before civil war was resumed with tragic consequences for the cause of neutrality. Had Kennedy lived to see the events in Southeast Asia after 1963, he probably would have judged the negotiated neutrality of Laos to be a failure. The neutral Laotian government of the early 1960s was far more fragile than the earlier coalition government of the late 1950s. The Pathet Lao controlled much more territory and never fully surrendered it to the central government. The Laotian army was too weak to prevent Vietnamese communists from using the Ho Chi Minh Trail; and as the war in Vietnam intensified, both North Vietnamese troops and American bombers violated Laotian sovereignty and conducted military operations in the northern and eastern portions of the country. At the height of the Vietnam War, neutrality in Laos was little more than a tacit recognition by the United States and North Vietnam that the fighting in Southeast Asia would not take place in Vientiane and some portions of the upper Mekong River valley. When South Vietnam finally fell in 1975, Laos and Cambodia, the two closest dominoes, fell with it. Laos became a communist regime dominated by its powerful Vietnamese neighbor.

Despite this disastrous result, Kennedy might have taken some satisfaction in the realization that events in Laos might have been even more unfortunate. There could have been a more serious Soviet-American confrontation over Laos in 1961 or 1962, and if that confrontation had spilled over to other regions of the world—Cuba and Berlin—it could have gotten out of hand. The United States might also have become involved in a large-scale land war in the remote Laotian jungles and mountains early in the 1960s, which would have posed even greater logistical obstacles than what it later faced in Vietnam. If such a land war had gone poorly, or if the Pathet Lao had turned to their North Vietnamese and Chinese allies for support, the United States might have been tempted to reconsider Pentagon plans for the use of tactical nuclear weapons in Southeast Asia. None of these dreadful alternatives came to pass while Kennedy was in office, and instead, the Laotian people enjoyed a temporary and imperfect cease-fire that lasted for a few years. Very often limited successes are all that foreign policy makers can expect; their satisfaction comes from knowing that even policies that have turned out badly could, after all, have been worse. For Lyndon Johnson, Kennedy's successor, and for the war in Vietnam, things would be worse, much worse.

Chronology of the Laotian Crises

1959

Spring Pathet Lao battalions, which were scheduled to be integrated into the Royal Laotian Army, return to northern provinces to resume guerrilla activity.

Dec 31 General Phoumi Nosavan takes power in a coup.

1960

Aug Revolt by Captain Kong Le results in new neutral government under Prince Souvanna Phouma. Phoumi and the Royal Army units loyal to him regroup in southern Laos.

Dec 3 Soviet airlift of supplies (food and fuel) from Hanoi to northern provinces of Laos begins.

Dec 11 In exchange for an alliance between Kong Le and the Pathet Lao, Soviets begin supplying arms and ammunition to the Kong Le forces.

Dec 16 Phoumi drives Kong Le from Vientiane. Souvanna Phouma goes into exile and a new pro-Western government under Prince Boun Oum and General Phoumi is formed.

1961

Jan Regular North Vietnamese units identified by U.S. intelligence as having entered northern Laos. Eisenhower decides to send six AT-6 bombers to Phoumi. U.S. sends in 400 special forces personnel.

Jan 19 During transition, Eisenhower and Kennedy discuss Laotian crisis.

Jan 22 British propose to Soviets a resumption of the ICC to supervise a cease-fire.

Jan 25 At first presidential press conference, Kennedy expresses desire to see a neutral Laos in the future.

Mar 9 Continued Kong Le/Pathet Lao military success evident as main road between Luang Prabang and Vientiane is cut, threatening both capitals.

Mar 20-21 National Security Council meets and plans are made for use of American troops in Laos. Limited military action is taken: task force in Okinawa put on alert, additional marines in Japan are readied, Seventh Fleet sends carrier task force to Gulf of Siam, supplies stockpiled in Thailand on Laotian border.

Mar 23 Kennedy begins press conference with long discussion of Laos focusing on external intervention of Soviets and North Vietnamese.

Mar 27 Kennedy meets with Gromyko and receives Soviet assurances that both superpowers want a neutral Laos.

Mar 28 Rusk at SEATO conference fails to obtain any support from France for possible U.S. military action in Laos.

Apr 1 Khrushchev responds favorably to British proposal for reactivation of ICC.

Apr 3 Russians agree that cease-fire should precede negotiations.

Apr 17 Bay of Pigs invasion.

(cont.)

(cont.)	
Apr 18	Kennedy orders the 400 "civilian" advisers to put on military uniforms and accompany the Royal Lao Army in combat zones.
Apr 24	Soviets and British announce reactivation of the ICC.
Apr 27	NSC considers escalation of U.S. military commitment to Laos.
May 3	Pathet Lao and Laotian government reach agreement on terms of cease-fire.
May 16	Geneva Conference convenes.
Jun 3-4	Kennedy and Khrushchev meet in Vienna, discuss Laotian cease-fire.
1962	
May	While Geneva Conference still in session, fighting takes place around Nam Tha, which falls on May 6. New series of NSC meetings consider American response.
May 12	Announcement of Seventh Fleet deployments to Gulf of Siam.
May 15	Announcement of reinforcements on Thai border with Laos.
May 25	Khrushchev announces continued support for a neutral Laos.
Jun 11	Souvanna Phouma having returned to Laos from Geneva succeeds in negotiating with Phoumi and Pathet Lao on cabinet composition of proposed national government.
Jul 9	New Laotian government issues statement of neutrality.
Jul 23	Geneva Declaration on the Neutrality of Laos signed.

Chapter 3 Documents

Document 3.1
Clark Clifford's Memorandum of Conference on January 19, 1961 Between President Eisenhower and President-Elect Kennedy on the Subject of Laos

The meeting was held in the Cabinet Room with the following men present: President Eisenhower, Secretary of State Christian Herter, Secretary of Defense Thomas Gates, Secretary of Treasury Robert Anderson, and General Wilton B. Persons.

With President-elect Kennedy were the new Secretary of State Dean Rusk, the new Secretary of Defense Robert McNamara, the new Secretary of Treasury Douglas Dillon, and Clark M. Clifford.

An agenda for the meeting had been prepared by Persons and Clifford. The subjects on the agenda had been recommended by the parties present at the conference and were arranged under the headings of "State," "Defense," and "Treasury." The first subject under the heading of "State" was Laos. President Eisenhower opened the discussion on Laos by stating that the United States was determined to preserve the independence of Laos. It was his opinion that if Laos should fall to the Communists, then it would be just a question of time until South Vietnam, Cambodia, Thailand and Burma would collapse. He felt that the Communists had designs on all of Southeast Asia, and that it would be a tragedy to permit Laos to fall.

President Eisenhower gave a brief review of the various moves and coups that had taken place in Laos involving the Pathet Lao, Souvanna Phouma, Boun Oum and Kong Le. He said that the evidence was clear that Communist China and North Vietnam were determined to destroy the independence of Laos. He also added that the Russians were sending in substantial supplies in support of the Pathet Lao in an effort to overturn the government.

President Eisenhower said it would be fatal for us to permit Communists to insert themselves in the Laotian government. He recalled that our experience had clearly demonstrated that under such circumstances the Communists always ended up in control. He cited China as an illustration.

At this point, Secretary of State Herter intervened to state that if the present government of Laos were to apply to SEATO for aid under the Pact, Herter was of the positive opinion that the signatories to the SEATO Pact were bound. President Eisenhower agreed with this and in his statement gave the impression that the request for aid had already come from the government of Laos. He corroborated the binding nature of the obligation of the United States under the SEATO Pact.

President Eisenhower stated that the British and the French did not want SEATO to intervene in Laos, and he indicated that they would probably continue to maintain that attitude. President Eisenhower said that if it were not appropriate for SEATO to intervene in Laos, that his next preference would be the International Control Commission. He was sure, however, that the Soviet Union did not want the ICC to go into Laos. President Eisenhower stated that if this country had a choice as to whether the task should be assumed by SEATO or the ICC, that he personally would prefer SEATO.

Secretary Herter stated that we possibly could work out some agreement with the British, if they could be persuaded to recognize the present government in Laos. The chances of accomplishing this, however, appeared to be remote.

Secretary Herter stated, with President Eisenhower's approval, that we should continue every effort to make a political settlement in Laos. He added, however, that if such efforts were fruitless, then the United States must intervene in concert with our allies. If we were unable to persuade our allies, then we must go it alone.

At this point, President Eisenhower said with considerable emotion that Laos was the key to the entire area of Southeast Asia. He said that if we permitted Laos to fall, then we would have to write off all the area. He stated that we must not permit a Communist take-over. He reiterated that we should make every effort to persuade member nations of SEATO or the ICC to accept the burden with us to defend the freedom of Laos.

As he concluded these remarks, President Eisenhower stated it was imperative that Laos be defended. He said that the United States should accept this task with our allies, if we could persuade them, and alone if we could not. He added that "our unilateral intervention would be our last desperate hope" in the event we were unable to prevail upon the other signatories to join us.

At one time it was hoped that perhaps some type of arrangement could be made with Kong Le. This had proved fruitless, however, and President Eisenhower said "he was a lost soul and wholly irretrievable."

Commenting upon President Eisenhower's statement that we would have to go to the support of Laos alone if we could not persuade others to proceed with us,

President-elect Kennedy asked the question as to how long it would take to put an American division into Laos. Secretary Gates replied that it would take from twelve to seventeen days but that some of that time could be saved if American forces, then in the Pacific, could be utilized. Secretary Gates added that the American forces were in excellent shape and that modernization of the Army was making good progress.

President-elect Kennedy commented upon the seriousness of the situation in Laos and in Southeast Asia and asked if the situation seemed to be approaching a climax. General Eisenhower stated that the entire proceeding was extremely confused but that it was clear that this country was obligated to support the existing government in Laos.

The discussion of Laos led to some concluding general statements regarding Southeast Asia. It was agreed that Thailand was a valuable ally of the United States, and that one of the dangers of a Communist take-over in Laos would be to expose Thailand's borders. In this regard, it was suggested that the military training under French supervision in Thailand was very poor and that it would be a good idea to get American military instructors there as soon as possible so the level of military capability could be raised.

President Eisenhower said there was some indication that Russia was concerned over Communist pressures in Laos and in Southeast Asia emanating from China and North Vietnam. It was felt that this attitude could possibly lead to some difficulty between Russia and China.

This phase of the discussion was concluded by President Eisenhower in commenting philosophically upon the fact that the morale existing in the democratic forces in Laos appeared to be disappointing. He wondered aloud why, in interventions of this kind, we always seem to find that the morale of the Communist forces was better than that of the democratic forces. His explanation was that the Communist philosophy appeared to produce a sense of dedication on the part of its adherents, while there was not the same sense of dedication on the part of those supporting the free forces. He stated that the entire problem of morale was a serious one and would have to be taken into consideration as we became more deeply involved.

Source: *The Pentagon Papers*, Gravel Edition, vol II, pp. 635-37

Document 3.2
Kennedy Press Conference,
selected passages, January 25, 1961

Question: Mr. President, you have spoken of the situation where there are crises in the world now. One of these crises is Laos. Do you have any hope that a political settlement can be negotiated there?

The President: Well, as you know, the British Government has presented to the Soviet Union—and to the best of my information an answer has not been received by the British—a proposal to reestablish the International Control Commission. We ought to know shortly whether there's any hope that that commission can be reestablished. As to the general view on Laos, this matter is of great concern to us. The United States is anxious that there be established in Laos a peaceful country—an independent country not dominated by either side but concerned with the life of the people within the country.

We are anxious that that situation come forward. And the United States is using its influence to see if that independent country, peaceful country, uncommitted country, can be established under the present very difficult circumstances.

Source: *Public Papers of the Presidents of the United States: John F. Kennedy, 1961*, p. 16.

Document 3.3
Kennedy Press Conference,
presidential statement and selected questions
pertaining to policy in Laos, March 23, 1961

The President: I want to make a brief statement about Laos. It is, I think, important for all Americans to understand this difficult and potentially dangerous problem. In my last conversation with General Eisenhower, the day before the inauguration on January 19, we spent more time on this hard matter than on any other thing. And since then it has been steadily before the administration as the most immediate of the problems that we found upon taking office. Our special concern with the problem in Laos goes back to 1954. That year at Geneva a large group of powers agreed to a settlement of the struggle for Indochina. Laos was one of the new states which had recently emerged from the French Union, and it was the clear premise of the 1954 settlement that this new country would be neutral—free of external domination by anyone. The new country contained contending factions, but in its first years real progress was made towards a unified and neutral status. But the efforts of a Communist-dominated group to destroy this neutrality never ceased.

In the last half of 1960 a series of sudden maneuvers occurred and the Communists and their supporters turned to a new and greatly intensified military effort to take over. These three maps (indicating) show the area of effective Communist domination as it was last August, with the colored portions up on the right-hand corner being the areas held and dominated by the Communists at that time; and now next, in December of 1960, three months ago, the red area having expanded; and now from December 20 to the present date near the end of March the Communists control a much wider section of the country.

In this military advance the local Communist forces, known as the Pathet Lao, have had increasing support and direction from outside. Soviet planes, I regret to say, have been conspicuous in a large-scale airlift into the battle area—over 100—1,000 sorties since last December 13th, plus a whole supporting set of combat specialists, mainly from Communist North Vietnam, and heavier weapons have been provided from outside, all with the clear objective of destroying by military action the agreed neutrality of Laos.

It is this new dimension of externally supported warfare that creates the present grave problem. The position of this administration has been carefully considered, and we have sought to make it just as clear as we know how to the governments concerned.

First, we strongly and unreservedly support the goal of a neutral and independent Laos, tied to no outside power or group of powers, threatening no one, and free from any domination. Our support for the present duly constituted government is aimed entirely and exclusively at that result. And if in the past there has been any possible ground for misunderstanding of our desire for a truly neutral Laos, there should be none now.

Secondly, if there is to be a peaceful solution, there must be a cessation of the present armed attacks by externally supported Communists. If these attacks do not stop, those who support a truly neutral Laos will have to consider their response. The shape of this necessary response will, of course, be carefully considered, not only here in Washington, but in the SEATO conference with our allies, which begins next Monday.

SEATO—the Southeast Asia Treaty Organization—was organized in 1954, with strong leadership from our last administration, and all members of SEATO have undertaken special treaty responsibilities towards an aggression in Laos.

No one should doubt our resolutions on this point. We are faced with a clear and one-sided threat of a change in the internationally agreed position of Laos. This threat runs counter to the will of the Laotian people, who wish only to be independent and neutral. It is posed rather by the military operations of internal dissident elements directed from outside the country. This is what must end if peace is to be achieved in Southeast Asia.

Thirdly, we are earnestly in favor of constructive negotiations among the nations concerned and among the leaders of Laos which can help Laos back to the pathway of independence and genuine neutrality. We strongly support the present British proposal of a prompt end of hostilities and prompt negotiations. We are always conscious of the obligation which rests upon all members of the United Nations to seek peaceful solutions to problems of this sort. We hope that others may be equally aware of this responsibility.

My fellow Americans, Laos is far away from America, but the world is small. Its two million people live in a country three times the size of Austria. The security of all Southeast Asia will be endangered if Laos loses its neutral independence. Its own safety runs with the safety of us all - in real neutrality observed by all.

I want to make it clear to the American people and to all of the world that all we want in Laos is peace, not war; a truly neutral government, not a cold war pawn; a settlement concluded at the conference table and not on the battlefield.

Our response will be made in close cooperation with our allies and the wishes of the Laotian Government. We will not be provoked, trapped, or drawn into this or any other situation; but I know that every American will want his country to honor its obligations to the point that freedom and security of the free world and ourselves may be achieved.

Careful negotiations are being conducted with many countries at the present time in order to see that we have taken every possible course to insure a peaceful solution. Yesterday the Secretary of State [Dean Rusk] informed the members and leaders of the Congress—the House and Senate—in both parties, of the situation and brought them up to date. We will continue to keep them and the country fully informed as the situation develops.

Question: Mr. President, can you tell us what reaction you may have had from the Russians, either directly or indirectly, perhaps through the British, with respect to the approach you suggest on this problem?

The President: The British have had a conversation with the Russians, but I think that it's impossible at the present time to make any clear judgment as to what the nature of the response will be. We are hopeful that it will be favorable to the suggestion that we have made—the suggestion that the British have made for a cease-fire and for negotiations of the matter.

Question: Mr. President, there have been reports that some portions of our Navy, some portions of our Marines, have been alerted and are moving toward that area. Could you tell us something of that, sir, and would it be safe to assume that we are preparing to back up our words as you have outlined them here?

The President: I think that my statement is clear and represents the views I wish to express at the present time, and I'm hopeful that it will be possible for us to see a peaceful solution arrive in a difficult matter, and I would let the matter rest at this point with that.

Question: Is there any kind of indicated deadline or time limit by which this Government will consider that further action is necessary unless hostilities have ceased in Laos?

The President: No time limit has been given, but quite obviously we are anxious to see an end to overt hostilities as soon as possible so that some form of negotiations can be carried on. And we are—but there has been no precise time limit set.

Question: Sir, I did not mean an ultimatum. I did mean in terms of an indicated time limit in our own minds if this drags on for a week or two weeks or three weeks, is there some time in there?

The President: Well, I think the matter, of course, becomes increasingly serious as the days go by, and that's why we're anxious to see if it's possible at the present time to reach an agreement on a cease-fire. The longer it goes on, the less satisfactory it is.

Question: Mr. President, that map would indicate that the Communists have taken over a good part of Laos. Have your advisors told you what the—how dangerous the military situation is there? Is there a real danger that the Communists will take over the whole kingdom?

The President: Well, quite obviously progress has been made on the—substantial progress has been made by the Communists towards that objective in recent weeks. And the capital—royal capital of Luang Prabang—has been in danger, and progress has been made southward towards the administrative capital of Vientiane. So that it is for this reason that we are so concerned and have felt the situation to be so critical.

Question: Yes, sir. Is there any—do you know how much time the supporters of the Laos Government might have for diplomacy? In other words, is there a danger of a quick takeover by the Communists in a matter of —

The President: I would say that we are hopeful that we can get a quick judgment as to what the prospects are going to be there. I think that every day is important.

Question: Mr. President, you mentioned earlier in your statement that there were dissident elements in Vietnam who were carrying on this warfare. There have been many reports of North Vietnamese troops involved. Do we have any intelligence or information that would bear out these reports?

The President: The phrase "dissident elements," I believe, referred to the internal group, and I also stated that there have been, has been evidence of groups from Viet Minh or North Vietnam who have been involved.

Question: Mr. President, there appears to be some national unawareness of the importance of a free Laos to the security of the United States and to the individual American. Could you spell out your views on that a little further?

The President: Well, quite obviously geographically Laos borders on Thailand, to which the United States has treaty obligations under the SEATO [Southeast Asia Treaty Organization] Agreement of 1954, it borders on South Vietnam—or borders on Vietnam to which the United States has very close ties, and also which is a signatory of the SEATO Pact. The aggression against Laos itself was referred to in the SEATO Agreement. So that, given this, the nature of the geography, its location, the commitments which the United States and obligations which the United States has assumed toward Laos as well as the surrounding countries—as well as other signatories of the SEATO Pact, it's quite obvious that if the Communists were able to move in and dominate this country, it would endanger the security of all, and the peace of all, of Southeast Asia. And as a member of the United Nations and as a signatory of the SEATO Pact, and as a country which is concerned with the strength of the cause of freedom around the world, that quite obviously affects the security of the United States.

Question: Mr. President, the United States has made the position all the way through on this that we want a neutral Laos. But isn't it true that Laos has a nonviable economy and it can't exist as an independent country?

The President: Well, I think it can exist. That was the premise under which the 1954 agreements were signed. It may require economic assistance, but there are many countries which are neutral which have received economic assistance from one side or the other, and many of those countries are in Southeast Asia and some of them are geographically quite close to Laos, so that I don't think that the final test of a neutral country is completely the state of its economy. The test of a neutral country is whether one side or another dominates it and uses it, a phrase I referred to, as a pawn in the cold war. We would like it to occupy a neutral category as does Cambodia.

Question: Mr. President, what is your evaluation of the theory that perhaps the Russians are so active in Laos to keep the Chinese Communists out?

The President: Well, I wouldn't attempt to make a judgment about a matter on which we have incomplete information. I think that the facts of the matter are that there has been external activity and that it has helped produce the result you see on the map, and this is of concern to us. I'm hopeful that those countries which have been supporting this effort will recognize that this is a matter of great concern to us and that they will be agreeable to the kind of proposals which we have made in the interests of peace.

Question: Mr. President, in the event that your strong efforts to reach a neutral Laos go unheeded, would you possibly consider it necessary then for SEATO to intervene, or would you spell out a little more clearly what would have to take place?

The President: I think a careful reading of my statement makes clear what the various prospects are and the critical nature of them.

Question: Mr. President, if these responses aren't forthcoming and aren't favorable on your proposals here, would you—and we have to shoot—would you use your Executive orders and authority, or is the purpose of Mr. Rusk going to the Senators in preparation of asking for a declaration of war in case it really becomes a shooting matter out there?

The President: I think that it would be best to consider it as I stated it in my statement.   The prospects, alternative responsibilities—I've stated them, I think, as clearly as today they can be stated. We will know a good deal more in the coming days.

Question: Mr. President, I have a question about conventional forces in relation to the Laos situation.   You have been reviewing the recommendations of your Secretary of Defense [Robert S. McNamara] on conventional forces.   Have you come to any decision on building them up, and have you found them adequate to deal with the Laos situation in case of —

The President: We will be sending a message on Monday or Tuesday on those changes we are going to make in defense, and at that time we'll give, I think, a more adequate response than I could give here to your question, because we're going to discuss the entire military budget.   Quite obviously, we are stretched around the world with commitments to dozens of countries and it does raise the question of our —whether a greater effort should not be made.

Question: Mr. President, could you tell us what in your opinion this country has obtained out of its roughly $310 million worth of aid sent in the past six or seven years to Laos?

The President: Well, Laos is not yet a Communist country and it's my hope that it will not be.

Source: *Public Papers of the Presidents of the United States: John F. Kennedy, 1961*, pp. 213-219.

_____

Document 3.4
Declaration on the Neutrality of Laos July 23, 1962

The Governments of the Union of Burma, the Kingdom of Cambodia, Canada, the People's Republic of China, the Democratic Republic of Viet-Nam, the Republic of France, the Republic of India, the Polish People's Republic, the Republic of Viet-Nam, the Kingdom of Thailand, the Union of Soviet Socialist Republics, the United Kingdom of Great Britain and Northern Ireland, and the United States of America, whose representatives took part in the International Conference on the Settlement of the Laotian Question, 1961-1962;

Welcoming the presentation of the statement of neutrality by the Royal Government of Laos of July 9, 1962, and taking note of this statement which is, with the concurrence of the Royal Government of Laos, incorporated in the present Declaration as an integral part thereof, and the text of which is as follows:

THE ROYAL GOVERNMENT OF LAOS,

Being resolved to follow the path of peace and neutrality in conformity with the interests and aspirations of the Laotian people, as well as the principles of the Joint Communiqué of Zurich dated June 22, 1961, and of the Geneva Agreements of 1954, in order to build a peaceful, neutral, independent, democratic, unified and prosperous Laos,

Solemnly declares that:

(1) It will resolutely apply the five principles of peaceful coexistence in foreign relations, and will develop friendly relations and establish diplomatic relations with all countries, the neighboring countries first and foremost, on the basis of equality and of respect for the independence and sovereignty of Laos;

(2) It is the will of the Laotian people to protect and ensure respect for the sovereignty, independence, neutrality, unity, and territorial integrity of Laos;

(3) It will not resort to the use or threat of force in any way which might impair the peace of other countries, and will not interfere in the internal affairs of other countries;

(4) It will not enter into any military alliance or into any agreement, whether military or otherwise, which is inconsistent with the neutrality of the Kingdom of Laos; it will not allow the establishment of any foreign military base on Laotian territory, nor allow any country to use Laotian territory for military purposes or for the purposes of interference in the internal affairs of other countries, nor recognize the protection of any alliance or military coalition, including SEATO;

(5) It will not allow any foreign interference in the internal affairs of the Kingdom of Laos in any form whatsoever;

(6) Subject to the provisions of Article 5 of the Protocol, it will require the withdrawal from Laos of all foreign troops and military personnel, and will not allow any foreign troops or military personnel to be introduced into Laos;

(7) It will accept direct and unconditional aid from all countries that wish to help the Kingdom of Laos build up an independent and autonomous national economy on the basis of respect for the sovereignty of Laos;

(8) It will respect the treaties and agreements signed in conformity with the interests of the Laotian people and of the policy of peace and neutrality of the Kingdom, in particular the Geneva Agreements of 1962, and will abrogate all treaties and agreements which are contrary to those principles.

This statement of neutrality by the Royal Government of Laos shall be promulgated constitutionally and shall have the force of law.

The Kingdom of Laos appeals to all the States participating in the International Conference on the Settlement of the Laotian Question, and to all other States, to recognize the sovereignty, independence, neutrality, unity, and territorial integrity of Laos, to conform to these principles in all respects, and to refrain from any action inconsistent therewith.

Confirming the principles of respect for the sovereignty, independence, unity and territorial integrity of the Kingdom of Laos and non-interference in its internal affairs which are embodied in the Geneva Agreements of 1954;

Emphasizing the principle of respect for the neutrality of the Kingdom of Laos;

Agreeing that the above-mentioned principles constitute a basis for the peaceful settlement of the Laotian question;

Profoundly convinced that the independence and neutrality of the Kingdom of Laos will assist the peaceful democratic development of the Kingdom of Laos and the achievement of national accord in that country, as well as the strengthening of peace and security of Southeast Asia:

1. Solemnly declare, in accordance with the will of the Government and people of the Kingdom of Laos, as expressed in the statement of neutrality by the Royal Government of Laos of July 9, 1962, that they recognize and will respect and observe in every way the sovereignty, independence, neutrality, unity and territorial integrity of the Kingdom of Laos.

2. Undertake, in particular, that

(a) they will not commit or participate in any way in any act which might directly or indirectly impair the sovereignty, independence, neutrality, unity or territorial integrity of the Kingdom of Laos;

(b) they will not resort to the use or threat of force or any other measure which might impair the peace of the Kingdom of Laos;

(c) they will refrain from all direct or indirect interference in the internal affairs of the Kingdom of Laos;

(d) they will not attach conditions of a political nature to any assistance which they may offer or which the Kingdom of Laos may seek;

(e) they will not bring the Kingdom of Laos in any way into any military alliance or any other agreement, whether military or otherwise, which is inconsistent with her neutrality, nor invite or encourage her to enter into any such alliance or to conclude any such agreement;

(f) they will respect the wish of the Kingdom of Laos not to recognize the protection of any alliance or military coalition, including SEATO;

(g) they will not introduce into the Kingdom of Laos foreign troops or military personnel in any form whatsoever, nor will they in any way facilitate or connive at the introduction of any foreign troops or military personnel;

(h) they will not establish nor will they in any way facilitate or connive at the establishment in the Kingdom of Laos of any foreign military base, foreign strong point or other foreign military installation of any kind;

(i) they will not use the territory of the Kingdom of Laos for interference in the internal affairs of other countries;

(j) they will not use the territory of any country, including their own, for interference in the internal affairs of the Kingdom of Laos.

3. Appeal to all other States to recognize, respect and observe in every way the sovereignty, independence and neutrality, and also the unity and territorial integrity, of the Kingdom of Laos and to refrain from any action inconsistent with these principles or with other provisions of the present Declaration.

4. Undertake, in the event of a violation or threat of violation of the sovereignty, independence, neutrality, unity or territorial integrity of the Kingdom of Laos, to consult jointly with the Royal Government of Laos and among themselves in order to consider measures which might prove to be necessary to ensure the observance of these principles and other provisions of the present Declaration.

5. The present Declaration shall enter into force on signature and together with the statement of neutrality by the Royal Government of Laos of July 9, 1962, shall be regarded as constituting an international agreement. The present Declaration shall be deposited in the archives of the Governments of the United Kingdom and the Union of Soviet Socialist Republics, which shall furnish certified copies thereof to the other signatory States and to all the other States of the world.

In witness whereof, the undersigned Plenipotentiaries have signed the present Declaration.

Done in two copies in Geneva this twenty-third day of July one thousand nine hundred and sixty-two in the English, Chinese, French, Laotian and Russian languages, each text being equally authoritative.

Source: *Bulletin of the Department of State*, 47 (July-December 1962), pp. 259-261.

Chapter 3 Notes

[1] Arthur M. Schlesinger, Jr., *A Thousand Days* (Boston: Houghton Mifflin, 1965), pp. 163-164.

[2] Bernard B. Fall, *Anatomy of a Crisis* (Garden City, N.Y.: Doubleday, 1969), p. 23.

[3] For additional background on Laotian history and political culture, see Hugh Toye, *Laos: Buffer State or Battleground* (London: Oxford University Press, 1968).

[4] Charles A. Stevenson, *The End of Nowhere: American Policy Toward Laos Since 1954* (Boston: Beacon Press, 1972), p. vii.

[5] George Ball, *The Past Has Another Pattern* (New York: Norton, 1982), p. 362.

[6] Fall, *Anatomy of a Crisis*, pp. 164-166. See also Roger Hilsman, *To Move a Nation* (Garden City, N. Y.: Doubleday, 1967), pp. 113-114.

[7] Arthur J. Dommen, *Conflict in Laos* (New York: Praeger, 1964), pp. 127-128.

[8] Ball, *The Past*, p. 362.

[9] Harold W. Chase and Allen H. Lerman, eds., *Kennedy and the Press* (New York: Thomas Y. Crowell, 1965), p. 9.

[10] Schlesinger, *Thousand Days*, p. 329.

[11] John Kenneth Gailbraith, Kennedy's ambassador to India. Quoted in Herbert S. Parmet, *JFK: The Presidency of John F. Kennedy* (New York: Dial Press, 1983), p. 141.

[12] Schlesinger, *Thousand Days*, p. 332.

[13] Quoted in Hilsman, *To Move a Nation*, p. 128.

[14] Roswell Gilpatric. Quoted in Parmet, *JFK*, p. 140.

[15] Hilsman, *To Move a Nation*, p. 130.

[16]Chase and Lerman, *Kennedy and the Press*, p. 53.

[17]Hilsman, *To Move a Nation*, p. 133.

[18]Parmet, *JFK*, p. 148.

[19]Quoted in ibid., p. 149.

[20]Ibid. See also Stevenson, *The End of Nowhere*, p. 151 (note 60).

[21]Parmet, *JFK*, p. 150.

[22]Stevenson, *The End of Nowhere*, p. 155.

[23]Ibid., p. 168.

[24]Ibid., pp. 168-170.

[25]Quoted in Stevenson, *The End of Nowhere*, p. 174.

[26]Hilsman, *To Move a Nation*, p. 150.

[27]Ibid., pp. 151-152.

[28]For a detailed discussion of the war powers controversy see David Gray Adler, "The Constitution and Presidential Warmaking," *Political Science Quarterly*, 103, no. 1 (Spring 1988), 1-36.

[29]Edward S. Corwin, *The President: Office and Powers 1787-1957*, 4th ed. (New York: New York University Press, 1957), p 171.

[30]Quoted in William Conrad Gibbons, *The U.S. Government and the Vietnam War: Part II 1961-1964* (Princeton, N.J.: Princeton University Press, 1986), pp. 30-31.

[31]Fulbright met with Kennedy on May 4, 1961, and expressed serious reservations about sending U.S. troops to Laos, though he was willing to use American forces to defend Thailand and South Vietnam. See Gibbons, p. 30. MacArthur recommended against any use of American ground forces in Southeast Asia. See Schlesinger, *Thousand Days*, p. 339.

[32]Quoted in Gibbons, T*he U. S. Government and the Vietnam War*: Part II, p. 31.

[33]Hilsman, *To Move a Nation*, p. 116.

[34]David Halberstam, *The Best and the Brightest* (New York: Random House, 1972), p. 115.

[35]Walter Isaacson and Evan Thomas, *The Wise Men* (New York: Simon & Schuster, 1986), p. 616.

[36]Theodore C. Sorensen, *Kennedy* (New York: Harper & Row, 1965), p. 309.

[37]Ibid., p. 644.

[38]Robert F. Kennedy, *Thirteen Days* (New York: New American Library, 1969), p. 120.

[39]Sorensen, *Kennedy*, p. 646. Emphasis in original.

[40]He did the same thing in connection with the Cuban missile crisis. See Kennedy, *Thirteen Days*, p. 124.

Chapter 4

Johnson and Escalation of the War in Vietnam

AMERICA'S COMMITMENT TO VIETNAM

Like Laos, Vietnam was part of French Indochina before the Second World War and, for most of the war, was occupied by the Japanese. When the war ended and the French attempted to reassert their colonial control over the region, they met with military resistance from nationalists who had gained considerable experience fighting against the Japanese occupation. Though the United States generally opposed the restoration of colonial empires after 1945, an exception was made in the case of Southeast Asia. The most prominent nationalist leader in Vietnam, Ho Chi Minh, was also a communist who fought against the French in order to create an independent and Marxist Vietnamese state. Where communist movements were involved, the United States took the side of colonialism.

Beginning in the Truman administration, and continuing under Eisenhower, substantial American military and economic assistance was provided to the French forces fighting in Vietnam. Moreover, a major public commitment to prevent the success of communist guerrilla movements throughout Southeast Asia was made. American foreign policy makers frequently expressed fears that a communist victory in Vietnam would endanger the stability of Vietnam's neighbors and the other countries throughout southern Asia. Those fears were given a memorable metaphor when President Eisenhower compared the fate of nations in the region to a row of dominoes: "You knock over the first one, and what will happen to the last one is the certainty that it will go over very quickly."[1]

The fear of falling dominoes on the part of American foreign policy makers was a logical consequence of the policy of containment adopted early in the cold war. Containment committed the United States to blocking Soviet, and later Chinese, expansion in order to restrict communism to those places in the world where it already existed. We could then await the collapse of Marxist regimes from their own internal economic and political stresses.[2] Containment meant that we did not need to fight and destroy the Soviet regime or Mao's China; we only needed to prevent their growth. By creating the NATO alliance in Western Europe and punishing North Korea for its invasion of South Korea, we could keep constant pressure on the Soviet Union and China, frustrate their global ambitions, and complicate their domestic problems. The difficulty with containment, at least as it was practiced in the 1950s and 1960s, was that it lacked discrimination. Communism was presumed to be monolithic, even after a serious split between the Soviet Union and China began to emerge. Every communist leader in the world was considered an agent of Soviet or Chinese power, even when they identified themselves with indigenous nationalist movements and were philosophically opposed to any and all foreign influence. Under containment, all communist revolutions were equally threatening to American security wherever they might occur.

The American concern for preventing the spread of communism was also fed by a recognition of the serious political repercussions that followed the fall of China to communist rule in 1949. That event shook Truman's presidency and contributed to the bitter recriminations of the McCarthy era when demagogues played on American fears of communist infiltration and world domination. Losing a country to communist control could have serious geopolitical consequences. It also carried with it the prospect of losing the White House, endangering civil liberties, and unleashing irrational public emotions.

Though Eisenhower clearly wanted to keep the dominoes of Southeast Asia standing as long as possible, his commitment to the French cause was not without its limits. When French forces suffered an embarrassing defeat at Dienbienphu in the spring of 1954, Eisenhower was forced to consider the use of American military power in Southeast Asia. In the end, he rejected all policy options that would have put U.S. troops into a guerrilla war in rugged Asian terrain.[3] Instead of an American war in 1954, there was an international conference in Geneva, a negotiated end to the fighting in the region, and a temporary partition of Vietnam at the seventeenth parallel. The newly created North Vietnam became a communist regime under Ho Chi Minh; in the south an austere Roman Catholic nationalist named Ngo Dinh Diem emerged as the leader of the new nation of South Vietnam. In America, Eisenhower learned that while losing a country to communism remained a potential political liability, losing half a country to communism in a remote corner of Asia was apparently acceptable to the American people. The loss of North Vietnam to communist control, and the mild public reaction that followed the Geneva accords in the United States, did not, however, lead to a reduction of America's involvement in Southeast Asia. Just the opposite occurred. The U. S. promise to prevent the spread of communism in the region was restated and reinforced by new treaty obligations under the Southeast Asia Treaty Organization (SEATO). Preventing the fall of the other half of Vietnam became a central foreign policy objective for Eisenhower and for his immediate successors.[4]

The 1954 Geneva accords called for free elections in all of Vietnam, but a year after the accords were signed, Diem announced, with the support of the United

States, that he would not allow elections in the south because he could not be sure that such elections would be free and fair. In fact, he knew that Ho Chi Minh would be the likely winner of national elections. Instead of working toward reunification, Diem used American assistance to begin the difficult task of building an effective army and an independent nation in South Vietnam. In many respects, he was poorly suited for that task. Though Lyndon Johnson, visiting South Vietnam as vice president in 1961, would compare Diem to Winston Churchill, Diem had very few of Churchill's leadership abilities and none of his commitment to genuine democracy.[5]

An intensely private and introspective individual, Diem was educated in French Catholic schools, served as a bureaucrat for the French colonial government, and lived for a number of years in exile in the United States. He had little in common with the Buddhist peasants who made up the majority of the South Vietnamese population, but was surprisingly adept at the conspiratorial maneuvering and fraud that passed for democratic politics in Southeast Asia. Diem pushed South Vietnam's first leader and former emperor, Bao Dai, aside, survived various coup attempts, and defeated a powerful Vietnamese version of the mafia called the Binh Xuyen. "Free elections" for the people of South Vietnam were held in 1955. In most polling places government officials carefully watched the balloting and took reprisals against those who voted the wrong way; in several sections of Saigon the number of votes cast for Diem exceeded the number of registered voters. Diem won the presidency by a 98.2 percent majority, even though some of his CIA advisers had suggested that stealing an election by more than 60 or 70 percent would be unseemly.[6] American officials in Washington who would later claim to be defending democracy in South Vietnam could hardly do so as long as Diem was in power. Even with Diem out of power, the absence of any democratic tradition in Southeast Asia, the long years of colonial rule and foreign occupation, and a culture that tolerated corruption and encouraged conspiracy would make it difficult to create or defend a Western-style democracy in South Vietnam. The most that could be said in favor of the government that the United States supported was that it was not communist.

In communist North Vietnam, Ho Chi Minh's new nation had its own problems with an economy devastated by years of war with the French and by the new boundary at the seventeenth parallel, which cut the north off from its traditional sources of rice. Efforts at an ideologically motivated land reform in North Vietnam resulted in the murder and internment of thousands of peasants and added to the economic disruption. Large migrations of Catholics who left North Vietnam and communists who left the south after the Geneva accords meant that both regimes had massive refugee problems on top of their other economic and political concerns. Ho's early expectations that national elections would be held in accordance with the Geneva agreements, and his confidence that he would win those elections, led his government initially to respect the 1954 cease-fire. Only later in the decade did North Vietnam begin actively and aggressively to support guerrilla forces in the south.

In his early years in power, Diem used American aid to build a well-equipped and well-funded military establishment, though the military leaders he placed in positions of command were chosen on the basis of their support for the government in Saigon rather than their independent judgment or leadership abilities.[7] He also managed to arrest, kill, or force into hiding many of the communist guerrillas who had remained in South Vietnam after the 1954 armistice. Those who escaped government forces, calling themselves the Vietcong, continued to fight against the government of South Vietnam using brutal tactics, including the assassination of local leaders, in order to intimidate villagers in remote sections of the country. For both Diem and the Vietcong in the early stages of South Vietnam's civil war, neither terrorism nor acts of repression won the lasting loyalty of peasants in rural villages where life remained a seasonal struggle to raise crops and a constant struggle to avoid the obvious dangers of offending either government officials or communist guerrillas.

Diem's early successes in consolidating power, sustaining American support, and fighting communist insurgents were short-lived. In Saigon, he remained powerful, but also isolated and aloof. Over time he increasingly depended on the advice and administrative assistance of his brother, Ngo Dinh Nhu, who ran the nation's secret police and, along with other family members, allegedly engaged in corruption. No major reforms in South Vietnam's economy or political structure were undertaken by Diem's government, and appointments and policies clearly favoring the nation's Catholic minority offended members of other religious groups. Reformers who wanted to see South Vietnam become a genuine democracy were frustrated by the absence of any progress in that direction, and Buddhist leaders were frightened by laws and policies that threatened their religious beliefs and practices. When a Buddhist priest protesting government crackdowns against his order set himself on fire in front of news cameras in the streets of Saigon, America and the world became painfully aware of how much resentment and resistance Diem's regime had engendered. Insult was added to political injury when the self-immolations were repeated and Diem's controversial sister-in-law, Madame Nhu, publicly referred to them as Buddhist "barbecues."[8] Outside of Saigon and South Vietnam's other major cities, the Vietcong gradually grew in strength as Diem's government became more unpopular and as supplies and reinforcements began to arrive from the north.

The Kennedy administration, after accepting neutrality in Laos, responded more forcefully to the deteriorating situation in South Vietnam. The number of American advisers in the country was increased, as was the level of U.S. foreign aid. Between November 1961 and December 1962, the United States increased the number of American advisers assigned to South Vietnamese military units from 948 to 11,300.[9] By the end of 1963, American military and economic aid totaled $500 million a year.[10] But even those high levels of aid and advice failed to stem the rising tide of communist guerrilla success in the Mekong Delta and other rural regions of South Vietnam. The South Vietnamese army, without good leadership, lost ground even as it became larger and better equipped. When they occasionally encountered large concentrations of Vietcong, as occurred in the village of Ap Bac in January 1963, the South Vietnamese could not make effective use of their superior numbers, modern equipment, and American technical assistance.[11] Peasants who had originally been indifferent to the Diem regime became hostile when they were forced to leave their villages and relocate to strategic hamlets that were supposed to provide for their security. The fortified villages of the strategic hamlet program took peasants away from what they valued most, their fields and the homes of their ancestors, and did so without having any noticeable impact on Vietcong attacks that were often carried out in stealth against remote army outposts, village leaders, and Diem supporters. The government and army of South Vietnam were losing the war by their own actions.

Recognizing the emerging problems in Vietnam and the importance of preventing a communist military victory in Southeast Asia, Kennedy appointed Henry Cabot Lodge as America's new ambassador in Saigon. Lodge, a former Republican senator from Massachusetts (who had been defeated by Kennedy), a former ambassador to the United Nations, and Nixon's vice-presidential running mate in 1960, was one of the most prominent Republicans in the nation when he took the assignment. His appointment by Kennedy, and his willingness to accept it, reflected the importance of the American commitment in Southeast Asia and the degree to which that commitment was beyond partisan dispute.

In the summer of 1963, just after arriving in Saigon, Lodge sent word to Washington that another crackdown against Buddhist leaders had taken place, with more than 1,400 monks placed under arrest. The ambassador also reported that a coup against Diem was being planned by a group of South Vietnamese generals, and he requested policy guidance from the administration. Unfortunately, the Lodge request arrived on an August weekend when many government officials were out of town—the president at his private home in Hyannisport, the secretary of state at a baseball game in New York, the secretary of defense on a mountain climbing excursion, and the deputy secretary of defense at a Virginia farm. The ambassador's cable was eventually delivered to Undersecretary of State George Ball during a Saturday golf game. Ball worked with the officials at the Department of State and the National Security Council staff who had not managed to escape for the weekend and prepared a response that criticized the growing influence of Diem's brother Nhu and gave Lodge the opening he sought to explore alternative leadership possibilities in South Vietnam. After clearing a draft of the State Department cable with the president, the Washington response was sent. The next day, Lodge, who favored an early end of the Diem regime, requested clarification of his new instructions and subsequently contacted the generals planning a coup without warning Diem about what might transpire.

On the following Monday, when most of the senior foreign policy makers were back in Washington, second thoughts were expressed about any attempt to overthrow Diem. Though Diem's faults were well known to Washington officials, it was not clear whether he could be replaced by a more effective leader. Other coup attempts had failed. If an American-approved coup did not succeed, the administration could easily have produced a foreign policy fiasco without creating any improvement in the security of South Vietnam. In the end, the August coup did not take place, and about the only lesson learned from the experience was the conclusion expressed by the president's national security adviser, McGeorge Bundy, that the United States government "should never do business on the weekend."[12]

The failure of the rumored August coup to materialize did nothing to alter the fundamental deficiencies and weaknesses of the Diem regime, and early in September President Kennedy sent a fact-finding mission to South Vietnam to bring back a firsthand report on the situation in Southeast Asia. When the mission returned to Washington, an experienced Marine Corps general reported to a meeting of the National Security Council that the war against the Vietcong was going well, while his State Department companion on the trip predicted that the Diem regime was nearing collapse. At the conclusion of their presentations, the president was forced to ask the mission members whether they had visited the same country.[13] A second, and higher-level, team, made up of Secretary of Defense Robert McNamara and Chairman of the Joint Chiefs of Staff Maxwell Taylor, went to South Vietnam later that month, and upon their return the president decided not to actively initiate a coup. Instead, the United States would use selective economic sanctions against the Diem regime, continue to encourage reform, and leave standing the impression that it would not oppose a change in the government of South Vietnam.

This subtle American policy had very little impact on events in Saigon, where the August coup conspirators finally executed their plans at the beginning of November, unaware that senior Washington policymakers no longer enthusiastically endorsed their cause. After capturing the presidential palace from which Diem had escaped, the fate of the coup was uncertain, but when Diem agreed to surrender and was promptly killed, a new era dawned in South Vietnam. It was not, however, an era of democracy and effective government. Instead, the coup leaders bickered, conspired against each other, and failed to form anything that resembled a stable regime. South Vietnam became what one official in the Johnson administration would later call "a country with an army and no government."[14] And the army was losing ground to the Vietcong. November 1963 was a critical turning point for American involvement in Vietnam, but our own ability to deal with the aftermath of the Diem assassination was severely limited by the need to deal with the aftermath of another assassination much closer to home.

JOHNSON AND THE AMERICAN COMMITMENT

When Lyndon Johnson unexpectedly became president following the assassination of John Kennedy in Dallas, Texas, late in November 1963, he inherited a domestic legislative agenda that was stalled in the Congress, a Democratic party that was divided over civil rights and social issues, and a nagging foreign policy problem in Vietnam. In the months before and after his 1964 landslide election over Barry Goldwater, Johnson would devote his considerable energies and political talents to completing Kennedy's New Frontier and initiating the domestic programs that would become known as the Great Society. Modeling himself after Franklin Roosevelt, Johnson thought that the powers of the presidency should be used to push forward major social and political reforms. But his legacy as a master of legislative relations, an innovator of government programs, and a builder of political coalitions would eventually be overshadowed by events in Southeast Asia. When Kennedy came to office in 1960, the foreign policy issue that Eisenhower thought most serious was the now largely forgotten crisis in Laos; when Lyndon Johnson decided not to run for reelection in 1968, the foreign policy issue that had led to the demise of his political career was Vietnam.

Predictions that South Vietnam was near defeat prior to the overthrow of the Diem regime, turned out to be slightly premature. Though Saigon suffered considerable instability, including several coups and coup attempts, in the months following Diem's death, the Vietcong were not yet prepared to deliver a death blow to the South Vietnamese army. Their success continued to be based on guerrilla tactics, sporadic large-scale battles, gradual domination of rural territory, and occasional acts of urban terrorism. The Johnson administration would have another year and a half before the imminent collapse of South Vietnam. During that period both the American involvement in the war and commitment to the survival of South Vietnam would deepen.

In January 1964, one of the Diem conspirators, General Nguyen Khanh, successfully overthrew his associates and took control of the South Vietnamese government. As with many of the earlier and subsequent changes in leadership, this one was at first greeted as an improvement over what had gone before. It was not. Stanley Karnow, who reported on events in Southeast Asia in the 1950s and 1960s and later wrote a popular history of the war in Vietnam, described Khanh this way, "Even in a society where scruples were scarce, he was distrusted, having built his career on switching his allegiance to whichever faction promised to fulfill his limitless ambitions."[15] Khanh's attempt to create a coalition that could rule South Vietnam in the early months of 1964 involved the killing, arrest, and trial of several of his fellow anti-Diem conspirators. Preoccupied with staying in power, Khanh had very few ideas about what to do with it. His one suggestion for fighting the growing strength of the Vietcong was an invasion of North Vietnam, which struck Washington observers as reckless and wholly unrealistic given the inability of South Vietnamese forces to secure territory in their own half of the country.

In early March, Johnson sent McNamara and Taylor back to Vietnam for another fact-finding mission, which produced more public promises that South Vietnam would win the battle against communist insurgents and some private reports that they would not be able to do so alone. At about the same time, William Bundy, the assistant secretary of defense and the national security adviser's older brother, prepared a memorandum for the president outlining further military steps that might be taken by the United States to advance the South Vietnamese cause. These included mining the harbor of North Vietnam's largest port, Haiphong, and bombing transportation centers, industrial facilities, and training camps throughout the north. The purpose of bombing North Vietnam would be twofold: It would, hopefully, slow the flow of men and matériel that freely moved from the north to the Vietcong in the south through the jungles and mountains of Laos, Cambodia, and both Vietnams. Also, bombing missions were expected to have important psychological benefits—bolstering the confidence of South Vietnamese officials, whose confidence almost always needed bolstering, and giving the North Vietnamese an incentive to negotiate some conclusion to the war. Throughout the fighting in Vietnam, it was always difficult to distinguish between what was partly a civil war in the provinces of South Vietnam and what was something between an infiltration and an invasion of the south by the forces of the north. Defeating the enemy in South Vietnam was considerably complicated by the problem of deciding who the enemy was. William Bundy, and others, in 1964 urged the president to consider North Vietnam as the principal opponent and the punishment of the North Vietnamese by aerial attack as an essential element in the defense of the south.

Bundy's memo also recognized that the actions he proposed might not be constitutional without a declaration of war or some other official act of congressional approval. For a president focused on an upcoming national election, Bundy's recommendations were politically sensitive. As the politics of 1964 developed, it appeared that Johnson would be running against Barry Goldwater, a conservative Republican from the Southwest, who would later be portrayed as too hawkish to be trusted with the foreign policy powers of the presidency. One not very subtle television commercial prepared for the 1964 campaign showed a small child picking the pedals off a flower while an announcer described some of Goldwater's more provocative foreign policy proposals and a large mushroom-shaped cloud rose in the background. But painting a negative portrait of Goldwater as a warmonger would be difficult, if not impossible, if Johnson was himself engaged in a major war in Vietnam. Johnson was also concerned that bombing North Vietnam might widen the war and increase the participation of Soviet and Chinese forces. The Bundy suggestions were rejected in the spring of 1964, but administration staff members at the Pentagon and the National Security Council began, on a contingency basis, to plan American bombing missions against North Vietnam and the wording of a congressional resolution that would authorize them. They would soon have occasion to use both.

In the summer of 1964, American destroyers equipped with CIA electronic surveillance equipment were engaged in secret intelligence-gathering missions in the Gulf of Tonkin off the coast of North Vietnam. The ships were well outside the three-mile territorial waters claimed by French colonial Indochina, but did operate within twelve miles of the North Vietnamese coast at a time when the twelve-mile limit was the standard measure for territorial waters claimed by China and many other nations of the world. One of the destroyers, the U.S.S. *Maddox*, on the morning of August 2, was attacked by three North Vietnamese patrol boats equipped with torpedoes that were launched against the American ship. Returning fire, the *Maddox*, along with planes from a nearby aircraft carrier, sank one of the North Vietnamese boats and damaged the other two. There were no American casualties. The next night, when the *Maddox* and a second destroyer sailed in the same waters, they initially reported another patrol boat attack. But after some frantic maneuvering and firing of weapons, the captain of the *Maddox* told his superiors that due to bad weather, low visibility, and a tense and overanxious crew, he could not be sure that a second attack had actually taken place.

Lyndon Johnson did not much care whether the August 3 attack had been real or not. He reported it to the American people as a second unprovoked assault on U.S. warships engaged in legitimate operations in international waters and proceeded to carry out the contingency plans that had been prepared months earlier. Reprisal bombings against North Vietnam were ordered and a draft resolution was sent to the Congress authorizing the president to "take all necessary measures" to respond to attacks on U.S. forces and to "prevent further aggression" in Southeast Asia. The Gulf of Tonkin resolution [Document 4.1] passed with overwhelming majorities in both the House and Senate and set the stage for a series of reprisal bombings that would be ordered after further attacks on U.S. military personnel at the end of 1964 and early in the new year. By the end of February 1965, after the Khanh government had been replaced by yet another coup, the United States was engaged in sustained bombing of North Vietnamese targets under a program ominously called Operation Rolling Thunder.

American bombing of North Vietnam, whether as punishment for incidents in the south or as part of an escalating military commitment, had relatively little effect on the conduct of the war. Targets for American attack were carefully chosen and restricted. Hanoi, the capital of North Vietnam, and other population centers were avoided; Haiphong harbor was not mined, and the ships at its docks, including those of U.S. allies Japan and Great Britain, were not attacked. Railroad bridges on the border with China were also exempted in order to avoid provoking a more direct Chinese participation in the war. Because of these limitations, and because the North Vietnamese economy was relatively underdeveloped, the bombing missions had only marginal consequences for the ability of the North Vietnamese to provide assistance to the south. As a psychological weapon, the bombing was even less effective. In the south it had no observable effect on the willingness of the South Vietnamese to form stable governments or effective fighting forces. In the north it galvanized the will of the people to resist American aggression and to sacrifice for a war that increasingly appeared to be a continuation of the fighting against French colonialism and Japanese occupation. Americans were becoming the new unwelcome foreigners seeking to dominate Southeast Asia.

The increased bombing had another consequence for America's growing commitment to the war. In order to carry out regular bombing missions, air bases in South Vietnam had to be protected from Vietcong attack. Early in 1965, General William C. Westmoreland, the new commanding officer in charge of American forces in Vietnam, requested marine deployments to provide protection for the airfields in Danang and elsewhere along the coast. In March, marines came ashore in a dramatic beach landing and set up defensive perimeters around various American facilities, adding to the burgeoning strength of American troops in the country and the number of military assignments that were carried out exclusively by forces of the United States. No longer merely advisers, American pilots flew missions in the north and south and American marine and army combat units provided protection for a variety of strategic locations in Vietnam. In addition, a vast array of support services, headquarters units, planning staffs, and advisory groups were stationed in Saigon and throughout the country, bringing the total American military presence to nearly 75,000.

In April, with the military situation in South Vietnam continuing to deteriorate, Westmoreland proposed that the marines be used in a more aggressive fashion to search out and destroy Vietcong forces near the bases they were assigned to guard. This was approved in a National Security Action Memorandum [Document 4.2] that also contained a presidential order that the change of mission not be made public. Lyndon Johnson was taking the United States deeper into war in Vietnam, but he was not yet prepared to do so openly. He did give a major speech at Johns Hopkins University, at about the same time he was secretly ordering a further expansion of the war, in which he outlined our reasons for fighting in Southeast Asia. [Document 4.3] We were there to keep the promises of a series of presidents to defend the independence of South Vietnam and to beat back the aggression of the North Vietnamese. These promises were important because they were related to larger goals and obligations. "The central lesson of our time is that the appetite of aggression is never satisfied. To withdraw from one battlefield means only to prepare for the next."[16] In the same speech Johnson also made a generous offer to provide a billion dollars in development aid for the Mekong River valley if the fighting in the region could be brought to a satisfactory conclusion. But in the spring and summer of 1965, there were no indications that the North Vietnamese or the Vietcong were interested in negotiations or in public works projects to create a Tennessee Valley Authority for the Mekong River. Johnson's interest in fully addressing the Vietnam issue was also limited. He and the Congress were occupied with many of the priority items on his Great Society agenda, and before any dramatic steps were taken in Southeast Asia, Johnson wanted some time to reexamine all of his options. At the end of July he would officially announce a decision to significantly increase U.S. forces in Vietnam. That decision would arguably be the most important made in the course of America's long involvement in Vietnam.

THE DECISION TO ESCALATE

Within the Johnson administration there was general agreement in the spring and early summer months of 1965 that a major decision regarding the future of Vietnam would have to be made. General Khanh had been replaced by Generals Thieu and Ky, but government instability in South Vietnam had become the norm, with little prospect of any significant improvement in the short term. Military losses for the forces of the south were widespread and expected to get worse. Desertions from the South Vietnamese army had become a serious problem, and Vietcong victories were redrawing the map of South Vietnam. When McNamara returned from his February inspection tour, he reported that 40 percent of the territory in the south was either fully or largely under communist domination. No longer restricted to the use of guerrilla tactics, larger units of enemy forces, sometimes combining guerrillas with North Vietnamese troops, were operating in the south. Reports from Director of the CIA John McCone, the embassy in Saigon, and the State Department concluded that the limited bombing of the north had shown no sign of weakening North Vietnamese support for the Vietcong or encouraging the North Vietnamese to negotiate a settlement compatible with the American objective of preserving an independent noncommunist South Vietnam.[17] Among the president's senior foreign policy advisers there was a basic consensus that without some change in American policy South Vietnam would collapse. No one could tell the president exactly when this would occur, or whether in the final stages it would be a result of internal political weakness or military defeat, but no one gave the president a rosy prediction for South Vietnam's future.

Four basic options for American action in South Vietnam were mentioned in a variety of memos written for the president and his senior advisers in the spring and summer of 1965. The first was simply to do nothing, just maintain the current level of U.S. assistance to South Vietnam and await events. Awaiting events almost certainly meant the defeat of the South Vietnamese army and the fall of one or more of the Southeast Asian dominoes. As a result, this option was uniformly rejected. It was, however, an important consideration in the 1965 deliberations because of the very real danger that events in South Vietnam would move faster than decision-making processes in Washington. It was this possibility that gave members of the Johnson administration working on the problem of Vietnam a serious sense of urgency.

The second option called for a limited American involvement in the ground war in the south and a major escalation of the bombing in the north. For a time, this was the option favored by Maxwell Taylor, the former chairman of the Joint Chiefs of Staff who had replaced Henry Cabot Lodge as American ambassador to South Vietnam when Lodge returned home to make an unsuccessful bid for the 1964 Republican presidential nomination. Though long associated with counterinsurgency warfare, Taylor believed that it would be futile to send American conventional forces to fight a guerrilla war in Asia and that far more could be done with American airpower. The arguments supporting a bombing escalation were the same arguments that William Bundy and others had used in getting the bombing of the north started. It was hoped that with sufficient punishment of the North Vietnamese, military progress in the south or meaningful negotiations with the north would eventually be achieved.

The problem with a strategy of depending on bombing alone was the risk it carried that the ground war in the south would be over before the suffering in the north had any significant effect. Furthermore, serious questions were raised about how a bombing escalation would affect world opinion and the willingness of the Soviets and Chinese to increase their assistance to North Vietnam. Throughout the air war in Southeast Asia, President Johnson was convinced that, at some point, American actions would create a much larger foreign policy crisis. According to one of his leading biographers, the president was "suspicious that the North Vietnamese had entered into secret treaties with the Communist superpowers," and "lived in constant fear of triggering some imaginary provision of some imaginary treaty."[18] Modifying the targets for American bombing missions against the north was a viable option throughout the 1965 Vietnam deliberations, but as our only response to the situation in South Vietnam, it was not taken seriously.

The final two options—taking over the ground war in the south and getting out of Vietnam all together—were the two broad policy proposals given the most careful consideration in the summer of 1965. Detailed memoranda were written in support of getting further in and all the way out of Vietnam. These memoranda were circulated and critiqued at the highest levels of government. Several sessions with the president's top advisers and formal meetings of the National Security Council were devoted exclusively to discussions of these two options. And both were championed by articulate and experienced presidential appointees.

Robert McNamara, the highly efficient secretary of defense who revolutionized Pentagon budgeting and procurement processes and introduced systematic analysis and planning to defense decision making had emerged as Johnson's most important foreign policy adviser. Throughout the spring and summer he worked with General Westmoreland and the Joint Chiefs of Staff on a plan for a major escalation of American involvement in the war. In a draft memorandum circulated among the senior officials in the administration, McNamara made his case for expanding the war. The goal for the United States, as McNamara saw it, was not to defeat the Vietcong but to demonstrate to them that they could not win a military victory in the south. This he argued would "turn the tide of the war."[19] The estimated commitment of American forces necessary to accomplish this mission was, accordₑ g to Westmoreland, 44 battalions, or roughly 200,000 servicemen. Raising troop deployments to this level in short order, and preparing for possible increases beyond 200,000, would involve calling up selected reserve units and extending tours of duty in all the military services. McNamara also proposed an expansion of the air war comparable to that proposed by Taylor. He wanted to mine and blockade the largest North Vietnamese ports, destroy vital transportation links between North Vietnam and China, target economically important facilities in the north, even if they were close to population centers, and eliminate the fighter aircraft and anti-aircraft missiles that the North Vietnamese had received from the Soviet Union.

Responding to McNamara's proposals at the end of June, McGeorge Bundy raised a number of probing questions. The totality of the program that the secretary of defense was outlining for Vietnam looked to Bundy to be "rash to the point of folly" and probably insufficient to accomplish the desired goal.[20] How do American conventional forces convince guerrillas that they cannot win? Westmoreland was arguing that the war in the south was entering what the Chinese revolutionary leader Mao Zedong had called the "third stage" of guerrilla warfare, when large-scale military operations would deal a final blow to the forces that had been progressively weakened by guerrilla attacks. But Bundy was skeptical. If the Vietcong were to abandon conventional warfare and go back into hiding, fighting only in small groups in remote locations, then the war could go on for a very long time without any clear-cut battles or American victories. And why were we confident that 200,000 soldiers would be enough for either third stage or continued guerrilla warfare? In taking over some of the missions now assigned to the South Vietnamese army, we were walking on "a slippery slope toward total US responsibility and corresponding fecklessness on the Vietnamese side."[21]

An even more devastating critique of the Defense Department plan was prepared by George Ball, who became the leading advocate in the Johnson administration for an American withdrawal from Vietnam. In Ball's estimate, the war was already lost and no deployment of American troops to a country where a French army numbering a quarter of a million had already been defeated would change that result. Ball joined Bundy in challenging the notion that the war was about to enter a conventional stage in which American forces would obviously be effective. He saw no evidence to indicate that the Vietcong and North Vietnamese would fight in a fashion that would be convenient for the United States. Everything learned from their long years of struggle against successive enemies suggested that they would do no such thing. And "no one had yet shown," Ball argued, "that American troops can win a jungle war against an invisible enemy."[22] [Document 4.4] American military involvement in Southeast Asia might postpone the eventual defeat of the South Vietnamese, but only if we were willing to engage in a protracted war with an open-ended commitment of American support. At some point, maintaining the credibility of our promises would become more important than the fate of South Vietnam and losing the war later rather than sooner would carry a much heavier price in terms of national prestige.

The problem for Ball was that he was asking for a withdrawal, or a negotiated settlement on whatever terms could be arranged, at a time when the American commitment to South Vietnam was already substantial. According to McNamara's assistant at the Pentagon, John McNaughton, maintaining American credibility and preventing a humiliating defeat was already 70 percent of the reason for continuing to fight in South Vietnam.[23] Secretary of State Rusk made much the same point in a private memorandum to the president responding to Ball's call for withdrawal: "The integrity of the US commitment is the principal pillar of peace throughout the world. If that commitment becomes unreliable, the communist world would draw conclusions that would lead to our ruin and almost certainly to a catastrophic war."[24] This was the same point that Johnson had made in his April speech at Johns Hopkins and a statement that reflected the logic of containment in its purest form. Maintaining a promise to stop the spread of communism in Southeast Asia was intimately related to similar promises made in Europe and elsewhere in the world. Failing to contain communism in one location would lead to challenges in other places and to a wobbling of both nearby and distant dominoes. Ball never denied the existence of an American commitment to South Vietnam, though he reminded the president that Eisenhower had publicly pledged to protect democracy in Southeast Asia and that nothing resembling democracy existed under Diem, Khanh, or any of their successors. Nor did Ball challenge the central arguments of the policy of containment. His basic point was that the commitment to stop communism in South

Vietnam had already failed and that it was far better to accept a small defeat today rather than a larger one tomorrow.

Despite the fact that Ball consistently gave the president bad news about Vietnam, Lyndon Johnson was impressed with his analysis, and late in June ordered both the Ball and McNamara proposals to be fully investigated and presented to the National Security Council. McNamara returned to Vietnam to consult with Taylor, Lodge (Taylor's designated successor who would shortly begin a second term as U.S. ambassador), Westmoreland, and others on the scene and prepare planning documents for the buildup he recommended. Ball remained in Washington, adjusting and refining his arguments for wider administration debate. A third option prepared by William Bundy called for a buildup in South Vietnam that was much smaller than the one that McNamara advocated and a trial period in which the effectiveness of American ground troops in the south and an intensified air war in the north might be tested.

McNamara's July visit to Vietnam reinforced his fears that South Vietnam was near collapse and that the United States would have to assume much larger military responsibilities in the war. He returned with a report that declared an American force of 200,000 adequate only for the time being and recommended that preparations be made for additional deployments, reserve unit activations, and substantial congressional appropriations to support these steps. A force level of 600,000 by 1966 was mentioned as what might be necessary for certain contingencies. On July 21, the president's senior foreign policy advisers met to consider McNamara's latest report. George Ball made his now familiar criticisms of what he saw as the beginning of a "perilous voyage." But when pressed by the president to come up with an alternative, Ball had nothing to suggest except some form of withdrawal with all the costs that would entail. The choice as Ball described it was not between promising courses of action, but between degrees of failure. Cutting our losses now was the least damaging alternative. Johnson questioned Ball carefully and gave him every opportunity to elaborate his views. He also invited reactions from others in the room who uniformly disagreed with the Ball proposal because of the harm that would be done to America's reputation as a reliable ally. Lodge even compared a surrender in Vietnam to the indulgence at Munich that helped to bring on World War II. The president ended the meeting without announcing any final decisions.[25]

The next day Johnson met with the Joint Chiefs of Staff, who thought that McNamara's recommendations might be too modest. The president raised all the questions that Ball, who was not in attendance, would have been likely to ask. How many troops would be enough to carry out our mission this year or next? Where would our deployments end? Would more unrestricted bombing have a significant impact? How many civilians would be killed? What Soviet or Chinese reactions might be provoked by our escalation? Would it be better to make a stand in Thailand or somewhere else in southern Asia? The answers he received were honest and sobering. No one promised that the steps being recommended would produce easy or immediate results. No one denied the risks they entailed.

The final National Security Council meeting on the question of escalation took place on July 27. There the president outlined five options: unrestrained bombing of the north; withdrawal; maintaining present force levels; McNamara's large-scale escalation, including a call-up of reserves and a request for major supplemental funding from the Congress; and a smaller escalation that more than doubled current deployments without calling up reserves or requiring immediate budget increases and without mining North Vietnamese harbors. Johnson described the fourth option as dangerously provocative to the Soviets and Chinese and outlined his reasons for considering the final option to be the best. Then he asked each adviser present if he was in agreement with his (Johnson's) decision. Everyone at the meeting, including the chairman of the Joint Chiefs of Staff, who had earlier argued for a larger escalation than the one McNamara had proposed, concurred with the president's choice.[26] Having decided to approve the deployment of approximately 100,000 additional servicemen to Vietnam, Johnson made sure that only the first half of those deployments was immediately announced to the public. The process of escalation had, nevertheless, taken a significant step, and within a year American forces were fully engaged in the longest and most controversial war in our modern history.

The predictions that Johnson heard in 1964 and 1965 that the war in Vietnam would be long and difficult turned out to be correct. American deployments to Southeast Asia increased for the next three years until they reached a peak of 580,000 in 1968. Even at that level, it was impossible to locate and defeat the Vietcong or stop their sources of supply from the north. The bombing of North Vietnam, which was intensified and periodically halted, failed to end the war in the south or bring North Vietnamese negotiators to the bargaining table. During the Buddhist holiday of Tet early in 1968, the Vietcong and North Vietnamese launched a massive assault on American forces in the field and a series of terrorist attacks on targets in Saigon. The Tet offensive was a military disaster for the communist forces because, for once, they fought in large concentrations that gave American troops an opportunity to utilize fully the superior firepower of modern weaponry. But the offensive was also a significant psychological victory for the insurgents. It demonstrated to Americans at home, who were increasingly critical of the war and who had an opportunity to watch its progress on the nightly news, that the fighting in Southeast Asia was far from being over and that three years of escalation had not yet brought us closer to success. Protests against the war grew more frequent and antiwar candidates were surprisingly successful in the early campaigning for the 1968 presidential nomination. Shortly after the Tet offensive, Johnson announced that he would not seek reelection in the upcoming presidential election and that a bombing halt was being ordered in conjunction with the initiation of the long-sought negotiations with the North Vietnamese. It would be four more years before the war was over for Americans and three more after that before fighting finally ended in Vietnam, but in 1968 the beginning of the end was proclaimed and the painful process of withdrawal had begun. The era in which we analyzed and agonized over what had gone wrong in Vietnam had also begun.

CONCLUSIONS

POWER

For many observers, what had gone wrong in the 1960s was the result of an imbalance in the relations between the executive and legislative branches and the gradual acceptance in the postwar era of an "imperial presidency."[27] Though the

Constitution clearly states that only Congress has the power to declare war, no declaration was voted or even debated for the fighting in Korea and Vietnam. In a host of other postwar incidents and confrontations American military forces had been used, or readied for use, without prior congressional concurrence. In the case of Vietnam, other than the ratification of the SEATO agreements and the passage of the Gulf of Tonkin resolution, the Congress had played a rather small role in the decisions committing the United States to the defense of South Vietnam. And when they did vote on the Tonkin resolution, members of Congress acted on the basis of an administration description of events in the waters off North Vietnam that was, at best, incomplete.

The withholding of information about the Gulf of Tonkin incident was not an isolated problem; secrecy pervaded executive branch decision making on Southeast Asia. American involvement in the coup that overthrew Diem was not made known to members of Congress or the American people. Bombing missions against the north that were publicly defended as one-time reprisals were planned within the Johnson administration as a coordinated effort to affect the conduct of the war in the south. Important decisions to change the mission of marine and army units in South Vietnam from defensive to offensive operations were kept classified, as were CIA activities against the North Vietnamese and various bombing missions against targets in Laos and Cambodia. How could the Congress play an equal and intelligent role in foreign policy decision making if presidents acted alone and failed to share vital information with the legislative branch? How could the constitutional language providing a congressional role in matters involving war and peace be made compatible with the realities of a cold war fought at a variety of intensity levels, on many fronts, against disparate enemies?

These questions dominated debates in the 1970s, when a series of laws and institutional reforms were carried out to make the Congress a more effective, and a more equal, partner in the conduct of foreign affairs. The Hughes-Ryan Amendment required all significant CIA covert operations to be officially approved in a presidential finding and reported to selected congressional committees. The Case Act required all executive agreements negotiated by the president to be recorded and made known to the Congress. Legislation regulating arms sales stipulated that all major transactions be reported to the Congress and be subject to congressional review. In addition, to requiring new executive branch disclosures, the Congress invested in a significant improvement of the professional expertise available to its members. Personal and committee staffs were enlarged throughout the decade and a number of new service organizations were created. The Office of Technology Assessment was established to answer member questions on a variety of scientific and technological problems, including those affecting Pentagon weapon systems, intelligence-gathering equipment, and other national security issues. The Congressional Budget Office was set up to monitor the national economy, federal spending, and the budget process so that Congress no longer depended exclusively on executive branch information and economic projections. The passage of new laws restricting presidential discretion in the expenditure of funds made it less likely that presidents could engage in large-scale military operations, as Johnson did after the escalation of the war in 1965, without going to Capitol Hill for specific spending approval. On a number of occasions in the 1970s, Congress used its power of the purse to dictate or restrict specific foreign policy actions. It passed laws forcing an end to any further bombing of Cambodia after a specified date, stopping all funding for fighting in Southeast Asia and denying any money to the CIA for intervention in the Angolan civil war.   After war broke out on Cyprus between Greek and Turkish factions, Congress embargoed arms shipments to Greece and Turkey against the wishes of the president and despite NATO commitments to both nations.

The most celebrated example of foreign policy reform legislation in the 1970s was the War Powers Resolution, passed in 1973 over President Nixon's veto. The act requires the president to report to the Congress within forty-eight hours of any action that puts American forces overseas in combat or combat-threatening situations. The Congress then has thirty days in which to authorize or prohibit the overseas commitment. When the Congress expresses its wishes in conjunction with the War Powers Resolution, it does so by joint resolution passed by the House and Senate but not requiring a presidential signature or permitting a presidential veto. The thirty-day deliberative period may be extended by an additional thirty days if the Congress so chooses, but if no action is taken by the end of the self-imposed congressional deadline, the president is obliged to withdraw from the overseas commitment he has initiated in a timely fashion. After the 1983 Chaddha decision by the Supreme Court ruled that legislative vetoes (joint resolutions negating executive branch actions) were unconstitutional, most of the teeth in the War Powers Resolution were removed. After that decision Congress could not stop a presidential deployment by joint resolution alone. Nor, presumably, would the failure of Congress to take action in a designated period, which might be called a silent legislative veto, pass constitutional scrutiny and force a president to end an overseas action. After 1983, about all that was left of the War Powers Resolution was the reporting requirement and the controversy over how the Congress could ensure itself a role in decisions about overseas combat engagements.

Each of the presidents who have served after Richard Nixon has expressed reservations about the constitutionality of the War Powers Resolution and has contributed to a mixed record of compliance with the forty-eight-hour reporting requirement. Part of the problem is a matter of definition. When are American forces in combat? Attacks on U.S. military personnel on or near the controversial naval and air stations in the Philippines have occurred on a number of occasions, and early in the Bush presidency American military aircraft in the Philippines provided assistance to the Acquino government when it was threatened by a coup. After the Iraqi invasion of Kuwait in 1990, American forces were sent to Saudi Arabia to deter a threatened attack against that country. In 1991, those forces, as part of a United Nations coalition, forced the Iraqis out of Kuwait. None of these events led to a formal war powers report. During the Reagan administration when marines were sent to Lebanon to serve as part of a multinational peacekeeping force, and when ships in the Persian Gulf endangered by the war between Iran and Iraq were temporarily placed under American protection, no war power reports were made. Later, when the marines came under attack in Lebanon and the ships in the Persian Gulf were hit by mines and missiles, the Congress debated these deployments and authorized them outside the procedures and provisions of the War Powers Resolution.

The forty-eight-hour reporting requirement has clearly created problems for presidents and members of Congress because of the uncertainty about what events should trigger the mandatory report; but it has also been criticized for granting too much power to the commander in chief. Under the War Powers Resolution it is recognized that the president may do anything deemed necessary in a military emergency for at least two days. In the nuclear age, when intercontinental ballistic missiles can travel thousands of miles in a matter of minutes, two days is a very long time. Even conventional military operations, like the invasion of Grenada or the American effort to remove Noriega from Panama, can be virtually over in forty-eight hours. Moreover, forcing a congressional debate about a foreign deployment at the outset of an international crisis almost guarantees legislative concurrence with the presidential action. In periods of perceived international danger, public opinion and congressional support traditionally rally behind the commander in chief, even if the actions he has taken are subsequently judged harshly. President Kennedy's standing in the polls rose when he announced the failure of the Bay of Pigs invasion in Cuba, as did President Carter's when American hostages were taken in Iran and when the rescue mission to release them ended in disaster. Asking the Congress to debate an overseas commitment shortly after it has begun may actually have the effect of enhancing rather than diminishing presidential power.

If the War Powers Resolution, before or after the Chaddha decision, had been law in the 1960s, it is doubtful that it would have had much relevance in the decision making concerning Southeast Asia. During the Kennedy and Johnson presidencies, both chief executives were confident that any immediate actions they chose to take in Laos or South Vietnam would have earned bipartisan support on Capitol Hill. If Kennedy and Johnson had fully reported their actions to the legislature in 1961 or 1965, it is highly unlikely that either of their decisions would have been opposed by majorities in the House and Senate. This does not, however, mean that a law requiring a formal congressional response to recent or pending military decisions would have been a meaningless reform. Part of Johnson's attraction to the modified escalation in July 1965 was the fact that by postponing a call-up of the reserves and a request for large congressional appropriations, there would be no immediate national debate over Vietnam. Johnson feared such a debate, not because he would lose it but because it would have distracted lawmakers from the controversial domestic agenda he was pushing and because even a few critics of the war in Vietnam, like Senator Wayne Morse, who voted against the Gulf of Tonkin resolution, would have raised embarrassing questions about the costs of the long-term commitment that the president was knowingly entering into. In 1965, Lyndon Johnson was a popular president and former majority leader of the Senate who could easily have weathered such criticism. Forcing him to do so would, presumably, have had little impact on the outcome of his decisions and might actually have strengthened bipartisan support for American actions in Southeast Asia. The fact that Lyndon Johnson chose to avoid a congressional debate on Vietnam in 1965 may indicate not an excess of executive power but an extreme sensitivity to legislative criticism and a strong desire to act on the basis of unchallenged consensus.

PROCESS

For critics of the war in Vietnam who explain its origin in terms of failures on the part of presidential advisers, foreign policy bureaucracies, and the decision-making processes they followed, the existence of consensus was at the heart of our problems. According to James C. Thomson, Jr., who worked for the National Security Council in the 1960s, the major problem with Vietnam decision making was the quality of advice the president received.[28] Johnson's advisers acted, too often, on the basis of shared, flawed, and unquestioned assumptions. They assumed that communism was monolithic, when in fact a Sino-Soviet split was beginning to take shape and the Vietnamese version of Marxism was leavened by nationalism and a long history of efforts to achieve independence from China and all other foreign nations. The president's advisers, with the significant exception of George Ball, also assumed that the nations of Asia and the world would behave like inanimate dominoes, falling automatically in response to a communist victory in Vietnam, when in fact the political, social, and cultural circumstances in the countries of Asia, and the rest of the world, varied enormously. There was some truth to the fear that one communist guerrilla success would lead to others, but only some. After the fall of South Vietnam in 1975, the neighboring nations of Laos and Cambodia were taken over by Marxist guerrilla movements that had long been assisted by the North Vietnamese. In the case of Cambodia, this brought the brutal Khmer Rouge to power, whose policies resulted in the deaths of something between one sixth and one third of that nation's population. The horrors in Cambodia were among the most tragic consequences of the wars in Southeast Asia, but the fears of endlessly falling dominoes, which played so large a role in the thinking about Vietnam, were unfounded. The process of communist expansion in southern Asia ended with the three nations that had been part of French Indochina.

In a broader criticism, Thomson observes that the decision making on Vietnam was made by advisers who lacked expertise in Asian history, culture, and language. Many of the State Department specialists on China and Asian affairs had been targets of McCarthy era witch-hunts following the fall of China and had either resigned or been fired. Those who stayed in office in the troubled 1950s obviously learned the lesson that communist movements in Asia must be resisted at all costs. The fact that many of the president's advisers had lived through the period of appeasement before the Second World War further reinforced their inclination to identify unpunished aggression, even the mixed version of infiltration and invasion practiced by the North Vietnamese, as a dire threat to global security. According to Thomson, there should have been more and better challenges to the assumptions underlying American policy in Vietnam and more knowledgeable policymakers in the senior ranks of the Johnson administration and in the bureaucracies that staffed their recommendations. Too many advisers told the president what he wanted to hear; too many reports from the military in Vietnam and officials in Washington were filled with wishful thinking and a bureaucratic use of language that disguised the human consequences of the war.[29] Someone should have broken the consensus that led us deeper into war in Vietnam and given the president honest, unvarnished, advice.

Lyndon Johnson did suffer because very few of his advisers had firsthand knowledge of Southeast Asia, but even if he had heard from additional experts on Vietnamese culture and Asian affairs, his mind may not have been changed. There are many types of expertise. If Lyndon Johnson and others were afraid of the consequences of losing a country to communism, that fear may have been based on their expert political judgment and their conviction that a return to McCarthyism might have accompanied a rapid withdrawal from South Vietnam or an overly dramatized escalation. Johnson expressed precisely such fears to one of his biographers, Doris Kearns.[30]   Could an expert on Asian affairs have assured Lyndon Johnson, who had spent his entire adult life in national politics, that the costs of acknowledging failure in Vietnam were politically acceptable? Furthermore, some of the basic assumptions about the war in Vietnam, though not all of them, were, in fact, questioned at the highest levels of the Johnson administration.

On the face of it, Johnson appears to have made a careful examination of the basic options he had in the summer of 1965. In addition to McNamara and the Joint Chiefs, who recommended a rapid and dramatic escalation, he heard from William Bundy, who proposed something much more modest. More importantly, he heard from George Ball, who provided him with a cogent argument against escalation and prescient predictions of what lay ahead if escalation took place. Thomson, who shared Ball's views on the war when he worked for the administration, argues that the critics of escalation became domesticated dissenters who were never taken seriously by the president. Ball disagrees. Though he accepts Thomson's assessment that too much credence was given to a simple-minded version of the domino theory, Ball believes that his arguments about the dangers of escalation were heard. His boss, Secretary of State Dean Rusk, who had very different views about Vietnam, thought that presidents should hear from a variety of points of view and never suppressed or censored the opinions of his undersecretary. The memos that Ball wrote in 1964 and 1965 were read and debated by senior administration officials. In the end, they were carefully considered by the president. Because of concern that Ball's dissent might leak to the press (which it did), he was occasionally described as a "devil's advocate" within the administration who was intentionally assigned the task of critiquing prevailing policy, but Ball makes it clear in his memoirs that, "not one of my colleagues ever had the slightest doubt about the intensity of my personal convictions. The devil, God knows, had plenty of lawyers; he was doing too well to need my services."[31]

Johnson appears to have studied the implications of both escalation and withdrawal without the need for a specially designated in-house critic. When he confronted Ball on July 21, he asked the questions about America's reputation as a loyal ally that his other advisers, including the secretary of state, found to be the biggest deficiency in an early departure from Vietnam. When he met with the Joint Chiefs of Staff the next day he probed them with the questions that Ball had raised about the open-ended nature of the military commitment they were recommending. In addition to George Ball, the president had a number of competent advisers who were asking difficult questions about policy in Vietnam. In a series of memos in 1965, McGeorge Bundy kept the president posted on what others in the administration were thinking and pointed out problems that needed to be addressed by the advocates of escalation.

Bundy, who in 1965 probably spent more time with the president than any other of the Vietnam advisers, is, however, not sure when the president made up his mind about what he was going to do. According to evidence assembled by political scientist Larry Berman, the July 21 meeting in which George Ball's proposals received their last high-level airing may have been staged.[32] Berman speculates that there may have been no real decision making at all in the summer of 1965. Instead, Lyndon Johnson could have been using the meetings of his senior staff and the National Security Council to build consensus for the limited escalation he had already decided to carry out. Ball's memos and arguments were important in this process because they gave Johnson ammunition to use against the secretary of defense and the Joint Chiefs of Staff and reasons to tone down their proposals.

Johnson's reasons for wanting a toned-down escalation and for going to great lengths to convince his advisers that it was the best course of action may have had more to do with his domestic agenda and the nature of his peculiar mixture of ambition and anxiety than with any objective analysis of the situation in Southeast Asia.

PERSONALITY

Throughout his life Lyndon Johnson dominated the people around him and used them in his rise to power. He boasted and bullied his way through school, served as a staff member for a Texas congressman while building his own political connections, exaggerated his association with Franklin Roosevelt when FDR was popular, and moved away from him when liberal policies became more controversial in the South. He lied about his "heroic" exploits in World War II, stole votes in a crucial Texas Democratic primary, and became a master manipulator of his Senate colleagues in the 1950s.[33] Tall and heavyset, Johnson had a commanding physical presence. While majority leader of the Senate, he had a habit of holding people by the lapels, putting his face directly in front or above theirs, and not letting go until the person he was talking to told Johnson what he wanted to hear. The extraordinary influence he had with the southern senators who chaired powerful Senate committees in the 1950s allowed him to push through the first major civil rights legislation since Reconstruction and earn a reputation as one of the most effective majority leaders in modern history.

But the characteristics that made him an extraordinary legislative leader may not have served him well in the White House. An accomplished compromiser, Johnson would naturally have been attracted to a middle course between Ball's proposed withdrawal from Vietnam and McNamara's full-scale escalation. A skillful builder of consensus, he may have intentionally appeared to keep an open mind in order to generate support among his advisers for a course of action that few of them originally advocated. A sensitive politician, he may have wanted to disguise the difficulty of the task that lay ahead in Vietnam in order to avoid a conflict with the competing priorities of the Great Society.

The importance of the Great Society programs to Lyndon Johnson and the fear that they would be lost to an expensive and unpopular war in Southeast Asia may well have been central to his thinking in the summer of 1965.[34] As his advisers described the situation in Southeast Asia, Johnson probably understood the risks inherent in any course of action involving Vietnam. If he followed Ball's advice, he would be losing a country to communism, giving an ideal issue to his right wing critics and perhaps an invitation to a revival of McCarthyism. If he carried out the major escalation that McNamara recommended, he would have faced the danger of Chinese or Soviet expansion of the war, and he would have been required to ask the Congress for special appropriations that would have competed with the dramatic increases in domestic spending he also wanted. As he told a biographer, "I knew the Congress as well as I knew Lady Bird, I knew that the day it exploded into a major debate on the war, that day would be the beginning of the end of the Great Society....I was determined to be a leader of war *and* a leader of peace."[35] Given the position he was in and his inclination to avoid the painful choices between war and peace, it may not be surprising that Lyndon Johnson looked for a way to navigate between the rocks of right wing resentment and the heavy seas of full-scale war.

But his middle course between withdrawal and escalation was not really a compromise decision. By electing to continue the process of escalation in 1965, Johnson was accepting a long-standing commitment to the defense of Southeast Asia and adding to an already substantial military force in South Vietnam. The decision made further escalations likely and offered no firm grounds for resisting them. His compromise did manage to mask, for a brief period of time, the size of the eventual commitment to Vietnam and the prospects for its success. But when that mask fell away, Johnson's credibility as both a leader of war and peace was lost and the standing of his presidency rapidly declined. Would Johnson have been better off accepting Ball's assessment of the situation in Vietnam and the humiliation of losing a country to communism in 1965, rather than the later and greater humiliation he encountered in 1968? From the vantage point of history, it seems apparent that he should have chosen early withdrawal, but that vantage point may impose an unfair standard by which to measure his actions.

Choosing withdrawal in 1965 would have been asking a great deal from any president and particularly of Lyndon Johnson. Despite his many successes in politics, Johnson was an extremely insecure individual, sensitive about the relatively humble origins of his family, the limits of his education at a Texas state teacher's college, and the social prejudices against his rural earthiness. Though a self-educated expert on a wide array of domestic issues and legislative procedures, he was not well versed in foreign affairs when he suddenly found himself in the presidency. To a man self-conscious of his limitations, the weight of the advice in favor of escalation would have been hard to push aside. As the columnist Tom Wicker pointed out in analyzing the Vietnam escalation decision, Johnson "would look around him and see in Bob McNamara that it was technologically feasible, in McGeorge Bundy that it was intellectually acceptable, and in Dean Rusk that it was historically necessary."[36] Had he chosen to support Ball's position, Johnson would have had to take a stand against his secretaries of state and defense, his national security adviser, and the Joint Chiefs of Staff. He would have had to renounce a series of promises made and sustained by three presidents from both political parties. He would have had to compromise a commitment written into a protocol of the SEATO treaty that had already taken hundreds of American lives. He would have had to challenge some of the basic assumptions that supported American foreign policy throughout the cold war. And he would have been expected, if he wanted his presidency and his domestic agenda to prosper, to bring the American people with him. That may be more than could be asked from any president, even one with Johnson's monumental manipulative skills.

Chronology of the Vietnam Decision

1950

Jul 26   Truman approves $15 million in military aid to the French fighting in Southeast Asia.

1954

Apr   Eisenhower rejects proposals to use U.S. military force to assist French forces in Vietnam.

May 7   French defeated at Dienbienphu.

July   Geneva accords end fighting in Southeast Asia and recognize the seventeenth parallel as a temporary dividing line pending national elections.

Sept 8   SEATO formed.

1955

July   U.S. supports Diem's refusal to participate in nationwide elections required under the Geneva accords.

1961

May   Vice President Johnson visits South Vietnam and calls for increased U.S. aid to Diem.

1962   Number of U.S. advisers in South Vietnam increases from 700 to 12,000.

1963

May–Jun   Buddhist protesters suppressed by Diem regime.

Nov 1–2   Diem overthrown and killed in Saigon coup.

Nov 22   Kennedy assassinated in Dallas, Texas. Johnson becomes president.

1964

Jan 30   New coup puts General Khanh in power.

Jun 2   New plans made for bombing North Vietnam at Honolulu conference.

Aug 2–4   Attacks and presumed attacks take place against U.S. destroyers off the coast of North Vietnam in the Tonkin Gulf.

Aug 7   Congress, by large majorities, passes Gulf of Tonkin resolution.

1965

Feb   McGeorge Bundy visits South Vietnam.

Feb 7   Vietcong attacks on U.S. installations leads to reprisal bombing.

Feb 24   Operation Rolling Thunder begins.

Mar 8   3,500 U.S. marines land in Danang to protect U.S. air bases.

Apr 1–2   After NSC policy review, Johnson approves use of marines for offensive search and destroy operations.

(cont.)

(cont.)	
Apr 7	Johnson gives speech at Johns Hopkins University explaining U.S. policy in Southeast Asia.
Jul 8	Henry Cabot Lodge reappointed as U.S. ambassador to South Vietnam.
Jul 21	Senior advisers meet to consider McNamara's escalation plans and Ball's proposals for withdrawal.
Jul 22	President meets with Joint Chiefs to discuss size of military commitment.
Jul 27	National Security Council meets to endorse president's decision on escalation.
Jul 28	Johnson officially approves Westmoreland request for 44 combat battalions.
Dec	U.S. troop strength in South Vietnam reaches 200,000.

Chapter 4 Documents

Document 4.1
The Tonkin Gulf Resolution,
August 7, 1964

To Promote the Maintenance of International Peace and Security in Southeast Asia

Whereas naval units of the Communist regime in Vietnam, in violation of the principles of the Charter of the United Nations and of international law, have deliberately and repeatedly attacked United States naval vessels lawfully present in international waters, and have thereby created a serious threat to international peace; and

Whereas these attacks are part of a deliberate and systematic campaign of aggression that the Communist regime in North Vietnam has been waging against its neighbors and the nations joined with them in the collective defense of their freedom; and

Whereas the United States is assisting the peoples of southeast Asia to protect their freedom and has no territorial, military or political ambitions in that area, but desires only that these peoples should be left in peace to work out their own destinies in their own way: Now, therefore, be it

Resolved by the Senate and the House of Representatives of the United States of American in Congress assembled

That the Congress approves and supports the determination of the President, as Commander in Chief, to take all necessary measures to repel any armed attack against the forces of the United States and to prevent further aggression.

Sec. 2. The United States regards as vital to its national interest and to world peace the maintenance of international peace and security in southeast Asia. Consonant with the Constitution of the United States and the Charter of the United Nations and in accordance with its obligations under the Southeast Asia Collective Defense Treaty, the United States is, therefore, prepared, as the President determines, to take all necessary steps, including the use of armed force, to assist any member or protocol state of the Southeast Asia Collective Defense Treaty requesting assistance in defense of its freedom.

Sec. 3. This resolution shall expire when the President shall determine that the peace and security of the area is reasonably assured by international conditions created by action of the United Nations or otherwise, except that it may be terminated earlier by concurrent resolution of the Congress.

Source: *Department of State Bulletin*, August 24, 1964, p. 268.

Document 4.2
National Security Action Memorandum No. 328, selected passages, April 6, 1965

On Thursday April 1, The President made the following decisions with respect to Vietnam:

1. Subject to modifications in light of experience, to coordination and direction both in Saigon and in Washington, the President approved the 41-point program on non-military actions submitted by Ambassador Taylor in a memorandum dated March 31, 1965.

2. The President gave general approval to the recommendations submitted by Mr. Rowan in his report dated March 16, with the exception that the President withheld approval of any request for supplemental funds at this time—it is his decision that this program is to be energetically supported by all agencies and departments and by the reprogramming of available funds as necessary within USIA.

3. The President approved the urgent exploration of the 12 suggestions for covert and other actions submitted by the Director of Central Intelligence under date of March 31.

4. The President repeated his earlier approval of the 12-point program of military actions submitted by General Harold K. Johnson under date of March 14 and re-emphasized his desire that aircraft and helicopter reinforcements under this program be accelerated.

5. The President approved an 18–20,000 man increase in U.S. military support forces to fill out existing units and supply needed logistic personnel.

6. The President approved the deployment of two additional Marine Battalions and one Marine Air Squadron and associated headquarters and support elements.

7. The President approved a change of mission for all Marine Battalions deployed in Vietnam to permit their more active use under conditions to be established and approved by the Secretary of Defense in consultation with the Secretary of State....

11. The President desires that with respect to the actions in paragraphs 5 through 7, premature publicity be avoided by all possible precautions. The actions themselves should be taken as rapidly as practicable, but in ways that should minimize any appearance of sudden changes in policy, and official statements on these troop movements will be made only with the direct approval of the Secretary of Defense, in consultation with the Secretary of State. The President's desire is that these movements and changes should be understood as being gradual and wholly consistent with existing policy.

Source: *The Pentagon Papers*, Gravel Edition, vol. III, pp. 702–703.

Document 4.3
Johnson's Address at Johns Hopkins University, selected passages, April 7, 1965

...The confused nature of this conflict cannot mask the fact that it is the new face of an old enemy.

Over this war—and all Asia—is another reality: the deepening shadow of Communist China. The rulers in Hanoi are urged on by Peiping. This is a regime which has destroyed freedom in Tibet, which has attacked India, and has been condemned by the United Nations for aggression in Korea. It is a nation which is helping the forces of violence in almost every continent. The contest in Viet-Nam is part of a wider pattern of aggressive purposes.

Why Are We in South Viet-Nam?

Why are these realities our concern? Why are we in South Viet-Nam?

We are there because we have a promise to keep. Since 1954 every American President has offered support to the people of South Viet-Nam. We have helped to build, and we have helped to defend. Thus, over many years, we have made a national pledge to help South Viet-Nam defend its independence.

And I intend to keep that promise.

To dishonor that pledge, to abandon this small and brave nation to its enemies, and to the terror that must follow, would be an unforgivable wrong.

We are also there to strengthen world order. Around the globe, from Berlin to Thailand, are people whose well-being rests in part on the belief that they can count on us if they are attacked. To leave Viet-Nam to its fate would shake the confidence of all these people in the value of an American commitment and in the value of America's word. The result would be increased unrest and instability, and even wider war.

We are also there because there are great stakes in the balance. Let no one think for a moment that retreat from Viet-Nam would bring an end to conflict. The battle would be renewed in one country and then another. The central lesson of our time is that the appetite of aggression is never satisfied. To withdraw from one battlefield means only to prepare for the next. We must say in Southeast Asia—as we did in Europe—in the words of the Bible: "Hitherto shalt thou come, but no further."

There are those who say that all our effort there will be futile—that China's power is such that it is bound to dominate all Southeast Asia. But there is no end to that argument until all the nations of Asia are swallowed up.

There are those who wonder why we have a responsibility there. Well, we have it there for the same reason that we have a responsibility for the defense of Europe. World War II was fought in both Europe and Asia, and when it ended we found ourselves with continued responsibility for the defense of freedom.

Our objective is the independence of South Viet-Nam and its freedom from attack. We want nothing for ourselves—only that the people of South Viet-Nam be allowed to guide their own country in their own way. We will do everything necessary to reach that objective, and we will do only what is absolutely necessary.

In recent months attacks on South Viet-Nam were stepped up. Thus it became necessary for us to increase our response and to make attacks by air. This is not a change of purpose. It is a change in what we believe that purpose requires.

We do this in order to slow down aggression.

We do this to increase the confidence of the brave people of South Viet-Nam who have bravely borne this brutal battle for so many years with so many casualties.

Source: *The Pentagon Papers*, Gravel Edition, vol. III, pp. 730–731.

Document 4.4
George Ball's Memo to LBJ
"A Compromise Solution in South Vietnam,"
selected passages, July 1, 1965

(1) A Losing War: The South Vietnamese are losing the war to the Viet Cong. No one can assure you that we can beat the Viet Cong or even force them to the conference table on our terms, no matter how many hundred thousand *white, foreign* (U.S.) troops we deploy.

No one has demonstrated that a white ground force of whatever size can win a guerrilla war—which is at the same time a civil war between Asians—in jungle terrain in the midst of a population that refuses cooperation to the white forces (and the South Vietnamese) and thus provides a great intelligence advantage to the other side....

(2) The Question to Decide: Should we limit out liabilities in South Vietnam and try to find a way out with minimal long-term costs?

The alternative—no matter what we may wish it to be—is almost certainly a protracted war involving an open-ended commitment of U.S. forces, mounting U.S. casualties, no assurance of a satisfactory solution, and a serious danger of escalation at the end of the road.

(3) Need for a Decision Now: So long as our forces are restricted to advising and assisting the South Vietnamese, the struggle will remain a civil war between Asian peoples. Once we deploy substantial numbers of troops in combat it will become a war between the U.S. and a large part of the population of South Vietnam, organized and directed from North Vietnam and backed by the resources of both

Moscow and Peiping.

The decision you face now, therefore, is crucial. Once large numbers of U.S. troops are committed to direct combat, they will begin to take heavy casualties in a war they are ill-equipped to fight in a non-cooperative if not downright hostile countryside.

Once we suffer large casualties, we will have started a well-nigh irreversible process. Our involvement will be so great that we cannot—without national humiliation—stop short of achieving our complete objectives. *Of the two possibilities I think humiliation would be more likely than the achievement of our objectives—even after we have paid terrible costs.*

(4) Compromise Solution: Should we commit U.S. manpower and prestige to a terrain so unfavorable as to give a very large advantage to the enemy—or should we seek a compromise settlement which achieves less than our stated objectives and thus cut our losses while we still have the freedom of maneuver to do so.

(5) Costs of a Compromise Solution: The answer involves a judgment as to the cost to the U.S. of such a compromise settlement in terms of our relations with the countries in the area of South Vietnam, the credibility of our commitments, and our prestige around the world. In my judgment, if we act before we commit substantial U.S. troops to combat in South Vietnam we can, by accepting some short-term costs, avoid what may well be a long-term catastrophe. I believe we tended grossly to exaggerate the costs involved in a compromise solution....

Source: *The Pentagon Papers,* Gravel Edition, vol. IV, pp. 615–619. (Emphasis is in original.)

Chapter 4 Notes

[1] Dwight Eisenhower speaking at an April 7, 1954 news conference. See Steven Ambrose, *Eisenhower the President* (New York: Simon & Schuster, 1984), p. 180.

[2] This was the thesis put forward in Kennan's X article. George F. Kennan, "The Sources of Soviet Conduct," *Foreign Affairs* (July 1947), 566–582.

[3] John Burke and Fred Greenstein, *How Presidents Test Reality: Decisions on Vietnam, 1954 and 1965* (New York: Russell Sage Foundation, 1989).

[4] For a review of the early American commitment to Vietnam, see Lloyd Gardner *Approaching Vietnam* (New York: Norton, 1988).

[5] Stanley Karnow, *Vietnam: A History* (New York: Viking, 1983), pp. 213–224.

[6] Ibid., pp. 223–224.

[7] Neil Sheehan, *A Bright and Shining Lie* (New York: Random House, 1988), p. 233.

[8] Karnow, *Vietnam,* p. 281.

[9] Larry Berman, *Planning a Tragedy* (New York: Norton, 1982), p. 29.

[10] Karnow, *Vietnam,* p. 681.

[11]Sheehan, *Bright and Shining Lie*, pp. 201-266.

[12]Quoted in Karnow, *Vietnam*, p. 288.

[13]David Halberstam, *The Best and the Brightest* (New York: Penguin, 1983), p 339.

[14]George Ball, quoted in Berman, *Planning a Tragedy*, p. 86.

[15]Karnow, *Vietnam*, p. 335.

[16]Lyndon Johnson, speech at Johns Hopkins University, April 7, 1965. See Document 4.3.

[17]Berman, *Planning a Tragedy*, pp. 51, 58–60 and 64–65.

[18]Doris Kearns, *Lyndon Johnson and the American Dream* (New York: Harper & Row, 1976), p. 282.

[19]Berman, *Planning a Tragedy*, p. 179.

[20]McGeorge Bundy, Memorandum for the Secretary of State, June 30, 1965. Reprinted as Appendix B in Berman, *Planning a Tragedy*, p. 187.

[21]Ibid. pp. 187–188.

[22]Ibid., p. 87.

[23]John McNaughton, draft for McNamara on Proposed Course of Action, March 24, 1965, Document 96 in *The Pentagon Papers*, New York Times Edition (New York: Bantam, 1971), p. 432.

[24]Quoted in Berman, *Planning a Tragedy*, p. 92. Rusk confirms this position in his memoirs, see Dean Rusk, as told to Richard Rusk, *As I Saw It* (New York: Norton, 1990), p. 448.

[25]For a full account of the July 21 meeting see George W. Ball, *The Past Has Another Pattern* (New York: Norton, 1982), pp. 399–402.

[26]Lyndon Johnson, *The Vantage Point* (New York: Holt, Rinehart, & Winston, 1971), p. 149.

[27]Arthur Schlesinger, Jr., *The Imperial Presidency* (Boston: Houghton Mifflin, 1973).

[28]James C. Thomson, Jr., "How Could Vietnam Happen? An Autopsy," *Atlantic Monthly*, 221 (1968), 47–53.

[29]Ibid.

[30]Kearns, *Lyndon Johnson*, p. 295.

[31]Ball, *The Past Has Another Pattern*, p. 384.

[32]Berman, *Plannina a Tragedy*, p. 106.

[33]See Robert Caro, *The Path to Power* (New York: Random House, 1982); and Robert Caro, *Means of Assent* (New York: Random House, 1989).

[34]See Berman, *Planning a Tragedy*, pp. 145–53.

[35]Kearns, *Lyndon Johnson*, p. 296.

[36]Quoted in Halberstam, *The Best and the Brightest*, p. 643.

Chapter 5

Nixon, Ford, and the Era Of Détente

RICHARD NIXON AND THE WORLD IN 1968

In most presidential elections, foreign policy plays a secondary role. Issues closer to home—the state of the economy, the quality of government services, debates about social justice and individual rights—usually have a higher priority in the minds of American voters. The 1968 presidential election was the exception; the dominant issue of the day was clearly Vietnam. The war in Southeast Asia, and the growing public protest against it, led Lyndon Johnson not to seek reelection. Candidates in the Democratic party primaries and delegates at the party convention in Chicago fought bitterly over what position to adopt on the conduct of the war. Peace candidates Eugene McCarthy, Robert Kennedy, and George McGovern garnered the majority of Democratic primary votes in 1968, but the nomination went to Johnson's chosen successor, Vice President Hubert Humphrey. In the Republican party, the presidential nomination went to the candidate with the most extensive foreign policy experience, Richard Nixon. Neither Nixon nor Humphrey offered radical alternatives to Johnson's policies in Vietnam, but both promised change. Details concerning the nature of that change were somewhat hard to come by.

Nixon's slogan was "peace with honor," an end to the Vietnam War in a manner that would not harm America's international reputation. Such a peace was more or less what Lyndon Johnson had been seeking since 1964. For both leaders, the major American interest in Southeast Asia was sustaining a general commitment to defend our allies against communist attack rather than any particular desire to help the people or government of South Vietnam. If American honor and reputation could be preserved, it might not be necessary to preserve also the independence of South Vietnam. Cynics have claimed that by the end of the Vietnam conflict all we really wanted was an American withdrawal from Southeast Asia that would not be followed by an immediate collapse of the South Vietnamese regime. If the south fell to conquest by the north after a "decent interval" following an American departure, that might be an acceptable outcome.[1] Nixon's own recollection is that he entered office with the expectation that hard-nosed negotiations with the North Vietnamese accompanied by threats to escalate American fighting would be sufficient to produce a diplomatic settlement to the years of war in Southeast Asia.[2] His initial actions in Vietnam were not dramatically different from those that had been taken by Lyndon Johnson. There were, however, some significant differences in tactics and in global strategy.

Nixon's secretary of defense, Melvin Laird, announced early in the administration that American troops would be gradually withdrawn from Southeast Asia as the South Vietnamese army, navy, and air force assumed greater responsibility for the conduct of the war. This process of "Vietnamization" was converted into a general principle for American foreign policy in a brief statement at a presidential press conference in Guam that subsequently became known as the Nixon Doctrine. According to the doctrine, the United States would continue to honor its treaty obligations and protect its major allies in Europe and Japan but would no longer take on the burden of ground warfare in developing nations threatened by communist takeover. Instead, the United States would sell arms, train armies, and offer assistance from a distance.

The policy of Vietnamization and the principles of the Nixon Doctrine made it difficult for the new administration to credibly threaten the North Vietnamese with an expanded war if they failed to negotiate an acceptable settlement. As a result, Nixon was reduced to a greater dependence on air power and a willingness to attack targets in Cambodia and Laos that had previously been considered out of bounds. Nixon was prepared to reduce American military strength in Southeast Asia and simultaneously reduce the inhibitions on how the remaining forces would be employed. At the strategic level, Nixon believed that if the United States were able to improve its relations with the communist governments in China and the Soviet Union, the resulting change in the international balance of power might isolate North Vietnam and put pressure on the North Vietnamese to be more forthcoming in the peace negotiations. For Richard Nixon, the road to peace in Vietnam was a winding one that went through Cambodia and Laos, with stops in Moscow and Beijing.

The president's expectations that American military force or superpower diplomacy would bring a rapid conclusion to the war were mistaken, but in the first year of his presidency, Nixon was taking a far broader view of the foreign policy problems facing the United States than were many of his fellow politicians. Preoccupation with Vietnam had led to the neglect of important changes that were taking place in Europe, in the Middle East, and within the communist world. In the decade of the 1960s, American ties to Europe had been weakened by the growth of independent nuclear arsenals in Britain and France, the emerging economic strength of the Common Market, and the desire of European leaders to escape the real or perceived dominance of the United States. When French President Charles deGaulle withdrew his military forces from the consolidated NATO command and ordered NATO headquarters to be moved from French soil, he signaled a new independence in foreign affairs that raised serious questions about future Atlantic alliance solidarity. In the Middle East a dramatic victory by Israel in the

1967 Six-Day War changed the political geography of the region. Ironically, military success made the prospects for peace and political negotiation in that troubled part of the world even more remote. Israeli occupation of the Sinai, West Bank, and Gaza and the growing economic power of the oil-rich Arab nations, which increasingly received their arms and military advice from the Soviet Union, made for a volatile mixture of regional and global politics. The changes in Europe and the Middle East that Nixon inherited at the outset of his administration were, however, far less important than the even greater changes taking place within the communist bloc.

Fears of a monolithic communist conspiracy to conquer the world, which fueled American concern about falling dominoes in the 1950s and 1960s, were no longer appropriate by the time Richard Nixon delivered his first inaugural address. During the Kennedy and Johnson years the Soviet Union and China (which may never have been as closely allied as the American public suspected) moved farther apart. The Soviet Union achieved effective strategic equality with the United States in the 1960s, but found it difficult to assert its leadership over an independent Mao Zedong. Minor skirmishes between Soviet and Chinese troops took place in 1968, and in May 1969, serious fighting broke out on the border between the two leading nations of the communist world. The depth of the Sino-Soviet split was obvious when, early in Nixon's presidency, the administration found it necessary to make contingency plans for the possibility of all-out war between the Soviet Union and China.[3] The world in the late 1960s was undergoing dramatic change and the traditional policies of the cold war were rapidly becoming outdated.

Though the United States had been distracted and disheartened by years of fighting in Southeast Asia and by public uncertainty about its purpose, the Soviet Union and China suffered more from their internal economic problems and increasingly open military clash. Responding to this new situation was far more important, in Nixon's view, than anything having to do with the war in Vietnam. The breakup of the communist bloc would give the United States important opportunities to promote peace and security in a reordered international balance of power. Richard Nixon was aware of these changes and entered office poised to take advantage of them. The policy he would pursue with the Soviet Union would be labeled détente, but that policy cannot be understood in isolation. Détente with the Soviet Union would not have emerged without a prior détente between the United States and the People's Republic of China.

THE OPENING TO CHINA

After the Chinese civil war ended in 1949 with a communist victory, American presidents had uniformly refused to recognize Mao and the Chinese Communist party as the legitimate rulers of China. Instead, the United States maintained close relations with Mao's opponent, Chiang Kai-shek, whose forces had retreated to Taiwan and other nearby islands off the coast of China. Chiang and his fellow Nationalist party leaders claimed to represent all the people of China and hoped for a political or military opportunity that would allow them to return to power on the mainland. The United States, from the presidency of Harry Truman on, shared those hopes and had no official dealings with the communist government in Beijing. This decision had broad implications. After the Korean War broke out, American naval vessels began regular patrols of the Taiwan Straits, and the United States made a public commitment to defend Taiwan from any mainland attack. When the tiny islands of Quemoy and Matsu, located between the mainland and Taiwan, were threatened during the Eisenhower administration, the United States used nuclear threats and the deployment of additional military forces to keep the islands in Nationalist hands. On the diplomatic front, the United States used its veto power in the United Nations Security Council to guarantee that there would be no resolution to remove the Nationalist delegate from China's seat as a permanent council member. Though there had been some internal discussions in various administrations about recognizing communist China, fear of conservative reaction to such a step kept all the presidents from Truman to Johnson from ever suggesting in public that they were planning to revise America's two-China policy. When Richard Nixon came to office, there were only a few vague hints that his presidency would be any different.

As a candidate, Nixon published an article in the fall 1968 edition of *Foreign Affairs* that reviewed the changes in Asian politics that could be expected when the Vietnam War was finally brought to an end. Nixon predicted that an American dialogue with mainland China could begin as soon as the Chinese abandoned their association with regional aggression and turned their energies to the substantial internal problems facing their country in the aftermath of the disastrous disruptions of the Cultural Revolution.[4] For Nixon, who had spent much of his early political career investigating communists in America and opposing the spread of communism throughout the world, the suggestion that the United States could begin discussions with the communist leaders of Red China was a major shift in policy. But Nixon's reference to that shift in an academic journal attracted relatively little attention. His decision to follow through on the proposal after he was elected to the presidency would rock international and domestic political alignments.

Nixon's approach to China in his first term was a mixture of cautious diplomatic overtures and secret presidential actions. Early on he authorized a new round of the direct talks between Chinese and American diplomats in Warsaw, where such talks had occasionally taken place between 1954 and 1967. He called on the State Department to study China policy and the implications of an American recognition of the communist regime. And, in a series of modest policy changes, he ordered the relaxation of selected trade and travel restrictions that had been put in place as barriers to contact between Chinese and American citizens. Beyond these public actions, Nixon attempted to send personal messages to the Chinese leaders inviting the initiation of a dialogue. Secretary of State William Rogers asked the leaders of Pakistan to help in this regard when he visited Islamabad in May 1969, and later that summer Nixon personally spoke to Pakistani leaders about the same subject. During his first presidential trip overseas, Nixon also approached Romanian ruler Nicolae Ceausescu for his assistance in conveying to the Chinese the new American desire to open discussions.

These private presidential requests were among the most sensitive pieces of information in the Nixon administration. The president understood that Taiwan had many friends in American politics and on Capitol Hill and that any leaks concerning his intention to offer improved diplomatic relations to the communist Chinese would have made it easy for opponents of such plans to mobilize an effective campaign against his efforts.[5] The United States was still at war in Vietnam and the Chinese were providing assistance to the North Vietnamese. Moreover, the long history of the two-Chinas policy, and the domestic political recriminations of the

McCarthy era against those who had favored an early recognition of Mao's regime, made any change extremely controversial. Nixon wanted to avoid that controversy until he was sure that China was just as interested as he was in a new political relationship. The Chinese, equally wary of their longtime American enemies, shared Nixon's desire to avoid publicity about the early steps in a possible rapprochement.

When Pakistani President Yahya Khan visited Beijing in November 1970, he took with him a new secret message from the Americans asking if it would be possible for a high-level administration official to visit China for private discussions. In the meantime, communication between China and the United States continued to be indirect and subtle. The United States was gradually removing or rescinding regulations that restricted contact between the two countries, and the Chinese were providing their own evidence of interest in improved relations. In April 1971, the Chinese invited an American Ping-Pong team that was taking part in international competitions in Japan to visit China. When the State Department approved visas for the visit, the American table tennis players ended up meeting high-ranking Chinese officials and attracting international media attention. At the end of April, an article published in *Life* magazine by China expert Edgar Snow contained a quote from Mao expressing his willingness to have Richard Nixon visit his country as a tourist or as president.[6] In private negotiations, plans for just such a visit were being made.

After the Chinese accepted the American request to send a high-level envoy, the administration was faced with an important decision about who that envoy should be. Nixon passed over his secretary of state and instead elected to send National Security Adviser Henry Kissinger. While on a tour of Asian capitals in 1971, news reports indicated that Kissinger had become ill and would be forced to rest in Pakistan. In fact, during his reported illness in Islamabad, Kissinger was actually on his way to a secret meeting with Chou En-lai in Beijing. The secrecy surrounding the early steps in the opening to China was extraordinary. The Kissinger mission ended with an understanding that Nixon was welcome to make his own trip to mainland China to discuss issues of mutual importance to the two nations. As soon as Kissinger returned to Washington, Nixon requested time on national television for a special announcement. The president surprised his audience by making a brief statement of his intention to visit China in the coming year. Richard Nixon, arguably the nation's most successful anticommunist politician, would travel to Beijing to meet with Mao Zedong and the rest of the Chinese leadership.

Public attention was immediately diverted from the continuing Vietnam War to the new possibilities opened up by an American dialogue with communist China. Euphoria about the upcoming talks overshadowed the substantial difficulties that existed in the initiation of any diplomatic relations between the United States and the People's Republic of China. The communist Chinese considered Taiwan to be a province of their nation in temporary rebellion from the central government in Beijing; the United States had long treated Taiwan as a separate and independent nation and even asserted that the government in Taipei was the legitimate government for all of China. During a second Kissinger trip to China the basic outline of the communiqué that would be issued during Nixon's visit was worked out. [Document 5.1] In essence, the Americans and Chinese agreed to disagree. The Shanghai communiqué was a summary of the often contradictory positions held by the two governments. Both were able to agree that the Taiwan issue should be resolved peacefully and that no nation (particularly the Soviet Union) should have hegemonic power in the Pacific, but those vague statements were all that the two nations could commit to paper.

Nixon's China trip was much more important for its symbolism than for its substance. The long era of silence between two powerful nations was brought to an end, the significance of the Sino-Soviet split was dramatically acknowledged, and talk of a new triangular diplomacy became possible. Nixon's hopes for Chinese assistance in bringing the Vietnam War to a rapid conclusion were not fulfilled, but the opening to China did change the focus of attention for American concerns in Asia. The future of Southeast Asia was no longer the most important U.S. priority. The promotion of security in the Pacific might no longer depend on the demonstrated American ability to contain communist expansion and might instead be based on the establishment of common interests and understandings between China and the United States. Even before the Vietnam War was over, Richard Nixon began to speak about a new "generation of peace" that was dawning in the world. Part of that new generation was the product of improved American relations with China, but an even more important part was the result of changes taking place in the relationship between the United States and the Soviet Union.

DÉTENTE WITH THE SOVIET UNION

The president's triumphant trip to China in February 1972 was followed in a matter of months by an equally dramatic presidential visit to Moscow, the first presidential trip ever to the Soviet capital. The Moscow summit took place despite an American decision to escalate the fighting in Southeast Asia and, for the first time, mine the harbors of North Vietnam. Once again, superpower relations proved to be more important than the lingering war in Vietnam. In Moscow, the American president and Soviet premier only briefly discussed events in Southeast Asia and spent most of their summit in serious negotiations and ceremonies that culminated in the signing of a number of significant agreements designed to limit strategic arms and the dangers of nuclear war.

The strategic arms limitation talks (SALT) were the cornerstone of détente in the Nixon era, but the issues dealt with in the talks were hardly new to the Nixon presidency. Throughout the 1960s, the arms race between the United States and the Soviet Union had been moving at a rapid pace. Both nations were building modern warheads and bombs for their growing numbers of intercontinental and submarine-launched ballistic missiles and for the long-range bombers developed during the 1950s. Moreover, from the mid-1960s on, both sides were seriously experimenting with antiballistic missile systems (ABMs) that promised to provide defensive capabilities against enemy missile attack. American strategists in the Johnson administration were highly suspicious of the value of ABMs. Antiballistic missiles would be expensive to build, difficult to operate, and likely to stimulate the construction of still larger offensive forces on the other side. At Johnson's brief 1967 meeting with Aleksei Kosygin in Glassboro, New Jersey, he urged the Soviet leader to join with Americans in negotiating a treaty to ban ABMs. Though Johnson's suggestion was initially rejected, in the following year the Soviet leadership accepted a general invitation for superpower discussions about strategic weapons, both offensive and defensive. The first session of these negotiations was scheduled to begin during the final summer of Johnson's presidency, but had to be cancelled after the Soviet invasion of Czechoslovakia. The question of limiting strategic weapons and defensive missile systems would be left to the next administration.

Richard Nixon was slow to reinstate the planned strategic arms limitation talks, and characteristically came to view them as part of a much larger endeavor. Nixon and Kissinger shared a desire to create an entirely new relationship between the United States and the Soviet Union. The goal in this new relationship was not only to reduce tensions between the two most powerful nations in the world, as the word *détente* suggests, but slowly to transform the Soviet Union from a dangerous promoter of international revolution into a reliable great power with a stake in maintaining the status quo. The Soviet Union could not be expected to make this transition easily or willingly. In order to induce dramatic changes in the way the Soviet Union conducted its international affairs, it would be necessary for the United States to make clear that any American cooperation in areas of Soviet concern would be linked to moderation in Soviet behavior and restraint in the support of revolutionary movements throughout the world. Nixon and Kissinger publicly defended these connections as their policy of "linkage."[7]

In some ways, linkage was little more than an explicit recognition of what had always been true. The Soviet invasion of Czechoslovakia had obviously been linked to the Johnson decision to cancel the beginning of SALT negotiations. But Nixon and Kissinger wanted to go beyond orchestrating American responses to objectionable Soviet actions in Eastern Europe or the third world. They wanted to replace responsive U.S. retaliations to Soviet actions with clear and early understandings about what was expected from the Soviet Union in exchange for American participation in security, economic, and political negotiations. The image of a link in a chain connecting separate issues was one way of describing how détente would alter relations between the superpowers. An even better image may be the spider's web. The emerging cooperation between the superpowers on a broad range of issues would, hopefully, create a complex network of agreements and negotiations between the two nations dealing with trade, scientific and cultural exchanges, regional security, and arms limitation that, taken together, would create binding incentives for cooperation and the peaceful resolution of disputes. In this web of agreements, SALT was the most important strand.

Official SALT negotiations began in November 1969 and included a series of negotiating sessions alternating between Helsinki and Vienna. Talking about the limitation of strategic weapons was difficult for both sides. The negotiations involved discussion of highly sensitive subjects by the representatives of normally hostile nations. In order to limit their offensive and defensive strategic forces, both sides had to reveal information about the numbers and capabilities of those forces. This was particularly difficult for the delegates on the Soviet side, who practiced strict secrecy in connection with any information related to national security, so strict that only some members of the Soviet delegation knew how many weapons their nation actually had.[8] The arguments against large-scale defensive systems were gradually acknowledged by both sides and various schemes for limiting ABMs were discussed. In the final 1972 agreement each side was allowed to have a relatively small number of antiballistic missiles located at two geographically restricted sites. (As a result of subsequent negotiations the number of such sites was reduced to one for each country.) Further limitations were placed on the radar and other equipment supporting ABMs to ensure that neither nation could easily or quickly expand its small ABM sites into a larger nationwide defensive system. The major sticking points in the negotiations involved the connection between defensive and offensive missiles and what should be counted in any offensive limitations. The Nixon administration insisted that any restrictions on ABMs be accompanied by limits on offensive strategic arms. The Soviets, who had a larger, and less capable, offensive missile force, argued that any discussion of limiting offensive systems should include the American tactical nuclear warheads in Europe and the French, British, and Chinese nuclear arsenals aimed at Soviet targets. SALT could not be isolated from alliance relations or the new triangular diplomacy.

Because SALT involved central issues in strategic doctrine, alliance politics, and the mutual vulnerability of the United States and the Soviet Union, it was obviously a negotiation that the president wished to follow closely. As was the case with the opening to China, important aspects of the SALT negotiations were handled in secret diplomacy by the president's national security adviser. In a series of "back-channel" communications and private meetings that bypassed the Department of State and the regular SALT negotiators, Kissinger worked out with Soviet diplomats in Washington and Moscow the basic framework of what came to be called SALT I. In addition to the treaty limiting ABMs to two locations in each country, a temporary freeze would be imposed on the total number of sea and land-based missile launchers each side would be allowed to possess. The SALT I limits on offensive weapons did not include any of the nuclear warheads deployed in Europe by the United States or its allies and did not restrict long-range bombers, a category in which the United States maintained a significant lead. Though the limitations on offensive arms were meant to be in effect for a relatively brief period while more permanent arrangements were negotiated, they were difficult to work out and controversial in American politics.

After Kissinger announced the basic outline for SALT I in May 1971, it took another year to finalize the details. Questions arose about how to count submarines under construction, whether new missiles built to replace old ones could be significantly larger than the ones they replaced, whether new sea-launched missiles could be deployed if older, land-based missiles were dismantled, whether the Soviet Union would be allowed to maintain several hundred extremely large land-based missiles, and how compliance with all of these complicated commitments could be verified. Some of these issues were technical and relatively minor, others were fundamental; several were left unresolved until the Moscow summit where Soviet leader Leonid Brezhnev and President Nixon held private discussions to settle the remaining differences. Neither leader was well versed in the arcane technicalities of nuclear armaments, and some of their summit agreements were hurried and confusing to the arms control experts working in Helsinki. Near the end of the summit, the official SALT negotiators were rushed to Moscow to convert the summit decisions into treaty language and witness the signing of the ABM Treaty, the Interim Agreement on Strategic Offensive Arms, and a document outlining the basic principles that would guide U.S.–Soviet relations [Document 5.2] and establish the framework for further strategic arms limitations and the development of détente.

Back in Washington, the temporary freeze on offensive missiles became the focus of considerable controversy because of what it failed to achieve. Even after SALT I, both superpowers would continue to maintain far larger nuclear arsenals than were needed for purposes of nuclear deterrence and the Soviets were permitted to keep and improve their fleet of very large land-based missiles that were theoretically capable of carrying many warheads each. Under the agreements, the Soviet

Union was permitted to have 2,358 missile launchers, while the United States could have only 1,710. Numbers of such launchers may not have been the best measure of strategic power, particularly since the United States was busy putting multiple warheads on many of its older missiles. (Nothing in the SALT I accords prohibited either side from taking advantage of this, the newest technological innovation in the arms race.) In the United States Senate, the deficiencies in the SALT I agreements were noted by Senator Henry Jackson and other senators in both political parties who feared the growth of Soviet strategic power and felt that the SALT negotiations had left the Soviets in a potentially superior position. Jackson, a conservative cold war Democrat, eventually decided to vote for the ratification of the ABM Treaty and the Interim Agreement, but only after the Senate approved an amendment requiring all future arms control negotiations between the United States and the Soviet Union to result in equal limits for both sides, and only after Richard Nixon had privately promised to fire selected members of the SALT negotiating team with whom Jackson had long disagreed.[9]

Nixon's successful trips to China and the Soviet Union helped him win reelection by a landslide in November 1972. The months just before and after that election also saw the conclusion of the war in Vietnam after a final and brutal round of bombings in the north. As his second term began, Nixon's national security adviser moved to the cabinet as secretary of state, and the fruits of the foreign policy efforts made by Nixon and Kissinger throughout the period from 1969 to 1973 appeared to ripen into a new era for American foreign policy. But their success carried with it the seeds of its own destruction and the high point of détente in 1972 and 1973 was also the beginning of its demise.

GERALD FORD AND THE DECLINE OF DÉTENTE

The secretive policymaking style and the fear of leaks that characterized Richard Nixon's international triumphs in his first term were part of a larger pattern that led to tragedy and his eventual fall from power. A special White House team of investigators, calling themselves the "plumbers," because they were given responsibility for discovering the sources of national security leaks, went on to perform illegal political espionage for the 1972 Nixon reelection campaign. Their late night break-in at the Democratic party headquarters in the Watergate office building, and the White House efforts to cover up official connections to the bungled burglary, became the focus of media and congressional investigations in 1973 and 1974 that ended with Richard Nixon's resignation in the midst of impeachment proceedings.

Building on the foreign policy breakthroughs of Nixon's first term was difficult, if not impossible, while the president and his White House staff were preoccupied with the Watergate investigations and while the powers of the presidency were under increasingly critical congressional and public scrutiny. Gerald Ford's assumption of the presidency after Nixon's resignation in August 1974 offered an opportunity for the restoration of an effective American foreign policy. Ford kept Kissinger as both his secretary of state and national security adviser and pledged to continue Nixon's policies in foreign affairs. Continuity was evidenced when Kissinger gave his most thorough public explanation of détente during the first few weeks of the Ford administration. [Document 5.3] But as the 1976 presidential campaign approached, criticisms of U.S.–Soviet relations were heard from both the left and the right. A number of factors contributed to the growing public disillusionment with Nixon era policies toward the Soviet Union. Taken together they signaled that détente was in decline.

Senator Jackson, who had serious reservations about the arms control process, also took a leading role in challenging other aspects of improved relations with the Soviet Union. When legislation came before the Congress to liberalize trade between the superpowers, Jackson co-sponsored an amendment with Congressman Charles Vanik that prohibited normal commercial dealings between the two countries unless the Soviet Union eased its restrictive policies on Jewish emigration. Soviet restrictions on religious freedom, political dissent, and open emigration were part of a long list of human rights violations that had been practiced in the Soviet regime since its creation. Détente was never directly aimed at the alleviation of those human rights abuses; it had the more narrow purpose of encouraging Soviet caution in international politics. The Jackson-Vanik amendment passed in both the House and Senate and was part of a 1973 trade bill that Nixon vetoed. When a slightly revised version became law the following year, the Soviet leadership rejected the trade agreement to which the amendment had been attached. Efforts to dismantle the restrictive commercial legislation of the cold war era and grant the Soviet Union most-favored-nation status and access to international credit ended in 1975. Aside from increased Soviet purchases of American grain, commerce between the two superpowers never developed the volume or scope that the advocates of détente had expected. The web of agreements envisioned by Nixon and Kissinger developed some gapping holes.

More importantly, the expected moderation of Soviet behavior on the international scene never fully materialized.[10] In the 1973 Middle East war, the Soviet Union took provocative action in support of Egypt and threatened to send troops unilaterally to the region to prevent the defeat of the Egyptian armies surrounded by Israeli forces. An active American response to this challenge, including a decision to place U.S. military forces on a temporary alert, brought the superpower crisis over the Middle East to a rapid conclusion. Kissinger's "shuttle diplomacy" to the various capital cities in the region eventually resulted in a lasting cease-fire and the beginning of a dialogue between Israel and some of its Arab neighbors. But the problems that arose in connection with the war provided a clear indication that the promised generation of peace, which Nixon had talked about during the 1972 presidential campaign, had lasted for less than a year.

Clients of both superpowers were still arrayed against each other in various parts of the world and dangers still existed that regional disputes would escalate into global confrontations. In the third world, the Soviets openly supported a Marxist faction in the Angolan civil war and encouraged Castro to send Cuban volunteers to train and assist a group of Angolan guerrillas. Elsewhere in the world, Marxist revolutionaries, with or without direct Soviet assistance, continued to threaten the stability of various nations in Asia and in Central and Latin America. In 1975, South Vietnam fell to the Vietcong and forces from the north, violating the 1973 cease-fire agreement. The fall of Saigon was quickly followed by communist takeovers in Laos and Cambodia, where weak governments were defeated by guerrilla movements allied with the North Vietnamese. The Nixon Doctrine and the mood of the nation in the wake of America's long involvement in Southeast Asia made it difficult, and in some cases illegal, for the United States to respond to these problems. In the case of Angola, Congress specifically prohibited the expenditure of any U.S. funds in that nation's civil war. With respect to events in Southeast Asia, by 1975 there was no public or congressional desire to rescue the government of South Vietnam or its immediate neighbors. The old cold war pattern of communist expansion in the third world was reemerging, and the fact that the United States needed to respond to that pattern indicated that détente was in trouble.

In Europe, the 1975 signing of the Helsinki Final Act should have marked one of the high points in the development of détente. Negotiated by the thirty-five nation Conference on Security and Cooperation in Europe (CSCE), the act settled a number of outstanding issues between the Eastern and Western blocs: It officially recognized the postwar European boundaries, endorsed the four-power agreement on Berlin that had been negotiated in 1971, recognized improved relations between the two Germanys that were the product of West Germany's own version of détente, Ostpolitik, set the stage for the hoped-for negotiation of conventional arms reductions in Central Europe, and committed all the European nations to respect fundamental human rights.[11] In America, President Ford's decision to go to Helsinki was widely criticized by conservatives and ethnic groups who feared that the agreements would be ineffective and hypocritical and involve dangerous concessions to the Soviet Union. For conservatives, the Helsinki Final Act was far too weak. It was not binding under international law and included no enforcement mechanism for the expected violations of human rights in the Soviet Union and the nations of Eastern Europe. For ethnic groups in the United States the decision to recognize existing European borders implied American acceptance of permanent Soviet domination of the Baltic republics, a sensitive issue in American domestic politics from the beginning of the cold war.

On the issue where the Soviet Union and the United States had made the most progress during the early years of détente, arms control, progress toward a follow on agreement to SALT I became bogged down in apparently endless negotiations and ominous suspicions that the Soviets were seeking military superiority over the United States. The Soviet arms control negotiators, who had abandoned their concerns about European nuclear weapons in the interests of completing the SALT I agreement, raised the same issue again in SALT II. The question of what to count as a strategic weapon was revived and further complicated by new technologies (the Soviet Backfire bomber and the cruise missile) that offered strategic capabilities in delivery systems that were technically classified as intermediate weapons.

The problem of what to count in SALT II had to be answered before either side could go on to the issue of what limits should be accepted on the weapon systems under discussion. Here Senator Jackson's reservations about SALT I produced additional difficulties. Since the Soviet Union had a much larger arsenal of missile launchers than the United States, reaching an agreement with equal limits meant that either the Soviets would have to dismantle many of their launchers before the Americans gave up any of theirs, or that equal ceilings for both sides would be set so high that very little arms control would actually take place. At his first summit with Soviet leaders in Vladivostok, President Ford accepted a basic framework for SALT II that included equal, but high, ceilings for both sides and only modest limitations on the deployment of multiple warheads. Even that agreement could not be completed until three years after Ford had left the White House and two years after the five-year interim SALT I agreement had officially expired.

During the mid-1970s, the whole process of arms control came under attack. Technology appeared to be moving much faster than diplomacy. Multiple warheads, officially referred to as multiple independently targetable reentry vehicles, or MIRVs, were unregulated by SALT I and largely unaffected by SALT II proposals. Yet their addition to the arsenals of both superpowers, along with significant improvements in missile accuracy, was making the danger of a preemptive first strike in a crisis situation significantly greater. A single launcher equipped with accurate MIRVs could now be expected to destroy many launchers on the other side. The premium for attacking first was raised and the SALT negotiators were unable to reduce it. The high ceilings approved at Vladivostok and the Soviet effort to modernize their strategic forces meant that the arms race had not been stopped or even significantly slowed. The Ford administration publicly revised upward its estimates of Soviet military spending and capabilities and changed the way the CIA would make such estimates in the future. The administration admitted that Soviet military power was growing. And at least some Washington officials claimed that the Soviets were secretly violating the arms control agreements they had already signed.[12]

The combination of arms control stagnation and Soviet third world adventurism made détente increasingly unpopular. In 1976, Ronald Reagan challenged President Ford for the Republican presidential nomination and used his campaign as a platform for criticizing the SALT negotiations and warning about the growing dangers of Soviet military superiority. Among the Democratic presidential candidates in 1976, the surprise winner was a one-term Georgia governor who attacked the Nixon-Ford administration for its failure to pay sufficient attention to violations of human rights within the communist world and among America's cold war allies. Both Reagan and Jimmy Carter promised a departure from the Kissinger era with its secret diplomacy, realpolitik, and indifference to the moral and ideological factors in foreign affairs. Kissinger, the hero of the 1972 summits, who went on to negotiate a conclusion to the American fighting in Vietnam and a successful disengagement of forces after the 1973 war in the Middle East, who survived the Watergate scandals and gave the transition between Nixon and Ford its most important continuity, was widely criticized by both liberals and conservatives as the Ford administration drew to a close.[13] In the final months before the 1976 presidential election, Ford's campaign advisers banished the word détente from the administration's vocabulary and tried to win the election by distancing the president from his own policies. Those efforts were not successful.

CONCLUSIONS

POWER

More than other strategies in the postwar era, détente depended on presidential power and public consensus. In order for an effective policy of linkage to be carried out, all aspects of relations between the two superpowers would have to be carefully monitored and adjusted in accordance with continuous assessments of what the Soviet Union was up to and which particular American carrot or stick might be used to influence their behavior. Linkage demanded rapid responses and decisive leadership. It also required a unified American foreign policy. If clear signals were to be sent to Moscow, they had to come from one source in Washington. Ironically, Richard Nixon's plans for a new generation of peace, and a powerful presidency to execute those plans, arrived on the American political scene at roughly the same time that the public and the Congress were inclined to impose new limits on the powers and prerogatives of the executive branch. The discovery of Nixon's misdeeds in connection with Watergate made that shift against the presidency more rapid and more pronounced.

Even before Watergate weakened Nixon's political standing and public confidence in the office he held, the differences between the legislative and executive branches over the conduct of foreign affairs were clearly evident. Much of the debate in the Nixon administration revolved around the issue of war powers. The period of détente was also the period of U.S. withdrawal from Vietnam, and for many American citizens and politicians of that day, bringing an end to the fighting in Southeast Asia was much more important than beginning a new era of improved superpower relations. Richard Nixon understood the public concern about Vietnam. Given the massive antiwar demonstrations that were staged in Washington following the 1970 incursions into Cambodia, he could hardly have been unaware of those concerns. He hoped that better relations with Moscow and Beijing would bring the war to a faster conclusion. There is relatively little evidence to suggest that détente produced the results in Southeast Asia that Nixon expected, certainly not in the time frame he wanted.

In the wake of Vietnam, Congress tried to make sure that there would be no more futile third world conflicts and no more exclusive presidential decisions to go to war. But the debate over war powers and the meaning of the Constitution had a broader context. For some members of Congress, and for many Americans, the lesson of Vietnam was that the United States should avoid entangling international commitments. During the cold war the United States had become the policeman of the planet, fighting communism in all of its forms and in every arena in which it appeared. The result of these contests did not appear to be a decisive victory for democracy. Instead, we had compromised our own political and moral values, formed alliances with unsavory regimes, sacrificed American lives for minor geopolitical gains, and killed thousands of innocent peasants who had no real understanding of twentieth-century ideological competition. We suffered from what Senator William Fulbright called an "arrogance of power"[14] that led us to take on excessive global responsibilities and make exaggerated assumptions about what America could and should do in the world. The lesson of Vietnam for many of the war's critics was that the United States should turn its attention inward, encourage democratic politics in the world by providing an example of democracy within its own borders, and minimize involvement in the sordid business of international politics.

This neo-isolationist agenda, which had strong roots in American culture and history, was in direct competition with the strategy of détente. Whereas the new isolationists wanted a partial American withdrawal from international relations, Nixon and Kissinger were calling for a more activist foreign policy that included the recognition of communist China, the transformation of relations with the Soviet Union, and the manipulation of economic, political, and military dealings among the great powers to maximize American advantage. The neo-isolationists wanted to reduce secrecy and presidential discretion in foreign affairs; Nixon and Kissinger wanted to increase them. The contest in the 1970s over which branch of government would dominate American foreign policy was also a contest over what the content of that policy would be.

By the end of his first term, it appeared that Nixon and détente were victorious. The president had made triumphant trips to China and the Soviet Union, signed a major arms control agreement with the Russians, assured the American people that an end to the Vietnam War was at hand, and won a landslide reelection against the Democratic antiwar candidate, George McGovern. But all of those triumphs failed to produce permanent changes in American politics and foreign affairs. The dramatic events of 1972 were the end, not the beginning, of a new foreign policy consensus. In part, the initiatives of Nixon's first term fell victim to the paralysis of the White House that accompanied the Watergate investigations and the president's slow slide toward resignation. But even without Watergate, it might have been difficult for Nixon to build on his early foreign policy successes.

So much was promised in connection with détente that public disappointment was almost inevitable. As Kissinger notes in his memoirs, "Nixon's penchant for hyperbole was unlikely to be restrained in an election year. He started out expressing the 'hope' for a generation of peace. Soon he came to claim it as an 'accomplishment.' And in the closing days of the 1972 election campaign he even escalated the goal to be a 'century of peace.'"[15] Those promises could not be fulfilled. The generation of peace that Nixon envisioned depended on an American public willing to ignore human rights violations in the communist world and develop extensive trade relations with their former adversaries. It further envisioned the manipulation of those trade relations to win concessions, particularly from the Soviets, in a continuing contest for influence throughout the third world. And if those manipulations failed, Nixon and Kissinger favored the use of covert action, and if need be military force, to prevent the victory of a Soviet-Cuban faction in Angola or the 1975 defeat of South Vietnam. While promising a generation of peace and an end to the cold war, Nixon and Kissinger were, in many ways, preparing to continue competition with the Soviet Union by other means.[16] Even without political scandal, they would have had a difficult time bringing the American public with them.

After the Watergate scandal and the ascension to office of an unelected chief executive, the task of building public support for a complicated and controversial set of foreign policies became nearly impossible. Ford struggled from the outset of his administration to sustain the foreign policies of Nixon's first term. But he was building on shifting sands and never had the full support of the American people or the Democratic Congress. Ford left office complaining that the imperial presidency had become an imperiled presidency.[17] Congress had gone too far in reclaiming its role in foreign affairs and ended up severely restricting the ability of the president to act decisively and independently in international affairs. But the competition between the branches of government in the 1970s, which is usually described as a contest over power, was also a contest about purpose. That contest had no clear resolution. Neither neo-isolationists in the Congress nor realists in the White House were able to convince the American public to adopt fully the foreign policy they preferred. The old cold war consensus was shattered by Vietnam and Watergate, but by the end of the Ford administration there was very little available to take its place.

Jimmy Carter would offer a foreign policy based on human rights and Ronald Reagan would call for a revival of traditional cold war anticommunism. Both of these alternatives would be controversial and neither would win lasting public support. Ronald Reagan would end his presidency with what appeared to be a second attempt at détente, complete with regular superpower summits, arms control agreements, and improved cultural and economic relations. The Reagan détente, unlike the version of détente promoted by Presidents Nixon and Ford, would be accompanied by dramatic changes in Soviet foreign and domestic policy that would revolutionize international politics in 1989.

PROCESS

The Nixon and Ford administrations were unusual both for their early pursuit of détente and for the procedures by which détente and the other foreign policies of that period were made. More than any other modern presidents, Nixon and Ford depended on a single foreign policy adviser. Henry Kissinger was Nixon's national security adviser from 1969 until the summer of 1973 and his secretary of state thereafter. For a time he held both positions and only surrendered his portfolio as national security adviser when President Ford made a number of cabinet changes and asked Kissinger's assistant, Brent Scowcroft, to assume the duties of NSC adviser. In the Ford administration as a senior cabinet officer, who was better known in the international community than the president, Kissinger had unquestioned access to the chief executive and more influence over foreign affairs than any secretary of state since George Marshall. Whether he worked in the White House or in the Department of State, Kissinger clearly took center stage in the foreign policy of the Nixon and Ford administrations.

Kissinger played that central role because Richard Nixon wanted it that way. In 1968, Nixon planned to be his own secretary of state. During the transition he appointed William Rogers, an old friend and a former attorney general in the Eisenhower cabinet, to take charge of the Department of State. Rogers was, in Kissinger's somewhat unkind judgment, one of the few secretaries of state "selected because of their President's confidence in their ignorance of foreign policy."[18] An ignorant, but loyal, secretary of state would help keep the foreign policy bureaucracies at bay while Nixon and his White House staff went about the business of developing and implementing the important international initiatives of the administration. By the late 1960s, it was common practice for presidents to have their own foreign policy advisers in the White House. The National Security Council could be called upon to coordinate the positions of the various departments, agencies, and organizations responsible for foreign affairs in the executive branch, but the National Security Council staff worked directly for the president and provided him with both independent evaluations of international problems and recommendations for policy actions. This use of the NSC staff had developed under Kennedy and Johnson and had existed in more informal ways under Eisenhower.[19] What was unique about the Kissinger tenure as special assistant to the president for national security affairs was the extent to which he emerged as the administration's chief foreign policy spokesman and the president's private negotiator on the opening to China, the details of détente, and the long negotiations that brought an end to the war in Vietnam.

Kissinger now believes that it is better to have the secretary of state, rather than the assistant for national security affairs, serve as the president's principal foreign policy adviser.[20] But at the time of his appointment to the Nixon White

House staff, he shared the president's distrust of the foreign policy bureaucracies and agreed with Nixon on the need for centralization of foreign policy decision making. Critics of the Johnson and Nixon administrations, concerned about an imperial presidency, concentrated their attention on defining the proper relationship between the president and the Congress in the conduct of foreign affairs and argued that balance needed to be restored between the two elected branches of government. Nixon and Kissinger took a very different view. They were much more concerned about the relationship between the president and the executive departments ostensibly under presidential control. They wanted to strengthen, not weaken, presidential power; the enemy of good policy was not the Congress but the bureaucracy.

Nixon was suspicious that officers in the foreign service, employees of the CIA, and some members of his own cabinet would oppose the dramatic changes he wanted to make in American relations with China and the Soviet Union. In the heated atmosphere of national debate over Vietnam, which had split the Democratic party and the foreign policy establishment, Nixon was probably correct in fearing resistance to some of his ideas. He may also have been concerned that those who agreed with his policy initiatives would claim credit for them after they achieved success. The combination of suspicion and jealousy led Nixon intentionally to concentrate power in the White House and maintain strict secrecy regarding the controversial aspects of his international agenda. Secrecy, Nixon believed, is essential to successful foreign policy: "Without negotiations in secret, there will be few agreements to sign in public. In some cases, it is simply the only way to conduct the business of international politics. Without secret negotiations we would not have been able to achieve the rapprochement with China, the arms control treaties with the Soviet Union in 1972, and the peace agreements with North Vietnam in 1973."[21]

Kissinger also approved of a White House centered foreign policy making system, but for slightly different reasons. As an academic analyst of foreign affairs before his appointment to the Nixon administration, Kissinger had written extensively about the weaknesses inherent in the bureaucratic nature of American foreign policy.[22] By training, and because of the structure of organizational rewards and punishments, bureaucrats tend to seek safety in collective decisions and in policies that minimize international and domestic political risks. They lack creativity, courage and vision—the qualities that Kissinger consistently associated with statesmanship—and seek instead objectivity, certainty, and stability. Almost all of Kissinger's academic writing on international politics touch on the theme of inevitable conflict between the statesman and the bureaucrat, between the need for innovation in foreign affairs and the modern organizational tendency toward predictability in domestic politics. Kissinger criticized the bureaucratization of American foreign policy and warned that we were wasting precious opportunities to make lasting progress on the international scene. The answer to our problems, if there was one, would have to come from extraordinary political leadership. As the president's trusted national security adviser, Kissinger had a chance to put his ideas into practice.

Though the White House centered foreign policy making system of the Nixon administration contributed to the successful opening to China, arms control, and détente, it was nevertheless widely attacked.[23] Critics claimed that depending on a small White House staff for the conduct of foreign policy had significant drawbacks. It meant that the number of issues that could be handled was necessarily small and affected by the preferences and abilities of the president's leading adviser. The Kissinger National Security Council staff gave relatively little attention to Africa, Latin America, and other parts of the developing world, unless they were threatened by leftist takeovers.[24] Only late in his tenure at the Department of State did Kissinger begin to deal with international economics and the new international politics of energy. The system of depending on a small White House staff also meant that the president was isolated from the considerable expertise available in the bureaucracy. Critics of the SALT I negotiations point out that the back-channel negotiations by Kissinger and the summit decisions reached by Brezhnev and Nixon were often vague and imprecise because the president and his national security adviser were understandably unfamiliar with the details of arms control.[25]

In Kissinger's defense, the limited agenda addressed by the Nixon NSC staff—negotiating an end to the Vietnam War and détente with China and the Soviet Union—arguably included the most important issues of the day. It certainly included the issues of greatest concern to the president. As for the trade-off between secrecy and expertise, Nixon and Kissinger fully understood what would be lost by maintaining secrecy in the early stages of policy development. They nevertheless consistently decided to sacrifice access to specialists in exchange for minimizing the dangers of leaks and early revelations of their initiatives. Together they had considerable expertise of their own in both the theory and practice of international relations and were convinced that together they could bring about dramatic changes in American foreign policy and perhaps in the structure of the international system. They gambled for high stakes.

PERSONALITY

Richard Nixon had always been a gambler. His leading biographer claims that his first campaign for the House of Representatives was financed by profits from poker games at which the future president showed remarkable skill.[26] After winning a seat in the House, Nixon gambled his reputation as a junior legislator when he took a leading role in the investigation of Alger Hiss and eventually proved that the distinguished diplomat's absolute denials of communist connections were suspect. He ran for the Senate after only two terms in the House and later became one of the youngest vice-presidential candidates in modern politics. When he was almost dropped from Eisenhower's ticket in 1952 because of allegations that he misused campaign funds, he gambled that he could go on national television and convince the American people of his innocence. His Checkers speech was a brilliant success. After losing the 1960 presidential election to John Kennedy and then a 1962 bid to become governor of California, he worked for six difficult years to stage one of the most impressive political comebacks in American history. Richard Nixon was a tenacious and ambitious politician who was willing to take great risks for the causes he believed in and to advance his own political career.

He was also an extremely insecure individual, highly sensitive to criticism and prone to see himself surrounded by enemies. Though Nixon clearly had a loving and devoted family, he had very few close personal friends. He was not a likable person, and never generated the kind of loyal following that Dwight Eisenhower or

Ronald Reagan was able to secure. Even his close associates who respected and admired his intellectual abilities and capacity for hard work were puzzled by his ability to win elections without winning public affection.[27] The nickname he acquired from his early California political campaigns, "Tricky Dick," stuck with him throughout his career and captured a side of his personality that many believed was always there. He was a loner. He liked to make decisions by himself after carefully reading detailed briefing materials. He sought to avoid direct confrontations with his cabinet officers and most of his White House aides. At the height of his political power he was served by a very small number of White House assistants who saw their duty as both carrying out his wishes and ignoring his occasionally vindictive instructions.[28]

The secrecy and concentration of power in the White House that were part of the foreign policy making process in the Nixon administration fit with the president's character. There may have been good reasons to suspect that members of Congress, or the bureaucracy, or some of the people in his own cabinet would have leaked sensitive information about China or détente. There were, in fact, damaging leaks in the Nixon era, including the publication of the *Pentagon Papers*. But there was also a personal obsession about hiding things from enemies in the press and opponents in the Democratic party, who, Nixon believed, were constantly seeking opportunities to embarrass his endeavors. There may have been requests from the Chinese and Russians to keep early negotiations about rapprochement and détente private, but there was also a desire on Nixon's part to stage surprise announcements of major diplomatic breakthroughs that would confound his critics in the media and the Congress. There may have been some efficiencies in working with a small group of trusted White House staff members who were in tune with the president's desires, but there was also a need to ensure that credit for success belonged to the president and not to others in his government. Henry Kissinger's most difficult dealings with Nixon came at a time when the president was beleaguered by Watergate and his national security adviser was becoming a major public figure in his own right.[29] In the Nixon White House the methods by which foreign policy decisions were made were always a reflection of the necessities of international politics, the troubled times of national controversy over Vietnam, and the defects in the president's character. Something of the same mixture led to the tragedies of Watergate.

Gerald Ford came to the White House in the aftermath of a major political scandal and without the benefit of an electoral victory to give his administration legitimacy. Before his appointment as vice president, he had been a senior member of the House of Representatives and a leader of the minority party in the legislature. Though hardly a national political figure, he was well known in Washington for his personal integrity and straightforward manner. Ford lacked experience and background in international politics and served in the White House for only two and half years. But his significant contribution to the presidency, to the nation, and to our standing in the world was a restoration of public trust and respect for the office he held.

Chronology of Détente

1969

Mar — Serious border fighting occurs between the Soviet Union and China.

Jul 21 — Some of the barriers to trade and contact between the U.S. and China are lifted.

Nov 7 — U.S. quietly ends 19-year-old policy of patrolling the Taiwan Straits.

Nov 17 — First official SALT negotiating session in Helsinki.

1970

Jan 20 — Resumption of talks between U.S. and Chinese diplomats in Warsaw.

Apr 30 — Nixon announces incursions into Cambodia to destroy North Vietnamese supply depots and headquarters.

1971

Apr 10 — U.S. Ping-Pong team visits China.

Apr 30 — Interview with Mao in which he invites Nixon to visit China is published in *Life* magazine.

May 20 — SALT breakthrough announced as a result of secret Kissinger diplomacy.

Jul 9–11 — Kissinger secret trip to Beijing.

Jul 15 — Nixon announces forthcoming presidential visit to China.

Sep 3 — Quadripartite Agreement on Berlin signed.

Oct 16–26 — Kissinger makes second trip to Beijing.

1972

Feb 21 — Nixon trip to China begins.

Feb 28 — Shanghai communiqué signed in Beijing.

May 26 — Signing of SALT I agreements at Moscow summit.

Jun 17 — Watergate break-in.

Oct 4 — Jackson-Vanik amendment introduced.

1973

May 17 — Senate Watergate investigating committee begins hearings.

Jun 16 — Brezhnev arrives in U.S. for second summit with Nixon.

Jul 31 — Bill of impeachment introduced in the House of Representatives.

Oct 5 — Yom Kippur War in the Middle East begins.

Oct 20 — "Saturday Night Massacre" in which Nixon fires Watergate special prosecutor Archibald Cox.

1974

Jun 27 — Nixon arrives in Moscow for third superpower summit.

Jul 24 — House Judiciary Committee begins debate on bill of impeachment.

Aug 8 — Nixon resigns; Ford becomes president.

Sep 19 — Kissinger, testifying before the Senate Foreign Relations Committee, explains the policy of détente toward the Soviet Union.

Nov 24 — Vladivostok accords outline the structure for SALT II.

Chapter 5 Documents

Document 5.1
The Shanghai Communiqué
February 28, 1972

President Richard Nixon of the United States of America visited the People's Republic of China at the invitation of Premier Chou En-lai of the People's Republic of China from February 21 to February 28, 1972. Accompanying the President were Mrs. Nixon, U.S. Secretary of State William Rogers, Assistant to the President Dr. Henry Kissinger, and other American officials.

President Nixon met with Chairman Mao Tse-tung of the Communist Party of China on February 21. The two leaders had a serious and frank exchange of views on Sino-U.S. relations and world affairs. . . .

The leaders of the People's Republic of China and the United States of America found it beneficial to have this opportunity, after so many years without contact, to present candidly to one another their views on a variety of issues. They reviewed the international situation in which important changes and great upheavals are taking place and expounded their respective positions and attitudes.

The Chinese side stated: Wherever there is opposition, there is resistance. Countries want independence, nations want liberation and the people want revolution—this has become the irresistible trend of history. All nations, big or small, should be equal; big nations should not bully the small and strong nations should not bully the weak. China will never be a superpower and it opposes hegemony and power politics of any kind. The Chinese side stated that it firmly supports the struggles of all the oppressed people and nations for freedom and liberation and that the people of all countries have the right to choose their social systems according to their own wishes and the right to safeguard the independence, sovereignty and territorial integrity of their own countries and oppose foreign aggression, interference, control and subversion. All foreign troops should be withdrawn to their own countries. The Chinese side expressed its firm support to the peoples of Viet Nam, Laos and Cambodia in their efforts for the attainment of their goal and its firm support to the seven-point proposal of the Provisional Revolutionary Government of the Republic of South Viet Nam and the elaboration of February this year on the two key problems in the proposal, and to the Joint Declaration of the Summit Conference of the Indochinese Peoples. It firmly supports the eight-point program for the peaceful unification of Korea put forward by the Government of the Democratic People's Republic of Korea on April 12, 1971, and the stand for the abolition of the "U.N. Commission for the Unification and Rehabilitation of Korea." It firmly opposes the revival and the outward expansion of Japanese militarism and firmly supports the Japanese people's desire to build an independent, democratic, peaceful and neutral Japan. It firmly maintains that India and Pakistan should, in accordance with the United Nations resolutions on the India-Pakistan question, immediately withdraw all their forces to their respective territories and to their own sides of the ceasefire line in Jammu and Kashmir and firmly supports the Pakistan Government and people in their struggle to preserve their independence and sovereignty and the people of Jammu and Kashmir in their struggle for the right of self-determination.

The U.S. side stated: Peace in Asia and peace in the world requires efforts both to reduce immediate tensions and to eliminate the basic causes of conflict. The United States will work for a just and secure peace: just, because it fulfills the aspirations of peoples and nations for freedom and progress; secure, because it removes the danger of foreign aggression. The United States supports individual freedom and social progress for all the peoples of the world, free of outside pressure or intervention. The United States believes that the effort to reduce tensions is served by improving communication between countries that have different ideologies so as to lessen the risks of confrontation through accident, miscalculation or misunderstanding. Countries should treat each other with mutual respect and be willing to compete peacefully, letting performances be the ultimate judge. No country should claim infallibility and each country should be prepared to re-examine its own attitudes for the common good. The United States stressed that the peoples of Indochina should be allowed to determine their destiny without outside intervention; its constant primary objective has been a negotiated solution; the eight-point proposal put forward by the Republic of Viet Nam and the United States on January 27, 1972 represents a basis for the attainment of that objective; in the withdrawal of all U.S. forces from the region consistent with the aim of self-determination for each country of Indochina. The United States will maintain its close ties with and support for the Republic of Korea; the United States will support efforts of the Republic of Korea to seek a relaxation of tension and increased communication in the Korean Peninsula. The United States places the highest value on its friendly relations with Japan; it will continue to develop the existing close bonds. Consistent with the United Nations Security Council Resolution of December 21, 1971, the United States favors the continuation of the ceasefire between India and Pakistan and the withdrawal of all military forces to within their own territories and to their own sides of the ceasefire line in Jammu and Kashmir; the United States supports the right of the peoples of South Asia to shape their own future in peace, free of military threat, and without having the area become the subject of great power rivalry.

There are essential differences between China and the United States in their social systems and foreign policies. However, the two sides agreed that countries regardless of their social systems, should conduct their relations on the principles of respect for the sovereignty and territorial integrity of all states, equality and mutual benefit, and peaceful coexistence. International disputes should be settled on this basis, without resorting to the use or threat of force. The United States and the People's Republic of China are prepared to apply these principles to their mutual relations.

With these principles of international relations in mind the two sides stated that:

- progress toward the normalization of relations between China and the United States is in the interests of all countries;
- both wish to reduce the danger of international military conflict;
- neither should seek hegemony in the Asia-Pacific region and each is opposed to efforts by any other country or group of countries to establish such hegemony; and
- neither is prepared to negotiate on behalf of any third party or to enter into agreements or understandings with the other directed at other states.

Both sides are of the view that it would be against the interests of the peoples of the world for any major country to collude with another against other countries, or for major countries to divide up the world into spheres of interest.

The two sides reviewed the long-standing serious disputes between China and the United States. The Chinese side reaffirmed its position: The Taiwan question is the crucial question obstructing the normalization of relations between China and the United States; the Government of the People's Republic of China is the sole legal government of China; Taiwan is a province of China which has long been returned to the motherland; the liberation of Taiwan is China's internal affair in which no other country has the right to interfere; and all U.S. forces and military installations must be withdrawn from Taiwan. The Chinese Government firmly opposes any activities which aim at the creation of "one China, one Taiwan," "one China, two governments," "two Chinas," an "independent Taiwan," or advocate that "the status of Taiwan remains to be determined."

The U.S. side declared: The United States acknowledges that all Chinese on either side of the Taiwan Strait maintain there is but one China and that Taiwan is a part of China. The United States Government does not challenge that position. It reaffirms its interest in a peaceful settlement of the Taiwan question by the Chinese themselves. With this prospect in mind, it affirms the ultimate objective of the withdrawal of all U.S. forces and military installations from Taiwan. In the meantime, it will progressively reduce its forces and military installations on Taiwan as the tension in the area diminishes.

The two sides agreed that it is desirable to broaden the understanding between the two peoples. To this end, they discussed specific areas in such fields as science, technology, culture, sports and journalism, in which people-to-people contacts and exchanges would be mutually beneficial. Each side undertakes to facilitate the further development of such contacts and exchanges.

Both sides view bilateral trade as another area from which mutual benefit can be derived, and agreed that economic relations based on equality and mutual benefit are in the interest of the peoples of the two countries. They agree to facilitate the progressive development of trade between their two countries.

The two sides agreed that they will stay in contact through various channels, including the sending of a senior U.S. representative to Peking from time to time for concrete consultations to further the normalization of relations between the two countries and continue to exchange views on issues of common interest.

The two sides expressed the hope that the gains achieved during this visit would open up new prospects for the relations between the two countries. They believe that the normalization of relations between the two countries is not only in the interest of the Chinese and American peoples but also contributes to the relaxation of tension in Asia and the world.

President Nixon, Mrs. Nixon and the American party expressed their appreciation for the gracious hospitality shown them by the Government and people of the People's Republic of China.

Source: *Department of State Bulletin*, March 20, 1972, pp. 435–438.

Document 5.2
Basic Principles of Relations Between the United States of America and the Union of Soviet Socialist Republics,
May 29, 1972

The United States of America and the Union of Soviet Socialist Republics,

Guided by their obligations under the Charter of the United Nations and by a desire to strengthen peaceful relations with each other and to place these relations on the firmest possible basis,

Aware of the need to make every effort to remove the threat of war and to create conditions which promote the reduction of tensions in the world and the strengthening of universal security and international cooperation,

Believing that the improvement of U.S.–Soviet relations and their mutually advantageous development in such areas as economics, science, and culture will meet these objectives and contribute to better mutual understanding and business-like cooperation, without in any way prejudicing the interests of third countries,

Conscious that these objectives reflect the interests of the peoples of both countries,

Have agreed as follows:

First. They will proceed from the common determination that in the nuclear age there is no alternative to conducting their mutual relations on the basis of peaceful coexistence. Differences in ideology and in the social systems of the United States and the U.S.S.R. are not obstacles to the bilateral development of normal relations based on the principles of sovereignty, equality, noninterference in internal affairs and mutual advantage.

Second. The United States and the U.S.S.R. attach major importance to preventing the development of situations capable of causing a dangerous exacerbation of their relations. Therefore, they will do their utmost to avoid military confrontations and to prevent the outbreak of nuclear war. They will always exercise restraint in their mutual relations and will be prepared to negotiate and settle differences by peaceful means. Discussions and negotiations on outstanding issues will be conducted in a spirit of reciprocity, mutual accommodation, and mutual benefit.

Both sides recognize that efforts to obtain unilateral advantage at the expense of the other, directly or indirectly, are inconsistent with these objectives. The prerequisites for maintaining and strengthening peaceful relations between the United States and the U.S.S.R. are the recognition of the security interests of the parties based on the principle of equality and the renunciation of the use or threat of force.

Third. The United States and the U.S.S.R. have a special responsibility, as do other countries which are permanent members of the United Nations Security Council, to do everything in their power so that conflicts or situations will not arise which would serve to increase international tensions. Accordingly, they will seek to promote conditions in which all countries will live in peace and security and will not be subject to outside interference in their internal affairs.

Fourth. The United States and the U.S.S.R. intend to widen the juridical basis of their mutual relations and to exert the necessary efforts so that bilateral agreements which they have concluded and multilateral treaties and agreements to which they are jointly parties are faithfully implemented.

Fifth. The United States and the U.S.S.R. reaffirm their readiness to continue the practice of exchanging views on problems of mutual interest and, when necessary, to conduct such exchanges at the highest level, including meetings between leaders of the two countries.

The two governments welcome and will facilitate an increase in productive contacts between representatives of the legislative bodies of the two countries.

Sixth. The parties will continue their effort to limit armaments on a bilateral as well as on a multilateral basis. They will continue to make special efforts to limit strategic armaments. Whenever possible, they will conclude concrete agreements aimed at achieving these purposes.

The United States and the U.S.S.R. regard as the ultimate objective of their efforts the achievement of general and complete disarmament and the establishment of an effective system of international security in accordance with the purposes and principles of the United Nations.

Seventh. The United States and the U.S.S.R. regard commercial and economic ties as an important and necessary element in the strengthening of their bilateral relations and thus will actively promote the growth of such ties. They will facilitate cooperation between the relevant organizations and enterprises of the two countries and the conclusion of appropriate agreements and contracts, including long-term ones.

The two countries will contribute to the improvement of maritime and air communications between them.

Eighth. The two sides consider it timely and useful to develop mutual contacts and cooperation in the fields of science and technology. Where suitable, the United States and the U.S.S.R. will conclude appropriate agreements dealing with concrete cooperation in these fields.

Ninth. The two sides reaffirm their intention to deepen cultural ties with one another and to encourage fuller familiarization with each other's cultural values. They will promote improved conditions for cultural exchanges and tourism.

Tenth. The United States and the U.S.S.R. will seek to ensure that their ties and cooperation in all the above-mentioned fields and in any others in their mutual interest are built on a firm and long-term basis. To give a permanent character to these efforts, they will establish in all fields where this is feasible joint commissions or other joint bodies.

Eleventh. The United States and the U.S.S.R. make no claim for themselves and would not recognize the claims of anyone else to any special rights or advantages in world affairs. They recognize the sovereign equality of all states.

The development of U.S.–Soviet relations is not directed against third countries and their interests.

Twelfth. The basic principles set forth in this document do not affect any obligations with respect to other countries earlier assumed by the United States and the U.S.S.R.

Source: *Department of State Bulletin*, June 26, 1972, pp. 898–899.

Document 5.3
Statement of Secretary of State Henry Kissinger to the Senate Foreign Relations Committee, selected passages, September 19, 1974

I. *The Challenge*

Since the dawn of the nuclear age the world's fears of holocaust and its hopes for peace have turned on the relationship between the United States and the Soviet Union.

Throughout history men have sought peace but suffered war; all too often deliberate decisions or miscalculations have brought violence and destruction to a world yearning for tranquility. Tragic as the consequences of violence may have been in the past, the issue of peace and war takes on unprecedented urgency when, for the first time in history, two nations have the capacity to destroy mankind.

The destructiveness of modern weapons defines the necessity of the task; deep differences in philosophy and interests between the United States and the Soviet Union point up its difficulty. These differences do not spring from misunderstanding or personalities or transitory factors:

- They are rooted in history and in the way the two countries have developed.
- They are nourished by conflicting values and opposing ideologies.
- They are expressed in diverging national interests that produce political and military competition.
- They are influenced by allies and friends whose association we value and whose interests we will not sacrifice.

Paradox confuses our perception of the problem of peaceful coexistence: If peace is pursued to the exclusion of any other goal, other values will be compromised and perhaps lost; but if unconstrained rivalry leads to nuclear conflict, these values, along with everything else, will be destroyed in the resulting holocaust. However competitive they may be at some levels of their relationship, both major nuclear powers must base their policies on the premise that neither can expect to impose its will on the other without running an intolerable risk. The challenge of our time is to reconcile the reality of competition with the imperative of coexistence.

There can be no peaceful international order without a constructive relationship between the United States and the Soviet Union. There will be no international stability unless both the Soviet Union and the United States conduct themselves with restraint and unless they use their enormous power for the benefit of mankind.

Thus we must be clear at the outset on what the term "détente" entails. It is the search for a more comprehensive relationship with the Soviet Union. It is a continuing process, not a final condition. And it has been pursued by successive American leaders though the means have varied as have the world conditions.

Some fundamental principles guide this policy:

- The United States cannot base its policy solely on Moscow's good intentions. But neither can we insist that all forward movement must await a convergence of American and Soviet purposes. We seek, regardless of Soviet intentions, to serve peace through a systematic resistance to pressure and conciliatory responses to moderate behavior.

- We must oppose aggressive actions, but we must not seek confrontations lightly.
- We must maintain a strong national defense while recognizing that in the nuclear age the relationship between military strength and politically usable power is the most complex in all history.
- Where the age-old antagonism between freedom and tyranny is concerned, we are not neutral. But other imperatives impose limits on our ability to produce internal changes in foreign countries. Consciousness of our limits is a recognition of the necessity of peace—not moral callousness. The preservation of human life and human society are moral values, too.
- We must be mature enough to recognize that to be stable a relationship must provide advantages to both sides and that the most constructive international relationships are those in which both parties perceive an element of gain. Moscow will benefit from certain measures, just as we will from others. The balance cannot be struck on each issue every day, but only over the whole range of relations and over a period of time.

II. The Course of Soviet-American Relations

In the first two decades of the postwar period U.S.–Soviet relations were characterized by many fits and starts. Some encouraging developments followed the Cuban missile crisis of 1962, for example. But at the end of the decade the invasion of Czechoslovakia brought progress to a halt and threw a deepening shadow over East-West relations.

During those difficult days some were tempted to conclude that antagonism was the central feature of the relationship and that U.S. policy—even while the Vietnam agony raised questions about the readiness of the American people to sustain a policy of confrontation–had to be geared to this grim reality. Others recommended a basic change of policy; there was a barrage of demands to hold an immediate summit to establish a better atmosphere, to launch the SALT talks [strategic arms limitation talks], and to end the decades-old trade discrimination against the Soviet Union, which was widely criticized as anachronistic, futile, and counterproductive.

These two approaches reflected the extremes of the debate that had dominated most of the postwar period; they also revealed deep-seated differences between the American and the Soviet reactions to the process of international relations.

For many Americans, tensions and enmity in international relations are anomalies, the cause of which is attributed either to deliberate malice or to misunderstanding. Malice is to be combated by force, or at least isolation; misunderstanding is to be removed by the strenuous exercise of good will. Communist states, on the other hand, regard tensions as inevitable by-products of a struggle between opposing social systems.

Most Americans perceive relations between states as either friendly or hostile, both defined in nearly absolute terms. Soviet foreign policy, by comparison, is conducted in a gray area heavily influenced by the Soviet conception of the balance of forces. Thus Soviet diplomacy is never free of tactical pressures or adjustments, and it is never determined in isolation from the prevailing military balance. For Moscow, East-West contacts and negotiations are in part designed to promote Soviet influence abroad, especially in Western Europe—and to gain formal acceptance of those elements of the status quo most agreeable to Moscow.

The issue, however, is not whether peace and stability serve Soviet purposes, but whether they serve our own. Indeed, to the extent that our attention focuses largely on Soviet intentions we create a latent vulnerability. If détente can be justified only by a basic change in Soviet motivation, the temptation becomes overwhelming to base U.S.–Soviet relations not on realistic appraisal but on tenuous hopes; a change in Soviet tone is taken as a sign of basic change in philosophy. Atmosphere is confused with substance. Policy oscillates between poles of suspicion and euphoria.

Neither extreme is realistic, and both are dangerous. The hopeful view ignores that we and the Soviets are bound to compete for the foreseeable future. The pessimistic view ignores that we have some parallel interests and that we are compelled to coexist. Détente encourages an environment in which competitors can regulate and restrain their differences and ultimately move from competition to cooperation.

A. *American Goals.* **America's aspiration for the kind of political environment we now call détente is not new.**

The effort to achieve a more constructive relationship with the Soviet Union is not made in the name of any one administration, or one party, or for any one period of time. It expresses the continuing desire of the vast majority of the American people for an easing of international tensions, and their expectation that any responsible government will strive for peace. No aspect of our policies, domestic or foreign, enjoys more consistent bipartisan support. No aspect is more in the interest of mankind.

In the postwar period repeated efforts were made to improve our relationship with Moscow. The spirits of Geneva, Camp David, and Glassboro were evanescent moments in a quarter century otherwise marked by tensions and by sporadic confrontation. What is new in the current period of relaxation of tensions is its duration, the scope of the relationship which has evolved and the continuity and intensity of contact and consultation which it has produced....

We sought to explore every avenue toward an honorable and just accommodation while remaining determined not to settle for mere atmospherics. We relied on a balance of mutual interests rather than Soviet intentions. When challenged—such as in the Middle East, the Caribbean, or Berlin—we always responded firmly. And when Soviet policy moved toward conciliation, we sought to turn what may have started as a tactical maneuver into a durable pattern of conduct.

Our approach proceeds from the conviction that, in moving forward across a wide spectrum of negotiations, progress in one area adds momentum to progress in other areas. If we succeed, then no agreement stands alone as an isolated accomplishment vulnerable to the next crisis. We did not invent the interrelationship; it was a reality because of the range of problems and areas in which the interests of the United States and the Soviet Union impinge on each other. We have looked for progress in a series of agreements settling specific political issues, and we have sought to relate these to a new standard of international conduct appropriate to the dangers of the nuclear age. By acquiring a stake in this network of relationships with the West the Soviet Union may become more conscious of what it would lose by a return to confrontation. Indeed, it is our expectation that it will develop a self-interest in fostering the entire process of relaxation of tensions....

Source: *Department of State Bulletin*, October 14, 1974, pp. 505–519.

Chapter 5 Notes

[1]Frank Snepp, *Decent Interval* (New York: Random House, 1977).

[2]Richard M. Nixon, *RN* (New York: Warner Books, 1978), pp. 469–472.

[3]Henry Kissinger, *White House Years* (Boston: Little, Brown, 1979), pp. 183–185, 764–65.

[4]Richard M. Nixon, "Asia After Viet Nam," *Foreign Affairs* (Fall 1968). Humphrey had also given hints that he would seek improved relations with mainland China. See *New York Times*, April 23, 1968.

[5]Richard Nixon, *In the Arena* (New York: Simon & Schuster, 1990), p. 327.

[6]Edgar Snow, "Conversation with Mao Tse-tung", *Life*, April 30, 1971.

[7]Nixon discussed linkage at his very first news conference as president. Nixon, *RN*, pp. 428–429.

[8]John Newhouse, *Cold Dawn: The Story of SALT* (New York: Holt, Rinehart & Winston, 1973), pp. 55–56.

[9]Gerard Smith, *Doubletalk: The Story of SALT I* (Garden City, N. Y.: Doubleday, 1980), pp. 441–445.

[10]This may have been a result of Jackson-Vanik, which removed any economic incentives for Soviet international concessions. See George Breslauer, "Why Détente Failed: An Interpretation," in *Managing the United States-Soviet Rivalry*, ed. Alexander George (Boulder, Colo.: Westview, 1983).

[11]John J. Maresca, "Helsinki Accord, 1975," in *U.S.–Soviet Security Cooperation*, ed. Alexander L. George et. al.(New York: Oxford University Press, 1988), pp. 106–122.

[12]International Institute for Strategic Studies, *Strategic Survey 1975* (London: IISS, 1976), p. 53.

[13]See, for instance, Warren G. Nutter, *Kissinger's Grand Design* (Washington D.C.: American Enterprise Institute, 1975); and Roger Morris, *Uncertain Greatness* (New York: Harper & Row, 1977).

[14]William Fulbright, *Arrogance of Power* (New York: Random House, 1966).

[15]Henry Kissinger, *White House Years*, p. 1255. This passage comes from a chapter in which Kissinger argues that these campaign exaggerations were not crucial in weakening détente.

[16]John Gaddis, *Strategies of Containment* (New York: Oxford University Press, 1982).

[17]Gerald R. Ford, "Imperiled, Not Imperial," *Time, November 10, 1980*.

[18]Kissinger, *White House Years*, p. 26.

[19]For a discussion of these issues, see I. M. Destler, "National Security Advice to U.S. Presidents: Some Lessons from Thirty Years," *World Politics* (January 1977).

[20]Kissinger, *White House Years*, p. 30.

[21]Nixon, *In the Arena*, p. 327.

[22]For a summary of Kissinger's views before going to Washington, see Stephen R. Graubard, *Kissinger: Portrait of a Mind* (New York: Norton, 1973); and John Stoessinger, *Henry Kissinger: The Anguish of Power* (New York: Norton, 1976).

[23]I. M. Destler, "Can One Man Do?" *Foreign Policy* (Winter 1971–1972).

[24]Morris, *Uncertain Greatness*, pp. 120–131 and 271.

[25]Tad Szulc, *The Illusion of Peace* (New York: Viking, 1978), pp. 77 and 579.

[26]Steven Ambrose, *Richard Nixon: The Education of a Politician* (New York: Simon & Schuster, 1982), p. 9.

[27]Bryce Harlow, "The Man and the Political Leader,", in *The Nixon Presidency*, ed. Kenneth W. Thompson (Lanham, Md.: University Press of America, 1987), p. 9.

[28]John Erlichmann, *Witness to Power* (New York: Simon & Schuster, 1982).

[29]Henry Kissinger, *Years of Upheaval* (Boston: Little, Brown, 1982), p. 7.

Chapter 6

Carter
and the
Panama Canal Treaties

THE LEGACY OF 1903

When Jimmy Carter was inaugurated as president of the United States in January 1977 and took his famous walk down Pennsylvania Avenue, the question of revising the existing treaties governing the Panama Canal was already more than twenty years old. It had been a serious issue for all five of Carter's immediate White House predecessors—from Dwight Eisenhower to Gerald Ford. For the people of Panama, it had been an issue much longer than that.

In 1903, the government of Colombia rejected an American offer to build a canal across the Central American isthmus, which was then under Colombian jurisdiction. Shortly thereafter, the citizens of Panama, the small Colombian province that occupied the narrow piece of territory between the Atlantic and the Pacific, revolted against the central government and formed an independent republic. It did so with the good wishes of policymakers in Washington and the assistance of eight American naval vessels. Within weeks of the Panamanian declaration of independence, a treaty was signed between the United States and the new nation giving the American government the right to build a canal across its territory and perpetual rights to administer both the canal and the lands adjacent to it.

The actual negotiation of the treaty was a matter of some dispute because the Republic of Panama was represented by a Frenchman, Philippe Bunau-Varilla, who had a financial stake in the construction of the canal and only vaguely defined authority to negotiate on behalf of the new Central American nation. When Panamanian leaders arrived in Washington and read the terms of what Bunau-Varilla had committed them to, which included a virtual grant of American sovereignty within the proposed Canal Zone, they refused to accept it. Bunau-Varilla then warned them that American protection, essential to the existence of their new nation, would be withdrawn unless they agreed to the negotiated terms. It is unlikely that

Bunau-Varilla made this threat with the knowledge or permission of the American government. The Frenchman, it would seem, was equally at home representing, or misrepresenting, both sides in these highly irregular international transactions. As a result of its questionable history, and the extraordinary powers granted to the United States over a ten-mile-wide strip of land that cuts across the center of Panama, the treaty has been resented by the Panamanian people from its inception.[1]

After the Second World War, in an era of worldwide decolonization, it became increasingly difficult for the United States to justify its relations with Panama. As nationalism within that country gathered strength, it brought with it vehement, and occasionally violent, anti-Americanism. In regional and global forums, Panamanian complaints about American imperialism received serious attention, interfering with the ability of American diplomats to win support for international initiatives in Latin America and the United Nations. All of this was occurring at the same time that the military significance of the canal was diminishing. In the decades after World War II, the United States elected to maintain large naval forces in both the Atlantic and the Pacific, including significant numbers of vessels permanently on patrol in the waters near Europe and the Far East. American naval power was kept close to those places on the globe where it might be needed quickly. As a result, for most foreseeable military contingencies, we no longer depended on an ability to rapidly transit the isthmus of Panama. Furthermore, by the 1960s, some of our most important warships—modern aircraft carriers and nuclear submarines—were either too large or too vulnerable to make effective use of a long and narrow canal. In an age of atomic weapons and intercontinental ballistic missiles, the canal itself was vulnerable to a Soviet nuclear attack from which there could be no effective defense.

International opposition to colonialism, a growing Panamanian nationalism, and a declining military significance for the canal all tended to make some modification of the 1903 treaty likely in the 1950s or 1960s. But while experts in international relations and Latin American affairs were able to recognize these trends and to begin thinking about new agreements between Panama and the United States, the American people and their representatives in Congress resisted efforts to change the status of our long-standing arrangements with Panama. In 1955, a number of revisions in the 1903 treaty were approved in Washington and Panama City, but they involved no fundamental changes. In 1958 and again in 1959, riots in Panama drew attention to the growing Panamanian dissatisfaction with the existing situation. The Eisenhower administration hoped to ease tensions between the two countries with a symbolic concession. Beginning in September 1960, a single Panamanian flag was to be flown within the Canal Zone at a prominent location near Panama City. Congress overwhelmingly and immediately condemned this decision, and a pattern of congressional resistance to executive concessions, a pattern that would remain unchanged for the next two decades, was established.[2]

In the winter of 1964, flag flying was again at the center of controversy in the Canal Zone. Because of sensitivity naturally surrounding symbols of sovereignty close to the canal, American administrators had previously banned the flying of either the Panamanian or American flag at schools and other public buildings within the zone. When a group of American students raised the Stars and Stripes outside their high school, violent demonstrations followed, resulting in more than twenty deaths and more than a hundred injuries. The rioting in 1964 also led to a temporary breakdown in diplomatic relations between the United States and Panama, and eventually a promise from President Johnson to reexamine the treaty issue. The subsequent negotiations were not very productive. In 1967, U.S. negotiators were prepared to accept a plan turning over control of the canal, with certain conditions, to the citizens of Panama; but when news of this proposal leaked, a public uproar in both Panama and the United States blocked any further progress.

Negotiations did not resume until Lyndon Johnson had been replaced by Richard Nixon and the government in Panama had been overthrown in a coup. The new Panamanian leader, General Omar Torrijos, continued discussions with the United States; and in 1974, during the Ford administration, Henry Kissinger and Panamanian Foreign Minister Juan Tack established the basic framework from which the 1977 treaties would emerge. Their agreements called for a new treaty to replace the 1903 document, ending U.S. "sovereignty" in the Canal Zone and granting Panamanian control of the canal after a transition period during which both nations would share responsibility for its administration. Efforts to convert the Kissinger-Tack formula into a treaty broke down for the same reason that earlier attempts by Eisenhower and Johnson to compromise with Panama also broke down—domestic political pressure. In 1976, Gerald Ford was fighting an uphill battle to win the presidential nomination from his own political party; and his principal opponent, Ronald Reagan, was getting applause every time he raised the issue of the canal. "We built it," Reagan told his cheering audiences, "we paid for it, it's ours, and we should tell Torrijos and company that we are going to keep it."[3] Gerald Ford eventually won his nomination, but he put off any resolution of the Panama question until after the election, an election he would lose.

Throughout the postwar years, when decisions about national flags, periodic rioting, and talk about renegotiation of the 1903 agreement briefly received public attention in the United States, opposition within the Congress and among the American people to any changes in the status of the canal was clearly evident. That opposition was bipartisan, including Democrats as well as Republicans, liberal labor unions as well as conservative patriotic organizations. The canal was, for its supporters, both a substantive and an emotional issue. Some worried about whether Panamanians could operate the canal; others saw dangers of a communist takeover in Central America. Many feared that the commerce traveling through the canal, or its occasional use by the U.S. Navy, or the safety of the Americans living and working in the Canal Zone would be threatened by any changes in the 1903 agreement.

For other supporters of the canal, the issue touched broader and more fundamental questions. American history textbooks for generations had described the canal as a triumph of American ingenuity, which it was. Europeans had failed in their various attempts to build a waterway across the isthmus, defeated by engineering problems they could not solve and tropical diseases they could not cure. Where the French and British failed, Americans succeeded. We built the canal, discovered the cause of yellow fever, and gave the American people a lasting source of national pride. That pride was a powerful political force, particularly when it was coupled with a fear that the power we demonstrated in building the canal might be waning. The Panama Canal was not only a symbol of past glories, it was also a symbol of future uncertainties. Would an America defeated in Vietnam be able to maintain control within "our" own hemisphere? Would we respond forcefully to the demands of an increasingly hostile third world? By 1976, the opposition to changes in America's relations with Panama was both more widespread and more deeply felt than many political observers realized. In the next three years the newly elected president from Georgia would be frequently, and painfully, reminded about exactly how strong that opposition had become.

In the 1976 presidential campaign Jimmy Carter tried to avoid making the canal a major issue. He told a reporter during the campaign that he "would not relinquish practical control of the Panama Canal Zone any time in the foreseeable future," but he also endorsed the Democratic party platform that expressed approval of the Kissinger-Tack principles.[4] By the time Carter had become president-elect, his views on Panama had changed and he was anxious to pursue the completion of the negotiations. He had learned about the 1903 treaty and the history of American relations with Panama, and he wanted to bring about a change in those relations. "We needed," he says in his memoirs, "to correct an injustice."[5] During the transition, the president-elect and his appointed foreign policy advisers decided to make the Panama Canal an early administration priority.[6] Sol Linowitz, a prominent expert on Latin American affairs and former ambassador to the Organization of American States, was appointed the president's special representative to the treaty negotiations. Because the appointment was for a relatively brief period, it required no Senate confirmation and thus no early confrontation with the Congress over canal policies. There would be ample opportunity for such confrontation as soon as the treaty was ready for Senate ratification.

NEGOTIATING WITH THE PANAMANIANS

The story of the Carter administration's actions in connection with the Panama Canal is really two different stories—a series of negotiations with representatives from the Republic of Panama and a subsequent series of negotiations with the Senate of the United States. The second of these negotiations was by far the more difficult, but the anticipated difficulties in dealing with the Senate made it imperative that the negotiations with Panama be completed as quickly as possible and that the final result of those negotiations be a treaty with at least some chance of receiving Senate approval.

The core of the problem in the negotiations was coming up with a way to satisfy Panama's basic demands—an end to American sovereignty in the zone, ownership of the canal, and freedom from American intervention—while at the same time satisfying legitimate American interests in keeping the canal open for the movement of international commerce and free from outside military domination. Johnson and Ford had already conceded to the Panamanian demands for eventual control of the canal and zone; what remained to be decided was when that control would be given and what rights the United States would have to defend the canal after Panamanian control began and during any period of transition that might be established. It was almost impossible to state those American rights without offending Panamanian nationalism; but leaving them out would have made the treaty completely unacceptable to the United States Senate. The problem for American negotiators was to find a workable agreement that would not include too much "offensive" or "unacceptable" language. They had their work cut out for them. They also had some obvious deadlines. They hoped to complete their negotiations so that Senate ratification could take place as soon as possible, well before the congressional elections of 1978. If it was obviously going to be hard for the Senate to approve the treaties, it would only get harder in the shadow of an upcoming election. A more artificial deadline was the expiration of Linowitz's appointment, which was used effectively to put pressure on Panama to resolve the final issues.

When Linowitz accepted Carter's temporary appointment, he joined Ellsworth Bunker, a senior American diplomat who had negotiated with Panama in both the Nixon and Ford administrations. Together they held a series of meetings with Panamanian officials in the winter of 1976–77 and the spring and summer of 1977. All the while they were carefully cultivating contacts with American senators whose advice they needed in establishing the limits of what would be politically acceptable in the ratification process. The American negotiators were given rather broad latitude to resolve differences with the Panamanians as they saw fit, providing that the final result was, in Carter's words, "generous, fair and appropriate."[7]

The key decision made by the negotiators was to divide the agreements between the United States and Panama into two separate treaties. One, the "Neutrality" Treaty, would deal with American concerns regarding the security of the canal and the preservation of the free movement of international commerce. [Document 6.1] This agreement would make it legitimate for the United States to use military force against a foreign power that attempted to close the canal; it would also have an indefinite duration and thus a painful resemblance to the tainted treaty of 1903. The other agreement, the "Panama Canal "Treaty, would deal with the return of the canal and zone to Panama and with the complicated administrative arrangements that would be in effect during the transition from American to Panamanian control. [Document 6.2] Linowitz and Bunker insisted that the neutrality questions be resolved first and canal administration issues second. This was difficult for the Panamanians to accept, but essential to the Senate, which would consider the agreements in the same order.

Throughout their early negotiations with Panama, Linowitz and Bunker could not be sure that their Panamanian counterparts were seriously committed to the negotiations. While all Panamanian nationalists wanted changes in the 1903 agreements, there were real political dangers for any Panamanian politician who entered into talks with the American government and failed to achieve all that might be expected. Opposition to American control of the canal and zone was passionate in Panama, and compromising with the Americans was a tricky political business. Progress in the negotiations, in the final analysis, depended on a recognition that both General Torrijos and President Carter were willing to take real risks in order to resolve the differences between their two countries. There was a natural uneasiness in the early negotiations as each side attempted to judge how far the other was willing to go. Would Torrijos compromise with "Yankee imperialists"? Would Carter fight domestic opposition from those who complained that he was giving away "our" canal?

Throughout the months of discussions in Panama and Washington, there were both breakthroughs and setbacks. By May, the basic framework of the Neutrality Treaty had been established and there was general optimism that the negotiations would succeed. The proposed language for the first agreement would guarantee the permanent neutrality of the canal, provide assurances that it would be open to all nations equally and at all times, and that the warships of both Panama and the United States would be permitted to transit the canal "expeditiously." This significant success was almost immediately followed by a serious setback. The Panamanian negotiators shocked their American counterparts by demanding huge payments from the United States, amounts in excess of $6 billion. The money was needed, they argued, as reimbursement for the decades of revenue Panama had lost while the canal and the zone were under American control. Linowitz explained that "it was wholly unrealistic to think that Congress would appropriate American taxpayers' money for the purpose of persuading the Panamanians to take away 'our' canal."[8] In the end, Linowitz's view would prevail and Panama would settle for increased revenues from the operation of the canal and a package of economic assistance made up of the normal kinds of American support for developing countries. Publicity surrounding the Panamanian demands, and the impression that they were attempting to extort large sums of money from the United States, did little to speed completion of the negotiations and gave treaty opponents added ammunition.

In the course of the negotiations, Carter's representatives agreed to reduce the transition period that had been contemplated in earlier discussions with the Johnson and Ford administrations from fifty years to less than twenty-five. The new Panama Canal Treaty would expire on December 31, 1999, and full Panamanian control of the canal would begin thereafter. During the remainder of the twentieth century, the United States would have primary responsibility for the protection and defense of the canal, but promised not to increase the numbers of its armed forces stationed in Panama. Control of the Canal Zone would revert to Panama as soon as the new treaty went into force, and Panamanian flags would fly throughout the zone. Special provisions were made for the fair treatment of American canal employees and their property and for the adjudication of disputes that might arise. Finally, the United States agreed not to build a new sea-level canal across Central America (an idea that was occasionally considered) without Panamanian concurrence.

All of this was agreed to only after extensive and, sometimes bitter, discussions. Delays continued to occur. Some were caused by misleading press reports that made one side nervous about the sincerity of the other. Additional problems arose from the negotiation, and renegotiation, of a multitude of minor details regarding the transfer of authority in the zone and the organizations that administered the canal. Panamanian translations of American proposals into Spanish often resulted in significantly different treaty language, reopening debate on issues that were thought to be resolved. Even on the last days of his temporary tenure as a negotiator, Linowitz was not sure that final agreement could be reached. On August 9, the day before his appointment officially ended, he called the White House suggesting that a press release be prepared explaining that the attempt to draft new treaties had failed and that Panama had refused to accept generous American terms. Within hours after making that call, a final round of negotiations and meetings with Torrijos produced a rapid resolution of the remaining differences between the two sides. Another call to the White House led to the preparation of a very different press release.

NEGOTIATING WITH THE CONGRESS

President Carter had played a relatively small role in the Panama Canal treaty negotiations. He and his senior cabinet officers, after reaching an early decision to make the canal a priority issue, gave broad discretion to the diplomats who dealt with Panama.[9] When Carter greeted Linowitz and Bunker on the White House lawn after their final, and successful, round of negotiations, he had not yet read the agreements to which he had been committed.[10] By Linowitz's account, though Carter was kept generally informed about the progress that was being made, only two minor issues toward the end of the negotiations required his personal attention.[11] Carter's involvement in the next stage of the treaty process—seeking the approval of two thirds of the members of the Senate—would be different. It would command enormous amounts of his time, energy, and political skill, and even with those efforts it would succeed by only the narrowest of margins.

The first action taken by the Carter administration was to lobby for time. The president and his advisers asked senators not to decide one way or the other on the canal issue until they had heard all the facts. There was a real possibility that the treaties could be defeated before they even came up for formal consideration. Public opinion polls in the summer of 1977 showed that 78 percent of the American people were against the treaties;[12] and treaty opponents, who had already mobilized their forces, were urging senators to renounce the newly negotiated agreements. In May 1977, months before the treaties were even signed, a professional survey indicated that twenty-five senators would definitely vote against ratification.[13] That number was dangerously large. The Constitution requires that treaties be ratified by two thirds of the senators voting. With all one hundred senators in attendance, thirty-four nays would be enough to kill the agreements; sixty-seven yeas were necessary to pass them. The administration needed all the time it could get to work out the daunting arithmetic of ratification.

The problems facing the administration in its campaign to win Senate approval had been foreseen. As early as April 1977, when progress in the negotiations made the completion of canal agreements likely, Hamilton Jordan, the political strategist who had put together Carter's remarkably successful bid for the 1976 Democratic nomination, was making plans for the Senate battle.[14] Jordan believed that the consistent majorities of Americans who were opposed to the new treaties with Panama in public opinion polls were actually shallow majorities. He hoped that a massive educational campaign could turn public opinion around, or at least move the negative numbers in the polls enough to permit wavering senators to go along with the president's wishes. He proposed the organization of a White House task force that would coordinate the administration's educational endeavors, focusing particular attention on the opinion and community leaders in those states whose senators were open to persuasion.

In the months that followed, literally thousands of Americans were invited to visit the White House to hear briefings on the treaties given by Linowitz, Bunker, Secretary of State Cyrus Vance, National Security Adviser Zbigniew Brzezinski, Secretary of Defense Harold Brown, Chairman of the Joint Chiefs of Staff General George Brown, and, very often, the president of the United States. A spectacular ceremony was scheduled for September 7, where eighteen Latin American heads of state witnessed the formal signing of the treaties by Carter and Torrijos. Endorsements for the agreements were sought, and won, from Gerald Ford, Henry Kissinger, Dean Rusk, John Wayne, and William F. Buckley, Jr. A committee of prominent citizens was formed to work for treaty ratification. On two occasions, Carter spoke to the American people in nationally televised "fire-side chats." By administration count, more than 1,500 personal appearances were made by treaty supporters in speaking engagements all across the country.[15] Trips were arranged for senators who wished to visit Panama. Before the ratification process had ended, almost half the Senate had gone to see the canal and General Torrijos for themselves.

Toward the end of the national debate, the White House task force began to work closely with those businesses that were dependent on the commerce that daily passed through the canal. It was widely understood by military experts, though rarely emphasized in public statements, that the canal could easily be closed by a few disgruntled Panamanians. Many of its locks were located in remote terrain and were vulnerable to the kinds of explosives readily available to terrorists throughout the world. When asked in Senate hearings to estimate the number of troops needed to defend the canal against a hostile Panamanian population, General Brown answered that it would take at least 100,000. Even that number of American armed forces might have been insufficient to protect the canal from sabotage or guerrilla attack. Throughout the Panama Canal debates there was a problem, as one White House staff member would later note, of putting across what was a counterintuitive argument—the best way to defend the canal was to give it to the Panamanians.[16] To some extent, the task force found the right audience for that argument when they began talking to those who had the most to lose from a sabotaged canal.

All of this activity by the administration did not mean that the battle to win ratification was clearly being won in the fall and winter of 1977. As a matter of fact, reports from the field were mixed. An administration count in December showed forty-five solid Senate votes for ratification, a big improvement in the level of support that had existed when the treaties were signed but well short of the sixty-seven that were needed.[17] Efforts to change public opinion were also mixed. Jordan's expectation that the public opposition to the treaties was shallow was turning out to be questionable. Polls did vary, and depending on how the question was asked, it was possible to find dramatic changes from the percentages that were recorded in the summer of 1977, but many citizens who were willing to go along with the treaties did so with little enthusiasm.[18] Just the opposite was true of the hard-core treaty opponents. They were highly motivated and did much more than oppose the treaties whenever they were interviewed by pollsters. They sent money to the organizations that were pledged to fight ratification and wrote letters and telegrams to their senators in numbers that no politician could easily ignore. Treaty opponents had their own list of well-known spokesmen, including Ronald Reagan, several former members of the Joint Chiefs of Staff and many leading conservative legislators—Jesse Helms, Philip Crane, Barry Goldwater, and Strom Thurmond. They also had a growing array of arguments against ratification.

The first of their arguments was a constitutional challenge. Several members of the House of Representatives who were opposed to the treaties went to court to block ratification. Their case was based on Article IV, Section 3, of the Constitution, which says that Congress (both houses) has the right to regulate and dispose of federal property. [Document 6.3] This clause, they argued, required action by the House of Representatives before the canal or the zone could be turned over to Panama. Other language in the Constitution giving the Senate the treaty ratification power and making treaties the supreme law of the land were regarded by most legal experts as sufficiently clear to make the Senate, and not the Congress as a whole, the legislative body that would decide the fate of the canal and zone. But even though the legal argument raised by members of the House was weak, it took months to resolve and an unsuccessful appeal to the Supreme Court before the issue was finally set aside. In the meantime, other objections to the treaties were raised.

News reports on September 16, 1977 claimed that the treaty-negotiating sessions had been bugged by the CIA and that Panamanian discovery of this fact had led to successful efforts to blackmail the American negotiators. Though there had been a clumsy attempt by someone to bug one of the negotiating sites, the rest of the story was speculation. Later allegations were made that members of Torrijos' family were involved in international narcotics transactions. In an extraordinary closed session of the Senate, administration officials revealed information they had about drug dealing in Panama. Though that information must have included damaging revelations about many officials in Panama, most senators were apparently satisfied that Torrijos was not directly involved in these activities. The bugging and drug accusations damaged ratification prospects, and when rumors were not making negative headlines, true stories were.

One of the biggest problems for the administration's ratification campaign was what went on in the Panamanian ratification debates. In Panama the treaty was put before the people in a national plebiscite scheduled for the end of October. Torrijos had made some painful compromises with the United States, particularly the language in the Neutrality Treaty that gave the United States the right to defend the canal after the year 2000 and preferential canal passage for American warships. Enthusiastic Panamanian officials trying to win popular support for the treaties gave speeches denying that the objectionable language existed or offering interpretations of the treaties that were wildly different from what Linowitz and Bunker had understood during the negotiations. Given the political interest in the issue, Panamanian speeches quickly found their way into American headlines, creating a crisis for the administration's public relations campaign. On October 14, at a hastily scheduled meeting between Carter and Torrijos, a statement was issued providing common interpretations of the most disputed treaty language. [Document 6.4] On the question of priority use of the canal for military vessels, Carter and Torrijos restated the provisions of the Neutrality Treaty, adding the clarification that in emergencies American naval vessels could "go to the head of the line." On the more controversial question of American military action to guarantee the canal's neutrality, both leaders agreed that action to defend the canal would be taken "in accordance with their respective constitutional processes," but that rights to defend the canal and keep it open to international passage should not be interpreted as "a right of intervention of the United States in the internal affairs of Panama."[19] This statement settled some of the interpretation problems in connection with the treaties and earned the administration a bit more time to make its case.

Throughout the second half of 1977, the administration focused its attention on key senators, legislators who held leadership positions or were so widely respected in the Senate that their support would tend to influence others. The administration needed the endorsement of Senate majority leader Robert Byrd and, after a long delay, got it in January 1978. Even more, it needed the support of prominent moderate Republicans and made special efforts to win the approval of Howard Baker, the Senate minority leader. Baker, like many of his colleagues, went to Panama in the fall of 1977. There he met with Torrijos and carried out his own private diplomatic negotiations. Baker came away from his meetings with Torrijos willing to vote for the treaties but only if the agreed-upon interpretations that Carter and Torrijos had announced on October 14 were incorporated into the text of the treaties. This was an important issue because Senate modification of treaties raises a number of controversies and complications.

The Senate has the right to give its "advice and consent" with regard to treaties in a variety of ways beyond merely voting to accept or reject them. It can offer amendments to the language of treaty documents. Such amendments usually require the concurrence of the other nations that have signed the treaty, and if that concurrence is not forthcoming may lead to rejection of the agreements. Opponents to the Panama Canal treaties would, in the course of Senate deliberations, offer dozens of so-called "killer" amendments, changes in treaty text that the Panamanians would clearly find unacceptable. Baker's amendments, which he offered in cosponsorship with Byrd, were not "killers" because they used language that was similar to that contained in the October 14 Carter-Torrijos statement, which the Panamanian people had seen before their plebiscite on October 23. Senators may also offer amendments to the treaty approval resolution. Such amendments, variously referred to as "understandings," or "conditions," or "reservations," are not made part of the treaty text and therefore have an ambiguous status in international law. They may, however, be politically important because they put the Senate on record regarding its interpretation of treaty documents. Whether understandings, conditions, or reservations—like amendments—need to be ratified by all parties to a treaty is not clear and would become a serious problem for Panamanian politicians during the finals days of Senate deliberations.

With Senators Byrd and Baker on board and their proposed amendments approved in February, the prospects for ratification were improving. On February 3, by a vote of 14 to 1, the Senate Foreign Relations Committee sent the treaties to the Senate floor. As floor debate began on the Neutrality Treaty, the president and his staff continued to lobby the remaining undecided senators. Throughout this period, Carter kept a notebook on his desk with information about each member of the Senate, whether he or she had a publicly announced position on the treaties, what contacts the administration had had with the senator and the leaders of his or her state, and what the president might say to persuade a particular senator. He called senators frequently and met with them in his office. As the Senate vote on the Neutrality Treaty got closer, the intensity of presidential lobbying increased proportionately, and the president faced difficult questions regarding how far he would go to win Senate approval. Accusations were widely made regarding "horse-trading" of various sorts in the final days of Senate deliberations on both the Neutrality and Panama Canal treaties. Senator Richard Schweiker, who voted against ratification, claimed that the best way to get a new bridge or federal project for your state was to remain undecided on the Panama question as long as possible.[20] Though it is always hard to document this kind of quid pro quo, Carter does mention in his memoirs that an Oklahoma desalinization plant, important to Senator Henry Bellmon, received last-minute presidential approval. In the final days of the ratification debate Carter notes, "I was not taking any chances."[21] The interests and concerns of all the undecided senators received special attention.

Senator James Abourezk of South Dakota negotiated with the administration for a change in energy policy that was particularly important to him. He did not get the president to endorse the energy policies he wanted, but by linking them to his Panama vote he did get national publicity for the positions he favored. Senator

James Sasser of Tennessee got an invitation to a White House country music concert where, according to Carter, "Tom T. Hall, Loretta Lynn, Conway Twitty, Larry Gatlin, and Charlie Daniels proved to be a lot of help to me and Panama."[22] Senator Samuel Hayakawa of California, a former college professor, was persuaded to vote for the treaties only after the president took the time to read his textbook on semantics and promised to meet regularly with him to discuss foreign policy issues. Several of the undecided senators could not be won over with federal funding or presidential favors; their votes came only after the administration agreed to support substantive amendments to the ratification resolution.

Carter very much needed and wanted the support of the two senators representing his home state of Georgia. Sam Nunn and Herman Talmadge finally agreed to support the treaties after receiving administration endorsement for an amendment they favored. The Nunn-Talmadge reservation addressed an issue not covered in the treaties, whether the United States would continue to have military bases in Panama after December 31, 1999. Senator Nunn, a respected expert on defense issues, wanted it made clear that nothing in the treaties would preclude a subsequent agreement between the United States and Panama to provide for American military bases in Panama in the twenty-first century. Carter went along with this modest change and won at least two critical votes for the treaties. He also endorsed minor understandings, conditions, and reservations put forward by other senators.

The line between innocuous amendments that could easily be given administration approval and substantive changes in the treaties that would threaten their acceptability to the Panamanians was not always easy to draw. Toward the end of the Senate debate the amendment process produced some serious dilemmas. As the number of senators committed to ratification grew closer to the magic number, sixty-seven, the president and the media turned their attention to the few remaining senators who did not have a firm public position on the treaties. One of them, Dennis DeConcini, serving in his first term as senator from the state of Arizona, proposed a controversial reservation.[23] It was not intended to be a "killer" amendment, but if it did not kill the treaties, it put them in critical condition. [Document 6.5]

DeConcini wanted to be blunt about American rights to defend the canal from domestic disturbances within Panama. His reservation was designed to make it clear that if the canal was closed or interfered with, the United States, acting independently, would have the right to "use military force in Panama." It was obvious that if the United States was going to defend the neutrality of the canal, such a defense might well involve the use of American armed forces in Panama. That was, after all, where the canal was located. DeConcini's reservation added little to the Neutrality Treaty that was not already there. The problem was that he wanted to be precise and explicit about what had previously been vague and implied. He was raising a sensitive issue, coming close to saying that the United States could intervene in Panama's domestic politics.

In one of the earlier White House briefings, the president's national security adviser had been asked what would happen after the year 2000 if the Panamanian government announced, without warning or justification, that the canal was being closed down for repairs. Brzezinski's answer was, "In that case, according to the Neutrality Treaty, we will move in and close down the Panamanian government for repairs."[24] This reply was understandably popular with those who were concerned about defense of the canal, but it also touched the exposed nerves of Panamanian nationalism. It was one thing for Brzezinski to answer a hypothetical question with an idea that was offensive to the Panamanians, it was something very different to make that idea a formal reservation to the treaties. Treaty language had intentionally been left ambiguous on the question of American military action in Panama after the year 2000. Carter and Torrijos had agreed in October that the United States claimed no right to intervene in the internal affairs of Panama, but the Neutrality Treaty gave both nations considerable leeway in defending the canal. Which was it to be, implied powers to take whatever action would be needed to keep the canal open, or explicit language that American military force could be used in Panama?

Efforts to persuade DeConcini to soften the language of his reservation failed, and the administration was forced to decide between going along with the Arizona senator's provocative language, which was supported by several other undecided senators, or risk losing the ratification battle. This was perhaps the most difficult decision in the entire ratification contest and there was very little time to make it. The president reluctantly accepted DeConcini's reservation. The stage was then set for final Senate action. On March 16, after twenty-two days of floor debate, broadcast live on public radio in the United States and in Panama, after hundreds of pages of committee hearings, the introduction of 192 proposed changes, 88 of which were voted upon, the roll call was taken. The count was sixty-eight senators in favor; thirty-two against. The administration had won approval for the Neutrality Treaty.

This hard-won victory did not, of course, put the Panama question to rest. The administration still needed Senate approval of the Panama Canal Treaty and legislation passed by both houses of Congress to implement some of the specific provisions in the two treaties. The DeConcini reservation complicated matters considerably. Torrijos was infuriated by the DeConcini language and threatened to withdraw his endorsement of the treaties. The Panamanian people had overwhelmingly approved the agreements in their October plebiscite, but now some Panamanian officials claimed that a new national vote would be necessary because of DeConcini's reservation, and this time the government might urge the people to vote against the treaties. Once again direct communication between Carter and Torrijos was needed to buy time for further negotiations. Special reservations for the second treaty were prepared that had the effect of weakening the DeConcini language. This had to be done delicately because both DeConcini and Torrijos were needed to bring the treaty ratification process to a successful conclusion. Hamilton Jordan, the president's personal adviser, went to Panama to calm Torrijos' fears, while Senate leaders put extraordinary pressure on DeConcini to accept some compromise. On April 18, the second Senate vote was taken and the result was identical to the first, sixty-eight to thirty-two. [Document 6.6]

Still the Panama issue did not go away. After the elections of 1978, the political costs of voting for the Panama canal "giveaway" were evident. Twenty senators who voted in favor of the treaties were up for reelection in 1978; only seven were returned to Washington to serve another term.[25] That political message slowed congressional approval for the implementing legislation, which was passed three days before the treaties went into effect. After decades of Panamanian humiliation under the terms of 1903, after years of serious bilateral negotiations, after months of ratification debate and still more months of legislative haggling over implementation, a new relationship was established between Panama and the United States on October 1, 1979.

CONCLUSIONS

POWER

Unlike some other chapters in this book, this case does not describe agonizing presidential decision making. Carter had no difficulty making up his mind on the central policy questions in connection with the Panama Canal. From the outset of his administration the president made it clear that he wanted to renegotiate the 1903 treaty and that he wanted the new arrangements governing the canal and zone to be fair and generous. For the most part he allowed his negotiators to work out the detailed treaty language that would accomplish these purposes. The challenge for the president in this case was not making a decision, but building a legislative coalition in support of an unpopular foreign policy initiative. In doing this, Carter confronted one of the major constitutional obstacles created by the Founders to check the independence of the executive in foreign affairs. Not only must presidents seek the advice and consent of the Senate before treaties become law, they must also win the approval of an extraordinary majority within that legislative body.

Given Carter's experience with the Panama treaties, it may be worthwhile to raise a question about whether the constitutional requirement for a two-thirds Senate majority on treaty ratification serves our nation well. Throughout American history, treaties have repeatedly been the source of bitter and divisive struggles between presidents and senators. George Washington encountered partisan resistance to agreements he thought necessary between the United States and Great Britain. Woodrow Wilson spent his last healthy months in the White House in a valiant, and ultimately unsuccessful, effort to win Senate endorsement for the treaty ending the First World War and creating the League of Nations. Jimmy Carter, later in his administration, would have to withdraw from Senate consideration a controversial SALT II arms control agreement with the Soviet Union because, at the time, it faced nearly certain defeat. Serious scholars and commentators have wondered, in response to these cases and others, about the wisdom of the two-thirds rule.[26] Are treaties so important that they must be approved by more than a simple majority of senators? Can the United States afford the inconvenience and embarrassment of having its duly elected presidents negotiate and sign international agreements only to have them rejected in a later stage of our democratic process? Do members of Congress have the time and expertise to make informed judgments on complicated and crucial matters of foreign policy?

Lloyd Cutler, who served as Carter's legal adviser during the last two years of his administration and took a leading role in efforts to mobilize Senate support for the SALT II agreements, saw the problems of treaty ratification from the president's perspective. Since leaving office, he has become a leading advocate of political reforms that would make it easier for the executive and legislative branches to work together in making foreign policy.[27] Cutler recommends that political parties be strengthened and that the terms of office for members of Congress be extended. House members would serve for four years and senators for eight, with all the representatives and half the senators running for office during presidential election years. He further proposes that members of Congress be permitted to serve in cabinet positions, and that the requirements for treaty ratification be changed to a 60 percent vote in the Senate or a simple majority in both houses.[28] The idea behind all of these changes is to make the two branches less separate than they have been in the past and more likely to feel part of the same government. These changes would not necessarily eliminate treaty ratification disputes, but they might make them less frequent and less divisive. Enacting Cutler's proposals would require amendments to the Constitution, which, like treaties, have to be approved by an extraordinary majority, two thirds of the Congress and three quarters of the state legislatures. As a result, there is little likelihood that such amendments will be adopted in the near future.

Even without constitutional amendments, presidents have, particularly since the Second World War, found a number of ways to circumvent the ratification process. Some presidents have signed treaties and then withheld them from Senate review in order to await a more favorable political climate. These unratified treaties have often been binding on the United States while they lingered in a legal limbo between branches of government. The SALT II Treaty, which never received a Senate vote, was treated for years as a binding limitation on American strategic deployments, until the Reagan administration formally renounced it in 1986.[29] Another way to avoid ratification debates, used extensively by postwar administrations, has been the negotiation of "executive agreements"—international obligations approved by the president without the advice and consent of the Senate. Between 1946 and 1976 more than 7,000 agreements were signed by the United States and foreign powers. Almost 95 percent of these were executive agreements requiring no Senate ratification.[30] Though many executive agreements involve minor issues and are negotiated pursuant to statutory authority which Congress knowingly grants to the executive branch, presidents have also used their power to negotiate executive agreements as a way of avoiding the politics of ratification. Jimmy Carter never proposed that the United States deal with the Panama issue by either of these methods. He wanted a permanent resolution of the problem, and there was no way to do that except by replacing the 1903 treaty with a new one; and there was no way to get a new treaty except by meeting the Constitution's demanding ratification requirements. In meeting those requirements the Carter administration obviously paid a very high political price. Perhaps the most important question raised by this case, in connection with the powers of the presidency, is whether that price was worth the prize it bought.

In considering that question, it is possible to look at what the ratification of the Panama Canal treaties tells us about presidential powers in two very different ways. From one perspective, this case shows what a determined president can do to get the Congress of the United States to carry out his policies in foreign affairs. Jimmy Carter did, after all, get the treaties he wanted ratified in the Senate and the enabling legislation for those treaties passed in both houses of Congress. He accomplished these objectives by using the full orchestra of presidential instruments of influence—the pomp and pageantry of an elaborate signing ceremony, the personal appeal of a party leader and chief executive asking individual legislators for their assistance, the active lobbying of the American people as a whole and the focused lobbying of commercial and opinion leaders in crucial states, the trading of executive favors for legislative votes, and the mobilization of the wide variety of people inside and outside government who were willing to offer their services in the ratification debate. All of this may be admired, particularly when one considers how low the odds of success were thought to be in 1977. But from another perspective, the difficulties that Carter overcame constitute proof of how weak the chief executive has become in the conduct of foreign affairs. That he had to resort to this sort of massive effort in order to achieve an objective of relatively minor importance in the overall scheme of world affairs suggests a presidency far less powerful than many believe it should be. Which is it, a powerful president able to move a reluctant Congress, or a painfully weak president spending his limited energies on a relatively unimportant foreign policy objective? How you answer that question depends, in part, on how important you believe the Panama Canal treaties to be and whether or not they were central to Carter's foreign policy agenda.

It is widely agreed by experts on Central America that without the new treaties America's ability to use and defend the canal would have deteriorated in the 1970s and beyond. On the day after the successful vote on the second treaty, Torrijos let it be known that had the vote gone the other way he would have closed the canal with military force.[31] Even if Torrijos had chosen to show restraint in that hypothetical situation, it would only have been a matter of time before dissatisfied Panamanians, within the government or without, elected to use violence against Americans and the canal. United States security interests in Central America could hardly have been served by a massive military buildup to protect an aging waterway. Given the problems the United States has had since 1978 in El Salvador and Nicaragua, it is hard to predict how we would have faired with yet another Central American crisis in the 1980s. The highly emotional response that many Americans had to questions concerning the canal suggests, however, that we would have been far more likely to use combat troops in Panama than we were willing to use them elsewhere in Central America.

The passage of the Panama Canal treaties did more than just prevent a potential Central American war. They also provided a symbol of a whole new American approach to Latin America and the third world. The treaties were generous and fair, just as Carter had directed, and they served as a message that the United States was no longer interested in real or imagined exploitation of the smaller and weaker nations in the hemisphere. Like Franklin Roosevelt's Good Neighbor policy and Kennedy's Alliance for Progress, the Panama Canal treaties inaugurated a new beginning for American relations with the nations of our region, or at least they could have. Linowitz points out in his memoirs that the administration failed to pursue this opportunity in the months that followed the ratification of the treaties, in part because the implementation votes lay ahead, and in part because the administration was thought to be so spent after its first battle in Panama that it had little energy to pursue the war that would have been necessary to bring about dramatic changes in American foreign policy.[32]

George Moffett, who worked in the Carter White House and later wrote an excellent book about the Panama treaties, explains why that war was never seriously fought. The American people were simply unwilling to support it. By 1977, the old cold war anticommunist foreign policy consensus had broken down in the aftermath of Vietnam and Watergate. Carter tried to build a new foreign policy consensus based on human rights and greater attention to "global" issues—nuclear proliferation, environmental quality, energy, arms sales and other problems confronting both the developed and the underdeveloped nations. Carter made a number of these global issues priority items on his foreign policy agenda and managed to produce some progress in a number of areas, particularly human rights. But although some of his policies in connection with global issues were popular, as a whole his foreign policy agenda failed to capture the public imagination. The victory in the battle over the Panama Canal treaties did not, therefore, mark the beginning of a new national consensus about international politics. In fact, it marked the opposite, the deepening of political divisions over foreign affairs. The treaties galvanized a patriotic right wing reaction against Carter that would contribute to the election of Ronald Reagan in 1980 and to a return to cold war foreign policy. At the end of his administration Carter himself would move away from his earlier emphasis on human rights and global politics in order to take a stronger and more traditional stand against Soviet aggression in Afghanistan. But by that time, Carter's administration, his party, and the public at large were divided over what direction American foreign policy should take. The early administration victory in the battle for ratification of the canal treaties was thus a victory not only against a reluctant Senate but also against a reluctant American public. In a democracy such victories are bound to be difficult.

PROCESS

How did the president win against such powerful forces? The process by which he built his temporary legislative coalition was one of the high points of the Carter administration. Carter won ratification for the Panama Canal treaties slowly, with the aid of carefully coordinated public lobbying. Unlike some presidents, Carter did not have the ability to make a single televised speech that would dramatically change public opinion. On an emotional issue like the canal there may have been no political communicator who had that ability. The president did make two TV presentations dealing with Panama, but they were not crucial parts of the administration's campaign for ratification. Instead, he focused his time and attention on convincing individual senators and the people at the state level who could influence their decisions.

Some senators were persuaded on the merits of the issue; some were fundamentally opposed from the outset and not susceptible to any persuasion; most prudently feared public opposition to the treaties and waited to see what the president would do. What he did was try to create a climate in which a vote for the treaties would not be an act of political suicide. Carter realized how unpopular the treaties were and consistently praised the courage of those who were willing to vote for them. Creating a favorable climate for the treaties, even for the courageous, was no easy task. The administration understood this, and aimed its message carefully, giving priority to the business and community leaders in the states of undecided senators. This strategy was dictated by the complexities of the canal issues. It took time to explain the military vulnerabilities of the canal and its locks. It took time to review the long history of Panamanian grievances and bipartisan negotiations. It took time to explain the subtleties and intricacies of the final treaty language. This was not an issue that could be condensed into a slogan (at least not for the proponents) or a series of thirty second clips on the evening news.

Telling the full story of why the Panama Canal treaties should be supported was, however, a time-consuming business, even if the message was directed to a narrowly selected audience. Carter was willing to invest that time and was reportedly very effective at the White House briefings. In winning support for the treaties in this way, he necessarily took himself away from other pressing matters. In his memoirs he notes the long list of issues that crossed his desk at the height of the ratification battle:

> ...a very serious nationwide coal strike, energy legislation, my upcoming trip to Latin America and Africa, a burgeoning crisis between Israel and Egypt plus an Israeli invasion of Lebanon, the United Nations Disarmament Conference, the midwinter Governors Conference, final approval of our complete urban program, a forthcoming trip by Brzezinski to China to work on normalization, war in the Horn of Africa, our proposals to prevent bankruptcy in New York City, negotiations with the British on air-transport agreements, a state visit by President Tito of Yugoslavia, final stages of the SALT negotiations, the Civil Service reform bill, the coming state visit of Prime Minister Takeo Fukuda of Japan, a decision about whether General Alexander Haig would stay on at NATO, F-15 airplane sales to Saudi Arabia, a visit by Israeli Defense Minister Ezer Weizman and preparations for an early visit by Prime Minister Begin, and a major defense speech at Wake Forest the day after the treaty vote.[33]

Those issues must have suffered from some presidential neglect during the ratification fight, for, as Carter confessed in his diary in March 1978, "It's hard to concentrate on anything except Panama."[34]

The president's staff and cabinet officers also made significant commitments of time and energy to the Panama lobbying effort. In what became a massive and well-coordinated endeavor, the Carter White House developed a particularly effective organization for getting their message across. The task force system of targeted White House briefings worked so well that shortly after the canal debates, the Carter White House created a permanent Office of Public Liaison that maintained a constant stream of White House visitors who heard substantive appeals on a variety of foreign and domestic policy initiatives. The president and his administration obviously did more than merely make their case to individual senators and influential citizens. They also did things that had nothing to do with the substance of the treaties. They massaged egos, traded votes, promised favors, put pressure on selected senators, cajoled Torrijos into staying calm, and, in general, did what needed to be done in order to win a two-thirds majority in the Senate. An administration frequently described as politically naive or inept may have made an error in making the treaties a priority issue, but once that decision was made, they showed real political skill in finding the right combination of arguments and actions to get sixty-eight senators to vote for two unpopular agreements.

Part of their success came, of course, from a willingness to compromise with the Senate, something that Woodrow Wilson had refused to do in his bid to win Senate approval for the Versailles Treaty. Those compromises varied in importance. The one with Senator Baker was constructive because it strengthened the treaties without going beyond what Torrijos was willing to accept. The compromise with Nunn on a secondary issue won an important vote at a reasonable price. DeConcini was another matter.

It is difficult to judge whether the negotiations over the DeConcini reservation were really about the substance of the treaties or DeConcini's desire to bask in the limelight as the last important uncommitted senator. There is also some question about whether the president should have been as personally involved in dealing with DeConcini as he was. Ironically, the very power of the presidency made it harder for the senator from Arizona to give ground. The more often he met with Carter and spoke with the reporters gathered on the White House lawn, the more important he became and the harder it was for him to relent on the language he had proposed. Relenting would have ended his access to presidential and media attention and made his amendment to the resolution of ratification only one of several that were passed without notice. Between the first and second treaty votes, the Senate leadership in private meetings apparently did better in dealing with DeConcini than the president had been able to do in their highly publicized encounters before the vote on the Neutrality Treaty.

PERSONALITY

Jimmy Carter never regretted the time and political capital invested in the Panama Canal treaties. He was sure that renegotiating the 1903 agreement was the right thing to do, whether the American public fully realized it or not. He believed that he had been elected to make the best decisions he could, and that, if he did so, the American people would respect his choices and reward him with reelection. This may sound a bit like a civics class cliché, but it also provides a fairly accurate description of Carter's personal political philosophy. One political scientist has labeled Carter a "trustee" president, defining a "trustee" as a political leader who sees himself representing the nation as a whole, rather than regional or organizational interests; an elected official who believes that he must exercise his own judgment about public policy, rather than follow current public opinion; a moralist concerned about corruption in politics who tries to do what is right, rather than what is expedient.[35] Carter is, in many ways, a classic trustee. Understanding what may have made him one requires an examination of the factors and events that shaped his personality and political career.

Raised in a religious family with a highly principled mother, Carter learned at an early age the importance of standing up for what one believes. Trained as an engineer, he developed skills in gathering facts, analyzing data, and finding the best solution for whatever problem was at hand. Apprenticed to a legendary taskmaster, Admiral Hyman Rickover, he learned to take on difficult assignments and strive to accomplish them. His revealing pre-presidential memoirs take their title from a Rickover admonition, "Why not the best?" To an unusual extent Carter's personal life and political career were full of obstacles that he single-handedly overcame and occasions when he was called upon to act as a guardian of the welfare of others.

After his father's death, when he gave up a promising career in the navy and took over the family business in Plains, he rescued it from near bankruptcy and built it into a prosperous enterprise. When he first entered public service, it was as a member of a county planning commission where he evaluated the proposals of developers and industrialists and tried to represent the broader environmental and community concerns. When he first sought elected office, he had to fight the corruption of a county courthouse politician who literally stole the primary election from him. When he served as Georgia's governor, he took an enlightened and progressive stand on racial issues, and pushed through the state legislature a series of administrative reforms that made state government more efficient and harder for special interests to influence. His political campaigns in general, and his run for the presidency in particular, were long shots begun with relatively little money, name recognition, or prospects for success. Carter's tenacity, hard work, honesty, and determination won out in almost all of his personal and political challenges and may have given him, and those around him, the impression that no task was too difficult.

Much that is central in Carter's personality and character can be seen in the actions he took in connection with the Panama Canal. It was completely in character for Carter to take on the Panama treaties early in his administration, even though conventional Washington wisdom had it that Panama was a second-term issue. It was also in character for Carter to devote his time to detailed briefings of senators and their influential constituents, believing that once the facts were known his position would prevail. It was completely in character for Carter to respond to the challenge of the long odds against ratification by redoubling his own efforts and refusing to back down. It was also in character for him to view the issue in terms of what was morally correct rather than what was momentarily popular. Carter was consistently enthusiastic about the rewriting of the Panama treaties. As his national security adviser observed, for Carter the issue "represented the ideal fusion of morality and politics; he was doing something good for peace, responding to the passionate desires of a small nation, and yet helping the long-range U.S. national interest."[36]

Six of the postwar presidents—Eisenhower, Kennedy, Johnson, Nixon, Ford, and Carter—found the Panama Canal on their foreign policy agendas. All of them took some steps toward reforming American relations with Panama, but all but one backed off when confronted with serious domestic opposition. Only Carter pursued the issue to its conclusion and produced a significant change. Those who believe that the new treaties represent an important accomplishment would have to conclude that Carter succeeded where his predecessors had failed. Those who believe that the price paid for the treaties in terms of domestic political rancor and lost opportunities was too high would have to conclude that Carter failed where his predecessors had succeeded in avoiding a controversial and costly issue. A large part of the explanation for either of these conclusions lies in the unusual ideas and idealism of our thirty-ninth president.

Chronology of the Panama Canal Treaties

1964

Jan 9   Riots in the Canal Zone over the flying of the U.S. flag.

Apr 3   Johnson administration begins renegotiation of the 1903 treaty.

1974

Feb 7   Agreement reached on Kissinger-Tack principles.

1977

Feb-Aug Negotiation of treaty provisions in Washington and Panama.

May 30   Panamanians issue demand for enormous U.S. payments.

Aug 10   Resolution of major issues announced by negotiators.

Sep 7   Elaborate signing ceremonies in Washington.

Oct 3   Members of the House go to court to block transfer of U.S. property to Panama unless approved by a vote in the House of Representatives.

Oct 14   Carter and Torrijos issue written agreement on interpretation of neutrality provisions.

Oct 23   Panamanian people approve treaty in plebiscite.

1978

Jan 30   Foreign Relations Committee sends treaties to the Senate floor.

Feb 1   Carter gives fireside chat on television.

Feb 8   Senate floor debate of Panama treaties begins.

Mar 13   Administration accepts Nunn-Talmadge reservation.

Mar 16   DeConcini amendment passed; Senate ratifies the Neutrality Treaty by vote of 68-32.

Apr 16   Court of Appeals rules that House of Representatives need not approve the transfer of the Canal Zone to Panama.

Apr 18   Senate ratifies Panama Canal Treaty by vote of 68–32.

Apr 19   Torrijos states that canal would have been closed by force if the Senate had failed to approve ratification.

May 15   Supreme Court allows decision of court of appeals to stand.

Jun 16   Carter travels to Panama to exchange official ratification notices with Torrijos.

1979

Jun 21   Passage of implementation legislation in the House (224–202).

Jul 26   Senate approves slightly different implementation provisions by a vote of 64–30.

Sep 27   Three days before treaties go into effect, Congress approves joint implementation provisions.

Chapter 6 Documents

Document 6.1
Treaty Concerning Permanent Neutrality and Operation of the Panama Canal,
selected passages, September 7, 1977

Article I

The Republic of Panama declares that the Canal, as an international transit waterway, shall be permanently neutral in accordance with the regime established in this Treaty. The same regime of neutrality shall apply to any other international waterway that may be built either partially or wholly in the territory of the Republic of Panama....

Article V

After the termination of the Panama Canal Treaty, only the Republic of Panama shall operate the Canal and maintain military forces, defense sites and military installations within its national territory....

Article VI

1. In recognition of the important contributions of the United States of America and of the Republic of Panama to the construction, operation, maintenance, and protection and defense of the Canal, vessels of war and auxiliary vessels of those nations shall, notwithstanding any other provisions of this Treaty, be entitled to transit the Canal irrespective of their internal operation, means of propulsion, origin, destination, armament or cargo carried. Such vessels of war and auxiliary vessels will be entitled to transit the Canal expeditiously....

Source: *Treaties and Other International Acts*, Series 10029, p. 11.

Document 6.2
Panama Canal Treaty,
selected passages, September 7, 1977

Article I
Abrogation of Prior Treaties and Establishment of a New Relationship

1. Upon its entry into force, this Treaty terminates and supersedes:

(a) The Isthmian Canal Convention between the United States of America and the Republic of Panama, signed at Washington, November 18, 1903;...

Article II
Ratification, Entry Into Force, and Termination

2. This Treaty shall terminate at noon, Panama time, December 31, 1999.

Article III
Canal Operation and Management

1. The Republic of Panama, as territorial sovereign, grants to the United States of America the rights to manage, operate, and maintain the Panama Canal, its complementary works, installations and equipment and to provide for the orderly transit of vessels through the Panama Canal. The United States of America accepts the grant of such rights and undertakes to exercise them in accordance with this Treaty and related agreements....

Article IV
Protection and Defense

1. The United States of America and the Republic of Panama commit themselves to protect and defend the Panama Canal. Each Party shall act, in accordance with its constitutional processes, to meet the danger resulting from an armed attack or other actions which threaten the security of the Panama Canal or of ships transiting it.

2. For the duration of this Treaty, the United States of America shall have primary responsibility to protect and defend the Canal....

Article XII
A Sea-Level Canal or a Third Lane of Locks

1. The United States of America and the Republic of Panama recognize that a sea-level canal may be important for international navigation in the future. Consequently, during the duration of this Treaty, both Parties commit themselves to study jointly the feasibility of a sea-level canal in the Republic of Panama, and in the event they determine that such a waterway is necessary, they shall negotiate terms, agreeable to both Parties for its construction....

Source: *Treaties and Other International Acts*, Series 10030, p. 10.

Document 6.3
Constitution of the United States of America,
selected passages relevant to the Panama ratification debate

Article II, Section 2

...He [the president] shall have Power, by and with the Advice and Consent of the Senate, to make Treaties, provided two-thirds of the Senators present concur...

Article IV, Section 3

...The Congress shall have Power to dispose of and make all needful Rules and Regulations respecting the Territory or other Property belonging to the United States; and nothing in this Constitution shall be so construed as to Prejudice any Claims of the United States, or of any particular State....

Article VI

...This Constitution, the Laws of the United States which shall be made in Pursuance thereof; and all Treaties made, or which shall be made, under the Authority of the United States, shall be the supreme Law of the Land; and the Judges in every State shall be bound thereby, any Thing in the Constitution or Laws of any State to the contrary notwithstanding....

Document 6.4
The Carter-Torrijos Understanding October 14, 1977

Under the Treaty Concerning the Permanent Neutrality and Operation of the Panama Canal [the Neutrality Treaty], Panama and the United States have the responsibility to assure that the Panama Canal will remain open and secure to ships of all nations. The correct interpretation of this principle is that each of the two countries shall, in accordance with their respective constitutional processes, defend the Canal against any threat to the regime of neutrality, and consequently shall have the right to act against any aggression or threat directed against the Canal or against the peaceful transit of vessels through the Canal.

This does not mean, nor shall it be interpreted as, a right of intervention of the United States in the internal affairs of Panama. Any United States action will be directed at insuring that the Canal will remain open, secure and accessible, and it shall never be directed against the territorial integrity or political independence of Panama.

The Neutrality Treaty provides that the vessels of war and auxiliary vessels of the United States and Panama will be entitled to transit the Canal expeditiously. This is intended, and it shall so be interpreted, to assure the transit of such vessels through the Canal as quickly as possible, without any impediment, with expedited treatment, and in the case of need or emergency, to go to the head of the line of vessels in order to transit the Canal rapidly.

Source: *Department of State Bulletin*, November 7, 1977, p. 631.

Document 6.5
The DeConcini Amendment March 16, 1978

Language approved by the Senate as a condition to the resolution of ratification of the Neutrality Treaty. Approved by a vote of 75–23.

Notwithstanding the provisions of Article V or any other provision of the treaty, if the Canal is closed, or its operations are interfered with, the United States of America and the Republic of Panama shall each independently have the right to take such steps as it deems necessary in accordance with its constitutional process, *including the use of military force in Panama*, [emphasis added], to reopen the Canal or restore the operations of the Canal, as the case may be.

Source: *Department of State Bulletin*, May 1978, p. 53.

Document 6.6
Excerpts from Senate Debate on the Panama Canal Treaty
April 18, 1978

Mr. HELMS... Mr. President, why is it that the President of the United States, the entire foreign policy apparatus, the power structure of academics, businessmen, and bankers, and the most powerful voices of the media have been unable to convince the American people that these treaties are in the best interests of the United States? Why is it that in the last 2 weeks or 10 days that even the supposed beneficiary of these treaties, the Republic of Panama, has balked at accepting the work of the Senate?

The fact is, Mr. President, that these treaties are still under a cloud. They originated under a cloud, they were negotiated under a cloud, they have been debated under a cloud....

Why are these treaties under a cloud? Why are they fatally flawed? They are fatally flawed because there has never been a meeting of the minds on the fundamental problem, which is the transfer of sovereignty. Now I realize that the notion of sovereignty has been ridiculed on this floor from the beginning, as something of no importance. But if the treaties founder, they will do so because that issue was never resolved. Sovereignty was not the issue, we were told over and over again; yet it is the issue upon which, even if the treaties succeed, we will come to grief.

For sovereignty is the question of ultimate power. It answers the question: Who has the right to decide what actions may take place within a defined territory? As long as the United States is free to exercise all the rights of a sovereign within the territory of the Canal Zone, there was no doubt that we could do whatever was necessary to defend it. There was no question of intervention in the internal affairs of Panama. There was no question of violating the territorial integrity of Panama.

But the moment the United States surrenders its sovereign rights, then everything that we do, every action, is subject to the will of Panama. It is as simple as that. When Panama is sovereign, Panama decides.

At the root of the problem is a fundamental unresolved contradiction that our negotiators failed to solve. The treaties are an attempt to paper over that contradiction.

The ultimate issue in sovereignty, of course, is the right to use force. That is what sovereignty is all about. There may be disputes about actions of a lesser level, but in the end, they come down to the issue of who has the right to use force.

The treaties attempt to pretend that there will never be any division of opinion between the United States and Panama on how the ultimate right to use force will be exercised. But that is an absurd supposition. It is an insult to the people of Panama. It assumes that they will be forever subservient to the desires of the United States.

That is why the people of Panama have been so disturbed over the past few weeks. The United States has made it clear that, despite the pretence of handing back sovereignty, we intend to keep the ultimate right to use force, even against the Panamanian people if necessary. There can be no other interpretation.

The President of the United States has said in writing that we intend to use force against any threat to the canal. I repeat, against any threat to the the canal. From the standpoint of the United States, I applaud his intention; but from the standpoint of the people of Panama, it can only mean that the President of the United

States intends to use force against the people of Panama if the President decides that the people of Panama are the threat.

Let us not pretend that it does not mean that. It does mean that. The DeConcini reservation simply makes manifest what is implicit in the formula of the treaties. The DeConcini reservation brings out into the open what is merely implied. And the attempt of the leadership to hide the true meaning of the treaties does a disservice to the people of the United States and people of Panama....

The President has written to the distinguished Senator from Massachusetts, and he attempts to assert both sides of the contradiction at the same time. He says, and I quote: "It is abundantly clear, therefore, that the United States can, under the the Neutrality Treaty, take whatever actions are necessary to defend the Canal from any threat regardless of its source."

That is what the President of the United States says: Any threat. Any threat. The President does not exclude threats which arise from the internal affairs of Panama. The President does not exclude threats which arise from within the integral territory of Panama. How can he exclude such threats? Is it not possible that such threats may be the most likely of all threats?

So the President is not excluding actions when the threat arises from Panama's internal affairs.

Nevertheless, the President has not abandoned the agreed-upon double-talk. He says: "The correlative part of the Memorandum of Understanding, embodied in the leadership amendment to the Neutrality Treaty, makes it quite clear that action of this character must be confined to the stated objective alone, and that it will not be interpreted as a right of intervention in the internal affairs of Panama."

What the President is saying is that any intervention in the internal affairs of Panama for the sake of defending the canal will not be interpreted as an intervention in the internal affairs of Panama.

Well, of course, the United States will not so interpret our intervention in the internal affairs of Panama; but can anyone have any doubt that Panama will interpret it as an intervention in the internal affairs of Panama?

The terms of the argument are contradictory. The President is trying to reconcile two opposites by declaring that they are not opposites. But the two propositions are mutually exclusive. And if the Senate of the United States attempts to assert both propositions at the same time, our whole relationship with Panama will come to grief....

So, Mr. President, I say again that if this Senate acts with wisdom, it will return these treaties to the negotiating table so that we can come up with a solution that will be acceptable to the Panamanians and acceptable to the American people, 72 percent of whom are in strong opposition to these treaties.

PRESIDING OFFICER. The Senator from Idaho (Mr. Church) is recognized for 10 minutes.

Mr. CHURCH. Mr. President, after 14 years of negotiations between the United States and the Republic of Panama, directed by four different Presidents of this country, and after 38 days of debate on these treaties in the Senate of the United States, we are asked to approve a motion to return this treaty to the Committee on Foreign Relations and to the President of the United States, in order that it might go back again to the bargaining table.

If there is one thing clear, it is this: Should the Senate adopt the motion of the distinguished Senator from Michigan, these treaties will not go back to the negotiating table. We will go back, instead, to a condition of deadlock and defiance. It just is not any longer possible for one country to maintain a colony in another against the wishes of the inhabitants of that country.

We began negotiations back in 1964, when 24 people died in riots in Panama, because the overwhelming sentiment of the Panamanian people finally flared into open flames. Since that time we have undertaken to negotiate at arm's length a just set of treaties, a fair bargain fairly arrived at.

As each Senator prepares to cast his vote on the pending resolution, let him consider that the treaty before us is right for the United States, right for the Republic of Panama, and right for the times in which we live. And let him take into account what his final vote will mean.

A vote against this treaty represents a vain attempt to preserve the past.

It represents a futile effort to perpetuate an American colony in Panama against the wishes of the Panamanian people, in an age when colonies have disappeared elsewhere, gone with the empires of yesterday.

It represents an ill-destined desire to cling to American ownership and control of an aging canal, which, by the end of this century, will be able to accommodate less than one-tenth of the commercial tonnage then on the high seas.

It represents a sentimental journey back to the era of Teddy Roosevelt, the Big Stick, and the Great White Fleet, in a day when our modern aircraft carriers and nuclear submarines can no longer even use the present canal.

It represents a dangerous folly that will exacerbate an old Panamanian grievance stemming from the Treaty of 1903, in an age when such grievances can readily deteriorate into endless harassment and guerrilla war.

But a vote for the treaty looks forward to a new day.

It would restore to Panama jurisdiction over her own soil and thus lay the basis for a close and friendly cooperation between the United States and Panama in the years ahead.

It would give us the best guarantee available of dependable use of the canal from now until the end of the century and beyond.

It would enhance the prospects for the construction of a sea-level canal to meet our naval and commercial needs of the 21st century.

It would protect our security interests by insuring that our right to go to the head of the line will be preserved in case of need, and by guaranteeing our right to defend the canal with military force if ever that should prove necessary.

It would create a sense of mutual respect and trust, nurtured from the knowledge that this is a just treaty, fair to both sides, which will make for better relations throughout the hemisphere and redound to our benefit everywhere in the world.

Yet the vote, Mr. President, will be a difficult one. Every Senator knows that ratification of these treaties will not be popular, given the deep division in public opinion. But the Senate was envisioned by our Founding Fathers as the legislative body where unpopular decisions might be made, when the long-term interests of the Nation demanded it.

Today I pray that the Senate will defeat this amendment, and then, by approving this treaty, will rise to its historic responsibility, as each Senator is called upon to put the country first—above personal and political considerations.

Mr. President, the moment of truth approaches. The outcome will either cast our future relations with Latin America and the developing world in a bright new light, or plunge it under a gathering shadow that could last for years to come....

Source: *The Congressional Record*, April 18, 1978, pp. S10500–S10515.

Chapter 6 Notes

[1]For a detailed account of the Panamanian revolution and the negotiation of the 1903 treaty, see David McCullough, *The Path Between the Seas* (New York: Simon & Schuster, 1977), pp. 361–402.

[2]George D. Moffett, *The Limits of Victory* (Ithaca, N.Y.: Cornell University Press, 1985), pp. 28–31.

[3]Jules Witcover, *Marathon: The Pursuit of the Presidency 1972–1976* (New York: Viking, 1977), p. 402.

[4]Sol Linowitz, *The Making of a Public Man* (Boston: Little, Brown, 1985), p. 149.

[5]Jimmy Carter, *Keeping Faith* (New York: Bantam, 1982), p. 155.

[6]Zbigniew Brzezinski, *Power and Principle* (New York: Farrar, Straus, & Giroux, 1983), p. 134.

[7]Linowitz, *Making of a Public Man*, p. 152.

[8]Ibid., p. 164.

[9]Cyrus Vance, *Hard Choices* (New York: Simon & Schuster, 1983), p. 144.

[10]Linowitz, *Making of a Public Man*, p. 176.

[11]Ibid., p. 164.

[12]Carter, *Keeping Faith*, p. 159.

[13]Moffet, *Limits of Victory, p. 74.*

[14]*Washington Post*, July 23, 1977.

[15]William L. Furlong and Margaret E. Scranton, *The Dynamics of Foreign Policymaking* (Boulder, Colo.: Westview, 1984), p. 141.

[16]Moffett, *Limits of Victory*, p. 41.

[17]Ibid., p. 94.

[18]For a detailed account of the public opinion data in connection with Panama and the steady opposition to the treaties, see ibid., pp. 112–137.

[19]William J. Jorden, *Panama Odyssey* (Austin: University of Texas Press, 1984), p. 480.

[20]Cecil V. Crabb, Jr., and Pat M. Holt, *Invitation to Struggle: Congress, the President and Foreign Policy*, 2nd ed. (Washington, D.C.: Congressional Quarterly Press, 1984), p. 90.

[21]Carter, *Keeping Faith*, p. 172.

[22]Ibid., pp. 175–176.

[23] Referred to here and in the press at the time as the DeConcini amendment or reservation, it was actually a Condition to the Senate Resolution on Ratification.

[24]Brzezinski, *Power and Principle*, p. 136.

[25]Of the twenty, seven chose not to seek reelection and six were defeated in either the primaries or the general election. Panama was an important issue in both 1978 and 1980 when eleven more senators who voted for the treaties were defeated.

[26]See, for instance, Edwin Borchard, "Should the Executive Agreement Replace the Treaty?" 53 *Yale Law Journal* 664 (1944); and "Treaties and Executive Agreements—A Reply," 54 *Yale Law Journal* 616 (1945).

[27]Lloyd N. Cutler, "To Form a Government," *Foreign Affairs* (Fall 1980).

[28]Lloyd N. Cutler, "Party Government Under the Constitution," in *Reforming American Government* , ed. Donald L. Robinson, (Boulder Colo.: Westview, 1985), pp. 93–109.

[29]Ironically, many members of Congress protested that presidential action.

[30]Loch Johnson and James M. McCormick, "Foreign Policy by Executive Fiat," *Foreign Policy*, 28 (Fall 1977), 117.

[31]Jorden, *Panama Odyssey*, pp. 623–26.

[32]Linowitz, *Making of a Public Man*, p. 205.

[33]Carter, *Keeping Faith*, p. 171.

[34]Diary entry March 13, 1978, ibid.

[35]Charles O. Jones, *The Trusteeship Presidency* (Baton Rouge: Louisiana State University Press, 1988), pp. 1–9.

[36]Brzezinski, *Power and Principle*, p. 137.

Chapter 7

Reagan and the Iran-Contra Affair

REVOLUTIONS AND THE REAGAN ADMINISTRATION

Two years after his landslide reelection in 1984, President Ronald Reagan became embroiled in one of the most controversial foreign policy scandals of the postwar era. On November 25, 1986, Attorney General Edwin Meese announced at a press conference that funds raised by secret arms sales to Iran, and controlled by members of the National Security Council staff, had been diverted to support the Nicaraguan contras fighting to overthrow the leftist Sandinista government in Managua.

Before that press conference, many of the important Reagan administration decisions about Iran and Nicaragua had been closely held secrets. Even today, after exhaustive executive, congressional, judicial, and media investigations, it is entirely possible that important facts related to these policies are still unknown to the American people. What we do know is that the Iran-contra affair involved two major foreign policy initiatives, carried out by a small circle of White House and administration officials, and that both policies failed to achieve their intended objectives before coming to a sudden end in November 1986. From that point on, investigators working for the Tower Commission, the House and Senate select committees, the major national media organizations, and the office of the special prosecutor have tried to unravel the tangled threads of Reagan White House connections to Iran and the Nicaraguan resistance movement. Those connections can only be understood in the context of events at the end of the Carter administration when two seemingly disconnected revolutions set much of the foreign policy agenda for the 1980s.

The first of the two revolutions took place in the Persian Gulf and saw the replacement of a loyal American ally, the Shah of Iran, with a fanatical religious leader, the Ayatollah Khomeini, who willingly flaunted long established standards of international law by sanctioning the capture and holding of American diplomatic hostages. Official American dealings with Iran were brought to an end as a result of the hostage crisis, and though the final months of the Carter presidency were spent in the successful negotiation of an agreement that would bring the hostages home, there was little hope in the early 1980s for anything like a return to normal relations between the United States and the Islamic republic established by Khomeini and his followers. Mutual distrust and suspicion characterized relations between the two countries; and though no new American hostages were taken in Iran, the Khomeini regime was indirectly involved in acts of political violence and kidnapping in Lebanon and elsewhere in the Middle East. Early in the third year of the Reagan administration, Iran was officially declared a state sponsor of terrorism and America's allies were publicly urged to cease all arms sales to Khomeini's government, a policy the United States was already following in protest against Iranian terrorism and in an effort to remain neutral in the war then being fought between Iran and Iraq.

The second revolution that set the stage for the Iran-contra affair took place in Nicaragua. In Managua, as in Tehran, an unpopular authoritarian ruler was overthrown by a broad-based revolutionary movement. As a result of a long history of human rights abuses, the United States had cut many of its ties with Nicaraguan dictator Anastasio Somoza before the revolution. When the revolution succeeded, we offered aid to the new Sandinista government; but early efforts to establish good relations between the United States and the revolutionary Nicaraguan regime quickly broke down. By the end of the Carter administration, it was clear that the Sandinista movement would be dominated by its Marxist-Leninist members and pose a threat to Nicaragua's neighbors in Central America.

Though separated by thousands of miles and involving radically different political cultures, the two revolutions of the late 1970s had a number of things in common. Both Somoza and the Shah were forced out of power by popular movements that gained strength from a virulent anti-Americanism. Both revolutionary movements blamed the United States for many of the past and present misfortunes suffered by the peoples of Iran and Nicaragua. Even when the revolutionaries were victorious, propaganda against the United States did not subside. Hatred for "American devils" and "Yankee imperialists" helped to sustain the legitimacy of weak regimes in Tehran and Managua and rationalized controversial domestic and international steps taken by Khomeini and the Nicaraguan revolutionary leader, Daniel Ortega.

As a result of the two revolutions, American confrontations with the Soviet Union in the Middle East and Central America were made more likely; and as the 1970s ended, many observers in the United States expected serious foreign policy challenges from both third world instability and the growing Soviet inclination to exploit it. The Soviet invasion of Afghanistan at the end of 1979 only added to those fears. The problems presented by anti-American revolutionary movements would not be easy to solve, and many years after the revolutions in Iran and Nicaragua, both Carter and Reagan would be judged harshly for the policies they pursued in the Persian Gulf and Central America.

Carter had been unwilling to use force to stop either the Khomeini or the Sandinista revolution and had, instead, searched in vain for some way to replace the departing dictators with moderate regimes.[1] Unfortunately, by the time the United States became seriously interested in pushing for progressive change in Iran and Nicaragua, most of the moderate political leaders in those countries had already joined the revolutionary movements. Carter could do little to prevent the rise of anti-American governments in the Persian Gulf and Central America, and appeared painfully impotent as American hostages were taken in Tehran and a predictable Marxist tilt took place in Managua. Carter's general response to these events was to back away from an early emphasis on human rights, which had characterized his administration, and move toward a more traditional foreign policy based on the need to contain Soviet power and influence in the world. Carter was defeated for reelection in 1980, in part because the public felt that his response to these revolutionary movements had been too weak and had come too late.

Reagan's failure was of a different sort. He was perfectly willing to use force to overthrow the Sandinista regime, more willing, in fact, than either the American public or their elected representatives. Between 1983 and 1986, many of the actions taken by his administration in support of the contras were secret and went against the legislated wishes of the Congress. In the case of Iran, Reagan and his advisers bungled a series of attempts to establish some dialogue with moderate Iranian officials and ended up selling arms to Iran in exchange for vague, and mostly unkept, promises that hostages held in Lebanon would be released.

Policy failure, though it is palpable in both the Reagan and Carter administrations, is not at the heart of the Iran-contra scandal. The real issues in the scandal involve the way that the foreign policy failures of the Reagan era were enacted—the people who made the decisions, the procedures that were followed, the agencies that took a leading role, and the congressional involvement that was largely absent. It is to these issues that we now turn.

THE IRAN INITIATIVE

Of the two sets of policies in the Iran-contra affair, the Reagan administration's dealings with Iran are by far the more complicated. They involved secret trips to Tehran, presidentially autographed Bibles, plane loads of missiles and spare parts, shady international arms dealers, captured and tortured kidnap victims, private Swiss bank accounts, and key pieces of information intentionally withheld from the Congress, the public, the secretaries of state and defense, and, most importantly, from the president of the United States.

Arms sales to Iran began in the summer of 1985 when Israeli officials approached Reagan's national security adviser, Robert McFarlane, with plans to sell missiles to Iran as a way of opening political discussions between the United States and moderate Iranians who might someday succeed Khomeini and as a way of bringing about the release of six Americans held hostage by factions in Lebanon sympathetic to the Ayatollah's revolutionary movement. Between August and November 1985, there were three shipments of missiles to Iran,[2] but only one American hostage was released.

These transactions raised controversial legal and policy questions. The resale of large quantities of American arms originally sold to Israel is prohibited by American law unless the transactions are approved by the president and reported to the Congress.[3] No reports were made to the House or Senate concerning the Israeli arms sales to Iran. Moreover, the attempt to establish relations with Iranian moderates and to secure the release of hostages held in Lebanon constituted "significant anticipated intelligence activities," which, by law,[4] must be approved in a formal presidential decision, called a *finding,* and reported in a timely manner to the intelligence committees of the House and Senate or to a small number of congressional leaders. In December 1985, after the first arms shipments to Iran had already been carried out by the Israelis with assistance from the CIA, the president signed a retroactive finding approving the completed transactions. The only presidentially signed copy of this finding was destroyed by Admiral John Poindexter, McFarlane's successor as national security adviser, after the Meese investigations of the administration had begun in November 1986. This finding unambiguously described the Iran initiative as an arms-for-hostages exchange, a proposition that the president had publicly denied shortly before Poindexter's decision to destroy the document.[5] The existence of the finding was known to very few members of the administration, and no information about the initiative was given to any member of Congress.

In addition to legal issues concerning the failure to make required reports to the Congress, the actions taken in 1985 raised serious policy questions about the wisdom of any continuation of the initiative. Were the Iranians with whom we were dealing really able to secure hostage freedom? Was the principal Iranian middleman in the arms sales, Manucher Ghorbanifar, who had failed several CIA polygraph tests and was judged to be thoroughly unreliable by the intelligence community, a well-chosen agent to serve in these transactions? Was the United States government, by dealing with Iran—a designated state-sponsor of terrorism—undermining its long-standing policy of refusing to negotiate with kidnappers and terrorists? Were we dangerously compromising our neutrality in the Iran-Iraq war, while hypocritically urging our allies to remain neutral in that conflict?

These questions were addressed in two formal meetings of the president's senior foreign policy advisers in December 1985 and January 1986. At those meetings, Robert McFarlane, who as former national security adviser continued to serve the president on selected policy issues, and the secretaries of state and defense all recommended the termination of arms shipments to Iran. The president heard their arguments, but after the meetings were over chose to continue the Iran initiative. This decision was promoted by Admiral Poindexter and his assistant, Lieutenant Colonel Oliver North, and by CIA Director William Casey. One of the kidnap victims in Beirut was the CIA station chief for Lebanon who was tortured and eventually killed by his captors. According to the president's chief of staff, Donald Regan, the decision to continue the initiative was the result of Reagan's understandable human impulse to do whatever he could to win the release of the Americans held hostage in Lebanon.[6] A second presidential finding authorizing arms sales to Iran "for the purpose of: (1) establishing a more moderate government in Iran, and (2) obtaining from them significant intelligence not otherwise obtainable, to determine the current Iranian Government's intentions with respect to its neighbors and with respect to terrorist acts, [and (3) furthering the release of the American hostages held in Beirut and preventing additional terrorist acts by these groups.]"[7] was signed on January 17, 1986. This document was withheld from the Congress and from the cabinet members who were opposed to the president's final decision.

During 1986 there were a series of arms sales to Iran[8] and some sharing of U.S. intelligence information useful to Iranian officials in the conduct of their war with Iraq. But none of these actions produced significant progress in ending the hostage situation in Lebanon. Though the Israelis continued to play some role in these transactions, the United States now made direct deliveries to Iran using ships and planes under the control of a retired air force general, Richard Secord, who was already working with Oliver North in the resupply of the contras. One hostage was released in July and another in early November; but late in the year, three new hostages were captured. Throughout 1986, the efforts of NSC staff members to win the release of the Beirut hostages became more desperate.

High-ranking U.S. officials flew secretly to Tehran bringing with them a presidentially inscribed Bible as a gift for Iranian leaders. In Tehran the American delegation found it impossible to carry out serious negotiations with Iranians who demanded much more than the administration could possibly deliver. Albert Hakim, a business partner of General Secord who was handling a number of the arms shipments to Iran, arranged new contacts with a "second channel" of Iranian intermediaries who promised better results for yet more arms shipments. During discussions with representatives of the second channel, North and Secord made false and misleading promises about American policy toward Iraq and Iran and permitted Hakim to pledge American support for the release of terrorists held in Kuwait, an outrageous misrepresentation of official government policy. As was the case with all the earlier aspects of this initiative, nothing was reported to Congress, very little was reported to members of the cabinet, and embarrassing details like the false promises made by North and Hakim were apparently not fully explained to the president.[9] All the while a steady flow of arms to Khomeini's Iran was taking place.

Whether arms sales to Iran were negotiated through the first or the second channel, with or without Israeli involvement, they invariably failed to produce an end to the Lebanese hostage problem or a beginning of genuine dialogue with Iranian moderates. About all the arms sales were able to produce were high profits for the middle-men carrying out the transactions. Those profits, amounting to millions of dollars, became the basis of what Oliver North described to the congressional investigating committees as a "neat idea"—the plan to use the funds generated in the Iranian arms sales to aid the contras fighting in Nicaragua. It was that idea, which Poindexter claims was never reported to the president, that would convert the failed Iranian initiative into the now familiar hyphenated scandal.

THE CONTRA CONNECTION

Secret aid to the contras managed by members of the Reagan administration went on much longer than the arms sales to Iran and involved more fundamental questions about the relationship between the executive and legislative branches in the conduct of foreign policy. The central issue for the Iran initiative was how much information the administration had to provide to the Congress about arms sales and ongoing covert activities and when that information should have been provided. The main issue with regard to Nicaragua was whether the president and members of his administration could defy clearly expressed congressional policy.

Early in the Reagan administration, Central America became a major focus of foreign policy attention. Nicaragua was condemned for its ties to Cuba and the Soviet Union, and El Salvador (a small Central American country on the Pacific coast north of Nicaragua) began to receive extensive administration assistance in an effort to suppress a communist guerrilla movement. President Reagan's first secretary of state, Alexander Haig, and others in the administration thought that El Salvador was an ideal location for an early administration foreign policy victory.

Unlike Vietnam or Afghanistan, El Salvador was in our own backyard, and though its government had a dubious human rights record, the administration believed that with enough outside support the Salvadoreans could defeat or at least stave off their leftist guerrillas. This was an opportunity for a dramatic reversal of the policies of the Carter era, and Haig hoped that widespread support for a policy of containing Central American communism could be won from the public and from the Congress. The administration made saving the government of El Salvador a major commitment, increased economic and military assistance to that country, and prepared to take covert action against the sources of supply for the Salvadoran rebels.

In December 1981, President Reagan signed a finding, which was properly reported to the Congress, authorizing CIA aid to the contras for the purpose of interdicting Nicaraguan arms flowing to the guerrillas in El Salvador. For the next two years, the CIA assistance given to the contras was justified by the need to stop Nicaraguan arms from entering El Salvador. The Sandinistas did provide aid to Salvadoran leftists, but the extent of that aid was sometimes exaggerated by the Reagan administration, and the CIA activities in support of the contras fighting on the southern border of Nicaragua were very difficult to explain in terms of their effect on the flow of arms to a country north of Nicaragua.

At the end of 1982, Congress passed the first Boland Amendment, which prohibited the use of federal funds for the specific purpose of overthrowing the Nicaraguan government. Administration assistance to the contras in the name of protecting El Salvador continued for some time after the first Boland Amendment became law but lost any semblance of credibility, when, in 1984, it was revealed that the CIA had played a role in the mining of Nicaraguan harbors and in the distribution of a training manual that called for the assassination of local Sandinista leaders. The contras were, in fact, attempting to overthrow the Nicaraguan government and the CIA was helping them. The language of the Boland Amendment, which was passed in one form or another each year after 1982, became much more restrictive after the training manual controversy. The version included in legislation signed by the president in October 1984, stated that "no funds available to the Central Intelligence Agency, the Department of Defense, or any other agency or entity of the United States involved in intelligence activities may be obligated or expended for the purpose or which would have the effect of supporting, directly or indirectly, military or paramilitary operations in Nicaragua by any nation, group, organization, movement, or individual."[10]

Between the passage of the October 1984 Boland Amendment and the congressional approval of $100 million in contra aid that became available in October 1986, no government funds could be provided to the contras without specific legislative language granting exemption from the sweeping Boland restrictions. During this period President Reagan publicly chided the Congress for its failure to fight communism in Central America and urged a change in policy. He was able to win some funding for limited amounts of nonlethal supplies in 1985, but made no progress in convincing the Congress to abandon the central principle in the Boland amendments. The will of the Congress was that the United States refrain from helping the forces fighting to overthrow the Sandinista regime. This was not, however, the president's will, nor was it his policy.

Members of the Reagan administration responded to the Boland restrictions by soliciting funds for the contras from foreign countries and private citizens and then funneling those funds to contra organizations in the form of cash, arms, and supplies. Beginning in the summer of 1985, Oliver North, a marine officer serving on the National Security Council staff, took charge of these efforts and recruited Richard Secord to handle the purchase and delivery of military supplies to Central America. The operation was a complicated one and the level of involvement of senior administration officials is still a matter of contention. According to information revealed during North's trial in 1989, Vice President George Bush may have participated in a plan to increase American foreign aid to Honduras as leverage to win Honduran support for the contra cause.[11]

Money for the contras came from a variety of nations and private donors. It was hard to keep track of all the contributions, and at least some of the money given to the contra movement was accidently deposited in the wrong Swiss bank account. North received some technical support from the intelligence community and the active encouragement of CIA Director William Casey, but was largely left on his own to make important decisions about the details of the contra resupply program. He kept McFarlane, and later Poindexter, informed about his activities, but misled congressional committees when asked in August 1986 about administration compliance with the letter and spirit of the Boland Amendment.[12]

General Secord leased planes, hired pilots, built an airfield in Costa Rica, and delivered weapons and supplies to contra camps in Central America. The exact legal status of his enterprise was obviously questionable. If he was acting as a private citizen, then he was probably guilty of violating the Neutrality Act and other laws that prohibit Americans from engaging in the unregulated international transfer of arms. If he was an official of the United States government engaged in a covert operation, as he would later claim in his testimony before Congress, then he may not have been subject to the usual regulations involving commercial arms transactions, but his actions would then have arguably been covered by the various Boland Amendments. Throughout the contra resupply program that North administered, very little effort was made to review the legality of the steps being taken by North, Secord, or any of the other participants.

At a NSC meeting in June 1984 several cabinet officers expressed concern that active White House funding of the contras in violation of the Boland Amendment could be an impeachable offense.[13] If foreign governments and private citizens had been urged to give money directly to the contra movement, there would have been much less cause for concern, but when Oliver North assumed a major role in the coordination of this fund raising and when money for the contras was given to Richard Secord for the purchase and delivery of arms, administration involvement became much more legally suspect. A legal opinion stating that the National Security Council was acting faithfully within the Boland restrictions was prepared by the staff counsel of the president's Intelligence Oversight Board (a group of civilians appointed by the president to act as an independent watchdog over intelligence organizations) after a brief and incomplete review of Oliver North's files in the summer of 1985.[14] But no substantive legal advice was sought from the Justice Department, the State Department, the White House counsel, or any of the other administration officials who could logically have been expected to render such an opinion. Nothing in the legislation creating the National Security Council suggests that it has the authority or the capacity to carry out covert operations. Indeed, North and Casey apparently believed that the advantage of managing such operations from the White House was precisely the fact that the NSC was outside regular legislative scrutiny and largely unmentioned in the laws of the 1970s designed to strengthen congressional oversight of covert activities.

The decision to mix funds from Iranian arms sales with the contra resupply operation greatly increased the likelihood that if one operation was discovered, both would be exposed. In the fall of 1986, events in Central America and the Middle East threatened the secrecy and security of both operations. On October 5, one of Secord's planes flying a contra resupply mission was shot down in Nicaragua, and the only surviving crew member, Eugene Hasenfus, was captured. Later that same month, Iranian factions critical of the negotiations that had taken place with members of the Reagan administration published a pamphlet outlining the main events in the Iran initiative and distributed it throughout Lebanon. It was only a matter of time before the information in those pamphlets was reported in the international press. On November 3, five days after the final shipment of 500 TOW missiles arrived in Iran and one day after hostage David Jacobsen was released, a Lebanese magazine revealed that a series of American arms shipments to Iran had taken place in 1985 and 1986. After a rather clumsy effort on the part of NSC officials to cover up the Iranian initiative led to congressional testimony and a presidential press conference in which mistaken and misleading statements were made, Reagan agreed to have his attorney general conduct an internal investigation. Though Poindexter and North had destroyed a number of important documents, members of Meese's staff were able to find an April 1986 memo in which North described the diversion of funds from the Iranian arms sales to the resupply of the contras, [Document 7.1] and both policies were then on their way to their ignominious conclusions.

CONCLUSIONS

POWER

At its core, the Iran-contra affair was a struggle between the president and the Congress over the power to control American foreign policy. As noted in earlier chapters, during the 1970s the Congress assumed a larger role in American foreign policy making. Among other things, Congress imposed new reporting requirements on the executive branch so that at least some members of the legislature would be told about sensitive intelligence and national security matters. During this same period the Congress made use of its power of the purse on several occasions to dictate particular foreign policy actions to presidents with whom the legislature disagreed. In the Iran-contra affair, the Reagan administration challenged both of these congressional instruments for gaining a greater role in foreign affairs. Clearly understood reporting requirements were ignored in both the sale of arms to Iran and the conduct of covert operations; and when congressional control over federal expenditures was used to prohibit aid to the contras, alternative funding sources were found for the policies that the legislature categorically refused to support. Both of these challenges raise important constitutional questions.[15]

Did the administration have a legal basis for withholding information from the House and Senate? The question is not unique to the Reagan administration and has been debated since the founding. John Jay points out in *Federalist 64* that the inability to keep secrets in the conduct of foreign affairs had been a serious defect in the Articles of Confederation: "So often and so essentially have we heretofore suffered from the want of secrecy and dispatch, that the Constitution would have been inexcusably defective, if no attention had been paid to those objects."[16] In Jay's view, though some foreign policy information was to be shared between the president and the Senate under the new Constitution, there would be occasions when the executive would wisely keep secrets:

> There are cases where the most useful intelligence may be obtained, if the persons possessing it can be relieved from apprehensions of discovery. Those apprehensions will operate on those persons whether they are actuated by mercenary or friendly motives; and there doubtless are many of both descriptions, who would rely on the secrecy of the President, but who would not confide in that of the Senate, and still less in that of a large popular Assembly. The convention have done well, therefore, in so disposing of the power of making treaties, that although the President must, in forming them, act by the advice and consent of the Senate, yet he will be able to manage the business of intelligence in such a manner as prudence may suggest.[17]

The selling of arms to Iran in exchange for hostages held in Lebanon hardly seems prudent in the aftermath, but the question remains whether the president can constitutionally keep secrets from the Congress, as Jay expected would be the case, or whether the chief executive must always comply with congressionally mandated reporting requirements. The legislation requiring committee notification about "significant anticipated intelligence activities" has a number of exceptions. It recognizes that prior notification may be impossible in some cases and permits timely notification after the fact, if the administration provides a statement explaining the reasons for delay. It also permits certain sensitive information about collection methods and sources to be withheld, and allows the president to restrict reporting to a group of eight congressional leaders if informing the full intelligence committees of the House and Senate is deemed dangerous to vital national interests. Furthermore, the preamble to the 1980 Intelligence Oversight Act[18] acknowledges that all compliance with the legislation must be consistent with the president's duties under the Constitution. This language suggests that there may be occasions when compliance is *not* consistent with the constitutional responsibilities of the chief executive.[19]

There are certainly precedents for the planning and execution of major military and intelligence operations about which the Congress has been kept in the dark. In Chapter 1, we noted that virtually all of the information related to the Manhattan Project was withheld from the Congress. But that was during the exceptional circumstances of world war. Perhaps a more pertinent precedent for the Iran-contra affair is President Carter's Iranian hostage rescue mission, which involved both military and covert intelligence operations that were unknown to members of Congress until after the mission had failed. Extraordinary secrecy in that case was justified by the need to protect the lives of the hostages and the CIA operatives in Iran who would have helped with later stages of the rescue mission. The decisions of the Reagan administration not to consult with Congress on the Iranian arms sales might have been justified on similar grounds if there were reasonable fears that a public revelation of the initiative would have endangered the hostages remaining in captivity or interfered with their forthcoming release. Neither the Tower Commission nor the congressional investigating committees accepted this interpretation of events. Both thought it far more likely that fear of political embarrassment rather than serious concern for the hostages guided the administration in its decision to withhold information about the Iranian arms sales for almost a year and a half.[20] This would have been even more true of the covert activities in Central America after Congressman Boland's legislation prohibiting such activity.

The general proposition that the executive may keep secrets from the Congress, whether established by principle or precedent, does not answer the specific question of whether the administration should have defied congressional reporting requirements in this case. What is, of course, implied in any presidential decision to withhold information from congressional committees or from congressional leaders is the assumption that sensitive information given to members of the legislature will leak. Indeed, Oliver North made the inability of the Congress to keep secrets, or sustain consistent policies, a theme in his testimony to the Iran-contra investigating committees and used it as his justification for the false testimony he gave to Congress in 1986. [Document 7.2]

It is usually difficult to prove the source of any leak, and while North is no doubt correct that members of Congress have released classified information to the media, so have members of the executive branch.[21] The prevalence of leaks in Washington is so great that the temptation is always present to keep debates over controversial policies within a very tight circle of advisers. In the case of the Iran initiative, important elements of the operation were not only withheld from members of Congress but were also withheld from senior cabinet officers ostensibly responsible for the administration's defense and foreign policies. In presidential decision making, some trade-off must always be made between the risk of premature disclosure and the need to air policy alternatives. The legislation requiring that foreign policy and intelligence information be reported to the Congress aims to put at least a few members of the legislature into the process of evaluating policy alternatives involving arms sales and covert operations. In electing to fully exclude congressmen and partially exclude cabinet officers from that process, the Reagan administration lost wise and cautionary counsel that might have brought the Iran initiative to an earlier and less damaging end.

The administration's aid to the contras during the period of strict Boland prohibitions involves a more fundamental challenge to the Congress than the issue of executive secrecy. Can the president constitutionally conduct a foreign policy that contradicts one of the laws he is sworn to uphold? Admiral Poindexter and Oliver North were never charged with violating the Boland Amendment and were found guilty by juries of crimes that were connected with the destruction of documents and misrepresentations made to congressional committees. Had they been tried for the actions directly related to the resupply of the contras, it might have been argued that because the Boland Amendment makes no specific mention of the National Security Council (though it does mention "any other agency or entity of the United States involved in intelligence activities"), the actions of the NSC staff were exempt from the provisions of that law. It could also be argued that because the funds raised for the contras came from private citizens and foreign governments—except, of course, the money diverted from the Iran initiative—those funds were not subject to regulation by the legislature. Without judging the legal soundness of these arguments, it can safely be said that the actions of the Reagan NSC staff in 1985 and 1986 violated the spirit of the Boland Amendment if not its letter. The Congress, through its power of purse, said that the United States should not provide aid to the contras; the president's agents gave them aid.

There is no question that in a genuine national emergency the president can claim extraordinary powers and act, as Lincoln did in 1861, in violation of the law. With southern states in revolt and the Congress not in session, Lincoln appropriated funds from the Treasury, which the Constitution clearly states can only be done by an act of Congress. He used those funds to pay for troops called to national service and the defense of Washington. Lincoln's eloquent defense of his action is frequently quoted, "By general law life and limb must be protected; yet often a limb must be amputated to protect a life; but a life is never wisely given to save a limb. I felt that measures, otherwise unconstitutional, might become lawful, by becoming indispensable to the preservation of the Constitution, through the preservation of the nation."[22] No national emergency remotely comparable to the Civil War existed in the mid-1980s. Contra aid was never a matter of necessity for the nation; it was merely the political preference of the president.

What, then, are we to expect when two branches of our government are at odds on a major foreign policy question and no national emergency exists? Such struggles are not a new phenomenon. George Washington's declaration of neutrality in the European wars that arose in the aftermath of the French Revolution sparked an intense debate about the constitutional language governing foreign affairs. Alexander Hamilton made the case for broad presidential powers in the conduct of foreign policy, while James Madison argued for a strict interpretation of constitutional language and a larger legislative role. As Louis Henkin has observed, "Madison...had the better of the argument from text and intent; history has tilted toward Hamilton."[23] Critics of this historical result fear the rise of an imperial presidency; its proponents praise the flexibility of the Constitution and its ability to adapt to America's transformation from an isolated frontier to a world power.

When the president and Congress dispute the substance of foreign policy and the limits of their constitutional powers, time is likely to force them toward some resolution. The electorate may change the officeholders in one of the two branches or make its wishes sufficiently clear that existing officeholders change their positions. The process of national debate and deliberation may also lead one of the branches to reconsider its policies as, in fact, occurred on the issue of contra aid when the Congress voted $100 million for the Nicaraguan resistance forces in the summer of 1986. In extreme cases, the impeachment process could be used by the Congress against a president resisting legislated policy.[24] All of these solutions obviously take time, and while the struggle between the branches goes on, there may be no easy constitutional remedy. There is, Justice Jackson wrote in one of the few Supreme Court opinions to consider legislative-executive relations in foreign affairs, "a zone of twilight in which [the president] and Congress may have concurrent authority, or in which its distribution is uncertain."[25] The Iran-contra affair, although raising important questions about the relationship between the branches in the conduct of foreign policy, may not produce lasting answers to those questions because it took place largely in Justice Jackson's constitutional twilight zone.

PROCESS

The constitutional issues raised by the Iran-contra affair were largely defused by President Reagan's willingness to admit that mistakes were made in connection with the foreign policies toward Iran and Nicaragua, and because he claimed personal ignorance of the most controversial mistake of the entire affair—the diversion of funds. Oliver North was fired after the Meese press conference and Admiral Poindexter resigned. Both were taken to court by the special prosecutor appointed to investigate the affair and both were found guilty by the juries that initially heard their cases of violating laws prohibiting the destruction of government documents and lying to Congress. Neither North nor Poindexter was able to produce conclusive evidence that the controversial actions connecting the Iranian initiative with the contra resupply operation were fully approved by the president, and Ronald Reagan's testimony in the Poindexter trial demonstrated an alarming degree of ignorance about the important decisions made in connection with Iran-contra.[26]

The limits in Reagan's knowledge about the Iran initiative and contra aid raise their own set of questions about the making of foreign policy in the Reagan era. What can the president be expected to know about the actions of his subordinates? What relationship should the National Security Council have with the executive departments responsible for foreign affairs? Who actually makes foreign policy—the president, his cabinet secretaries, their bureaucratic assistants, or the members of the president's White House staff?

Some of these same issues were raised in the conclusion to Chapter 4 when we discussed Henry Kissinger's role in the Nixon and Ford administrations. But the issues in Iran-contra are different. When Kissinger was Nixon's national security adviser, he acted with the knowledge and approval of a president well versed in international politics who chose, for his own reasons, to run foreign policy from the White House and to ignore the Department of State and other federal bureaucracies. Kissinger rarely made an important decision or statement that was not part of a strategy worked out in close consultation with the president. In the case of the Reagan administration, it is not clear whether the president fully understood the implications of what Oliver North was doing or the general foreign policy framework to which his actions belonged. In the absence of presidential direction, foreign policy in the Reagan administration was made by informal processes that were severely criticized by the commission established by President Reagan to investigate the affair.

According to the Tower Commission, the national security decision making processes of the Reagan administration were seriously deficient. [Document 7.3] Record keeping about important decisions was haphazard; excessive secrecy prevented an adequate airing of policy implications; coordination with relevant agencies and departments took place only at the cabinet level and, even at that level, was incomplete; warnings from the intelligence community about dangers in dealing with a particular Iranian middleman were unheard or ignored; and emerging problems in both the policies toward Iran and Nicaragua went unrecognized and unaddressed because neither policy ever received formal and systematic review.[27] The problem, according to the Tower Commission, with both the arms-for-hostages policy in Iran and the arms-for-revolution policy in

Central America was the absence of normal and effective decision-making procedures.

But what is normal and what is effective in the making of foreign policy
decisions? The National Security Council was created to enhance the coordination
of policy and encourage the sharing of foreign policy responsibility. It was originally intended to be a check on presidential power. Under President Roosevelt
during the Second World War, it was thought that too many important decisions
were made by the chief executive alone, or negotiated by his personal emissaries,
and not communicated to the departments and agencies responsible for the conduct
of foreign affairs. The National Security Council, legislated into existence by the
National Security Act of 1947, was designed to ensure that presidents would have
periodic meetings with their senior foreign and defense policy advisers in which
the major issues of the day would be discussed. The language of the 1947 act is
clear:

> The function of the Council shall be to advise the President with respect to the
> integration of domestic, foreign, and military policies relating to the national security
> so as to enable the military services and the other departments and agencies of the
> Government to cooperate more effectively in matters involving national security.[28]

Even though the president retained the ultimate responsibility in foreign affairs and
the power to dictate policies for his administration, at least the NSC would ensure
that those policies were made known to appointed officials and coordinated among
the departments and agencies of the federal government.

Throughout the postwar period, the National Security Council has been used
in a wide variety of ways reflecting a variety of presidential styles. Eisenhower had
frequent and formal meetings of the council; Truman, particularly in the period
before the Korean War, only occasionally scheduled or attended such meetings.
Both Truman and Eisenhower had national security advisers who were rarely seen
in public and whose names are nearly forgotten. In their administrations the
president's security adviser served as a clerk for the council and was not expected
to offer independent policy recommendations. Under Kennedy and Johnson, and
even more so under Nixon, the national security adviser took a much more prominent role in the foreign policy process and became an important presidential
assistant in his own right. The council itself became less important as the adviser
and the NSC White House staff grew in influence. In some administrations the
council was replaced by institutions and procedures not anticipated in the 1947
legislation. During the Cuban missile crisis, President Kennedy worked with a
group of advisers that called itself the executive committee of the NSC, or ex com,
when no such committee existed in law or practice. During the Vietnam War
Lyndon Johnson met for lunch on Tuesdays with his secretaries of defense and state
and his national security adviser and used those occasions, rather than NSC
meetings, for serious policymaking in foreign affairs.

Ronald Reagan had more national security advisers than any other president
and never established a consistent pattern for foreign policy coordination. When
his administration began, the national security adviser was Richard Allen, the
president's foreign policy assistant during the campaign. Allen reported to presi-

dential counselor Edwin Meese, not directly to the president, and kept a low profile while Secretary of State Alexander Haig took the leading role in shaping the administration's early international initiatives. In the first year of the Reagan administration, however, very little presidential attention was given to Allen, Haig, or any foreign policy adviser. The president and the senior members of the White House staff were devoting their time and energy to the tax and budget cuts that dominated the domestic agenda in 1981. Allen was replaced by Judge William Clark, a Reagan associate from California who knew the president well but had little experience in foreign affairs. When Clark was appointed secretary of the interior, his national security duties were taken over by McFarlane and then Poindexter. After Poindexter's resignation, Reagan had two more national security advisers, Frank Carlucci and Colin Powell.

In the critical period of decisions connected to Iran-contra, members of the NSC staff operated without sufficient supervision. By taking an active role in the resupply of the contras, Oliver North was challenging the Congress and its Boland amendments. That challenge may have been worth taking, but its implications were never fully debated at the senior levels of the Reagan administration. In promoting and carrying out the secret arms sales to Iran, North was risking serious political embarrassment for the administration if it were ever discovered that arms were being traded for hostages. This question was raised at the highest levels of the administration, but after several cabinet secretaries expressed serious objections to any dealings with Iran they were subsequently excluded from full information about further policy developments. By merging the two operations with the diversion of funds, North was multiplying the chances of being caught and the price that would be paid if secrecy were ever lost.

President Reagan knew something about both policies. He signed findings approving the arms-for-hostages plan, though he tended to think of it, and remember it, as an opening to Iranian moderates. He frequently and fervently stated his opposition to the Boland amendments and worked to keep the contras going until the Congress could be persuaded to change its mind on contra funding. But apparently, President Reagan did not know very much about the details of either policy or the connections between them. His secretaries of defense and state also remained ignorant about a number of relevant details. The president's national security advisers in 1985 and 1986—McFarlane and Poindexter—who did know what was going on, failed to fully inform Reagan, Caspar Weinberger, and George Shultz. They also failed to stop North from taking excessive risks. During the transition between the two national security advisers and after the disastrous secret trip to Tehran, McFarlane did recommend that North be removed from the NSC and reassigned to less sensitive duties, but Poindexter failed to follow through on that recommendation.[29]

In North's testimony to the Iran-contra committees and in some of the subsequent analysis of the affair, there is considerable speculation about the role CIA Director William Casey may have played in North's activities.[30] North claims that Casey was fully aware of what he was doing and encouraged him to persevere. Casey reportedly wanted to see the creation of a White House covert action capability that would be outside the CIA and beyond the reach of congressional interference.[31] What Casey may have thought about how the president would control such a covert capability was never determined, but McFarlane and Poindexter may have given North less supervision than was necessary because they thought Casey was doing so. Casey's death in the midst of the Iran-contra investigations, and before he had an opportunity to testify, leaves a number of unanswered questions about his contribution to the affair and how sensitive foreign policy and intelligence decisions were actually made in the Reagan White House.

PERSONALITY

Critics of the Reagan administration find it hard to believe that Poindexter, McFarlane, Casey, and others knowledgeable about the diversion of funds and the many controversial aspects of Iran-contra would have kept the president uninformed about such politically dangerous details. Reagan has consistently said he did not know about the diversion, and several observers close to the Reagan National Security Council staff find it plausible that he would not have known this essential information.[32] They attribute the president's limited knowledge of North's activities to more than lax procedures in the administration of the National Security Council. At its heart the Iran-contra affair cannot be understood without coming to grips with President Reagan's unusual personal qualities.

Ronald Reagan was probably the most ideological president in recent American experience. He came to office with strongly held beliefs on a number of domestic and foreign policy issues that did not change throughout his administration. While president he was capable of stubbornly sticking to his convictions, even when those convictions were widely criticized in the nation at large and within his own administration. During the deep recession of 1982 he resisted the advice of Wall Street commentators and his own budget director that major new taxes would have to be considered in order to avoid dangerous deficits. Reagan chose, instead, to live with mounting national debt. Before he gave his 1983 speech announcing the strategic defense initiative, Reagan overruled Defense Department experts who argued that effective ballistic missile defense was not possible. When SDI became extremely controversial in the Congress and when Soviet Premier Gorbachev urged him to give it up in a major arms control agreement, he stuck with the program he had initially recommended.

The portrait of Reagan as a strong and ideologically motivated leader is, however, incomplete and must be balanced with observations frequently made by his closest associates. Ronald Reagan, unlike most governors, presidents, or national political candidates rarely gave orders to his subordinates. People working for him found him to be pleasant and intelligent but remarkably unassertive. Reagan conveyed warmth and self-confidence but very little of the energy and ambition to get things done that characterize most politicians. He delegated authority widely and trusted those to whom he made delegations. When American planes late one night were attacked off the coast of Libya and returned fire, the president's advisers chose not to wake him with news of the attack or the American response. That incident became a symbol of the president's detachment from the day-to-day affairs of state.

Like Dwight Eisenhower, Ronald Reagan came to political office late in life and used his age and amiable personality to build broad public trust and support.

As noted in Chapter 2, recent scholarship has demonstrated that Eisenhower was an activist president who behind the scenes was fully in control of his cabinet officers and White House staff. Reagan was not.[33] He apparently trusted his assistants and associates to carry out his wishes without feeling the need to state those wishes in precise language or bothering to check on their implementation. He often communicated his views to those around him by telling stories and anecdotes rather than giving specific instructions. Uncomfortable in situations where he was expected to have detailed knowledge of a complicated subject, Reagan preferred prepared speeches or informal discussions to press conferences and debates. According to one of his biographers, he was a "passively decisive" individual.[34] A prominent political scientist makes much the same point when he describes the Reagan administration as a "committed Presidency" run by a "detached President."[35] Those phrases capture a contradictory quality in Reagan's character without really explaining it.

What does explain Reagan's passivity and detachment? Some observers argue that Reagan's childhood as the son of an alcoholic salesman who had considerable difficulty holding a job may have made him an unusually private individual who uses his likable nature to hide his true feelings and avoid rejection. Others point to the president's background as an actor and remind us that in much of his adult life he was accustomed to reading other people's scripts and doing his job by effectively playing a solitary part rather than directing the action of others.[36] Acting demands that an individual respond to an audience and somehow convert the imaginary into the believable. Throughout his presidency, Ronald Reagan used his skills as a communicator to win approval for the programs and policies of his administration, and whether he did so in nationally televised speeches, weekly radio broadcasts, or face-to-face meetings with members of Congress, he was remarkably successful. In this regard he was nearly the opposite of his predecessor, who gave his attention to the facts and figures of the policymaking process and too often expected that if the right decision were made, public relations would take care of itself. But just as Carter paid a political price for concentrating on the details of policy, Reagan paid a very high price for leaving those details to others. More than most presidents his success depended heavily on the character and capabilities of those who worked for him. In the case of Iran-contra they let him down.

Chronology of the Iran-Contra Affair

1981

Dec   Reagan signs a finding authorizing covert CIA support of the contras in order to interdict Nicaraguan arms flowing to rebels in El Salvador.

1982

Dec 21   First Boland Amendment becomes law.

1984

Jan 20   State Department declares Iran to be a state-sponsor of terrorism.

Feb 21   McFarlane warns Reagan that contra movement is running out of money.

Mar – Apr   Public revelations of CIA role in the mining of Nicaraguan harbors leads to congressional demands for end of all aid to the contras.

Mar 16   William Buckley, CIA station chief in Beirut, is kidnapped by pro-Iranian extremists in Lebanon. From May 1984 to May 1985 five more Americans will be kidnapped in Lebanon.

May   McFarlane persuades Saudis to contribute to contra cause.

Sep   Congress learns about CIA manual with assassination instructions.

Oct 12   President signs legislation with strengthened Boland Amendment.

1985

Jun 3   Kidnap victim William Buckley reported killed.

Jul   North takes over control of funds for the contras. Israelis approach McFarlane about possibility of opening an American-Iranian political discourse. Reagan approves sale of TOW anti-tank missiles to Iran.

Aug 20   Israel sends 96 TOW missiles to Iran

Sep 13   Israel ships 408 more TOWs to Iran; kidnap victim Peter Weir is released.

Nov 24   CIA arranges for shipment of 18 Hawk antiaircraft missiles to Iran.

Dec 4   McFarlane resigns as NSC adviser and is replaced by Poindexter.

Dec 5   Reagan signs retroactive "finding" authorizing arms sales to Iran.

Dec 7   NSC has full-scale discussion of arms sales to Iran. Shultz and McFarlane oppose continued sales.

1986

Jan 7   NSC reconsiders arms sales to Iran. Shultz and Weinberger oppose sales.

Jan 17   Reagan signs finding approving additional arms shipments to Iran. Copies of this document are not sent to NSC members who opposed arms sales.

Feb   U.S. ships 1,000 TOWs to Iran in two shipments and supplies Iran with intelligence information about Iraq. No hostages are released.

(cont.)

(cont.)	
Apr	North writes memo that mentions plan to use $12 million of Iran profits for the contras.
May 23	508 TOWs and spare parts for Hawk missiles shipped to Israel for Iran.
May 25	McFarlane, North, and others travel to Iran and attempt to negotiate additional hostage releases. Mission fails.
Jun 26	Congress approves $100 million in contra aid.
Jul 26	Beirut hostage Father Jenco freed.
Aug 3	U.S. sends Iran Hawk spare parts.
Aug 6	North in testimony before Congress denies that he has raised money for the contras or offered them military advice.
Sep – Oct	Three new hostages taken in Lebanon.
Oct 5	NSC staff members begin discussions with representatives of the second channel to Iran. In Nicaragua, contra resupply plane is shot down and Hasenfus is taken prisoner.
Oct 29	Another 500 TOWs sent by Israel to Iran.
Nov 2	Hostage Jacobsen is released.
Nov 3	Lebanese magazine *Al Shiraa* reveals U.S. arms shipments to Iran.
Nov 12–19	North and others prepare inaccurate chronologies of events.
Nov 19	Reagan at press conference gives erroneous and misleading information about arms to Iran.
Nov 21	CIA Director Casey appears before Congress to testify. Meese suggests to president the need for internal investigation. North begins shredding documents.
Nov 23	North admits to Meese that money was diverted to contras.
Nov 25	Meese makes public announcement of diversion; North fired, Poindexter resigns.

Chapter 7 Documents

Document 7.1
Oliver North's April 1986 Memorandum (the diversion memo)

Background.—In June 1985, private American and Israeli citizens commenced an operation to effect the release of the American Hostages in Beirut in exchange for providing certain factions in Iran with U.S.-origin Israeli military material. By September, U.S. and Israeli Government officials became involved in this endeavor in order to ensure that the USG would:

- not object to the Israeli transfer of embargoed material to Iran;
- sell replacement items to Israel as replenishment for like items sold to Iran by Israel.

On September 13, the Israeli Government, with the endorsement of the USG, transferred 508 TOW missiles to Iran. Forty-eight hours later, Reverend Benjamin Weir was released in Beirut.

Subsequent efforts by both governments to continue this process have met with frustration due to the need to communicate our intentions through an Iranian expatriate arms dealer in Europe. In January 1986, under the provisions of a new Covert Action Finding, the USG demanded a meeting with responsible Iranian government officials.

On February 20, a U.S. Government official met with an official in the Iranian Prime Minister's office—the first direct U.S.-Iranian contact in over five years. At this meeting, the U.S. side made an effort to refocus Iranian attention on the threat posed by the Soviet Union and the need to establish a longer term relationship between our two countries based on more than arms transactions. It was emphasized that the hostage issue was a 'hurdle' which must be crossed before this improved relationship could prosper. During the meeting, it also became apparent that our conditions/demand had not been accurately transmitted to the Iranian government by the intermediary and it was agreed that:

- The USG would establish its good faith and bona fides by immediately providing 1,000 TOW missiles for sale to Iran. This transaction was covertly completed on February 21, using a private U.S. firm and the Israelis as intermediaries.
- A subsequent meeting would be held in Iran with senior U.S. and Iranian officials during which the U.S. hostages would be released.
- Immediately after the hostages were safely in our hands, the U.S. would sell an additional 3,000 TOW missiles to Iran using the same procedures employed during the September 1985 transfer.

In early March, the Iranian expatriate intermediary demanded that Iranian conditions for release of the hostages now included the prior sale of 200 PHOENIX missiles and an unspecified number of HARPOON missiles, in addition to the 3,000 TOW's which would be delivered after the hostages were released. A subsequent meeting was held with the intermediary in Paris on March 8, wherein it was explained that the requirement for prior deliveries violated the understanding reached in Frankfurt on February 20, and were [sic] therefore unacceptable. It was further noted that the Iranian aircraft and ship launchers for these missiles were in such disrepair that the missiles could not be launched even if provided.

From March 9 and until March 30, there was no further effort undertaken on our behalf to contact the Iranian Government or the intermediary. On March 26, [the official in the Prime Minister's office] made an unsolicited call to the phone-drop in Maryland which we had established for the purpose. [He] asked why we had not been in contact and urged that we proceed expeditiously since the situation in Beirut was deteriorating rapidly. He was informed by our Farsi-speaking interpreter that the conditions requiring additional material beyond the 3,000 TOW's were unacceptable and that we could in no case provide anything else prior to the release of our hostages. [The Iranian official] observed that we were correct in our assessment of their inability to use PHOENIX and HARPOON missiles and that the most urgent requirement that Iran had was to place their current HAWK missile inventory in working condition. In a subsequent phone call, we agreed to discuss this matter with him and he indicated that he would prepare an inventory of parts required to make their HAWK systems operational. This parts list was received on March 28, and verified by CIA.

Current Situation.—On April 3, Ari Gorbanifahr [sic], the Iranian intermediary, arrived in Washington, D.C. with instructions from [his Tehran contact] to consummate final arrangements for the return of the hostages. Gorbanifahr was reportedly enfranchised to negotiate the types, quantities, and delivery procedures for materiel the U.S. would sell to Iran through Israel. The meeting lasted nearly all night on April 3–4, and involved numerous calls to Tehran. A Farsi-speaking CIA officer in attendance was able to verify the substance of his calls to Tehran during the meeting. Subject to Presidential approval, it was agreed to proceed as follows:

- By Monday, April 7, the Iranian Government will transfer $17 million to an Israeli account in Switzerland. The Israelis will, in turn, transfer to a private U.S. corporation account in Switzerland the sum of $15 million.
- On Tuesday, April 8 (or as soon as the transactions are verified), the private U.S. corporation will transfer the $3,651 million to a CIA account in Switzerland. CIA will then transfer this sum to a covert Department of the Army account in the U.S.
- On Wednesday, April 9, the CIA will commence procuring $3.61 million worth of HAWK missile parts (240 separate line items) and transferring these parts to. . . This process is estimated to take seven working days.
- On Friday, April 18, a private U.S. aircraft (707B) will pick-up the HAWK missile parts at . . . and fly them to a covert Israeli airfield for prepositioning (this field was used for the earlier delivery of the 1000 TOW's). At this field, the parts will be transferred to an Israeli Defense Forces' (IDF) aircraft with false markings. A SATCOM capability will be positioned at this location.
- On Saturday, April 19, McFarlane, North, Teicher, Cave, [C/NE], and a SATCOM communicator will board an aircraft in Frankfort, Germany, enroute [sic] to Tehran.
- On Sunday, April 20, the following series of events will occur:
- U.S. party arrives Tehran (A-hour) — met by Rafsanjani, as head of the Iranian delegation.
- At A+7 hours, the U. S. hostages will be released in Beirut.
- At A+15 hours, the IDF aircraft with the HAWK missile parts aboard will land at Bandar Abbas, Iran.

Discussion.—The following points are relevant to this transaction, the discussions in Iran, the establishment of a broader relationship between the United States and Iran:

- The Iranians have been told that our presence in Iran is a 'holy commitment' on the part of the USG that we are sincere and can be trusted. There is great distrust of the U.S. among the various Iranian parties involved. Without our presence on the ground in Iran, they will not believe that we will fulfill our end of the bargain after the hostages are released.

- The Iranians know, probably better than we, that both Arafat and Qhadhaffi are trying hard to have the hostages turned over to them. Gorbanifahr specifically mentioned that Qhadhaffi's efforts to 'buy' the hostages could succeed in the near future. Further, the Iranians are well aware that the situation in Beirut is deteriorating rapidly and that the abilitiy [sic] of the IRGC [Iranian Revolutionary Guard Corps] to effect the release of the hostages will become increasingly more difficult over time.

- We have convinced the Iranians of a significant near term and long range threat from the Soviet Union. We have real and deceptive intelligence to demonstrate this threat during the visit. They have expressed considerable interest in this matter as part of the longer term relationship.

- We have told the Iranians that we are interested in assistance they may be willing to provide to the Afghan resistance and that we wish to discuss this matter in Tehran.

- The Iranians have been told that their provision of assistance to Nicaragua is unacceptable to us and they have agreed to discuss this matter in Tehran.

- We have further indicated to the Iranians that we wish to discuss steps leading to a cessation of hostilities between Iran and Iraq. . . .

- The Iranians are well aware that their most immediate needs are for technical assistance in maintaining their air force and navy. We should expect that they will raise this issue during the discussions in Tehran. Further conversation with Gorbanifahr on April 4, indicates that they will want to raise the matter of the original 3,000 TOW's as a significant deterrent to a potential Soviet move against Iran. They have also suggested that, if agreement is reached on TOW's, they will make 200 out of each 1,000 available to the Afghan resistance and train the resistance forces in how to use them against the Soviets. We have agreed to discuss this matter.

- The Iranians have been told and agreed that they will receive neither blame nor credit for the seizure/release of the hostages.

- The residual funds from this transaction are allocated as follows:

- $2 million will be used to purchase replacement TOW's for the original 508 sold by Israel to Iran for the release of Benjamin Weir. This is the only way that we have found to meet our commitment to replenish these stocks.

- *$12 million will be used to purchase critically needed supplies for the Nicaraguan Democratic Resistance Forces. This materiel is essential to cover shortages in resistance inventories resulting from their current offensives and Sandinista counter-attacks and to 'bridge' the period between now and when Congressionally-approved lethal assistance (beyond the $25 million in 'defensive' arms) can be delivered.* [Emphasis added.]

The ultimate objective in the trip to Tehran is to commence the process of improving U.S.-Iranian relations. Both sides are aware that the Iran-Iraq War is a major factor that must be discussed. We should not, however, view this meeting as a session which will result in immediate Iranian agreement to proceed with a settlement with Iraq. Rather, this meeting, the first high-level U.S.-Iranian contact in five years, should be seen as a chance to move in this direction. These discussions, as well as follow-on talks, should be governed by the Terms of Reference (TOR) (Tab A) with the recognition that this is, hopefully, the first of many meetings and that the hostage issue, once behind us, improves the opportunities for this relationship. Finally, we should recognize that the Iranians will undoubtedly want to discuss additional arms and commercial transactions as 'quids' for accommodating our points on Afghanistan, Nicaragua, and Iraq. Our emphasis on the Soviet military and subversive threat, a useful mechanism in bringing them to agreement on the hostage issue, has also served to increase their desire for means to protect themselves against/deter the Soviets.

RECOMMENDATION

That the President approve the structure depicted above under 'Current Situation' and the Terms of Reference at Tab A.

Approve _____   **Disapprove** _____

Source: From the files of The National Security Archive, 1755 Massachusetts Avenue N.W., Washington, D.C. This copy of the diversion memo was found in Oliver North's White House files in the course of the Meese investigations. There is no indication on the copy recovered by Meese and his associates that the president ever saw the memo or checked the approve/disapprove blanks.

Document 7.2
Testimony of Lieutenant Colonel Oliver North
to the Iran-Contra Committees of the House and Senate,
selected passages, July 9, 1987

As you all know by now, my name is Oliver North, lieutenant colonel, Marine Corps.

I came to the National Security Council six years ago to work in the Administration of a great President. As a staff member, I came to understand his goals and his desires. I admired his policies, his strength and his ability to bring our country together. I observed the President to be a leader who cared deeply about people and who believed that the interests of our country were advanced by recognizing that ours is a nation at risk in a dangerous world, and acting accordingly. He tried, and in my opinion succeeded, in advancing the cause of world peace by strengthening our country, by acting to restore and sustain democracy throughout the world and by having the courage to take decisive action when needed.

I also believed that we must guard against a rather perverse side of American life, and that is the tendency to launch vicious attacks and criticism against our elected officials. President Reagan has made enormous contributions, and he deserves our respect and admiration.

The National Security Council is, in essence, the President's staff. It helps to formulate and coordinate national security policy. Some, perhaps on this committee, believe that the N.S.C. was devoid of experienced leadership. I believe that is wrong. While at the N.S.C. I worked most closely with three people—Mr. Robert C. McFarlane, Adm. John Poindexter and C.I.A. Director William Casey.

There is nearly a century of combined public service by these three men.

As a member of the N.S.C. staff, I knew that I held a position of responsibility, but I knew full well what my position was. I did not engage in fantasy that I was the President or Vice President, or a Cabinet member, or even the director of the National Security Council. I was simply a staff member with a demonstrated ability to get the job done. Over time, I was made responsible for managing a number of complex and sensitive covert operations that we have discussed here to date. I reported directly to Mr. McFarlane and to Admiral Poindexter. I coordinated directly with others, including Director Casey.

My authority to act always flowed, I believed, from my superiors. My military training inculcated in me a strong belief in the chain of command. Insofar as I can recall, I always acted on major matters with specific approval, after informing my superiors of the facts as I knew them, the risks and the potential benefits. I readily admit that I was action-oriented, that I took pride in the fact that I was counted upon as a man who got the job done. And I don't mean this by way of criticism, but there were occasions when my superiors, confronted with accomplishing goals or difficult tasks, would simply say, "Fix it, Ollie," or "Take care of it."...

During 1984, '85 and '86, there were periods of time when we worked two days in every one. My guess is that the average workday lasted at least 14 hours. To respond to various crises, the need for such was frequent, and we would often go without a night's sleep, hoping to recoup the next night or thereafter. If I had to estimate the number of meetings and discussions and phone calls over that five years, it would surely be in the tens of thousands. My only real regret is that I virtually abandoned my family for work during these years. And that work consisted of, my first few years on the staff, as a project officer for a highly classified and compartmented national security project which is not a part of this inquiry.

I worked hard on the political military strategy for restoring and sustaining democracy in Central America and in particular El Salvador. We sought to achieve the democratic outcome in Nicaragua that this Administration still supports, which involved keeping the contras together in both body and soul. We made efforts to open a new relationship with Iran and recover our hostages. We worked on the development of a concerted policy regarding terrorists and terrorism and a capability for dealing in a concerted manner with that threat. We worked on various crises such as T.W.A. 847, the capture of Achille Lauro, the rescue of American students in Grenada and the restoration of democracy on that small island, and the U.S. raid on Libya in response to their terrorist attacks....

I believe that this is a strange process that you are putting me and others through. Apparently the President has chosen not to assert his prerogatives, and you have been permitted to make the rules. You call before you the officials of the executive branch, you put them under oath for what must be collectively thousands of hours of testimony. You dissect that testimony to find inconsistencies and declare some to be truthful and others to be liars.

You make the rulings as to what is proper and what is not proper. You put the testimony which you think is helpful to your goals up before the people and leave others out. It's sort of like a baseball game in which you are both the player and the umpire. It's a game in which you call the balls and strikes and where you determine who is out and who is safe. And in the end you determine the score and declare yourselves the winner. From where I sit, it is not the fairest process.

One thing is, I think, for certain: that you will not investigate yourselves in this matter. There is not much chance that you will conclude at the end of these hearings that the Boland Amendments and the frequent policy changes therefore were unwise, or that your restrictions should not have been imposed on the executive branch. You are not likely to conclude that the Administration acted properly by trying to sustain the freedom fighters in Nicaragua when they were abandoned. And you are not likely to conclude by commending the President of the United States, who tried valiantly to recover our citizens and achieve an opening with strategically vital Iran.

It is also difficult to comprehend that my work at the N.S.C., all of which was approved and carried out in the best interests of our country, has led to two massive parallel investigations, staffed by over 200 people. It is mind-boggling to me that one of those investigations is criminal and that some here have attempted to criminalize policy differences between coequal branches of government and the executive's conduct of foreign affairs.

I believe it is inevitable that the Congress will, in the end, blame the executive branch. But I suggest to you that it is the Congress which must accept at least some of the blame in the Nicaraguan freedom-fighters matter.

Plain and simple, the Congress is to blame because of the fickle, vacillating, unpredictable, on-again-off-again policy toward the Nicaraguan democratic resistance, the so-called contras.

I do not believe that the support of the Nicaraguan freedom fighters can be treated as the passage of a budget. I suppose if the budget doesn't get passed on time again this year, there will be, inevitably, another extension of a month or two. But the contras, the Nicaraguan freedom fighters, are people, living, breathing, young men and women who have had to suffer a desperate struggle for liberty, with sporadic and confusing support from the United States of America.

Armies need food and consistent help. They need a flow of money, of arms, clothing and medical supplies. The Congress of the United States allowed the executive to encourage them to do battle and then abandoned them.

The Congress of the United States left soldiers in the field unsupported and vulnerable to their Communist enemies. When the executive branch did everything possible, within the law, to prevent them from being wiped out by Moscow's surrogates in Havana, in Managua, you then had this investigation to blame the problem on the executive branch. It does not make sense to me.

In my opinion, these hearings have caused serious damage to our national interests. Our adversaries laugh at us, and our friends recoil in horror. I suppose it would be one thing if the intelligence committees wanted to hear all of this in private and thereafter passed laws which, in the view of Congress, make for better policies, for better functioning of government, but to hold them publicly, for the whole world to see, strikes me as very harmful.

Not only does it embarrass our friends and allies, with whom we have worked, many of whom have helped us in various programs, but it must also make them very wary of helping us again.

I believe that these hearings, perhaps unintentionally so, have revealed matters of great secrecy in the operation of our Government. And sources and methods of intelligence activities have clearly been revealed, to the detriment of our security....

Source: *Joint Hearings Before the Senate Select Committee on Secret Military Assistance to Iran and the Nicaraguan Opposition and the House Select Committee to Investigate Covert Arms Transactions with Iran*, Part I, July 7, 8, 9 and 10, 1987, pp. 187–192.

Document 7.3
The Tower Commission Report,
selected passages, 1987

Part IV What Went Wrong

The arms transfers to Iran and the activities of the NSC staff in support of the Contras are case studies in the perils of policy pursued outside the constraints of orderly process.

The Iran initiative ran directly counter to the Administration's own policies on terrorism, the Iran/Iraq war, and military support to Iran. This inconsistency was never resolved, nor were the consequences of this inconsistency fully considered and provided for. The result taken as a whole was a U.S. policy that worked against itself.

The Board believes that the failure to deal adequately with these contradictions resulted in large part from the flaws in the manner in which decisions were made. Established procedures for making national security decisions were ignored. Reviews of the initiative by all the NSC principals were too infrequent. The initiatives were not adequately vetted below the cabinet level. Intelligence resources were underutilized. Applicable legal constraints were not adequately addressed. The whole matter was handled too informally, without adequate written records of what had been considered, discussed, and decided.

This pattern persisted in the implementation of the Iran initiative. The NSC staff assumed direct operational control. The initiatives fell within the traditional jurisdictions of the Departments of State, Defense, and CIA. Yet these agencies were largely ignored. Great reliance was placed on a network of private operators and intermediaries. How the initiative was to be carried out never received adequate attention from the NSC principals or a tough working-level review. No periodic evaluation of the progress of the initiative was ever conducted. The result was an unprofessional and, in substantial part, unsatisfactory operation. . . .

B. Failure of Responsibility

The NSC system will not work unless the President makes it work. After all, this system was created to serve the President of the United States in ways of his choosing. By his actions, by his leadership, the President therefore determines the quality of its performance.

By his own account, as evidenced in his diary notes, and as conveyed to the Board by his principal advisors, President Reagan was deeply committed to securing the release of the hostages. It was this intense compassion for the hostages that appeared to motivate his steadfast support of the Iran initiative, even in the face of opposition from his Secretaries of State and Defense.

In his obvious commitment, the President appears to have proceeded with a concept of the initiative that was not accurately reflected in the reality of the operation. The President did not seem to be aware of the way in which the operation was implemented and the full consequences of U.S. participation.

The President's expressed concern for the safety of both the hostages and the Iranians who could have been at risk may have been conveyed in a manner so as to inhibit the full functioning of the system.

The President's management style is to put the principal responsibility for policy review and implementation on the shoulders of his advisors. Nevertheless, with such a complex, high-risk operation and so much at stake, the President should have ensured that the NSC system did not fail him. He did not force his policy to undergo the most critical review of which the NSC participants and the process were capable. At no time did he insist upon accountability and performance review. Had the President chosen to drive the NSC system, the outcome could well have been different. As it was, the most powerful features of the NSC system—providing comprehensive analysis, alternatives and follow-up—were not utilized.

The Board found a strong consensus among NSC participants that the President's priority in the Iran initiative was the release of U.S. hostages. But setting priorities is not enough when it comes to sensitive and risky initiatives that directly affect U.S. national security. He must ensure that the content and the tactics of an initiative match his priorities and objectives. He must insist upon accountability. For it is the President who must take responsibility for the NSC system and deal with the consequences.

Beyond the President, the other NSC principals and the National Security Advisor must share in the responsibility for the NSC system.

President Reagan's personal management style places an especially heavy responsibility on his key advisors. Knowing his style, they should have been particularly mindful of the need for special attention to the manner in which this arms sale initiative developed and proceeded. On this score, neither the National Security Advisor nor the other NSC principals deserve high marks.

It is their obligation as members and advisors to the Council to ensure that the President is adequately served. The principal subordinates to the President must not be deterred from urging the President not to proceed on a highly questionable course of action even in the face of his strong conviction to the contrary.

In the case of the Iran initiative, the NSC process did not fail, it simply was largely ignored. The National Security Advisor and the NSC principals all had a duty to raise this issue and insist that orderly process be imposed. None of them did so.

All had the opportunity. While the National Security Advisor had the responsibility to see that an orderly process was observed, his failure to do so does not excuse the other NSC principals. It does not appear that any of the NSC principals called for more frequent consideration of the Iran initiative by the NSC principals in the presence of the President. None of the principals called for a serious vetting of the initiative by even a restricted group of disinterested individuals. The intelligence questions do not appear to have been raised, and legal considerations, while raised, were not pressed. No one seemed to have complained about the informality of the process. No one called for a thorough reexamination once the initiative did not meet expectations or the manner of execution changed. While one or another of the NSC principals suspected that something was amiss, none vigorously pursued the issue.

Mr. Regan also shares in this responsibility. More than almost any Chief of Staff of recent memory, he asserted personal control over the White House staff and sought to extend this control to the National Security Advisor. He was personally active in national security affairs and attended almost all of the relevant meetings regarding the Iran initiative. He, as much as anyone, should have insisted that an orderly process be observed. In addition, he especially should have ensured that plans were made for handling any public disclosure of the initiative. He must bear primary responsibility for the chaos that descended upon the White House when such disclosure did occur.

Mr. McFarlane appeared caught between a President who supported the initiative and the cabinet officers who strongly opposed it. While he made efforts to keep these cabinet officers informed, the Board heard complaints from some that he was not always successful. VADM [Vice Admiral] Poindexter on several occasions apparently sought to exclude NSC principals other than the President from knowledge of the initiative. Indeed, on one or more occasions Secretary Shultz may have been actively misled by VADM Poindexter.

VADM Poindexter also failed grievously on the matter of Contra diversion. Evidence indicates that VADM Poindexter knew that a diversion occurred, yet he did not take the steps that were required given the gravity of that prospect. He apparently failed to appreciate or ignored the serious legal and political risks presented. His clear obligation was either to investigate the matter or take it to the President—or both. He did neither. Director Casey shared a similar responsibility. Evidence suggest that he received information about the possible diversion of funds to the Contras almost a month before the story broke. He, too, did not move promptly to raise the matter with the President. Yet his responsibility to do so was clear.

The NSC principals other that the President may be somewhat excused by the insufficient attention on the part of the National Security Advisor to the need to keep all the principals fully informed. Given the importance of the issue and the sharp policy divergences involved, however, Secretary Shultz and Secretary Weinberger in particular distanced themselves from the march of events. Secretary Shultz specifically requested to be informed only as necessary to perform his job. Secretary Weinberger had access through intelligence to details about the operation. Their obligation was to give the President their full support and continued advice with respect to the program or, if they could not in conscience do that, to so inform the President. Instead, they simply distanced themselves from the program. They protected the record as to their own positions on this issue. They were not energetic in attempting to protect the President from the consequences of his personal commitment to freeing the hostages.

Director Casey appears to have been informed in considerable detail about the specifics of the Iranian operation. He appears to have acquiesced in and to have encouraged the operation. Because of the NSC staff's proximity to and close identification with the President, this increased the risks to the President if the initiative became public or the operation failed.

There is no evidence, however, that Director Casey explained this risk to the President or made clear to the President that Lt Col North, rather than the CIA, was running the operation. The President does not recall ever being informed of this fact. Indeed, Director Casey should have gone further and pressed for operational responsibility to be transferred to the CIA.

Director Casey should have taken the lead in vetting the assumptions presented by the Israelis on which the program was based and in pressing for an early examination of the reliance upon Mr. Ghorbanifar and the second channel as intermediaries. He should also have assumed responsibility for checking out the other intermediaries involved in the operation. Finally, because Congressional restrictions on covert actions are both largely directed at and familiar to the CIA, Director Casey should have taken the lead in keeping the question of Congressional notification active.

Finally, Director Casey, and to a lesser extent, Secretary Weinberger, should have taken it upon themselves to assess the effect of the transfer of arms and intelligence to Iran on the Iran/Iraq military balance, and to transmit that information to the President.

Source: *Report of the President's Special Review Board* (February 26, 1987).

Chapter 7 Notes

[1]For excellent accounts of Carter administration policy toward Iran and Nicaragua, see Gary Sick, *All Fall Down* (New York: Random House, 1985); and Robert A. Pastor, *Condemned to Repetition* (Princeton, N.J.: Princeton University Press, 1987).

[2]Approximately 500 TOW antitank missiles were sent to Iran in two shipments. A shipment of eighteen Hawk antiaircraft missiles did not meet Iranian expectations and were returned.

[3]Arms Export Control Act. This law requires that a report be made to Congress of any arms transfer or retransfer in excess of $14 million and that the receiving country give written assurance that it will not retransfer American arms without American permission. In addition, the act was amended in August 1986 prohibiting the transfer of arms to any country on the State Department's list of nations sponsoring terrorism, a list that included Iran.

[4]Two pieces of legislation contain reporting requirements for covert operations: the National Security Act of 1947, Section 501 (amended in 1980), which is quoted above; and the Hughes-Ryan Amendment to the Foreign Assistance Act (passed in 1974). The texts of these laws are reprinted in the appendix of Loch Johnson, *A Season of Inquiry* (Chicago: Dorsey Press, 1988), pp. 283–285.

[5]*Report of the Congressional Committees Investigating the Iran-Contra Affair with the Minority Report*, abr.ed., Joel Brinkley and Stephen Engelberg, eds.(New York: Times Books, 1988), p. 269.

[6]Don Regan, *For the Record* (New York: Harcourt Brace Jovanovich, 1988), pp. 10–11.

[7]*The Chronology*, prepared by the National Security Archive (New York: Warner Books, 1987), p. 239–240. The bracketed third purpose was added to the original draft of this finding at the insistence of CIA counsel.

[8]Fifteen hundred TOW missiles were shipped in three deliveries of 500 each, as well as three shipments of Hawk missile spare parts.

[9]There is some contradictory evidence on this point. See William S. Cohen and George J. Mitchell, *Men of Zeal* (New York: Viking, 1988), p. 219.

[10]*The Chronology*, p. 66.

[11]"Bush Joined Efforts by Reagan Aides to Solicit Arms for Contras During Ban," *Washington Post*, April 7, 1989.

[12]*Report of the Congressional Committees Investigating the Iran-Contra Affair*, pp. 128–129.

[13]Ibid., p. 39.

[14]Ibid., pp. 122–123.

[15]For a review of constitutional issues raised by the Iran-contra affair, see a special issue of the *Houston Journal of International Law* (Fall 1988).

[16]Alexander Hamilton, John Jay, and James Madison, *The Federalist* (New York: Modern Library, 1937), p. 420.

[17]Ibid., p. 419.

[18]This is the informal name for Section 501 of the National Security Act of 1947, which was amended in 1980 to provide for greater accountability in intelligence activities.

[19]This issue was raised by Senator Daniel Moynihan in William Casey's confirmation hearings. For a brief summary of their exchange, see Bob Woodward, *Veil* (New York: Simon & Schuster, 1987), pp. 81–83.

[20]This was the conclusion reached in *The Tower Commission Report* (New York: Times Books, 1987), pp. 74–75; and *Report of the Congressional Committees Investigating the Iran-Contra Affair*, p. 354, with the minority report dissenting on the seriousness of congressional leaks, p. 451.

[21]For a summary of alleged congressional leaks of sensitive foreign policy information, see Bruce Fine, "The Constitution and Covert Action," *Houston Journal of International Law* (Fall 1988), pp. 53–68.

[22]Letter to Albert G. Hodges from *The Complete Works of Abraham Lincoln*, eds. John Nicolay and John Hay, (New York: Francis D. Tandy Co., 1894), vol. X, pp. 65–66.

[23]Louis Henkin, "Foreign Affairs and the Constitution," *Foreign Affairs* (Winter 1987/88), p. 292.

[24]It is not clear, however, that a conflict over foreign policy could be counted as a high crime or misdemeanor. The House Judiciary Committee dropped from its bill of impeachment against Richard Nixon an article dealing with the secret war in Cambodia that the Nixon administration conducted at a time when Congress had restricted funding for such a purpose.

[25]*Youngstown Sheet & Tube Co.* v. *Sawyer* (1952).

[26]"Reagan Testifies He Told Aides 'We Don't Break the Law,'" *Washington Post*, February 23, 1990, p. A11.

[27]For a summary of the Tower Commission findings, see *Tower Commission Report*, pp. xvii–xix.

[28]Quoted in *Tower Commission Report*, p. 7.

[29]Michael A. Ledeen, *Perilous Statecraft* (New York: Scribner's, 1988), pp. 1996–198.

[30]See, for instance, Woodward, *Veil*; and Michael Anderson, *Revolution* (New York: Harcourt Brace Jovanovich, 1988).

[31]*Report of the Congressional Committees Investigating the Iran-Contra Affair*, p. 361.

[32]See for instance, Constantine Menges, *Inside the National Security Council* (New York: Simon & Schuster, 1988), and Ledeen, *Perilous Statecraft* .

[33]Fred I. Greenstein, "Ronald Reagan—Another Hidden-Hand Ike?" *PS: Political Science and Politics* (March 1990), pp. 7–12.

[34]Quoted in Menges, I*nside the National Security Council*, p. 385

[35]Bert Rockman, "The Style and Organization of the Reagan Presidency," in *The Reagan Legacy*, ed. Charles O. Jones, (Chatham, N.J.: Chatham House, 1988), p. 8.

[36]Menges, *Inside the National Security Council*, p. 385.

Chapter 8

Bush
and the
Invasion of Panama

1989

On December 20, 1989, the armed forces of the United States invaded Panama in the largest military operation undertaken with American combat troops since the war in Vietnam. There were many reasons why the Bush administration decided to use force to resolve its problems with Panama, and there was a long train of events that led to the brief military confrontation. But the most important observation about the operations against Manuel Noriega during the final month of the first year of the Bush presidency involves the reasons for military action that were absent. The invasion of Panama had nothing to do with communism, or the threat of communism, or any American treaties or promises to contain that threat. The Panama decision came at the end of a year in which the communist world, and the entire international order, underwent dramatic and fundamental change. The year 1989 will be remembered as a major turning point in modern international relations and in the conduct of American foreign policy. Events in Panama, which had a significant impact on many American and Panamanian lives, will be a minor footnote to the revolutionary events that took place elsewhere in the world.

During the spring and summer of 1989, a student-led democratic movement emerged in China, raising expectations that there would soon be major political reforms in the world's most populous country. Those expectations were shattered by the brutal crackdown at Tiananmen Square, but democratic revolutions elsewhere in the world produced more lasting results. In the year that ended with the invasion of Panama, the political map of Eastern Europe was redrawn as the communist parties that had been in power for more than four decades surrendered to popular protest movements. First in Poland and Hungary, then in Czechoslovakia, and then East Germany, where the Berlin Wall was dismantled, and finally in Bulgaria and Romania, rulers and ruling parties fell like the much talked about dominoes of the 1950s. But instead of tilting toward communism, these dominoes leaned, to varying degrees, in the direction of democracy and market capitalism. In the Soviet Union, where Mikhail Gorbachev continued to propose controversial domestic reforms, the end of the Soviet system of European satellites was accepted without military resistance. In 1989, the Soviet empire in Eastern Europe collapsed, and because of internal problems with ethnic minorities and a stagnant economy, the USSR appeared to be unable, for the foreseeable future, to reclaim meaningful control over the dominions it surrendered.

President George Bush was not the maker of these events, but his administration benefited enormously from the widespread outbreak of peace and democracy that occurred in the first year of his presidency. Soviet military power did not, of course, completely disappear in 1989, and serious problems remained for the two superpowers to work out in the negotiation of strategic arms reductions and the reordering of European military and political arrangements. But in 1989, the longest and most dangerous confrontation of the cold war era, the confrontation of NATO and Warsaw Pact forces in central Europe, came to an end. Thereafter, the chances of war between the United States and the Soviet Union would be greatly diminished and the agenda for American foreign policy would be radically rewritten.

For decades the threat of war with the Soviet Union and the need to maintain a credible defense of Europe were central concerns for American foreign policy makers. According to some estimates, between one third and one half of the roughly $300 billion being spent each year on American defense in the late 1980s were devoted to NATO and European security.[1] At the end of the decade more than 300,000 American troops were stationed in Europe, where if fighting broke out, they were sure to be among the first casualties. Confrontations elsewhere in the world, in Korea, Vietnam, and a host of lesser military and covert operations, were given added salience because of fears that a crisis in a remote corner of the world would escalate to a global conflict and because a psychological connection was drawn between relatively minor third world foreign policy issues and superpower commitments in central Europe. This is precisely what happened in Vietnam where arguments for an early American withdrawal failed, in part because of concerns that the defeat of a SEATO nation would undermine the NATO alliance.

After 1989, the third world ceased to be seen as simply an arena for superpower competition, and a host of secondary problems rose in importance on the list of priorities in American foreign policy. When George Bush completed his first year in the White House, American hostages were still being held in Lebanon, terrorists continued to pose a threat to executives and tourists traveling abroad, debts to developing countries added to the burdens of America's troubled financial institutions, the international competitiveness of the U.S. economy was seriously at issue, instability in the Middle East, Latin America, southern Asia, and the horn of Africa posed unique regional problems, and drugs from a variety of international sources were crossing American borders in alarming volume. In public opinion polls Americans no longer listed the Soviet Union as their major foreign policy concern. Instead, they identified terrorism, economic competitiveness, and drugs as the most important threats to the nation's security.[2] Later in the administration, the Middle East would become the focus of foreign policy attention, but in 1989 events in Panama involving drugs, dictatorship, and the safety of Americans living abroad forced Panama to the forefront of presidential concern.

The use of American military power to overthrow Panamanian dictator Manuel Noriega is worth examining in some detail because it is the first major post–cold war crisis. But the origins of America's problems with Noriega have a long history that is deeply rooted in the cold war, when competition with international communism and the fear of Soviet expansion shaped American thinking about events throughout the third world.

MANUEL NORIEGA

Manuel Antonio Noriega took command of the Panama Defense Forces and effective control of the nation of Panama in December 1983, about two and a half years after Omar Torrijos, the popular military dictator during the negotiation of the Panama Canal treaties, died in a plane crash. Noriega was not at all like the charismatic, temperamental, and highly political Torrijos. Born from the out of wedlock liaison between an alcoholic civil servant and the family maid, Noriega became an orphan when his mother died or disappeared before his fifth birthday. He grew up in urban poverty without the benefits of parental support or social status. Unusually short and severely pockmarked, he suffered as an object of school yard jest. From early in life, his acne-damaged complexion earned him the nickname *cara de piña*, "pineapple face." Poor, small, disfigured, and tainted in a macho society by his close association with an older half brother who was openly homosexual, Noriega would seem an unlikely candidate for success in Latin American military or political circles.[3]

But his humble origins and hard life as a child may have made Noriega a more ambitious and a more devious competitor in the conspiracies of Panamanian politics. While still a student, Noriega told a classmate that Machiavelli's *The Prince* was his favorite book and wrote a paper praising the insights of the Italian philosopher of power politics.[4] As an adult he wrote his own book on psychological warfare arguing that Genghis Khan, the Mongol conqueror, was one of the earliest and best practitioners of that art.[5] From Machiavelli and Genghis Khan, Noriega would have learned the need to combine shrewdness with brutality and understanding of human nature with disregard for moral restraint. He learned his lessons well. His rapid rise in the ranks of his nation's military service was the result of cunning, hard work and a penchant for double-dealing. Noriega began his military training by simultaneously working for both Panama and the United States. Recruited by the CIA as a young cadet, Noriega went through a military academy in Peru filing reports about which students and instructors had discernible leftist leanings. First placed on the CIA payroll around 1960, Noriega would remain in the service of the American intelligence community off and on for the next quarter century.[6] But America would never have any real claim to Noriega's loyalties, nor would any other country. Noriega's services belonged to whomever was able to promote his interests and pay his price.

After completing his training, Noriega took up duties in the Panamanian National Guard, which was later renamed the Panama Defense Forces (PDF). In a small nation without hostile neighbors, and plenty of American troops to defend the Panama Canal, there was little need for a large professional military service. Costa Rica, Panama's northern neighbor and the most stable and prosperous nation in Central America, was also the only country in the region without a military establishment. Unfortunately, none of the other countries in Central America followed the Costa Rican example. In Panama, during the decades after the Second World War, the military grew in size and power. Many of its officers, including Noriega, took training courses in the United States and developed a variety of professional skills without absorbing any of the lessons in civil-military relations that are part of the American tradition. The National Guard/PDF emerged in the postwar era as Panama's most important institution. Its members worked as soldiers, sailors, pilots, policemen, intelligence agents, border guards, and presidential protectors. By the time of the Torrijos coup in 1968, the National Guard was the nation's army, navy, air force, coast guard, CIA, FBI, secret service, border patrol, police force, and drug enforcement administration all rolled into one. Most nations have military organizations; in Panama, the military organization had a nation. Though Torrijos permitted the election of civilian politicians and plebiscites on various issues, including the Panama Canal treaties, he ruled for more than a decade from his position as senior military commander. The full power of that position would not, however, be demonstrated until it was occupied by Manuel Noriega.

Noriega was a participant in the coup that put General Torrijos in power and sided with Torrijos again in the following year when a countercoup tried to unseat him. As a result of these services, Noriega was promoted from commander of a provincial military district to head of the nation's military intelligence. From that vantage point he was able to collect information about prominent persons throughout the country and keep tabs on every aspect of the Torrijos regime. From the beginning of his rule, Torrijos was interested in negotiating a revision of the 1903 treaty with the United States and made that his highest foreign policy priority. He was often openly anti-American and reestablished relations with Castro's Cuba in order, in part, to goad his American counterparts in the treaty negotiations. Domestically he instituted mildly socialist reforms of agriculture, health care and education, and liberalized Panamanian banking laws, making the nation a haven for dubious and illegal business transactions. During the 1970s Torrijos tripled the membership of the armed forces and vastly expanded the nation's civil service. Government became more important in Panamanian society during the Torrijos regime, and the military became more important in the nation's government. Meanwhile, drugs and drug money flowed through the country ever more freely and American officials who wanted simultaneously to maintain good relations with Panama and stop the flow of illegal drugs were presented with a dilemma.

During the Carter administration, Noriega was reportedly removed from the CIA payroll because of his links with drug trafficking and other questionable activities, but he continued to provide occasional services for the American government. His intelligence agents captured a number of Colombian drug dealers and arranged for their extradition to the United States. This won Noriega credit in Washington and also made it easier for him to demand substantial bribes from other drug dealers who were set free.[7] When the exiled Shah of Iran briefly stayed in Panama, Noriega was assigned the task of providing protection and charged exorbitant fees for his services while secretly recording all the phone calls made by the Shah and his entourage.[8] Throughout this period, problems in Panama involving drugs and corruption were overshadowed by larger questions. The Senate in the course of its ratification debate over the Panama Canal treaties held highly unusual secret sessions on drug trafficking in Panama; it may well have heard evidence against Noriega. But for the majority of U.S. senators, and for the Carter administration, the involvement of Panamanian officials in illegal activities was less important than the resolution of the strategic issues surrounding the future of the canal. In the interest of creating new arrangements for the canal's operation and security, Noriega could be overlooked.

When Noriega replaced Torrijos as dictator of Panama, his actions became harder to ignore. Noriega had none of Torrijos' charisma or earthy charm and no ambitions for major accomplishments in foreign or domestic affairs. Torrijos often referred to Noriega as "my gangster." When he came to power, Noriega ruled by fear rather than persuasion and for himself rather than the Panamanian people. As his nation's leading intelligence officer, Noriega had been a shadowy figure, little known to the outside world, but as Panama's acknowledged ruler, he became the focus of national and international attention. His lifestyle, like his complexion, did not show well in public. Throughout his military career Noriega had been associated with scandalous behavior. From time to time he drank heavily, womanized freely, kept a number of mistresses, was accused of rape, accumulated a substantial personal fortune from a modest officer's salary, and reportedly participated in acts of torture. Insecure and fearful of his personal safety, Noriega at the end of his rule kept an erratic schedule, organized phony motorcades and helicopter movements, used tape-recorded phone conversations to disguise his whereabouts to electronic eavesdroppers, and slept in a variety of homes. Fascinated by religions and the occult, he maintained an eclectic set of spiritual beliefs and superstitious practices. According to one of his hired psychic consultants, Noriega was "a Christian, a Rosicrucian, a Freemason, a Buddhist, a Taoist, a man protected by God and the Son of God."[9] In Panama and in his international travels Noriega sought out mediums, astrologers, mentalists, witch doctors, and tarot card readers. When his homes and offices were raided during the American invasion, soldiers found objects suggesting that the Panamanian dictator was an active practitioner of voodoo who cast spells on Ronald Reagan, George Bush, and the entire U.S. Congress.[10] These religious beliefs and practices were not unusual in Central America, but they often made it difficult for American officials to understand Noriega's personal behavior. It was easier to understand his ruthless pursuit of power.

Noriega was intelligent, well informed about persons and events within his nation, and brutal in his treatment of those who opposed his rule. A self-trained expert on psychological warfare, Noriega was extremely adept at the manipulation and management of those around him. Domestically he foiled repeated coup attempts, restricted freedom of expression, staged phony elections, ordered the torture and murder of his most serious political enemies, and organized a group of street thugs, called the "dignity battalions," to carry out special tasks that he did not want associated directly with the PDF. Internationally he managed in the early years of his dictatorship to maintain good relations with the United States despite mounting evidence of his drug connections and corruption. He did so by continuing to provide information and arrests for the American drug enforcement agencies, whose administrators regularly praised his "cooperation" in the war on drugs, and by making himself useful to the foreign policy objectives of the Reagan administration.[11]

Though earlier in his career Noriega had helped to sell arms to the Sandinistas, in the Reagan era he joined the contra cause and provided arms and assistance to the forces fighting communism in Central America. According to documents filed in connection with the trial of Oliver North, Noriega personally made a $100,000 contribution to the contras in July 1984.[12] At the same time he was helping the White House fight communism in Nicaragua, he was improving Panamanian relations with Cuba, assisting a Marxist revolutionary group in Colombia called M-19, opening new ties with Libya, and enjoying his resumed payments from the CIA—reported in the early 1980s to be between $100,000 and $200,000 a year.[13] Throughout his career Noriega skillfully played communist against anticommunist, Castro against the CIA, Colombian drug dealers against U.S. drug investigators, and foreign interests against those of Panama. Panama under Noriega became a haven for all sorts of unsavory characters and transactions. The whole nation, observed an American who worked with Noriega in the 1980s, was "a brothel for intelligence agencies, arms merchants, drug dealers, and soldiers of fortune."[14] Getting rid of Noriega would not be easy.

DEPOSING THE DICTATOR

The Panamanian elections of 1984 were completely controlled by the PDF and the results were the product of predictable fraud. Popular Panamanian nationalist and former president Arnulfo Arias was defeated by the candidate Noriega and his lieutenants chose for the presidency, Nicolás Barletta.[15] The results were suspect. According to the journalist and author of a book on Noriega, John Dinges, the slogan in Panama was always "It's not who wins that counts; it's who counts that wins."[16] In the aftermath of the elections Noriega's and the PDF's control over the country tightened and the repression of dissident forces became more frequent and more deadly. The popular opposition leader Hugo Spadafora, returning to Panama from Costa Rica, was captured, tortured, and beheaded. His headless body was stuffed in a mailbag and deposited on Costa Rican territory just across the border between the two states. When President Barletta announced plans to appoint an independent commission to investigate the Spadafora murder, he was forced to resign.

The U.S. government raised no serious objections to these actions, in part because of Noriega's assistance to the contras. Just as the Carter administration had overlooked Panamanian problems in the interest of getting the canal treaties ratified, the Reagan administration ignored obvious threats to Panamanian democracy in the interest of promoting democracy elsewhere in Central America. Members of Congress, who were under the impression that no aid was being provided to the contras as a result of the Boland amendments, saw no need to look the other way.

Congressional efforts to focus attention on Noriega emerged from an unlikely alliance of a southern conservative and a Massachusetts liberal. Senator Jesse Helms of North Carolina had been one of the most vocal critics of the Panama Canal treaties and fought their ratification with all of his considerable energy. When members of the Spadafora family brought the story of torture and murder in Panama to the senator's attention, he used it to embarrass Noriega and raise questions about the steps being taken to implement the canal treaties. In June 1986 front page stories in the *New York Times* by investigative reporter Seymour Hersh revealed Noriega's connections to the Spadafora murder and to other illegal activities.[17] Three months later Senator Helms introduced an amendment to the appropriations legislation that funded the intelligence community requiring the director of the CIA to prepare a report on the involvement of the PDF in violations of human rights, drug trafficking, arms trafficking and money laundering. One of his co-sponsors for the amendment, which passed 53–46, was Senator John Kerry of Massachusetts. Kerry, like Helms, was a member of the Senate Foreign Relations Committee and, after the 1986 elections, the chairman of its Subcommittee on Terrorism, Narcotics and International Communications. Unlike Helms, Kerry was a liberal Democrat who almost always voted on the opposite side of the North Carolina conservative. On the issue of drugs in Panama, however, they joined forces and became the Senate's leading critics of U.S. associations with Noriega. Helms protested Noriega's human rights record and warned about the future of the canal; Kerry made Noriega's drug dealing and the reputed drug dealing of the contras the focus of a number of subcommittee investigations. In 1986 and 1987, the two senators co-sponsored a series of legislative actions aimed at halting apparent American indifference to drug trafficking in Panama. Other senators, including Edward Kennedy and Alfonse D'Amato, also spoke out against Noriega.

The major antidrug legislation passed in 1986 suspended half of the annual foreign aid to twenty-four countries, including Panama, that were believed to be involved in drug-related activities. The law required that the aid be withheld unless the president certified by March 1, 1987 that each of the countries named in the legislation was fully cooperating with U.S. antidrug efforts. When President Reagan certified that Panama was in compliance with the requirements of the law, Helms and Kerry offered a resolution rejecting Reagan's report and calling for a halt to all further American aid to Noriega's regime. [Document 8.1] The resolution passed, but because of technicalities in the foreign aid legislation, it was not binding on the Reagan administration. Senate rejection of the president's report did, however, provide a symbolic victory for the growing congressional opposition to nations and national leaders known to participate in the international drug trade. American support for the Noriega regime was becoming harder to defend.

In the summer of 1987 public revelations by former Noriega associate Díaz Herrera about the rigged elections of 1984 and the corrupt practices of the PDF led to riots and demonstrations in Panama. As a kind of "fruity effigy," pineapples were hung from telephone poles in Panamanian cities.[18] Some observers of the Panamanian protests in 1987 thought they were similar to the kind of public outcry that had toppled Ferdinand Marcos in the Philippines during the previous year. Instead, on July 10, a date known as "Black Friday" in Panama, Noriega cracked down even harder against his opposition. Fifteen hundred protesters were arrested and hundreds were injured by riot police using live ammunition. Herrera's home was stormed and he was arrested. The Reagan administration could no longer tolerate Noriega's behavior. In 1987 his annual CIA payments were suspended and diplomatic protests were lodged publicly and privately against his violations of human rights and disrespect for democratic processes.[19] During the summer, American economic and military assistance programs were suspended, and in January 1988 Assistant Secretary of Defense Richard Armitage went to Panama to suggest that Noriega step down.[20] But none of the words spoken against Noriega by senior officials in Washington or members of Congress had the kind of impact that would accompany actions taken in February by two district attorneys in Florida.

Independent criminal investigations, one in Miami and one in Tampa, conducted in the mid-1980s produced convincing legal evidence that high officials in Panama, including Manuel Noriega, were directly involved with the Colombian

Medellín cartel in the trafficking of narcotics and the laundering of drug profits. In February 1988 grand juries in both Florida cities issued indictments against Noriega. Knowledge of the ongoing investigations and pending indictments had been available in Washington for some time, but may never have reached President Reagan's attention.[21] At meetings of Reagan foreign policy advisers, no decision was made to set the Justice Department investigations aside and attempt to solve the Noriega problem through diplomatic channels alone. By the time the indictments were debated in Washington, information assembled against Noriega was widely known by members of the prosecutorial teams and the citizens in Florida who had served on the grand juries. If the indictments had been shelved in Washington, it is likely that such a decision would have leaked to the press. Under such circumstances, and in the aftermath of the Iran-contra affair, it was difficult for members of the Reagan administration to do anything but go along with the Florida district attorneys.

Three weeks after the indictments were made public, Eric Delvalle, the Panamanian president who had replaced Barletta, fired Noriega as commander of the PDF. His action had little effect. Noriega ignored the decision, forced Delvalle into hiding, and replaced him with a more compliant president, Manuel Solis Palma. The Delvalle decision did, however, manage to produce considerable confusion about who actually ruled in Panama. When the State Department announced that the United States considered Delvalle to be Panama's legitimate head of state, lawyers in the United States representing opposition groups in Panama went to court to take control of Panamanian assets in American banks and prevent their use without Delvalle's permission. Even before the United States officially imposed sanctions against Noriega, private attorneys using the American legal system were able to produce a major banking crisis in Panama. On March 11, the Reagan administration added to Noriega's troubles by announcing that all payments due Panama for use of the canal would be held in escrow until the Delvalle government was fully restored. In April, after another failed coup attempt against Noriega, Reagan declared a state of emergency in U.S.–Panamanian relations and imposed further economic sanctions against Panama. [Document 8.2]

Throughout the spring and summer of 1988, members of the Reagan administration debated additional steps against Noriega. Secretary of State George Shultz and his controversial assistant for Latin American policy Elliott Abrams urged military action. They were resisted by Pentagon officials, including the general in charge of American forces on the scene, who worried about the safety of the canal and our ability to protect the many Americans still living and working in Panama. Instead of authorizing military action, President Reagan approved a plan to negotiate Noriega's departure in exchange for dropping the Florida indictments. George Bush, caught between his obligations as a loyal vice president and the demands of his campaign for the 1988 Republican presidential nomination, publicly broke with the president and criticized the negotiations, which, in any case, were unsuccessful. When diplomacy failed to end the Noriega regime, the president approved a CIA plan to sponsor covert action against Noriega. The new coup planning involved support for opposition groups in Panama and Panamanian exiles in the United States. Shortly after it was reviewed by members of Congress in accordance with established legal procedures, a detailed description of the plan appeared in the *Washington Post*. The Reagan administration and the Senate Select Committee on Intelligence publicly argued about who was responsible for the leak. There were good reasons to suspect that Reagan officials had revealed their own plan to the press. In the fall of 1988, with an approaching presidential election, there was considerable political pressure to play down problems in Panama and to blame the Democratic Congress for interfering with an American-sponsored coup. When George Bush won the election, the future of American relations with Panama remained unresolved and uncertain.

BUSH AND THE INVASION DECISION

For the first eleven months of 1989 the Bush administration tried various means for ending the Noriega problem. The sanctions imposed by President Reagan remained in effect and over time did considerable damage to the relatively weak Panamanian economy. But they were never fully enforced and had very little impact on Noriega's financial gains from illegitimate dealings. Panama was able to replace some lost American aid with assistance from Cuba, Libya, and other nations. Noriega remained in power. President Bush did approve new covert actions for Panama, involving propaganda and psychological warfare against Noriega, but a CIA radio transmitter designed to broadcast opposition news and information was discovered by the PDF and an American CIA agent was captured and imprisoned.

     In May 1989, new elections in Panama offered a unique opportunity to remove Noriega in a peaceful fashion, or at least focus international attention on his dictatorship. Preoccupied with more pressing problems in the early months of a new presidency and busy making appointments to key foreign policy positions, the members of the Bush administration initially gave little attention to the upcoming elections in Panama. But after some congressional pressure, led by Senator Richard Lugar, who had been the senior American observer in the crucial 1986 elections in the Philippines, the White House arranged for a team of American observers to monitor the polling in Panama.[22] Other teams sponsored by international organizations and independent groups, including one led by former president Jimmy Carter, also went to Panama for the May voting. The Senate and House Intelligence committees reportedly approved $10 million in covert support for candidates and organizations campaigning against Noriega.[23] When fraud, violence, and intimidation were practiced on a scale that was obvious to all the outside observer groups, the people of Panama and the people of the world knew instantly what had happened. Carter, whose support for the canal treaties had won him many Panamanian friends, took a leading role in denouncing the elections and the Noriega regime. When the brutal beatings of opposition candidates by members of Noriega's dignity battalions were captured by news cameras and broadcast throughout the world, they provided a powerful visual image of the depths of the Noriega dictatorship. The May elections did not end Noriega's rule, but they weakened his standing in world opinion and demonstrated that he governed without popular support. After the elections, the Bush Administration worked with the Organization of American States (OAS) to orchestrate diplomatic pressure against the Noriega regime.

     In July, the commander of U.S. armed forces in Panama, General Frederick Woerner who had cautioned against the use of American military power in the fight against Noriega, was replaced by General Maxwell Thurman, whose nickname was "Mad Max." Thurman was instructed at the time of his appointment to begin making plans for an American mission to remove Noriega.[24] The decision to carry out such a mission had not been made, but Noriega's outrages were such that contingency planning and precautionary steps were clearly necessary. Many of the dependents of American military personnel stationed in Panama went home or moved to safe housing on military bases, the number of troops in Panama was increased from 10,000 to 12,000, base personnel were put on a higher state of alert and military exercises off the bases, which were permitted under the terms of Panama Canal treaties, took on a greater significance.

The contingency plans for an operation against Noriega fell roughly into three categories.[24] At the lowest level of American military action, a commando raid could have been used to capture Noriega, bring him to one of the American bases, and fly him to Florida to face drug charges. There were a number of problems with this option. Noriega's extreme care in disguising his whereabouts meant that a small-scale raid could not be carried out successfully without excellent intelligence on Noriega's location. That information was very hard to come by. American intelligence about Noriega was rarely as good as Noriega's sources about American activities. Moreover, a simple plan to remove Noriega did nothing to change the structural problems in Panama. The PDF would still have remained the nation's most powerful institution, and the new leader of the country would most likely have been one of Noriega's cronies, rather than President Delvalle or the winner of the May elections. The other two options were aimed against the PDF rather than Noriega alone and involved either moderate or major invasions of the country. The moderate invasion would have used the American forces already in Panama to neutralize PDF units in and near the nation's major cities, making it impossible for Noriega to get any military protection and difficult for him to escape capture. This option would, however, have left some provincial PDF forces intact and raised the danger that the invasion would be followed by guerrilla fighting in Panamanian jungles or possible attacks against the Panama Canal. The third option was the invasion that would actually take place at the end of the year. It involved nearly twice as many troops as the moderate plan, but gave the best prospects for neutralizing the PDF completely. Planning and preparation for that option took place throughout the fall.

As tensions between the United States and Panama rose, a final coup attempt almost ended Noriega's dictatorship without the need for any offensive American military operations. In the fall of 1989, one of Noriega's trusted associates, Major Moises Giroldi, began plotting a coup. Giroldi's plan was simple; he would choose a time when he was alone or in a small group with Noriega and together with a few friends capture the dictator and announce his retirement. Catching Noriega off guard would be relatively easy, but in order keep him in captivity, it was crucial that loyal units of the PDF be prevented from coming to his rescue. Before the coup, Giroldi approached American officials in Panama and requested that U.S. troops use their regularly scheduled exercises to block various roads and bridges by which PDF forces might come to Noriega's assistance. Rumored coups in Panama were fairly common in 1988 and 1989 and American intelligence officers had relatively little information about Giroldi, except that he was one of the senior officers in the PDF. General Thurman was afraid that the proposed coup might be a trick by Noriega to embarrass the U.S. and the new commander of American forces in Panama. Limited American support for the coup was, however, authorized at senior levels of the Bush administration. When confusion arose regarding the timing of the coup and when American troops failed to block all the routes for Noriega's possible rescue, Giroldi's prospects for success were significantly diminished. He and his co-conspirators did manage to hold Noriega prisoner for a number of hours, but chose not to kill him or immediately turn him over to U.S. authorities. Giroldi's hesitancy and American failures to take his coup attempt more seriously saved Noriega. The dictator was rescued by loyal troops flown into Panama City. Giroldi was tortured and killed.[26]

The elections of May 1989 demonstrated that Noriega had no popular support. The failed coup attempt of October showed that even his most trusted associates were potential enemies. In the United States, congressional criticisms of the American failure to support the October coup more fully made it easier for members of the Bush administration to contemplate more active methods of removing Noriega from power. Everyone was tired of the Panama problem and anxious to see it solved. By the end of 1989, Noriega was becoming more isolated, more insecure, and more outrageous in his behavior toward the United States. Americans stopped at PDF roadblocks in Panamanian cities were subjected to arbitrary searches, detainments, and threats. On the last weekend before Christmas, incidents involving American servicemen and their families tipped the scales in favor of military invasion.

On Friday, December 15, Noriega promoted himself, declaring that he would henceforth be known as Panama's "maximum leader," with newly declared powers that ended the last illusions of constitutional government in Panama. These added powers were necessary, according to Noriega, to control domestic resistance and respond to the "state of war" that now existed with the United States. The first casualty of that war occurred the next day when a marine lieutenant was killed by PDF soldiers manning a roadblock near Noriega's headquarters. A naval officer and his wife who witnessed the killing were subsequently arrested. The officer was beaten and his wife was threatened with sexual abuse. When President Bush was informed of these events he reportedly told his senior foreign policy advisers reviewing plans for an invasion, "Let's do it.... It will only get worse."[27] December 16 was a Panamanian holiday commemorating the anniversary of Noriega's assumption of power in 1983. The attacks on Americans in Panama that day made it the last such holiday that Noriega would enjoy.

The decision to invade was made on Sunday, December 17, in the president's office in the residential section of the White House. In attendance were Secretary of State James Baker, Vice President Dan Quayle, White House Chief of Staff John Sununu, National Security Adviser Brent Scowcroft, his deputy Robert Gates, Secretary of Defense Dick Cheney, Chairman of the Joint Chiefs of Staff Colin Powell, Lieutenant General Thomas Kelly, and Marlin Fitzwater, the president's press secretary.[28] At the meeting, the president's military advisers, Powell and Cheney, outlined the plans for a large-scale invasion of Panama in some detail. The president reportedly asked why a smaller, more surgical strike could not be arranged to simply capture Noriega. Defense Department officials explained the problems with that option and their preference for an attack that would neutralize the PDF and destroy Noriega's power base. Colin Powell, as national security adviser late in the Reagan administration, had reportedly opposed using American military power to resolve the Panamanian situation, but as President Bush's chairman of the JCS, he carefully reviewed the contingency planning and after the attacks on December 16, endorsed the need for an invasion.[29] President Bush had reached the same conclusion.

In order to maintain secrecy about the upcoming invasion, the president carried out his routine schedule on December 19, including attendance at a White House Christmas party. Early in the evening, about six hours before the operation was scheduled to begin, he personally made phone calls to tell selected members of Congress what was about to happen. Similar courtesy calls were made later in the evening to allied leaders and to Latin American heads of state. The president spent most of the night in the White House situation room reviewing initial reports from Panama and preparing for a public announcement of the invasion that he delivered early the next morning. [Document 8.3] At the Pentagon, Secretary of Defense Cheney monitored events but tried to interfere as little as possible in the execution of the carefully prepared military plans.

In all, 22,000 American troops took part in the invasion, which began at 1:00 A.M. on December 20. Operation Just Cause, as it was called, involved coordinated attacks on targets throughout the cities and rural regions of Panama, the largest landing of paratroopers since the Second World War, and the first ever combat support missions for the F-117A stealth attack aircraft. Twenty-three Americans died, including three civilians. More than 300 were wounded, many as a result of misdirected friendly fire or low level paratroop jumps. Casualties for the Panamanians were much higher; conservative estimates suggest that there were between 220 and 300 Panamanians deaths during the invasion.[30] In addition, large sections of the country suffered extensive property damage from days of uncontrolled looting that followed the neutralization of the PDF, which was Panama's police force as well as its army. The main objective of the operation, the capture of Noriega, did not occur until January 3. Noriega's intelligence service reportedly warned him about the forthcoming invasion several hours before it began,[31] but the dictator had heard such warnings before and took no special precautions as he spent the night at a PDF officer's club with one of his mistresses. His first knowledge that this rumored invasion was real came when he heard gunfire in the early morning hours; he immediately moved to a different location in a borrowed car. After several days of eluding American patrols, Noriega finally sought asylum in the papal embassy. While awaiting his fate, he reportedly watched world news on cable television and saw coverage of the fall of the Romanian government and the killing of Romania's dictator, Nicolai Ceaucescu.[32] Outside the embassy he heard the constant blaring of rock music from the radios of American soldiers patiently awaiting his surrender. After several days of negotiations Noriega agreed to turn himself over to American authorities.

In the aftermath of the invasion, Panama rapidly withdrew from the limelight of American foreign policy. The opposition leaders who were beaten and denied victory in the May elections took office and began the slow and difficult process of rebuilding a viable economy and establishing a democratic regime. Noriega went to jail in Florida, hired attorneys, and started the long litigation that could be expected to accompany a case as celebrated and controversial as the arrest of a foreign leader by an invading American army. The Congress took up special foreign aid legislation to help pay for the restoration of portions of the country damaged by the invasion and the subsequent looting. The passage of that legislation did not, however, occur until well into 1990 as a result of extraneous amendments that slowed the legislative process. Panama only briefly took center stage in the drama of American foreign policy—once during the debate over the canal treaties and again at the height of Noriega's rule and removal from power. When the invasion was over, President Bush and his foreign policy advisers went back to dealing with the much more important events taking place in Europe and the Soviet Union and the emerging problems in the Middle East. The American public went back to not paying much attention to what went on in the Central American nations that are among our nearest neighbors.

CONCLUSIONS

POWER

American action against Noriega involved several critical presidential decisions in both the Reagan and Bush administrations. George Bush approved limited American military support for the October 1989 coup and full support for the large-scale invasion carried out in December. Both decisions were necessarily kept secret until just before or just after their execution and involved no meaningful congressional participation. The president did inform leading members of Congress about the pending invasion of Panama hours before it occurred, but the War Powers Resolution was not implemented and no formal congressional approval of the invasion was sought. Like the Reagan era military operations against Libya and Grenada, the action against Panama was over quickly and widely supported by the American people. Even if the full provisions of the War Powers Resolution, including the constitutionally suspect legislative veto, had been implemented, there is little reason to believe that Congress would have restricted anything that the Bush administration wanted to do in Panama. Where the mission assigned to American military forces is popular, and when it can be accomplished in short order with moderate casualties, the president may feel free to act on the basis of his powers as commander in chief. A conflict with the Congress is hard to imagine when these conditions are met.

In the future, the number of such situations is likely to be limited. There are a great many military dictators in the world (though there are fewer today than there were ten years ago), but not very many of them are as easy for the American people to dislike as was Manuel Noriega. By 1989, Noriega's widely reported drug dealing and corruption, his outrageous disrespect for democratic processes, and his eccentric lifestyle made him an outcast without influential friends in American politics or meaningful support in the international community. When other dictators fell from power—Somoza in Nicaragua, the Shah in Iran, and Marcos in the Philippines—they had, even at the end, a few loyal supporters in the Congress and within the American foreign policy elites. In the months before the invasion of Panama, Noriega had no such support. There were international protests against the invasion in Latin American nations and elsewhere and general criticisms of American imperialism and disregard for the principles of international law, but outside of Libya's Qaddafi and Cuba's Castro there was no outpouring of sympathy for Noriega. The general was an easy target.

Other factors in America's relations with Panama contributed to making the invasion a quick and relatively painless success. When military action was ordered, the United States already had 12,000 well-equipped troops in Panama, many of whom were familiar with the targets they would be ordered to take and the terrain in which they would be expected to operate. The system of bases built by the United States for the protection of the canal made the logistics of rapid reinforcement and resupply of the forces in Panama unusually smooth. Moreover, knowledge that some sort of military operation might be necessary had given U.S. commanders ample time to conduct careful planning and preparation for the operation that was finally ordered in December. In domestic politics, the decision to invade received widespread and almost automatic support because of Noriega's behavior toward Americans and the many attempts that had already been made to remove him from power. The invasion of Panama was clearly seen by the American public as a last resort in a long, drawn-out struggle in which a variety of lesser means had been exhausted. In December 1989, the commander in chief had the unchallenged power to act alone in ordering an invasion of Panama because of months and years of apparent U.S. powerlessness in the earlier attempts to depose the dictator.

Ronald Reagan, like his successor, made several important decisions designed to bring down the Noriega regime. He maintained official recognition of President Delvalle as Panama's head of state, even after Delvalle had been removed from office by Noriega; he imposed a series of economic sanctions against the Panamanian government; he instructed the State Department to negotiate a deal in which the United States would cancel Noriega's indictments if he would immediately resign; and, when those negotiations failed, Reagan ordered the CIA to prepare plans for an anti-Noriega coup. Among all of these actions, the economic sanctions were the most potent weapon in the war against Noriega. Sanctions did not destroy the Noriega regime, but they did weaken it.

American economic sanctions against Panama were put in place by executive order, without a congressional vote, under emergency powers granted to the president by the International Emergency Economic Powers Act and the National Emergencies Act. On other occasions, most notably the imposition of sanctions against South Africa in the mid-1980s, the Congress has passed special legislation restricting American citizens from engaging in certain economic activities with particular foreign nations and businesses in those nations. With regard to Panama, the president acted on the basis of general legislation granting the chief executive substantial control over international commerce after a public declaration that a state of emergency exists in U.S. relations with a particular country. The laws currently in effect are revisions of the Trading with the Enemies Act passed in 1917 at the outset of the First World War. Implementation of the provisions in the 1917 law and its successors has been controversial and subject to a number of criticisms.[33]

Very often presidential orders to restrict trade with a particular country are controversial because it is claimed that they hurt U.S. businesses more than they hurt the nations we seek to harm. The Carter administration's embargo against grain sales to the Soviet Union after the Soviet invasion of Afghanistan is a frequently cited example. The embargo may have inconvenienced the Russians, who were forced to find suppliers for their food needs elsewhere in the world, but the inconvenience was manageable as long as some of the other major grain exporting nations were willing to sell their products to Soviet buyers. To American farmers who lost years of expected overseas sales, the harm done was more than a matter of inconvenience. Ronald Reagan, no friend of the Soviet Union in his early years in office, ended the grain embargo in 1981 and promised not to use agricultural exports as a weapon in international politics.

In addition to restricting trade, presidents have the power to issue executive orders freezing foreign assets in American banks and financial institutions, thus preventing many ordinary business transactions from taking place. This was a major element in the Reagan sanctions against Noriega and was also used by President Carter in his efforts to punish Iran after American diplomats were taken hostage in that country. When Iraq invaded Kuwait in the summer of 1990, President Bush immediately froze both Iraqi and Kuwaiti assets under the same legislative authority. In the case of Panama, private attorneys using civil litigation were able to place some of Panama's government accounts under the exclusive control of President Delvalle even before President Reagan froze those assets using his emergency powers. In all of these cases considerable disruptions of the target economies took place, because all of the nations involved happened to have substantial holdings in the United States and were particularly vulnerable to American financial power. Not all countries have such vulnerability, and the precedents set by Carter, Reagan, and Bush have worried some observers who fear that in the future those countries experiencing or expecting political difficulties with the United States will elect to minimize their business and financial transactions with corporations and institutions based in the United States. There is little evidence to suggest that this has already happened, but it must be recognized that the frequent use of emergency powers to impose economic sanctions is bound to have domestic economic costs. These trade-offs make the imposition of economic sanctions a course of action that presidents must take with great care.

PROCESS

The decisions by Presidents Reagan and Bush to impose economic sanctions and order an invasion of Panama were not controversial. In both cases they responded to obvious provocations with retaliations that were widely supported by their advisers, by the Congress, and by the American people. President Bush's decision to approve the invasion came after years of frustrating dealings with Noriega and only when the safety of Americans living in Panama was clearly threatened. Faced with the situation in December 1989 in which one American had been killed and others were arrested or harassed, the president acted decisively. He ordered the use of American military power to protect U.S. citizens and to remove an unpopular dictator who had been indicted for criminal activities. In the United States there was not much dispute about the president's decision. By December 1989 a broad-based anti-Noriega consensus had developed in American politics. That consensus facilitated presidential action, but the consensus was not itself a presidential creation.

If we take a wider view of American relations with Noriega, we see that presidential attention to problems in Panama came late in the day and that an unusually large and diverse group of participants in the foreign policy process played a role in the efforts to expose and then depose Manuel Noriega. In dealing with Panama the United States exhibited a wide distribution of power over foreign affairs, and some highly unusual political alliances and policymaking contributions. Seymour Hersh, a *New York Times* reporter, gave rumored accusations against Noriega national credibility in a series of articles in the summer of 1986. Senators

Kerry and Helms, generally about as far apart on the political spectrum as possible, worked together to increase public attention about drug trafficking and human rights violations in Panama. Two district attorneys in Florida simultaneously developed cases before grand juries that resulted in Noriega's indictment and provided a legal confirmation that the evidence against him was substantial. Private attorneys working for Panamanian opposition groups got American courts to enforce economic sanctions against Panama weeks before President Reagan officially decided to impose them. Former President Jimmy Carter led a respected observation team during the Panamanian elections and publicly denounced Noriega's disregard for democratic processes. All of these individuals contributed to the shift in U.S. policy toward Panama from friendship, to opposition, to invasion. An invasion of Panama would have been hard to imagine without the public revelations of Noriega's drug dealing, the official indictments against him, the bipartisan support for stopping the flow of drugs into the country, and the recognition that less radical means of getting rid of Noriega—sanctions, diplomatic pressure, elections, and covert actions—had all been tried.

Until the last year and a half of the Reagan presidency, the variety of individuals and groups who were pushing for a tougher American stand against Noriega met resistance from the officials responsible for American foreign policy. It is relatively easy to explain the eventual decisions to impose sanctions against Panama and then to use military force to protect American lives in that country; it is much harder to explain the long period of time in which the United States paid, tolerated, and worked with Manuel Noriega. Members of the American intelligence community and diplomatic corps knew, or suspected, for many years that Noriega was engaged in gun running, drug trafficking, and double-dealing. They chose not to give that information public exposure and to continue American relations with Panama's intelligence service, its notorious leader, and the country's eventual dictator.

Doing business with dictators has been part of American foreign policy since the Second World War, when we were allied with Stalin's Soviet Union. In the cold war era, there were a number of reasons and rationalizations for maintaining good relations with nations across the globe that had little experience of, or appreciation for, democratic institutions and values. Iran was a strategically important country occupying territory between the Soviet Union and the Persian Gulf. The Shah of Iran, who had a less than perfect record on human rights, was a loyal ally of the United States who received our support until the revolution of 1978 removed him from power. The Philippine islands contain some of the most important American naval and air bases in the Pacific. Ferdinand Marcos, the Filipino president who refused to leave office when his two elected terms were complete, had official American support until the elections of 1986 demonstrated his weakness. Throughout Central and Latin America in the decades of the cold war, the United States maintained good relations with a variety of military and civilian dictators. We sometimes did so with serious misgivings, but more often than not, we were pleased with the stability that dictatorial regimes offered and with the expectation that stable governments would prevent communist takeovers. We were willing to overlook the absence of democracy in exchange for the promise that communism would be avoided.

The American acceptance of Noriega was more complicated than some of the other compromises that were made during the cold war. Noriega had no ideology and was never suspected of intellectual sympathy with the communist cause. He did deal with Cuba, and he provided aid to the Sandinistas and the M-19 rebels in Colombia; but those actions were taken for money or for political leverage, not for revolutionary ideals. When American intelligence officers realized that Noriega was double-dealing and providing information to Cuba at the same time that he was spying on Castro for the United States, they understood how embarrassing his behavior would be if it were publicly known. They were convinced that the information he gave us was far more useful than any information he might simultaneously be giving to the Cubans.[34] As it became evident that Noriega not only did business with Cuba but was heavily involved in the international drug trade, other compromises had to be accepted. Noriega was a known facilitator of the illicit movement of drugs and drug money, but he occasionally cooperated with U.S. antidrug investigations, arrested dealers who were operating in Panama, or pointed out narcotics production facilities in his country. Decisions were once again made that Noriega's assistance was valuable enough to justify tolerance of his own involvement in money laundering and drug trafficking. Throughout our dealings with Noriega, we consistently accepted painful trade-offs in our relations with the unsavory intelligence chief and dictator. Such trade-offs are at the core of the foreign policy making process.

Presidents and their advisers are almost never presented with clear-cut problems in which right is obviously on one side and wrong on the other. Difficult choices are almost always required. During the Carter administration, the desire to create new treaties for the Panama Canal led to a willingness to overlook certain aspects of behavior among senior officials in the Panamanian military. For President Reagan the need to defeat rebels in El Salvador and overthrow the Sandinista regime in Nicaragua had the same consequences as the Carter concentration on the future of the canal. Both administrations placed issues of ideological and strategic importance above public exposure and protest of corruption and criminal activity. Both were aware of the compromises they were making and both had reasons for making the choices they did. Throughout the cold war, preventing the spread of communism more than any other factor tilted the scales in American foreign policy in favor of overlooking otherwise objectionable activities on the part of our ostensibly democratic partners.

After the revolutionary changes on the international scene that took place in 1989, it became much harder to make or justify the kind of choices that were commonplace in the decades before the collapse of communism in Eastern Europe. This is apt to make the process of foreign policy making more open and more chaotic. In the years that lie ahead there will be fewer good reasons to hide the misbehavior of our friends and allies and less desperation to maintain their assistance and friendship. The large number of participants who contributed to the change in U.S. policy toward Panama are likely to find more issues on which they can exercise their influence. Foreign policy considerations in the post–cold war era will be harder to distinguish from traditional domestic issues, and the line between them, always difficult to draw, is likely to become more blurred. Political scientists have for some time made use of an awkward label for the emerging foreign policy agenda, calling the new issues in American foreign policy "intermestic."[35]

Panama was an American intermestic military intervention. The importance of fighting drugs in domestic politics was combined with the need to protect citizens living and working abroad and the traditional American interests in the safety of the canal. All of these factors contributed to the invasion decision. But the ease with which George Bush ordered the invasion of Panama and the praise with which it was greeted will be hard to duplicate in the future. Problems like Noriega will be unlikely to fester in future administrations for as long as Panama did in the later years of the cold war. The secret compromises of the cold war intelligence agencies are more likely to become public controversies in the years ahead. And the trade-offs that will always be part of the foreign policy making process will be harder to make.

PERSONALITY

George Bush had personal reasons to be concerned about the trade-offs made in America's early dealings with Noriega. Having come to office with more experience in the federal government and in foreign affairs than any president since Richard Nixon, Bush had a long and close association with many of the difficult foreign policy problems of the 1970s and 1980s. In addition to his eight years in the vice presidency, George Bush had served as a representative in Congress, as chairman of the Republican party during the Watergate investigations, as special envoy to China, as ambassador to the United Nations, and as director of the Central Intelligence Agency. He is the only president of the United States who was previously in charge of the nation's intelligence service.

The appointment of George Bush as CIA director during the Ford administration was highly controversial. CIA directors usually have professional experience in the collection or analysis of intelligence information. Bush had neither. He was the first director who had previously held elective office as well as a high-ranking position in a national political party. He was widely criticized for his partisan background and lack of relevant intelligence experience. At the time of the appointment, congressional committees in the House and Senate were just completing extensive investigations into abuses of power and violations of individual rights by the intelligence agencies. The investigations had uncovered American-sponsored assassination attempts against Castro and other world leaders, unauthorized interception of international communications, illegal investigations of American citizens in the United States, and FBI efforts to disrupt the civil rights movement and discredit its leaders.[36] The task of restoring intelligence community morale and effectiveness in the wake of these scandalous revelations fell to George Bush. Because Gerald Ford lost the 1976 election to Jimmy Carter, Bush had relatively little time to carry out that mission, but he is widely praised for the service he rendered to the CIA during a difficult period.

In December 1976, as part of his duties as CIA director, George Bush had his first meeting with Manuel Noriega. At the time there was some tension in CIA relations with Noriega because of his alleged involvement in terrorist bombings near American facilities in Panama and because the Panamanian intelligence service had evidently paid American servicemen for classified materials that revealed U.S. efforts to spy on the Panamanian military. It was a complicated affair in which both sides had reason to be embarrassed. Noriega, while still on the payroll of the CIA, was evidently bribing Americans into revealing that the CIA was collecting information on Noriega and the Panamanian military government. At the time of the meeting George Bush may also have had access to information concerning Noriega's involvement in arms sales and the drug trade. According to one report, the major issue raised by Bush in December 1976 was not bombs, or spies and counterspies, or illegal activities, but whether or not Torrijos (who had recently visited Cuba) was a communist.[37] Assured that he was not, the meeting ended with no action taken to criticize or punish Noriega.

The two men met a second time in 1983, when, as vice president, Bush made an official visit to Panama and requested assistance from Panamanian officials in the Reagan administration's efforts to support El Salvador and oppose the Sandinista regime in Nicaragua. At the meeting the vice president also mentioned new allegations about Panamanian money laundering.[38] As with their previous encounter, this one produced no open and direct criticisms of what the American government knew, or suspected, about Noriega's personal involvement with drugs and drug money. During the 1988 presidential campaign, the previous connections between Noriega and Bush were a potential political liability. It turned out to have little effect on the election because Democratic candidate Michael Dukakis made only a brief mention of the issue in one of the candidate debates and because the vice president publicly criticized President Reagan's efforts to negotiate a deal with Noriega. The latter action helped to defuse attacks on Bush for being weak and wimpish and helped to distance him from his old intelligence agency associations.

How was President Bush affected by those old associations? We can only speculate that during his first year in office he found the Noriega problem a nagging reminder of the compromises in American foreign policy that had once been commonplace. There were sound policy reasons for supporting coups against Noriega and for ordering an invasion of Panama, but there may also have been personal and political reasons. The fight against international communism was coming to an obvious turning point in 1989, if not an end, and the old trade-offs made in the name of anticommunism no longer appeared to be necessary or wise. The rising tide of American resentment about what drugs were doing to our society guaranteed that domestic and international questions involving illegal drugs would remain major political issues in the years to come, perhaps eclipsing fear of the Soviet Union and global communism. Noriega was a troublesome holdover from the days when drug dealing could be ignored in the interest of ideological battles in the Western Hemisphere. As the world entered an era when ideology would be far less important, George Bush, perhaps more than other recent presidents, would have felt the need to separate himself from the old compromises that he and others had so often and so easily made. The invasion of Panama gave him a dramatic opportunity to do so.

Chronology of the Panama Invasion

1986

Jun   *New York Times* articles attack Noriega for human rights and drug violations.

Sep   Helms resolution calls for CIA report on Panama and Noriega.

1987

Apr 3   Senate passes Helms-Kerry resolution rejecting presidential certification that Panama is cooperating in the war on drugs.

Jun 11   Revelations that Noriega rigged 1984 elections touch off riots.

Jul 10   "Black Friday," Noriega's crackdown on opposition forces.

Dec   Assistant Secretary of Defense Richard Armitage delivers message of protest to Noriega.

1988

Feb 4   Grand juries in Miami and Tampa indict Noriega for drug trafficking and money laundering.

Feb 25   President Delvalle fires Noriega, but is soon replaced by a Noriega crony.

Mar   Lawsuits filed on Delvalle's behalf tie up Panamanian assets in the U.S. and creates banking crisis in Panama.

Mar 11   U.S. places Panama Canal payments to Panama in escrow.

Mar 16   Failed coup attempt against Noriega.

Apr 8   Reagan imposes economic sanctions against Panama.

Mar–May   Shultz and Abrams urge Reagan to use military force against Noriega but fail to convince Reagan.

May 22   President approves deal with Noriega (resignation for cancelled indictments) which Bush publicly criticizes.

May 25   Deal with Noriega collapses.

Jul   Reagan approves CIA covert operation against Noriega. News of CIA plan leaked to *Washington Post*.

1989

Apr 6   Noriega learns location of transmitter. CIA agent is imprisoned.

May   Noriega annuls election won by opposition. Bush recalls U.S. ambassador and dispatches 1,800 additional troops to Panama.

Jul 22   U.S. commander in Panama replaced; plans for invasion begin.

Oct 3   Giroldi coup fails to overthrow Noriega.

Dec 15   Noriega declares himself "maximum leader."

Dec 16   U.S. serviceman killed in Panama; witnesses arrested and harassed.

Dec 17   Bush orders invasion of Panama and seizure of Noriega.

Dec 20   U.S. forces invade at 1 A.M.

1990

Jan 3   Noriega surrenders to U.S. authorities.

Chapter 8 Documents

Document 8.1
Excerpts from Senate Floor Debate on S.J. Res. 91
April 3, 1987

Mr. HELMS. Mr. President, I ordinarily do not serve as a promoter of magazine subscriptions, and maybe I am not even doing that when I refer to the January issue of *Reader's Digest*, on page 136. I hope that every Senator, after he has voted—correctly or incorrectly—on the pending joint resolution, will read about Mr. Noriega.

The title of the article is "Will This Man Control the Panama Canal?" I ask unanimous consent that the article be printed in the Record at the conclusion of my remarks.

The PRESIDING OFFICER. Without objection, it is so ordered....

Mr. HELMS. Mr. President, it is an enlightening article, and it tells what we are doing when we act as a bunch of wimps in the Senate and refuse to stand up for the law that we voted for unanimously last year.

I would hate to be running for reelection and having voted to table the previous joint resolution, because it puts the Senators who voted to table in the position of saying, "I will bluster about the drug problem, but I won't do anything about it." That is what it amounts to.

Furthermore, the law specifically requires that the President of the United States certify that the countries involved in whatever resolution happens to be before us—and this one happens to be Panama—has "cooperated fully" during the past year. If anybody believes that Panama has "cooperated fully" during the past year, I want to take them out to Senator D'Amato's State and sell them a little interest in the Brooklyn Bridge.

Furthermore, even casual observers know that the Panama Defense Forces [PDF] control the levers of power in Panama. Dozens of press accounts over the past year have pointed out the role of the PDF and General Noriega in drug trafficking, in money laundering, and all the rest of it; and it is pouring into the United States, corrupting our society. If we do not start doing something beyond talking, it is going to bring down this society. Panama, as well as Mexico and the Bahamas, is a major transshipment point for cocaine from South America into the United States.

While we are awaiting the arrival of the distinguished Senator from Massachusetts, let me just say, Mr. President, that there are more than 125 banks in Panama with more than $30 billion—that is not million, billion—in deposits. It is a situation made to order for criminals with large amounts of American cash from drug trafficking to launder.

The Panamanian banking system is high on secrecy—they will not give us any information—and low on accountability, and yet the State Department sent to this Senate, by way of a routine detour at the White House, certification that Panama has "cooperated fully" with our antidrug efforts.

In the first place, that is a falsehood. This Senator is not going to vote in favor of a certification that is a falsehood.

Bank secrecy laws in Panama protect criminals against disclosure. Both the Customs Service and the DEA confirm that the problem of drug money being laundered in Panama is increasing and not decreasing.

As an indication of the vast amount of drug money flowing through Panama, it's been reported that the National Bank of Panama transferred over $1.5 billion to the Federal Reserve Bank of Miami last year. Some estimates conclude that as much as 50 percent of these dollars were from illicit narcotics trafficking and had been laundered through Panama.

Senators should know that Panama last year broke off negotiations with the United States over a Mutual Legal Assistance Treaty which is essential to crack down on money laundering. The State Department points to the Panama drug legislation passed on December 30 of last year as cooperation and soft peddles the lack of progress on the Mutual Legal Assistance Treaty.

The certification process means full cooperation over the preceding 12 month period not potential cooperation over the coming year. The process is retrospective not prospective. A law passed in Panama one day before the end of last year can hardly be taken as an example of full cooperation and we will have to carefully examine the effectiveness of this new law over the course of this year in order to make a determination as to its value in enforcement.

There are a number of glaring cases which reflect corruption at the highest levels of the Panamanian Government and involvement in drug trafficking. Last year, one of General Noriega's personal pilots was killed allegedly over a drug deal gone sour. Two more of his personal pilots are currently in U.S. jails serving time for involvement in drug trafficking.

The former Secretary-General of the Panamanian Defense Forces, Col. Julian Melo, who has been one of General Noriega's closest advisers, was caught smuggling large quantities of ethyl ether into Panama and from there into Colombia. This chemical is used in the production of cocaine and is considered an important indicator in cocaine investigations. Colonel Melo was discharged from the Panama Defense Forces [PDF], but he was never prosecuted for his involvement in smuggling this chemical which is so critical to cocaine manufacturing. He lives openly in comfortable retirement in Panama. In addition to his smuggling operations, the Customs Service has confirmed that he received over $2 million for protection of illegal narcotics operations in Panama and was never tried for this....

Mr. President, there is no doubt in the mind of this Senator that Panama has not "cooperated fully" in the fight on drugs—in fact, they have hardly cooperated at all. We can no longer defend the Panamanian regime under General Noriega.

I invite any Senator to read the law that we passed last year. It does not leave any loopholes for us to slide off and compromise and turn the other way.

It says that the country, in this case Panama, must be certified to have "cooperated fully" in stopping drug trafficking in the eradication of crops, in stopping money laundering, and all the rest, and Panama has not.

Anybody who votes to table this joint resolution will be making a serious mistake....

The PRESIDING OFFICER. The Senator from Connecticut.

Mr. DODD. Mr. President, I thank my colleague for yielding.

Mr. President, very briefly what we are talking about here basically is a resolution that will condemn one man.

None of us want to be referred to as carrying the brief for General Noriega. The brief we have is a joint resolution that we are carrying 100 to nothing.

The real question here is: "Do we want to cut $12 million in 1987 and $15 million in 1988 money to Panama?"

We have 5,000 young Americans down in Panama. We have our southern command in Panama. We have the Panama Canal that is very important in Panama.

All are important issues.

I think it is worthwhile to note here, and the distinguished Senator from Kansas made this point, what our report says about several other countries.

On Argentina, for which the Senate has no resolution: "Argentina is becoming a major transit country for cocaine."

I turn to Brazil. "Recent reports indicate that Brazil is being used in all facets of illicit international drug trafficking."

And further: "Unofficial estimates indicate that Paraguay is becoming a major drug producing country."

The point is that we picked out three countries, and we have by doing so indirectly said all these other countries are doing fine.

Most countries, unfortunately, are not doing very well, either in the consumption battle or cutting out the supply.

All I would like to suggest to my colleagues here is that while we have much to be concerned about in dealing with Panama and other countries, there has to be a better way of handling it than by tying up all the issues with Panama on account of a single issue....

The implications of tying up all our interests in Panama on this single question would be broad in scope and serious.

It seems to me there has to be a better way of dealing with this than just a joint resolution that will cut off aid and not take into consideration the implications it would have for the southern command, for the strategic importance of Panama, and for our relationship with that country.

If we want the entire relationship with that nation to be determined on this single issue, then vote against tabling this joint resolution. That is an easy vote because you will be attacking a general in that country.

If you are concerned, however, about our relationship with this country, one of the most strategically important nations in this hemisphere, then I urge you to vote to table this joint resolution and provide us a better opportunity to deal with this question, as the Senator from Kansas has pointed out, in an authorization bill, where we could confront the full range of issues related to Panama.

Source: *Congressional Record*, April 3, 1987, pp. S4504 – S4512.

Document 8.2
President Reagan's Executive Order No. 12635
April 8, 1988

By the authority vested in me as President by the Constitution and laws of the United States of America, including the International Emergency Economic Powers Act (50 U.S.C. 1701 *et seq.*), the National Emergencies Act (50 U.S.C. 1601 *et seq.*), and section 301 of title 3 of the United States Code,

I, RONALD REAGAN, President of the United States of America, find that the policies and actions in Panama of Manuel Antonio Noriega and Manuel Solis Palma constitute an unusual and extraordinary threat to the national security, foreign policy, and economy of the United States and hereby declare a national emergency to deal with that threat.

Section 1. I hereby order blocked all property and interests in property of the Government of Panama that are in the United States, that hereafter come within the United States, or that are or hereafter come within the possession or control of persons located within the United States. For purposes of this Order, the Government of Panama is defined to include its agencies, instrumentalities and controlled entities, including the Banco Nacional de Panama and the Caja de Ahorros.

Sec. 2. Except to the extent provided in regulations which may hereafter be issued pursuant to this Order:

(a) Any direct or indirect payments or transfers from the United States to the Noriega/Solis regime of funds, including currency, cash or coins of any nation, or of other financial or investment assets or credits are prohibited. All transfers, or payments owed, to the Government of Panama shall be made into an account at the Federal Reserve Bank of New York, to be held for the benefit of the Panamanian people. For purposes of this Order, the term "Noriega/Solis regime" shall mean Manuel Antonio Noriega, Manuel Solis Palma, and any agencies, instrumentalities or entities purporting to act on their behalf or under their authority.

(b) Any direct or indirect payments or transfers to the Noriega/Solis regime of funds, including currency, cash or coins of any nation, or of other financial or investment assets or credits, by any United States person located in the territory of Panama, or by any person organized under the laws of Panama and owned or controlled by a United States person, are prohibited. All transfers, or payments owed, to the Government of Panama by such persons shall be made into an account at the Federal Reserve Bank of New York, to be held for the benefit of the Panamanian people. For purposes of Section 2(b), "the United States person" is defined to mean any United States citizen, permanent resident alien, juridical person organized under the laws of the United States, or any person in the United States.

Sec. 3. Sections 1 and 2 shall not be deemed to block property or interests in property of the Government of Panama, including, but not limited to, accounts established at the Federal Reserve Bank of New York as described in section 2, with respect to which transactions are authorized by, or on behalf of, the recognized representative of the Government of Panama as certified by the Secretary of State, or are otherwise authorized in regulations which may hereafter be issued pursuant to this Order. Section 2 shall not be deemed to prohibit interbank clearing payments.

Sec. 4. The measures taken pursuant to this Order are intended to extend the effectiveness of actions initiated in cooperation with the Government of Panama and its President, Eric Arturo Delvalle, and are not intended to block private Panamanian assets subject to the jurisdiction of the United States or to prohibit remittances by United States persons to Panamanian persons other than the Noriega/Solis regime....

This Order shall be transmitted to the Congress and published in the Federal Register.

Source: 53 *Federal Register* 12134, April 12, 1988.

Document 8.3
President Bush's Address to the Nation
December 20, 1989

My fellow citizens. Last night, I ordered U.S. military forces to Panama. No president takes such action lightly. This morning, I want to tell you what I did and why I did it.

For nearly two years, the United States, the nations of Latin America and the Caribbean have worked together to resolve the crisis in Panama. The goals of the United States have been to safeguard the lives of Americans, to defend democracy in Panama, to combat drug trafficking and to protect the integrity of the Panama Canal Treaty.

Many attempts have been made to resolve this crisis through diplomacy and negotiations. All were rejected by the dictator of Panama, General Manuel Noriega, an indicted drug trafficker.

Last Friday, Noriega declared his military dictatorship to be in a state of war with the United States and publicly threatened the lives of Americans in Panama. The very next day, forces under his command shot and killed an unarmed American serviceman, wounded another, arrested and brutally beat a third American serviceman, and then brutally interrogated his wife, threatening her with sexual abuse. That was enough.

General Noriega's reckless threats and attacks upon Americans in Panama created an imminent danger to the 35,000 American citizens in Panama. As president, I have no higher obligation than to safeguard the lives of American citizens.

And that is why I directed our armed forces to protect the lives of American citizens in Panama and to bring General Noriega to justice in the United States.

I contacted the bipartisan leadership of Congress last night and informed them of this decision. And after taking this action, I also talked with leaders in Latin America, the Caribbean and those of other U.S. allies.

At this moment U.S. forces, including forces deployed from the United States last night, are engaged in action in Panama. The United States intends to withdraw forces newly deployed to Panama as quickly as possible.

Our forces have conducted themselves courageously and selflessly. And as commander-in-chief, I salute every one of them and thank them on behalf of our country. Tragically, some Americans have lost their lives in defense of their fellow citizens, in defense of democracy. And my heart goes out to their families. We also regret and mourn the loss of innocent Panamanians.

The brave Panamanians elected by the people of Panama in the elections last May, President Guillermo Endara and Vice Presidents Calderon and Ford, have assumed the rightful leadership of their country.

You remember those horrible pictures of newly elected Vice President [Guillermo] Ford, covered head to toe with blood, beaten mercilessly by so-called dignity battalions. Well, the United States today recognizes the democratically elected government of President Endara. I will send our ambassador back to Panama immediately.

Key military objectives have been achieved. Most organized resistance has been eliminated. But the operation is not over yet. General Noriega is in hiding.

And nevertheless, yesterday a dictator ruled Panama and today constitutionally elected leaders govern.

I've today directed the secretary of the Treasury and the secretary of state to lift the economic sanctions with respect to the democratically elected government of Panama and, in cooperation with that government, to take steps to effect an orderly unblocking of Panamanian government assets in the United States.

I am fully committed to implement the Panama Canal Treaties and turn over the canal to Panama in the year 2000. The actions we have taken and the cooperation of a new democratic government in Panama will permit us to honor these commitments. As soon as the new government recommends a qualified candidate—Panamanian—to be administrator of the canal as called for in the treaties, I will submit this nominee to the Senate for expedited consideration.

I am committed to strengthening our relationship with the democratic nations in this hemisphere. I will continue to seek solutions to the problems of this region through dialogue and multilateral diplomacy. I took this action only after reaching the conclusion that every other avenue was closed and the lives of American citizens were in grave danger.

I hope that the people of Panama will put this dark chapter of dictatorship behind them and move forward together as citizens of a democratic Panama with this government that they themselves have elected. The United States is eager to work with the Panamanian people in partnership and friendship to rebuild their economy.

The Panamanian people want democracy, peace and the chance for a better life in dignity and freedom. The people of the United States seek only to support them in pursuit of these noble goals.

Thank you very much.

Source: *Weekly Compilation of Presidential Documents*, December 25, 1989, pp. 1974–1975.

Chapter 8 Notes

[1]Estimates of the costs involved in the U.S. commitment to NATO are difficult to make because the U.S. defense budget is normally divided by service and function rather than geographic region, but with more than 325,000 troops in Europe and substantial portions of the Atlantic fleet and U.S. airlift capacity devoted to European resupply in the event of war, estimates of one third to one half are reasonable. For estimates of the cost of replacing a portion of the U.S. European force, see Richard L. Kugler, "Theatre Forces: The Future of the U.S. Military Presence in Europe," in *American Defense Annual 1988–89*, ed. Joseph Kruzel,(Lexington, Mass.: Lexington Books, 1988), p. 97.

[2] For a review of changes in public opinion on foreign policy in the late 1980s, see Daniel Yankelovich and Richard Smoke, "America's 'New Thinking,'" *Foreign Affairs* (Fall 1988), 1–17. In a September 1989 *New York Times*/CBS News poll, 54 percent of the respondents cited drugs as an important issue facing the nation. Only 1 percent thought

war and the threat of war with the Soviet Union was the most important issue on the national agenda. *New York Times*, September 28, 1989, p. 26.

[3]Two recent books describe Noriega's life and associations with the United States: Frederick Kempe, *Divorcing the Dictator* (New York: Putnam's, 1990); and John Dinges, *Our Man in Panama*, (New York: Random House, 1990). Dinges gives a slightly different account of Noriega's parents than the one summarized above (p. 31).

[4]Kempe, *Divorcing the Dictator*, pp. 45–46.

[5]Dinges, *Our Man in Panama*, pp. 251–52.

[6]Kempe *Divorcing the Dictator*, p. 26. Dinges suggests that Noriega may have worked for the United States even earlier during the Eisenhower administration.

[7]Kempe, *Divorcing the Dictator*, pp. 90–95.

[8]For an account of the Shah's complaints about security in Panama, see Mohammed Reza Pahlavi, the Shah of Iran, *Answer to History* (New York: Stein & Day, 1980), pp. 29–32. See also William Shawcross, *The Shah's Last Ride* (New York: Simon & Schuster, 1988), pp. 317–318 and 324–326.

[9]Kempe, *Divorcing the Dictator*, p. 2.

[10]William Branigin, "Army Reveals Details of Noriega's Lair of Magic," *Washington Post*, December 26, 1989, p. A14.

[11]The Reagan administration certified to the Congress that Panama was cooperating in the war on drugs in the spring of 1987.

[12]Stipulated in the Oliver North trial documents, Kempe *Divorcing the Dictator*, p. 165.

[13]Dinges *Our Man in Panama*, p. 51; Kempe *Divorcing the Dictator*, p. 162. See also Seymour Hersh, "Our Man in Panama," *Life* (March 1990).

[14]Joel McCleary, quoted in Kempe, *Divorcing the Dictator*, p. 173.

[15]The State Department acknowledged in its annual report on human rights that the 1984 elections had been rigged. "Country Reports on Human Rights Practices for 1985" *Report Submitted to the Committee on Foreign Affairs House of Representatives and the Committee on Foreign Relations U.S. Senate by the Department of State* (February 1986), 640.

[16]Dinges, *Our Man in Panama*, p. 41.

[17]Articles by Seymour Hersh appeared in the *New York Times* on June 12, 13, and 22. The first on June 12 was particularly embarrassing to Noriega because it was published while he was visiting the United States on official business.

[18]Kempe, *Divorcing the Dictator*, p. 225.

[19]Ibid., p. 223.

[20]Steve C. Ropp, "Panama's Defiant Noriega," *Current History* (December 1988), pp. 417–418.

[21]There are conflicting reports about Reagan's early awareness of the indictments. See Kempe, *Divorcing the Dictator*, p. 226.

[22]"Lugar Urges Crackdown on Noriega," *Washington Post*, April 22, 1989, p. A8.

[23]"Taking Aim at Noriega," *U.S. News and World Report* May 1, 1989, pp. 40–41.

[24]"Long Road to the Invasion of Panama," *Washington Post*, January 14, 1990, p. 1.

[25]Kempe, *Divorcing the Dictator*, p. 11.

[26]Kevin Buckley, *Panama: The Whole Story* (New York: Simon & Schuster, 1991), pp. 193–208.

[27]"Doing the Inevitable," *New York Times*, December 24, 1989 p. 9.

[28]Buckley, *Panama*, pp. 229–231.

[29]"The Conversion of Gen. Powell," *Washington Post*, December 21, 1989, p. A31.

[30]There is considerable controversy about the number of Panamanian casualties, which may be much higher than 300. These figures are from "Inside the Invasion," *Newsweek*, June 25, 1990, pp. 28–31. Buckley reports estimates of 1,000 civilian casualties, p. 264.

[31] "Inside the Invasion," p. 30.

[32]Kempe, *Divorcing the Dictator*, p. 411.

[33]For a review of presidential powers and international economic policy, see Barry E. Carter, *International Economic Sanctions* (Cambridge: Cambridge University Press, 1988).

[34]Dinges, *Our Man in Panama*, pp. 233–234.

[35]For an early use of the term, see Bayless Manning, "The Congress, the Executive and Intermestic Affairs: Three Proposals," *Foreign Affairs* (Winter 1977), 306–324.

[36]Loch Johnson, *A Season of Inquiry* (Chicago: Dorsey Press, 1988).

[37]Dinges, *Our Man in Panama*, pp. 88–90.

[38] Ibid., pp. 162–164.

Epilogue

The War with Iraq

Though the fighting in Panama in December 1989 was the largest American military operation since Vietnam, it held that distinction for a very short time. Late in the summer of 1990, Saddam Hussein moved thousands of Iraqi troops to the border between his nation and Kuwait. To the surprise of most international observers, Middle East experts, and members of the Bush administration, Hussein proceeded to order a full-scale invasion of his small but wealthy neighbor. After an easy victory against the Kuwaiti army, Iraqi officials announced that Kuwait would henceforth be designated the nineteenth province of Iraq. It was a disastrous decision.

President Bush responded to the Iraqi invasion immediately with a simple statement. The unprovoked conquest of Kuwait by Iraq, the president said, "will not stand."[1] The United States and the international community would work to force an Iraqi withdrawal. The president dispatched American air, sea, and land forces to protect Saudi Arabia and the other oil-rich nations on the desert peninsula between the Red Sea and the Persian Gulf from any further Iraqi military moves. Diplomatic efforts at the United Nations and among America's European allies and Arab friends gradually produced a coalition of nations committed to denying Hussein the fruits of his aggression.

For almost the first time since its creation, the United Nations Security Council became the focal point for much of this diplomatic activity. Not since the Korean War (which broke out at a time when the Soviet Union was boycotting UN meetings) had the members of the Security Council met to discuss a major threat to the peace without the fear that a veto by one of the permanent council members would block any meaningful response. In the new atmosphere of improved relations between the United States and the Soviet Union, both former cold war rivals agreed on the need to maintain stability in the Middle East and prevent Hussein from using his substantial armed forces for blackmail or conquest. Britain and France joined in this endeavor; China remained on the sidelines. With no real danger of a veto, the path to effective United Nations action was open.

Between August and November 1990, the Security Council passed a series of resolutions condemning Iraq's invasion of Kuwait and imposing economic sanctions against Hussein's regime. The early sanctions included an embargo against any Iraqi oil exports, a move that cut off Iraq's only major source of foreign currency. Throughout the fall months the sanctions were gradually tightened to include virtually every product and method of transportation into and out of Iraq and occupied Kuwait. The sanctions were enforced with the full cooperation of Iraq's neighbors (though they were least effective on the border with Jordan) and by the use of American naval power in the Persian Gulf. When it appeared that sanctions alone would not force rapid Iraqi compliance with the resolutions calling for the restoration of an independent Kuwait, the United States announced in early November that it would double its troop deployments to Saudi Arabia and scrap plans to rotate the soldiers already there. On November 29, the Security Council passed resolution 678 authorizing the use of "all necessary means," including military force, to get Iraq out of Kuwait. The resolution gave Hussein a month and half to remove his troops peacefully, but if he failed to do so, UN military operations could begin after January 15, 1991. The United States played a leading role in the passage of the resolutions and in the building of a multinational military force in the Middle East capable of enforcing them.

The president also built a domestic coalition in support of his objectives. Ironically, it was harder for President Bush to persuade the Congress and the American people of the wisdom of his decisions than it was to convince the members of the Security Council, the major European powers, and the moderate Arab states. Though there was widespread public and congressional approval of the president's early commitments to the security of Saudi Arabia and the enforcement of economic sanctions against Iraq, the closer the United States moved toward actual fighting in the Middle East the stronger the public and congressional opposition became. At highly publicized hearings before the Senate Armed Services Committee, chaired by Democratic Senator Sam Nunn, witnesses warned that a war with Iraq might well be costly for U.S. troops and for the future stability of the region. Moreover, a variety of military and foreign policy experts testified that the uncertain consequences of war could probably be avoided since the economic sanctions imposed by the United Nations would eventually cripple the Iraqi economy. As the January 15 deadline approached with no sign of Iraqi compliance with the terms of Resolution 678 and no progress in a final round of diplomatic negotiations between Secretary of State James Baker and the Iraqi foreign minister, members of Congress were forced to take a position on the impending war.

In an historic session both chambers considered resolutions supporting the president's authority to use force against Iraq and alternate resolutions that called for a longer testing of economic sanctions before military operations would begin. After serious, lengthy, and passionate debate, both houses voted to authorize military operations to remove Iraqi forces from Kuwait. When the January 15 deadline passed without a voluntary Iraqi withdrawal, Desert Shield (the code name for the defense of Saudi Arabia) became Desert Storm (the Pentagon's designation for operations to liberate Kuwait). The storm began with a massive air war against military targets in Iraq and Kuwait. Carried on live international television, the war became a media spectacle complete with continuous expert commentary, live coverage of Iraqi Scud missiles traveling through the night skies, and videotape of highly accurate U.S. munitions destroying military facilities throughout Iraq. Air power could not, by itself, dislodge the Iraqi troops from Kuwait, and after weeks of heavy bombardment the air war was followed by a swift and successful ground campaign that finally liberated a plundered and war-ravaged Kuwait.

It is probably too soon to write a detailed case study of the war in the Persian Gulf, and certainly too soon to evaluate its long-term consequences. But a number of the events in the months before and after the fighting broke out are worth discussing at the conclusion of this book because they are related to the issues and themes that have been explored in the preceding chapters.

POWER

The Gulf war provides a classic example of the conflict between presidential and congressional powers in foreign affairs. President Bush stated on several occasions during the Gulf crisis that he had sufficient authority under the Constitution and the Charter of the United Nations to send U.S. troops to Saudi Arabia, to enforce an international economic embargo against Iraq, and to use American military power to remove Iraqi forces from Kuwait. "Saddam Hussein should be under no question on this," he told the press on January 9, 1991, three days before the House and Senate approved their resolutions of support. "I feel that I have the authority to fully implement the United Nations resolutions."[2] The president welcomed the congressional support he eventually received, but he denied that there was a constitutional requirement that his actions undergo prior legislative review. In taking this position, Bush was reiterating the traditional postwar executive interpretation of the Constitution and the president's foreign policy powers under its provisions. The problem with this position, as we have seen in a number of the cases, is that it discounts, and even ignores, the constitutional language giving Congress the power to declare war.

In the weeks and months preceding the January 15 deadline many members of Congress, including liberals, moderates, and conservatives, called for a formal vote on the pending military operations in the Persian Gulf. Democrats like Edward Kennedy wanted the Congress brought into special session during the late year holiday recess and given an opportunity to consider Gulf policies; Republicans like Richard Lugar wanted the Congress to carry out its formal constitutional responsibility and vote a declaration of war against Iraq. Though President Bush consulted with various members of the legislature, and particularly the leadership in the House and Senate, he refused to call a special session to consider issues in the Persian Gulf. "I cannot consult with 535 strong-willed individuals," he told reporters during a news conference on November 30. "Nor does my responsibility under the Constitution compel me to do that."[3] The Democratic leaders of the House and Senate, who also had the power to bring the members of Congress back to Washington, refused to take that action. As the January deadline approached, the constitutional provisions giving the legislature the power to declare war appeared to be irrelevant.

Several disgruntled members of Congress who wanted a chance to block the president's plans went to court in order to force the administration to comply with the constitutional procedures governing war and peace. Their case was dismissed. Similar cases had been initiated during the 1980s in connection with American military operations in Grenada, Libya, and Lebanon, and the U.S. decision to protect ships in the Persian Gulf during the Iran-Iraq war. In the case involving Iraq's invasion of Kuwait, as in all the other attempts to resolve the war powers issue in the courts, the presiding judge ruled that a small group of Congressmen cannot sue the executive branch in order to ensure compliance with the Constitution. The issue is, the courts have consistently said, a political question to be settled by the two elected branches of government. If Congress wants to stop the president from entering an expected war, it must do so by using its own legislative authorities.

Early in January, when the 102nd Congress officially convened, the issue of policy in the Persian Gulf finally became an active legislative question. In a remarkably frank and solemn debate, which ended on Saturday, January 12, members of both chambers considered alternative Persian Gulf proposals. In the House a bipartisan group of Democrats and Republicans sponsored a resolution expressing support for Security Council Resolution 678 and the use of force against Hussein after January 15. A second resolution put forward by the House Democratic leadership urged the administration to continue sanctions against Iraq and maintain a defensive posture in Saudi Arabia. At that time, the American people were deeply divided about the prospect of a war in the Middle East and each of the resolutions under consideration had substantial public support.

In an unusual procedure, the Speaker of the House, Thomas Foley, left his place as the presiding officer of the House of Representatives and spoke from the floor as a member representing one district in the state of Washington. He called upon all members of the House to set aside their partisan and ideological alignments and vote their conscience on the question put before them. The House then voted to support the president and his policies by a majority of 250 to 183. In the Senate the margin of support for President Bush was narrower, 52 to 47, and more partisan; but both bodies ended the debate by giving the executive a free hand in the use of force against Iraq. It was the first time a Congress had made such a grant of power since the aftermath of the Gulf of Tonkin incident in the Johnson administration. Though the language of the resolution passed in the House and Senate stated that the congressional action with regard to Iraq was consistent with the War Powers Resolution, the executive branch continued to regard the provisions of the 1973 war powers legislation as an unconstitutional infringement on presidential authority.

In a number of the cases reviewed in earlier chapters the question of presidential and congressional powers in deciding to take the nation to war has been controversial. It remains so. The issue will, in all likelihood, never be fully or finally resolved. The successful completion of Desert Storm and the relatively light allied casualties that it entailed may make the use of military power a more attractive instrument in the conduct of American foreign policy, but the circumstances surrounding our operations in the Middle East, like those surrounding the invasion of Panama, may not repeat themselves very often.

Hussein, like Noriega, took actions that denied him any effective support in the world community. His clear violation of the UN prohibitions against aggression, the reported atrocities that were committed in occupied Kuwait, and the potential economic consequences of his ability to control a large portion of the world's known oil reserves, made Hussein an international outlaw. The only sympathy he received for any of his actions in late 1990 and early 1991 came from radical Palestinian and Arab nationalist groups who were too weak to rescue Iraq from the combined economic power of the UN membership and the substantial military power of America and its coalition partners. Hussein's efforts to convert the issue of Iraqi conquest of Kuwait into a struggle between Israel and the Arab world failed when the Israelis chose not to respond to the Scud missile attacks from which they suffered throughout the allied campaign. Denied his claim to leadership of the Arab movement, Hussein was isolated and unable to withstand the air and ground attacks that the United States and the coalition brought to bear.

Is this a harbinger of things to come? Will there be a new world order in which the UN Security Council will regularly address important international controversies and have the United States supply the presidential leadership and military muscle needed to make and enforce its decisions? For now, such a fundamental change in international politics is hard to envision. Even in the relatively clear-cut case of a nation violating international law and threatening the economic interests of the developed world, the people of the United States and their congressional representatives had serious reservations about whether or not American lives should be risked in the worthy cause of punishing Iraq. If the world is to have a new order, the old American Constitution and the long legacy of disputes it has produced over issues of war and peace will limit the ability of American presidents to lead that order.

PROCESS

The debate about war powers and the Persian Gulf was carried out in public, in the courts, and on the floor of the House and Senate where it was finally resolved, in this case, by the casting of recorded votes. We know the arguments that were put forward and the positions that prevailed; it is all a matter of public record. We know much less about the decision-making process within the Bush administration concerning the Gulf war. Nevertheless, several preliminary observations are worth making.

To an unusual extent the foreign policy team during the Bush administration has appeared to work well as a group and provide the nation with consistent and effective foreign policy management. Throughout the weeks and months before the war with Iraq began, and after the fighting was underway, the administration spoke with one voice—Iraq must leave Kuwait. Pressures from the Soviet Union and France to negotiate with the Iraqis and accept less than a total withdrawal were opposed. Proposals from the Congress to rely primarily on economic sanctions against Iraq were defeated. And temptations to extend the aims of the war once military victory was assured were resisted. More than most of the postwar administrations we have examined, the Bush presidency has been characterized by an absence of open conflict and competition between cabinet officers and the White House and among the president's principal foreign policy advisers. There are a number of explanations for this phenomenon.

Unlike most recent presidents, George Bush came to the White House with extensive experience in a variety of national security policy making positions. As a former ambassador to the United Nations, U.S. representative in China, director of the CIA, and vice president for eight years, Bush knew more about the foreign policy making institutions of the national government at the time of his election than any other modern president, with the possible exception of Dwight Eisenhower. President Bush wanted a foreign policy making team that could work together and avoid the divisive public debates that he had seen in a number of previous administrations.

The president appointed an impressive group of senior advisers who were also people with whom he had long personal and professional connections. His secretary of state, James Baker, had been Bush's campaign manager in both the unsuccessful bid for the Republican nomination in 1980 and the winning campaign in 1988. Baker was an old friend from Texas politics and an associate throughout the Reagan years. Secretary of Defense Dick Cheney had been White House chief of staff under Gerald Ford when Bush held a number of appointed positions within that administration. At the time of Cheney's appointment, following former Texas Senator John Tower's failure to win confirmation, the president and the secretary of defense had known each other for many years. Colin Powell, the chairman of the Joint Chiefs of Staff, was another member of the Reagan administration who took on new responsibilities under President Bush. Finally, the president's national security adviser, Brent Scowcroft, is the only person to hold that office on two separate occasions. Scowcroft was Ford's special assistant for national security affairs after Henry Kissinger relinquished that title. Bush, because of his long years in Washington, was able to assemble an unusually experienced and able group of advisers in foreign affairs who knew each other and the president before the administration began. Once in office they gave the impression that they were loyal and reliable team members who shared the president's desire for consensus and consistent policy.

But appearances in presidential politics are not always a reliable reflection of reality. In one of the first published accounts of the Bush administration's foreign policy decision making, *Washington Post* investigative reporter Bob Woodward suggests that there was more disorder and dissent in the upper ranks of the Bush foreign policy team than was evident to outside observers.[4] In particular, he reports that Colin Powell was dissatisfied with the quality of decision making in connection with the Gulf war. According to Woodward, the important decision for the Bush administration was not the initiation of an air war after the January 15 deadline, but the much earlier October decision to double U.S. forces in the Middle East region from approximately 250,000 to nearly half a million military personnel. It was that decision that gave the administration an offensive military option that the president was fully prepared to use. At that time, well before any congressional hearings had publicly raised the issue of using sanctions rather than military force, Powell advocated a policy of containment—defending against any further Iraqi aggression and letting the sanctions run their course. In Woodward's account, that option never got a full airing at the highest levels of the Bush administration where the disposition toward the use of force was an early presidential preference. By October 1990, apparently the president had made up his mind that force would be used to get Hussein out of Kuwait. The rest of that year and the early weeks of 1991 were devoted to building international and domestic support for that decision.

The Woodward account of foreign policy decision making in the Bush administration was controversial when it first appeared. The president dismissed it as Washington gossip, pointing out that some of the information in the book was not correct and that most of it was based on interviews with unnamed sources.[5] He reaffirmed his pleasure with the performance of Powell and all of his national security advisers at an impromptu news conference during a photo opportunity. "They are not going to divide us on this," he told the White House press corps.[6] In responding to the Woodward revelations the president was confronting a problem that all presidents encounter in the organization and administration of their policymaking systems. Chief executives want their assistants to perform two very different functions. They need to hear alternative proposals for action and frank discussion about existing situations and pending decisions. Diversity of opinion and well-argued options give presidents meaningful choices. But once decisions are made, the people working for the administration are expected to change immediately from forceful advocates of alternative courses of action to loyal supporters of the prevailing policy. Smooth shifts from diversity to unity, from giving candid advice to promoting a common cause, are hard to manage and strain the ability of any president to maintain an effective team of foreign policy advisers. In most administrations, diversity in policy options is purchased at the price of consistency in implementation, and vice versa. The tension between the two is almost impossible to resolve. For scholars interested in how decisions are made, there is the added difficulty of penetrating the secrecy that naturally surrounds the private deliberations in the early stages of policy formulation.

The dispute about what really went on in the inner circles of the Bush administration concerning the war with Iraq should make us cautious about reaching any firm conclusions concerning recent events in American foreign policy. The cases in this book have been based on the available evidence about what went on in the various presidential administrations and the judgments of scholars who have studied that evidence in detail. But final conclusions are hard to come by. The existing evidence will always be incomplete and subject to interpretation. Even after hundreds of people took part in the Iran-contra investigations carried out by congressional committees and the office of the special prosecutor, after thousands of pages of documents were reviewed, and after most of the available participants were interviewed and questioned under oath, there are still significant gaps in what we know about foreign policy decision making in the Reagan administration. Some of those gaps may be filled in at a later date if new documents or evidence become available, but many issues surrounding the affair are likely to remain open to discussion and debate for decades.

PERSONALITY

If it is difficult to know fully what goes on within the inner circles of a particular administration, it is even harder to know what goes on in the mind of an individual leader. Throughout the cases we have examined, the conclusions about presidential personality have been more brief and tentative than those dealing with power and process. This is not because personality is unimportant. It is, however, the hardest source of presidential behavior for which to gather reliable evidence and reach definitive conclusions.

At a certain level of generality, the personal qualities of presidents and their impact on policy are easy to identify. We know that Jimmy Carter was morally committed to a number of his policy initiatives and believed that relinquishing American ownership of the Panama Canal was the right thing to do. We know that Lyndon Johnson was manipulative in his dealings with his staff and members of Congress and may not have told those around him everything he planned to do in Vietnam. Long before his presidency began Richard Nixon was suspicious of the bureaucracies and the press and was likely to make his most important decisions in secrecy. Throughout his political career Harry Truman was a blunt and decisive person who may have been inclined to endorse quickly the recommendations of his advisers on the atomic bombing of Japan. But all of these men are complicated individuals whose behavior at any particular moment is bound to reflect mixed motives and the complex interaction of personal qualities and political forces that are almost impossible to unravel completely. Can we really know for sure what Harry Truman's heart-felt private thoughts about the bombing of Hiroshima and Nagasaki may have been? Or when Lyndon Johnson made up his mind that American troops would have to be used to prevent the fall of South Vietnam? Or what made Jimmy Carter take a moral stand on some issues and a realistic position on others? Or whether Richard Nixon's foreign policy secrecy was primarily based on legitimate fear of leaks or excessive distrust of those around him? Connecting obvious personal qualities to specific policy outcomes involves some of the most sensitive judgments made by students of foreign affairs.

Moreover, the personal qualities of presidents are not always obvious. Despite the fact that candidates for the presidency are engaged in long national campaigns that put them constantly in the public spotlight, and despite the fact that after their election they become the focus of nearly continuous media attention, it is often surprisingly difficult to know who they really are. In the case of President Bush and the war with Iraq, many Washington observers did not expect his dogged determination to get Hussein out of Kuwait. Because of his consistently loyal support for President Reagan throughout his vice presidency and his long years of service to other presidents, some members of the media thought that George Bush lacked a forceful independent personality. They labeled him a "wimp" in the 1988 campaign. Two years later, he turned out to be anything but wimpish in his response to the Gulf crisis.

George Bush is far from being the only president to be seriously misunderstood by the press and the public. Dwight Eisenhower was thought by many to be detached from policy decisions and ineffective as a chief executive when he left office in 1960. More recent research has shown that he was extremely active behind the scenes throughout his presidency and that he intentionally cultivated an image of detachment. He did so in order to maintain his popularity with an American public that likes its presidents to be above the political manipulation that is an essential part of the job.[7] In other words, we often misunderstand presidents because the holders of that office hide their actions and motives from public view and because our expectations about presidential performance may be overly idealistic. New technologies in information distribution do not necessarily help. In fact, in the age of television and instant communications, we may actually experience a false sense of intimacy with our political leaders. We see them daily, hear detailed reports about their movements, listen to their public statements, and even get clinical reports about their medical condition. But do we really know them? Or are we manipulated by images carefully created by campaign officials and White House staff members who do nothing but cultivate favorable media attention?

Because human behavior, and the institutions that humans create, are inherently complex, even when we have honest information about presidents and their decisions, it is often difficult to put that information in its proper context. Understanding American foreign policy and the processes and persons that make it requires a constant digging for more and better information and a careful effort to give all the available information a thorough and balanced analysis. The cases in this book are far from being the last word on the issues or individuals they describe. They may, however, provide an adequate introduction to the intricate connections between presidents, the administrations they lead, the powers they hold, and the foreign policies they create.

NOTES

[1]Presidential statement, August 5, 1990.

[2]Presidential press conference, January 9, 1991.

[3]Presidential press conference, November 30, 1990.

[4]Bob Woodward, *The Commanders* (New York: Simon & Schuster, 1991).

[5]"Bush Defends Gen. Powell," *Washington Post*, May 3, 1991, p. A16.

[6]Ibid.

[7]Fred Greenstein, *The Hidden-Hand Presidency: Eisenhower as Leader* (New York: Basic Books, 1982).

Selected Bibliography

AMERICAN FOREIGN POLICY
AND THE PRESIDENCY

Allison, Graham. *Essence of Decision*. Boston: Little, Brown, 1971.

Ambrose, Stephen. *Rise to Globalism*, 5th ed. New York: Penguin, 1988.

Barber, James David. *Presidential Character*. Englewood Cliffs, N.J.: Prentice Hall, 1972.

Corwin, Edward S. *The President: Office and Powers 1787–1957*, 5th ed. New York: New York University Press, 1984.

Destler, I. M. *Bureaucrats, Presidents and Foreign Policy*. Princeton, N.J.: Princeton University Press, 1974.

George, Alexander. *Presidential Decisionmaking in Foreign Policy*. Boulder, Colo.: Westview, 1980.

Henkin, Louis. *Foreign Affairs and the Constitution*. New York: Norton, 1972.

Isaacson, Walter, and Evan Thomas. *The Wise Men*. New York: Simon & Schuster, 1986.

Kennan, George. *American Diplomacy*. Chicago: University of Chicago Press, 1951.

Kissinger, Henry. *American Foreign Policy*. New York: Norton, 1969.

Lord, Carnes. *The Presidency and the Management of National Security*. New York: Free Press, 1988.

Neustadt, Richard. *Presidential Power and the Modern Presidents*. New York: Free Press, 1990.

Prados, John. *Keepers of the Keys*. New York: William Morrow, 1991.

Rubin, Barry. *Secrets of State*. New York: Oxford University Press, 1985.

THE HIROSHIMA DECISION
AND EISENHOWER'S ARMS CONTROL POLICIES

Bundy, McGeorge. *Danger and Survival*. New York: Random House, 1988.

Eisenhower, Dwight D. *The White House Years: Mandate for Change*. Garden City, N.Y.: Doubleday, 1963.

Herken, Greg. *Counsels of War*. New York: Knopf, 1985.

Hewlett, Richard G., and Jack M. Holl. *Atoms for Peace and War 1953–1961*. Berkeley: University of California Press, 1989.

Rhodes, Richard. *The Making of the Atomic Bomb*. New York: Simon & Schuster, 1986.

Rostow, W. W. *Open Skies*. Austin: University of Texas Press, 1982.

Sherwin, Martin J. *A World Destroyed*. New York: Knopf, 1975.

Stimson, Henry L., and McGeorge Bundy. *On Active Service in Peace and War*. New York: Harper & Bros., 1948.

Truman, Harry S. *Memoirs: Year of Decision*. Garden City, N.Y.: Doubleday, 1955.

Williams, Robert C., and Philip L. Cantelon, eds. *American Atom*. Philadelphia: University of Pennsylvania Press, 1984.

Wyden, Peter. *Day One*. New York: Simon & Schuster, 1984.

LAOS AND VIETNAM

Ball, George. *The Past Has Another Pattern*. New York: Norton, 1982.

Berman, Larry. *Planning a Tragedy*. New York: Norton, 1982.

Burke, John, and Fred Greenstein. *How Presidents Test Reality: Decisions on Vietnam 1954 and 1965*. New York: Russell Sage Foundation, 1989.

Dommen, Arthur. *Conflict in Laos*. New York: Praeger, 1964.

Fall, Bernard B. *Anatomy of a Crisis*. Garden City, N.Y.: Doubleday, 1969.

Gibbons, William Conrad. *The U.S. Government and the Vietnam War*, 2 vols. Princeton, N.J.: Princeton University Press, 1986.

Halperstam, David. *The Best and the Brightest*. New York: Random House, 1972.

Hilsman, Roger. *To Move a Nation*. Garden City, N.Y.: Doubleday, 1967.

Karnow, Stanley. *Vietnam: A History*. New York: Viking, 1983.

Kerns, Doris. *Lyndon Johnson and the American Dream*. New York: Harper & Row, 1976.

Rusk, Dean. *As I Saw It*. New York: Norton, 1990.

U.S. Department of Defense. *The Senator Gavel Edition: The Pentagon Papers*, 4 vols. Boston: Beacon, 1972.

Van De Mark, Brian. *Into the Quagmire*. New York: Oxford University Press, 1991.

DÉTENTE

Bell, Coral. *The Diplomacy of the Kissinger Era*. New York: St. Martin's, 1977.

Gaddis, John. *Strategies of Containment*. New York: Oxford University Press, 1982.

Garthoff, Raymond. *Détente and Confrontation*. Washington, D.C.: Brookings, 1985.

George, Alexander, et al., eds. *U.S.–Soviet Security Cooperation*. New York: Oxford University Press, 1988.

Kissinger, Henry. *White House Years*. Boston: Little, Brown, 1979.

———. *Years of Upheaval*. Boston: Little, Brown, 1982.

Morris, Roger. *Uncertain Greatness: Henry Kissinger and American Foreign Policy*. New York: Harper & Row, 1977.

Newhouse, John. *Cold Dawn: The Story of SALT*. New York: Holt, Rinehart & Winston, 1973.

Nixon, Richard. *RN: The Memoirs of Richard Nixon*. New York: Grosset & Dunlap, 1978.

Smith, Gerard. *Doubletalk: The Story of SALT I*. Garden City, N.Y.: Doubleday, 1980.

Stoessinger, John G. *Henry Kissinger: The Anguish of Power*. New York: Norton, 1976.

Szulc, Tad. *The Illusion of Peace*. New York: Viking, 1978.

PANAMA CANAL TREATIES AND THE INVASION OF PANAMA

Buckley, Kevin. *Panama: The Whole Story*. New York: Simon & Schuster, 1991.

Carter, Jimmy. *Keeping Faith*. New York: Bantam, 1982.

Dinges, John. *Our Man in Panama*. New York: Random House, 1990.

Hogan, J. Michael. *The Panama Canal in American Politics*. Carbondale: Southern Illinois University Press, 1986.

Jorden, William J. *Panama Odyssey*. Austin: University of Texas Press, 1984.

Kempe, Frederick. *Divorcing the Dictator*. New York: Putnam's, 1990.

Linowitz, Sol. *The Making of a Public Man*. Boston: Little, Brown, 1985.

Moffett, George D. *The Limits of Victory*. Ithaca, N.Y.: Cornell University Press, 1985.

Woodward, Bob. *The Commanders*. New York: Simon & Schuster, 1991.

IRAN-CONTRA

Anderson, Martin. *Revolution*. New York: Harcourt Brace Javanovich, 1988.

Cohen, William S., and George J. Mitchell. *Men of Zeal*. New York: Viking, 1988.

Draper, Theodore. *A Very Thin Line*. New York: Hill and Wang, 1991.

Johnson, Loch. *America's Secret Power*. New York: Oxford University Press, 1989.

Ledeen, Michael. *Perilous Statecraft*. New York: Charles Scribner's, 1988.

Menges, Constantine. *Inside the National Security Council*. New York: Simon & Schuster, 1988.

The National Security Archives. *The Chronology*. New York: Warner Books, 1987.

U.S. Congress. *Report of the Congressional Committees Investigating the Iran-Contra Affair*. Washington, D.C.: U.S. Government Printing Office, 1987.

U.S. Presidential Commission. *The Tower Commission Report*. Washington D.C.: U.S. Government Printing Office, 1987.

Woodward, Bob. *Veil*. New York: Simon & Schuster, 1987.